A Courtship after Marriage

A Courtship
after Marriage

*Sexuality and Love in Mexican
Transnational Families*

Jennifer S. Hirsch

UNIVERSITY OF CALIFORNIA PRESS
Berkeley · Los Angeles · London

The author and publisher would like to thank the following, who have kindly given permission to use copyrighted material: *Culture, Health and Sexuality,* for material first published in *Some Traditional Methods Are More Modern Than Others: Rhythm, Withdrawal, and the Changing Meanings of Sexual Intimacy in the Mexican Companionate Marriage* 2001, 3 (4): 413–28; The Russell Sage Foundation, for permission to reprint material from *En El Norte La Mujer Manda: Gender, Generation, and Geography in a Mexican Transnational Community,* first published in *Immigration Research for a New Century,* Foner, Rumbaut, and Gold, eds. (New York: Russell Sage Foundation), 2000. The author and publisher would also like to thank the International Union for the Scientific Study of Population (IUSSP) for the assistance provided at the Seminar on Social Categories in Population Research, organized by the IUSSP Committee on Anthropological Demography and the New Arab Demography Project of the Social Research Center at the American University in Cairo, Egypt, 15–18 September 1999, at which portions of this research were first presented as well as *Urban Anthropology and Studies of Cultural Systems and World Economic Development* for material first printed in that journal.

The cover illustration is from a mid–twentieth century Mexican wall calendar and is reproduced courtesy of Gusano de Luz, a manufacturer and wholesaler of greeting cards, postcards, and calendars with Mexican themes and calendars with nostalgic images of Mexico. For more information contact Gusano de Luz at http://www.gusanodeluz.com.mx or Gusano de Luz, S. A., Amores 43, 03100 Mexico City, México, telephone/fax + (525) 687-0313.

University of California Press
Berkeley and Los Angeles, California

University of California Press, Ltd.
London, England

© 2003 by
The Regents of the University of California

Library of Congress Cataloging-in-Publication Data

Hirsch, Jennifer S.
    A courtship after marriage : sexuality and love in Mexican transnational families / Jennifer S. Hirsch.
        p. cm.
    Includes bibliographical references (p.) and index.
    ISBN 978-0-520-22871-9 (pbk. : alk. paper)
    1. Marriage—Mexico. 2. Marriage—Georgia—Atlanta Region.
3. Man-woman relationships—Mexico. 4. Man-woman relationships—Georgia—Atlanta Region. 5. Mexicans—Sexual behavior. 6. Mexican Americans—Georgia—Atlanta Region—Sexual behavior. 7. Companionate marriage—Mexico. 8. Companionate marriage—Georgia—Atlanta Region.
I. Title.
HQ562 .H57 2003

306.81'0972—dc21   2002154938

Manufactured in the United States of America

13   12   11   10   09   08   07

10   9   8   7   6   5   4

For John, Isaac, and Jacob

Jennifer: Now that [your daughter] is going to get married... soon, what do you advise her to look for in marriage?

Eva: What I advise her, all the time, is that she not get pregnant right away when they are just married. Later, if they can't get along, I don't want her to say "I am just here for the kid"—that is, that she would feel tied, bound. On the contrary, she has hardly gone out to dances, she has never had any fun, so...[she should have] a year or two, if they have any money, to have fun, to get out, to enjoy what you could call a courtship after marriage. If they get married and are then tied down by a baby on the way, they will be thinking all the time, well, if it hadn't been for that, I wouldn't have gotten married.

J: por ejemplo ahora que se va a casar [tu hija]...pronto se va a casar ¿que es lo que le aconsejas a ella que busque en el matrimonio?

E: Yo lo que le aconsejo todo el tiempo es que nunca salga embarazada luego luego recien casada, porque no quiero que despues si no hace vida con él, despues diga por el hijo estoy, o sea que ella sienta que es una amarradera, una atadura ahi, sino que ella al contrario y como nunca ha salido a un baile, nunca se ha divertido que al contrario un año, dos años si tiene un cinco se divierta, se paseen, se disfruten lo que es todavía se puede decir que un noviasgo despues de casados, porque si se casan ya atados a un bebe que viene o por asi decir despues van a estar todo el tiempo no pues si no hubiera sido por esto no me hubiera casado.

Contents

Illustrations

MAPS

Tables

Acknowledgments

The long list of those to whom I feel an intellectual debt begins with Constance Nathanson. With her warm friendship and steadfast guidance, a set of fuzzy questions about gender, reproduction, and migration grew into a proposal, which then grew from funded research into a data set, and now finally from a dissertation into a book. For Connie's careful readings of countless drafts, for the perception and clarity with which she sees the social context of gender, sexuality, and reproduction, for her dry wit, and for her insistence that I let go of my love for semicolons, I am more grateful than I can begin to say. Gillian Feeley-Harnik and Peggy Bentley also provided valuable input at various stages of this project, as did Ken Hill, Sidney Mintz, Henry Mosley, Robert Schoen, and Rebecca Wong. For their companionship at Johns Hopkins University, thanks also to Patti Ringers, Laura Oaks, and Elizabeth Van Den Kerkhof.

Long before I began my Ph.D. at Johns Hopkins, the Program in Women's Studies at Princeton was a thrilling place to study in the late 1980s, and I would like to thank the faculty there for helping me turn adolescent struggles with identity into a critique of gender as a socially constructed phenomena. In particular, Christine Stansell, Natalie Zemon Davis, and Michael Jiménez opened my eyes to the historically specific weaving and unweaving of gender, power, and sexuality, providing an initial push toward the questions within which this book is framed. Thanks also to Suellyn Preston at Trinity School and to Sharri

Grossman (who first led me to wonder about women's lives around the world by reading Pearl Buck novels to us students) at Village Community School.

All the intellectual excitement in the world, of course, is no good without money for books, computers, and a dry place to sit while reading. I have received generous support from many institutions. The Labouisse Fellowship Committee at Princeton University supported my first research trip to Mexico, and both they and the Fundación Mexicana Para La Planeación Familiar (Mexfam), whose staff graciously allowed me to observe them at work and patiently answered my naive questions in beginner's Spanish, deserve much of the credit (though none of the blame) for my enduring interest in cultural and social influences on reproductive health in Mexico. Thanks also to Laura Legorreta for facilitating my introduction to Mexfam so many years ago.

At Johns Hopkins, I received support from sources both within and outside the university. These included a fellowship from 1991 to 1995, provided through a training grant to the Hopkins Population Center from the Demographic and Behavioral Sciences Branch of the National Institute of Child Health and Human Development, a postcertified scholarship from 1995 to 1998 from the Department of Population and Family Health Sciences (formerly the Department of Population Dynamics), and support for fieldwork in Mexico from the Andrew Mellon Foundation through a grant to Population Dynamics. Outside the university, this research was supported by fellowships from the National Science Foundation Program in Cultural Anthropology (SBR-9510069) and the International Migration Program at the Social Science Research Council. A personal thanks go to Carolyn Makinson at Mellon, Stuart Plattner at NSF, and Josh DeWind at SSRC for their openness to work that crosses so many disciplinary lines.

Here at Emory, the Department of International Health has provided a congenial environment in which to sit, write, and think. I would like to thank especially the department chair, Reynaldo Martorell, for his support. I am grateful for his vision of public health as an endeavor that includes room for a theoretically inclined anthropologist. By trying to teach my students that theory can help them do better applied work, I have striven to assure Reynaldo that his faith in the value of my contribution is not misplaced. The Department of International Health has also provided material support for the making of this book, by providing the funds for the preparation of the photographs, drawings, and maps in the pages that follow and by providing me with a student, Molly Brady, who in a week did a better job of checking the references than I could have done in a month. Thanks also to Sandra Smith for administrative and moral support, to Maria Sullivan for her good cheer and meticulous attention to detail, to Khaleelah Muwwakil for photocopying, to Jeanne Moseley for endless trips to the library and for reminding me, along with my other advisees in the 2002 cohort, why I love to teach, to Moshe Haspel for producing the maps of Georgia and metro Atlanta, to Emory Biomedical media for their patient and lovely handling of the photos and drawings and to Jenny Higgins, Christina Nyhus, and Laurie Helzer for research assistance along the way. In the School of Public Health, I would also like to thank Joan Herold, Deb McFarland, Shannon Shelton, Aryeh Stein, and Claire Sterk, and in the wider Emory community, I appreciate the support and friendship shown by Carla Freeman, Peter Brown, Bruce Knauft, and Carol Worthman in the Anthropology Department, and Mary Odem and Frances Smith Foster in the Women's Studies Program.

Thanks are due as well to Carlos del Río, director of Emory's AIDS International Training and Research Program. Since coming to Emory it has been my pleasure to serve as associate director of the Emory AITRP (NIH#1 D43 TW01042–02), and I am grateful for Carlos's friendship, epidemiological acuity, and perspective on being a Mexican migrant of a very different sort, as well as for the opportunity to work with students who, when they return to Mexico, Vietnam, Armenia, and the Republic of Georgia, will make important contributions to the fight against HIV/AIDS. Particular thanks to two AITRP trainees, Eric Folch Viadero and Isabel Hernández Ramos, for checking the spellings of words in Spanish.

With ideas and money, however, there was still the actual work to be done, and I would not have been able to move from proposed research to a book had not many people been generous with time and advice. Foremost among those are former Mexican Consul Teodoro Maus, Professor Arthur Murphy at Georgia State University, Sister Barbara Harrington, formerly of Mercy Mobile Health Care, and others at MMHC, and Father Carlos García Carreras and María de Jesus Castro at the Misión Catolica de Nuestra Señora de las Americas. Thanks also to Fryda Sanchez, both for her meticulous transcriptions and for her perceptive and entertaining commentary on the material therein. I am also grateful to the Apostolado Hispano of the Catholic Archdiocese of Atlanta and to members of the many organizations providing health and social services to Atlanta's growing Latino community for the time they took to meet with me during the preliminary phases of my fieldwork. While I was still collecting data and later as I wrote my dissertation, it was a pleasure to share work in progress with colleagues in the Sexuality Research Seminar at El Colegio de México in Mexico City (I benefited particularly from Ivonne Szasz's thoughtful comments), the Post Field Seminar at Emory University's Anthropology Department (where I have been pleased to see those first tentative interchanges with Daniel Smith and Holly Wardlow develop into ongoing collaborations), Mercy Mobile Health Care, and the Atlanta Latinas Working Group.

The warm reception I received in many homes as I was collecting data for this book has confirmed for me that every positive stereotype about Mexican hospitality is true. To Evita García de Lujambio and her sons Alan and Pepe and her daughter-in-law Blanca, many thanks for the delicious meals, for sharing the warmth, peace, and graciousness of your home when I was far from my own, for receiving my father, husband, and son with the same *cariño* you always extended to me, and for your apt observations about life in your particular corner of the world. Thanks as well to the family of Miguel Lopez, who kindly received me in their home during the first several weeks of my fieldwork in Degollado. To Cathie and Enrique Pani and Erika Pani and Pablo Rivera in Mexico City, and to Gloria Briceño in Guadalajara, thank you for being my family in Mexico.

Those who deserve the most credit for whatever I may have learned during the fieldwork are those who provided me with the material I present in the pages that follow. This includes two families in El Fuerte with whom I frequently stayed overnight, as well as the many women and men who opened their homes and their hearts to me, who fed me, listened to me, answered my questions, entertained me with their stories and jokes, let me hold their beautiful children, and in general welcomed me into their lives, both in Degollado and El Fuerte and while at home in Atlanta. Because of the need to protect confidentiality, I cannot thank them by name, but to all of them, *muchísimas gracias por lo que me enseñaron y la confianza y cariño que me brindaron. Aprendí tanto con ustedes, como profesora y como mujer, y espero haber representado sus historias con fidelidad.*

Finally, even with wonderful teachers, generous resources, and willing informants, I would not have reached the point of writing these words were it not for the many people who have stood beside me along the way. First on this list are my parents, Ellen and David Hirsch, for their love, support, and generosity. Their generosity certainly includes the twelve years of private school tuition and four years at Princeton, along with the many other pleasures of life on West 12th Street and Roaring Brook Lake. Perhaps more importantly, their generosity also includes the fact that since I learned to talk they have encouraged me to ask questions and have shown a belief in my ability to find interesting answers that to this day sustains me in moments of doubt. As María notes in Chapter 8, children "don't just live on food.... They have to feel that they have your help." It is for that help, in particular, that I am grateful. (And in a family where food is love, all the delicious meals have emphasized the pleasure they take in providing that help.) To my brother, Andrew, and my sister, Jessica, for their love, and for teaching me the many important lessons that one learns from having siblings.

In *Mother Nature* (1999), Sarah Hrdy explains that an "allomother" is someone other than the biological parent who supplements that parental care and thus contributes to the healthy development of a child. Although very different from the sense in which she meant it, I cannot help thinking that any woman would be fortunate to have had as many "allomothers" as I have. Their belief in my potential and interest in my progress has been like having a personal pep squad. Among them, Judy Felton, Froma Benerofe, and Suzy Hirsch deserve special mention, but thanks also to the other Vassar Girls from the class of 1963, and to the other members of the New York Freudian Society, all of whom have provided me with such wonderful models of adult womanhood, as well as to Christine Stansell and Constance Nathanson (yes, these last two deserve to be mentioned twice). Gloria Emerson also belongs on this list— Gloria, who teased me, taught me, and took care of me at Princeton, and who with her inimitable prickly good humor opened my eyes and prodded me to do something useful for others. I hope that I have not been, and shall not be, a disappointment to her in that regard.

I cannot imagine more delightful companions with whom to share my years at Princeton than Kathleen Clark, Neely Holt McNulty, Caitlin Halligan, Dawn Jahn Moses, and Amy Mayer. The friendships we share have been among my most abiding joys, and as the years have passed I have come to count their husbands—especially David Dean— as among my dearest fictive kin. A special thanks to Kathleen, with whom it has been a delight to share the pleasures and trials of producing both a book and a child at the same time. In the hard red clay of Georgia, too, where to my surprise we have put down deep roots, I am grateful to Hannah Baker Hitzhusen, Rabbi Debra Landsberg, and Lori de Ravello. Further afield, a warm thanks to Elizabeth Armstrong, Pat Lanning, and Alicia Glen for their support.

I would also like to thank Nancy Foner, Tom Fricke, Susan Greenhalgh, Matt Gutmann, Susan Newcomer, and Simon Szreter for kind words of encouragement over the past several years. If I accomplish during the course of my career even a small part of what any of them has, I shall be satisfied indeed, and I hope that I remember to emulate them as well in terms of their generosity with praise for junior scholars. Thanks also to Linda Anne Rebhun for her careful reading of the manuscript and to Naomi Schneider, Suzanne Knott, Annie Decker, Sarah Skaggs, Alexandria Giardino, Sierra Filucci, and an anonymous reviewer at the University of California Press.

I remember as a child listening to the soundtrack from *Fiddler on the Roof*, hearing the voices of my imagined forebears as Tevye sang to Golde about love and change. It was not long ago that my kin and my husband's were part of the huddled masses yearning to be free. On my side, the Rosens and Karps are from Minsk, the Greenfields from Tulchin (near Kiev), and the Hirshkowitzes (later shortened to Hirsch in a burst of upward mobility) from a nameless town in the former Austro-Hungarian Empire. On my husband's side, the Santellis and the Vitaros hail from Cerizano in Calabria, and the Van de Erves from Holland and Norway. Although none endured the terrors of the Rio Grande or the desert at night, Ellis Island was no picnic either, and in spite of the myth about my paternal grandmother's family arriving from Russia with a spare set of china for Passover, and the odd doctor (on his side) or rabbi (on mine), we both come from people who worked with their hands—butchers, milkmen, seamstresses, and tailors, whose hours at labor produced material objects rather than just words on paper. Although our families' journeys and those I write about here are separated by decades, by geography, and by political circumstances, I have been drawn to this story in part by a feeling of fellowship with these brave seekers, a shared sense of diaspora—although, of course, to the Mexican men and women with whom I spoke there could be no one who looks more American than I do, with my green eyes, fair skin, and blue-eyed child. I hope that the grandchildren of Rosa, María, Lucha, Mercedes, and the rest will find real opportunities here in the decades to come—and I hope just as fervently that, unlike previous groups of immigrants, they will be able to do so without turning their backs quite so firmly on the language and lore of the land from which they came.

Finally, my thanks go to John Santelli, with gratitude for his love, for our shared commitment to public health as social justice, for teaching me to steer a sailboat with my foot when the water is calm, and for his steady hand on the wheel when the water is rough. Some might consider it a mixed blessing to live with a feminist academic who is writing a book on love and marriage, and I appreciate his occasional reminders that, bargaining theory aside, it would be helpful to start out from the assumption that we are on the same team. It is to him, to Isaac—who has fulfilled the blessing of his name by daily enriching our life with laughter—and to Jacob, my delicious baby, that I dedicate this book.

CHAPTER I

Introduction

Older women in Degollado, Jalisco, frequently complained to me about girls these days: "No tienen vergüenza," they would tell me—"They don't have any shame." These women, born in the 1930s and 1940s, would tell me that in the days when they courted, girls only eloped against their will, carried off at gunpoint on horseback. Now, they told me again and again, the girls are in the lead, dragging their boyfriends by the hand when they run off without their parents' permission. Men and women in this community talked about how the social construction of gender changes with migration, in addition to generation: when asked how life might be different for their sisters and brothers in the United States, they told me that people say that *en el norte la mujer manda* (in the United States, women give the orders).

In this book, I describe generational and geographic changes in social constructions of gender, sexuality, and reproduction, arguing that declining fertility in this transnational community must be understood in the context of a redefinition of marriage and sexuality. I explain the changes in relationship goals and in sexual and reproductive health practices through reference to structural changes such as migration patterns, increased access to education, and women's greater economic opportunities in the United States as well as to women's and men's desires to craft specific types of relationships. Learning about companionate marriage in this Mexican transnational community deepens our understanding of changing patterns of sexuality and fertility, but the implications go beyond the specific Mexican case: the rise of an ideal of companionate marriage is a key factor in explaining declining fertility rates in the developing world in this century, just as it was in the fertility declines in Europe and North America a century earlier.[1]

Migration has also influenced intimate behaviors in this transnational community; the generational changes were at least in part due to the increasing integration of the sending communities into international migration circuits. I set out initially to compare the sexuality and reproductive health practices of Mexican women in Mexico to those among their peers in the United States, and there are important differences between how Mexican women in Atlanta and their sisters in Mexico negotiate courtship and marriage—differences that affect their sexuality and reproductive health practices and their fertility goals. However, contrasts between the two social locations can only be understood within the context of transformations over time in marriage, sexuality, and reproduction.

GENDER AND SEXUALITY

This project is at its heart an exploration of the cultural and social determinants of reproductive behavior, and of how contraceptive use is best understood in the context of sexual and social relationships rather than being solely seen as a reflection of demographic preferences and health choices.[2] This interest in situating reproductive health practices such as fertility control and the prevention of sexually transmitted diseases within their larger cultural meanings draws on developments in the fields of demography, anthropology, and public health. Within demographic studies of fertility and reproduction, there has been a growing attention to explanatory models that place the individual in a specific relationship and social context.[3] Cultural anthropology has also demonstrated a renewed interest in fertility (as exemplified by the focus of the 1998 meetings of the Anthropological Association of America, which had population issues as their theme), but feminist social science has long focused on gender and the body.[4] Ethnographers working in diverse contexts have presented overwhelming evidence that sexual and reproductive behaviors must be understood within specific social, cultural, and historical contexts, rather than as automatic reflections of the desired number of children or knowledge about how to protect one's health.[5] Largely as a result of our inability to stem the rising tide of HIV infection, in more recent years the social aspects of physical relationships have attracted increased attention in public health as well.[6]

Gender

More than two decades of social science research has developed gender as an analytical category that, similar to social class or ethnicity, operates as a form of social stratification and as a source of identity.[7] Gender in this sense is both an individual property (for example, people act out gender identities) and a characteristic of social organizations. In the past decade, scholars working in this area have increasingly recognized that gender is fundamentally a relational concept rather than a property of women.[8] My focus is on how gender structures women's options and identities, but I included men because it is not possible to understand how gender is understood and negotiated only by talking to women.

Social constructionism portrays gender as the historically variable product of global processes such as colonialism and capitalism and of local social structures such as kinship.[9] Research conducted by social historians has demonstrated the variability of gender regimes, as well as how women and men have questioned and challenged ideas about gender as a way of working for more general social change.[10] Gender inequality may constrain women's options, but it does not determine them; women and men maneuver within its constraints, as they do within those of race and class.[11] In this study, the focus is particularly on changes in marriage as an institution within which gender is negotiated. Connell suggests that a study of any gendered institution should focus on three aspects: affectivity (he calls it "cathexis"), labor, and power. Affectivity draws our attention to people's feelings and emotional expectations about marriage. Labor corresponds here to the question of who does what work—the gendered organization of production and reproduction. Power addresses the question of decision making, autonomy, and control of the other person, the possibility of physical violence, and control over the family's resources. Connell's framework corresponds remarkably well with the range of women's and men's comments about marriage. This study looks at both ideal and actual marriages, reflecting an underlying interest both in changing marital ideologies and in the diversity of gendered practices.[12]

Sexuality

Anthropologists have contributed greatly to the idea that sexuality is socially constructed—in other words, that "physically identical sexual acts may have varying significance and subjective meanings depending on how they are defined and understood in different cultures."[13] Sexuality is conceptualized here as the culturally variable meanings, ideas, and practices attached to physical relationships between people. Sexuality here includes both public performative aspects (the Sunday promenade of single women around the plaza) and private, more intimate, moments such as sexual relations with a spouse or confession to a priest.

Many of the women in the study talked about their own sexuality as more "*abierta*" (open) than women's sexuality was in their mothers' day, but I am not arguing here that an era of sexual liberation has arrived in Mexico or in Mexican communities in the United States. Rather, I draw on the work of scholars such as Foucault and Giddens who direct our attention to the ways in which discourses about sexuality transmitted via social forms such as sex education and soap operas come to stand alongside older, more obvious, institutional forms of regulating sexuality.[14] A young woman may say that she feels freer than women of the past to don a baby-doll nightie or to have oral sex, but her inclination to do so is not an expression of a less inhibited sexuality so much as it is a product of the way her most intimate desires are shaped by widespread messages about modern intimacy. The family and the Catholic Church continue to enforce vigorously some norms about sexuality, but these institutions now compete for people's attention with more diffuse but no less powerful messages about proper marital sexuality.

A primary objective here is to describe changes in shared meanings of sexuality, but it is of paramount importance to show the intertwining of cultural meaning and social inequality, and so I attend both to the macrolevel forces that construct sexuality and to the microlevel ways that people use this construction.[15] Both gender and sexuality are culturally constructed, but this construction is a starting place, offering individual actors a menu of possibilities for thinking about their bodies and relationships. As we watch people go about the business of living meaningful lives, we should attend carefully to how people choose among these meanings, the ways in which some have a greater latitude of choice than others, and the fact that these meanings may be differentially advantageous to people depending on their social position and the other resources to which they have access. If we think only about culturally constructed meanings, rather than exploring how these meanings are woven together with social structure, we run the risk of—in Farmer's eloquent terms—"conflating structural violence with cultural difference."[16]

This focus on individual strategizers who create sexual meanings, maneuver within constructions of sexuality, and use sexual and reproductive resources to achieve their goals is exemplified by recent anthropological work on homosexuality and by Bledsoe's work on reproduction and family structure in Africa.[17] This study, however, fills a much-needed gap in the anthropological literature on sexuality by examining marital heterosexuality. The focus (at least in the Western world) has primarily been on small urban groups—for example, homosexuals and commercial sex workers—whose sexuality is "visible" because it is perceived as problematic. It has certainly been important to explore these marginal sexualities, both in their own right and for what can be learned about oppression and resistance in the social construction of sexuality, but it is equally worthwhile to turn our theoretical and ethnographic gaze toward that which has seemed so normal as to be invisible—the sexuality research equivalent of "studying up."[18] This study also breaks new ground by focusing on how sexuality in a developing world community is influenced by historical processes, applying insights such as those of D'Emilio about the relationship between structural change and sexuality to people's lived experience of heterosexual intimacy.[19]

In public-health research on sexual behavior, culturally variable aspects of sexuality have more often been on the independent variable side of the research equation, while the dependent variables under study have been specific behaviors such as condom use or anal sex. In this project, sexuality is on both sides of the equation: I examine the structural and cultural factors that have contributed to changes in marital sexuality and the ways in which these changes in marital sexuality, combined with migration, have affected more traditional public-health outcomes such as condom use and fertility control practices. In their sexual relationships, people express multiple, concurrent forms of desire—desire for a certain number of children, desire to protect one's own health, desire to be a certain kind of person, and, of course, desire for love and pleasure. Therefore, we will not understand the social context of sexual behavior if we fail to listen to the sighs, the whispers, and the dreams through which people express these longings.

COMPANIONATE MARRIAGE AND BARGAINING THEORY

There are two reasons that it is important to understand more about what marriage means to the Mexican women and men in this study of gender, sexuality, and reproductive health. First, marriage is a crucial social and economic institution to examine in order to understand how gender is constructed and reconstructed. Second, much of women's sexual and reproductive behavior in these Mexican communities takes place in the context of marriage, so one approach to exploring the meanings of these behaviors is to study the relationships in which they take place.[20] (From the point of view of public-health research on reproductive health, this emphasis on relationships, rather than individual decision making, is itself a relative innovation.[21]) Asserting that marriage is a core institution for the reproduction of gender does not make it clear, however, what exactly one must look at to see how marriage is gendered. One approach is to use bargaining theory, which underlies a great deal of recent research on the processes through which women negotiate for sexual and reproductive health practices in relationships of unequal power.[22]

The bargaining perspective combines structure and agency by directing attention to strategies forged with varied resources to reach culturally constructed goals in the context of socially shaped constraints.[23] Resources could include material, social, and psychological factors, such as a driver's license, transnational family networks, and the confidence that without a man one could *salir adelante con mis hijos* (carry on ahead [to support] my children). Bledsoe, Browner, and Lewin, Nathanson and Schoen, Gonzalez de la Rocha, and Hoodfar look at the gendered nature of opportunity structures and, in particular, at how women use their sexual and reproductive resources when access to other resources is limited.[24] In the words of Nathanson and Schoen: "A critical dimension of variation among settings is the extent to which access to economic security and social position is controlled by men.... To the degree that women are economically dependent on men,... women's power in the heterosexual marketplace will be a function of the value attached to their sexual and reproductive resources."[25] I set out to examine under what circumstances sexual access and reproduction are resources for women and how they use them in those circumstances.

Constraints also vary; in this context, the pressure to demonstrate *vergüenza* (shame) in certain situations can be a key constraint on women's social and sexual behavior, as can other beliefs about proper sexual behavior. Other potential constraints include gender-specific economic opportunities, social class, and legal status of residence (for Mexicans in the United States). Goals vary as well; while Nathanson and

Schoen suggest that "women have goals of economic security and social status," this study incorporates the insights of Sobo to include relationship (affective) goals.[26] Indeed, the way that the affective goal of creating a certain kind of marriage (which in turn undoubtedly also relates to economic security and social status) shapes women's sexual and reproductive health practices became a central focus of this study. Bringing together resources, constraints, and goals, this study concentrates on one particular set of strategies: sexual and reproductive health practices. Obviously, women rely on a variety of strategies to achieve their goals, but the object of this study is to understand the meanings behind the choices women make about what they do with their bodies.

The principal attraction of bargaining theory is its focus on people as active agents who use culture instead of merely acting it out. I avoid problematic assumptions about a universal rational actor by thinking about strategies as reasoned instead of rational. Reasoned means that behavior is understood as maximizing within the context of certain commonly held unchallenged beliefs. Crow refers to this as "hidden rationality"; he explains that "it is possible to understand as rational behavior that which seems to the untutored observer unthinking or even bizarre."[27] In this case, the content of those beliefs deals with appropriate masculine and feminine behaviors and sexual relationships. Bargaining theory focuses attention on the material and ideological factors that constrain people's lives and on the way they maneuver within those constraints. It also highlights the gendered inequities of marriage without denying that women still have some room to negotiate—that is, it looks at women as perhaps less powerful, but certainly not powerless.

The appropriateness of bargaining theory in diverse cultural contexts needs further exploration, and so I take a critical approach, exploring whether Mexican women conceive of their sexuality or fertility as something they can manage—that is, in what ways are these women sexual subjects (as opposed to objects) who understand their bodies to be individual as opposed to group property? Furthermore, the complexity of the stories presented here suggests that while the metaphor of bargaining is a useful one within which to understand marital processes, the idea that there is one bargain that is struck and to which a couple holds, which is how this theory has been applied in quantitative analyses, may obscure more than it reveals.[28] Rather, we should think of multiple bargains, changing resource levels, and constant renegotiation—and we should remember that this is more than a two-sex game, that bargaining occurs not just between women and men in bed but also in the confessional, over the kitchen table, and on the way to pick up the tortillas, and that the threat of violence, sexual and otherwise, may obviate the possibility of any real bargaining.

A culturally grounded application of bargaining theory also directs us to develop a more complex understanding of what men and women seek to get out of a marriage. My discussion of marriage should be read *against* the tradition of measuring gender hierarchy by concentrating on inequalities in the household division of labor and the distribution of resources.[29] Questions of who does what work in a marriage and who receives what benefits are key ones, but all too often this framework reduces a complex relationship to differential time spent on child care and laundry.[30] Surely women's marital goals extend beyond getting men to share the housework, just as men's surely go beyond having their wives available to bring them a cold beer. It is important that a Mexican woman now might expect her husband to help sweep the house (and a much more easily measured indicator of social change than feelings), but the sweeping speaks both to the immediate question of whose job it is to get the dirt off the floor and to the larger question of what other sorts of exchanges (labor and otherwise) are assumed within the marital project. Others have made this same critique of research that focuses on the power dynamics between couples to the exclusion of affective aspects of relationships. As Sobo suggests, studies that look at reproductive health practices in terms of strategies and negotiation have overemphasized the material aspects of women's relationships and neglected the ways that the search for love and identity affect women's decisions.[31] Inhorn also gives a fine examples of these more nuanced portrayals of intimate relationships as sites of both love and power struggles.[32] It is especially important to include the range of men's subjectivity, to break down simplistic ideas about a homogeneous masculinity. Nencel talks about how gender studies in Latin America have tended to approach men's subjectivity as insignificant and irrelevant in the face of their greater social power.[33]

The way that women and men are motivated by emotion and desire is one of my central interests here, but their emotion and desire must be culturally and historically situated. The attention I pay to the affective aspects of relationships is perhaps my most significant break with previous studies that have used the bargaining perspective. The context within which a Mexican man might agree to sweep the floor—which is not so much a total redefinition as it is a loosening of gendered task boundaries—is part of a larger shift in the meaning of marriage. These changes in the minutiae of social reproduction help us see transformations in the emotional landscape in which bargaining takes place. It is this terrain within which people struggle to make bargains that feel more or less fair. These intimate relationships are not becoming unbound by gender; rather, they are becoming bound in new ways, by new ideals of masculinity and femininity.

COMPANIONATE MARRIAGE

The difference between older and younger women's discussion of marital ideals can be broadly described as a shift of emphasis from *respeto* (respect) to *confianza* (trust). Younger women's and men's descriptions of how marriage draws strength from emotional and sexual intimacy find striking historical and contemporary parallels around the world in discussions of companionate marriage. The term "companionate marriage" is borrowed from descriptions of social changes in the early part of the century in the United States and Western Europe. As Simmons writes:

> A spate of literature outlining the new "companionate marriage," one based on friendship and sexual satisfaction, appeared in the 1920s, followed by more technical marriage manuals and popular medical advice in the next decade.... They [reformers] sought harmony between the sexes by reforming what seemed the most oppressive elements of Victorian marriage.... Companionate marriage represented the attempt of mainstream marriage ideology to adapt to women's perceived new social and sexual power. This power was manifested, as one man observed, in "the increasing subordination of... maternity to sexuality... of love to passion, of procreation to recreation."[34]

Those who wrote about and advocated this new form of marriage focused particularly on affective aspects of the relationship. Simmons notes the two key assumptions about marriage: "that intense psychological companionship, or friendship, should characterize relations between husband and wife and that the sexual aspect of this intimacy was particularly important."[35]

Both Trimberger and Gordon note that these American discussions about intimacy and sexual pleasure represented a depoliticizing of earlier, more radical or even utopian ideas about the possibilities for remaking relationships between men and women on more egalitarian terms.[36] Trimberger describes how bohemians such as Max Eastman and Floyd Dell shared with others in their community in turn-of-the-century Greenwich Village an ideal that "women's sexual fulfillment would be equal to men's.... Moreover, heterosexual intimacy would entirely eliminate separate spheres for men and women. Rather, women would share the public interests of men, and men would share the private domestic life that had previously been defined as predominantly female."[37] In the more conservative United States of the 1920s and 1930s, all that remained of this initial enthusiasm for reinventing men's and women's relationships was the ideology of companionate marriage, which focused on sexual intimacy and friendship but sidestepped questions about underlying disparities in power between men and women.

These ideas about the ways that sexual intimacy could strengthen the marital bond were picked up by early birth control advocates searching for a way to make the services they offered seem a socially stabilizing, rather than a revolutionary, force.[38] Similar ideas about the productive nature of sexual intimacy were rediscovered by North American sex therapists in the 1970s. In *The Pleasure Bond: A New Look at Sexuality and Commitment,* Masters and Johnson argue that a tie based on emotion is at the core of a healthy marriage: "The search for pleasure—and pleasure is an infinitely deeper and more complex emotional matter than simply sensual gratification—continues throughout life. The quality of marriage is determined by whether the pleasure derived exceeds the inevitable portion of displeasure that human beings must experience in all their associations.... To them [a married couple], it seems a matter of elementary logic: love leads to sex, which leads to greater love, which in turn leads to better sex—and so it goes."[39] Giddens discusses how these ideas about sexuality's role in relationships have become part of popular wisdom in the United States. He notes, for example, that Lillian Rubin's research with married American women found that "far more is anticipated sexually of marriage...by both women and men, than was normally the case in earlier generations. Women expect to receive, as well as provide, sexual pleasure, and many have come to see a rewarding sex life as a key requirement for a satisfactory marriage."[40] Giddens argues that heterosexual marriages are just one type of intimate relationship in which people are bound together by choice and pleasure rather than commitment and obligation. He describes these relationships as a new, modern form of voluntary (and quite unstable) kinship connection, based on affect rather than blood or obligation.

Giddens's work suggests that the idea that mutual sexual pleasure and satisfying emotional intimacy are the foundation of a strong relationship has become widespread. Though he does not take up the issue of the globalization of this ideology, the idea that sexual and emotional intimacy is at the core of the marital bond in low-fertility, largely neolocal societies seems to have become a sort of native theory of kinship on an increasingly global scale. Inhorn has discussed how emotional bonds expressed through sexual intimacy unite infertile couples in modern Egypt. Jane and Peter Schneider have explored the connections between the fertility decline in Sicily and local inflections of this modern sexuality. John Gillis has written about similar changes related to the English fertility decline.[41] Elizabeth Bott, comparing middle-class and working-class British families in 1957, found a similar ideal among the middle-class families, who "had a less rigid division of labor, stressed the importance of shared interests and joint recreation, and placed a good deal of emphasis on the importance of successful sexual relations."[42] Others working on marriage in locations as diverse as Papua New Guinea, Nepal, Brazil, Spain, the People's Republic of China, and Nigeria have noted how couples talk about the role of sexual closeness and emotional intimacy in building marriage.[43]

Skolnik discusses three ways in which structural transformation in the United States has promoted this particular move toward a more companionate marital ideal. First, she notes the effect of economic change: a shift from an industrial to a service economy and the concomitant feminization of the workforce, increasing opportunity costs of fertility to women, and later age at first marriage for both men and women. Second, she notes the effect of demographic changes on marriage: declines in infant mortality and increased adult life expectancy mean that most adults who marry can expect to survive their children's childhoods and to spend a greater portion of their adult life as a married couple without children. Third, she discusses what she calls "psychological gentrification," a sort of change in mentality, due to rising rates of higher education and a variety of other cultural and economic changes, in which Americans became "more introspective, more attentive to inner experience.... Above all, they became more attentive to the emotional quality of relationships."[44] These demographic and cultural changes in early-nineteenth-century Europe and North America have striking parallels in late-twentieth-century Mexico. The forces mentioned by Skolnik are important, but I also show how companionate marriage has been promoted by other changes in Mexico such as neolocal households and individual strategies for social mobility.

John Caldwell was one of the earliest demographers to describe a similar change in the developing world. Discussing Nigeria in the 1970s, he notes what he calls "the emotional nucleation" of the family. He attributes this microlevel ideological change in turn to more macrolevel cultural influences such as European religious missionaries, the social effects of education, the media, and the transformation of sexuality into a domain for consumer satisfaction. Furthermore, he asserts that it is this cultural change—rather than any economic or social change—that is the key attitudinal precondition for fertility decline.[45] Critiquing Caldwell, Veena Thadani writes that the evidence presented by both Caldwell and Lawrence Stone (who makes an argument similar to Caldwell's about the rise of affective individualism in *The Family, Sex and Marriage in England, 1500–1800*) could just as easily be used to support an argument for the interrelatedness of structural change and ideological transformation. She argues that Caldwell's and Stone's perceptive descriptions of changes in the emotional texture of family life are insufficient evidence for their argument that ideological change alone is the driving force behind social and demographic change. Rather, she notes how "relationships between ideas and social structure are reciprocal, as are the causal connections between them."[46] Following her lead, I take the structural and cultural changes to be mutually reinforcing.

Mexican companionate marriages share with the North American construct an emphasis on the importance of sexual intimacy, but they manifest at the same time a number of uniquely Latin American features, such as a continued emphasis on maternity (albeit redefined) and an ongoing distinction between women of the street and of the house. This brief exploration of factors related to companionate marriage in the United States is not meant to suggest that Mexico is undergoing some sort of linear, predetermined modernization process—an idea that, as has been noted by others, has beset demographic studies of fertility decline.[47] Here, I am showing how both as a reaction to local social changes and to demonstrate their awareness of a broader global interweaving of gender and modernity people use intimate relationships to act out modern gendered identities.

MODERNIZATION, MODERNITY, AND GENDER

One of the main themes in my story is the way younger Mexican men and women in both urban Atlanta and rural Mexico are striving to reinvent intimate relations as a way of expressing that they are modern people. It is necessary, therefore, to explain what I do and do not mean through the use of this word "modern." Occasionally those I interviewed would themselves use the Spanish equivalent, *moderno*—and I think particularly of a man in Atlanta who told me, "Soy un hombre moderno" (I am a modern man). When asked what that meant, he said that it meant he likes to be with his wife, to spend time with her. The implicit contrast (and critique) was to an antediluvian style of *machismo* in which social life was highly gender-segregated and a man's domestic priority was to control his wife and children rather than to enjoy their company. Far more frequently, though, men and women would simply insist to me that they were different than their parents and grandparents and that these differences were writ particularly clearly in their gendered (and sexual) interactions with one another.

In common usage, the word modern implies a contrast with the traditional, a description of the way things are now in comparison to how they have been in the past. The Mexican women and men I spoke with, however, were not just telling me that their lives and loves were different than those of their parents'. Their point was that these relations were *better*—supposedly freer from constraint, more pleasurable and satisfying, perhaps even in some way more prestigious. The prestige of modernity is so omnipresent a feature of our intellectual landscape as to be invisible; it has become one of our unexamined habits of thought. We may accept without questioning that to describe something as modern means to suggest that it is superior to what has gone before. This belief in the possibility of progress is part of what Harvey, drawing on Habermas, describes as the "project of modernity":

> The *project* of modernity came into focus during the eighteenth century.... The idea was to use the accumulation of knowledge generated by many individuals working freely and creatively for the pursuit of human emancipation and the enrichment of daily life. The scientific domination of nature promised freedom from scarcity, want, and the arbitrariness of natural calamity. The development of rational forms of social organization and rational modes of thought promised liberation from the irrationalities of myth, religion, superstition, release from the arbitrary use of power as well as from the dark side of our own human natures. Only through such a project could the universal, eternal, and the immutable qualities of all humanity be revealed. Enlightenment thought...embraced the idea of progress, and actively sought that break with history and tradition which modernity espouses. It was, above all, a secular movement that sought the demystification and desacralization of knowledge and social organization in order to liberate human beings from their chains.[48]

Around the world, individuals claim membership in this project of modernity by asserting in a variety of ways that they, too, are modern people. Strategies for building a modern identity can include shifting consumption practices, pressing for political change, or converting to

Christianity.[49] In Latin America, gender has been a particularly critical discourse through which people make claims about having a modern identity.[50] Gender has also been a central focus of social science researchers who, by using gender as a lens to explore the cultural and social implications of the vast transformations the region has experienced in the past fifty years, have been perhaps unwitting participants in this same modernist project.[51] Of all the work on gender and modernity in Mexico, Gutmann's *The Meanings of Macho* is notable for the way he manages to do three things simultaneously: he explores how people use a gendered discourse to create modern identities; he examines the social, economic, and political factors that have reshaped the circumstances within which gender relations are negotiated; *and* he manages to convey a healthy skepticism about the project of modernity by showing that change is not necessarily progress. It is precisely this double take on gender and modernity, this idea that one could look simultaneously at modernity as a cultural construction and as a product of social transformations that has both costs and benefits, that I seek to emulate here.

Although they would, to be sure, discuss the changes in Degollado and El Fuerte in very different terms, María and Pilar are certainly participants in this gendered project of modernity. They described to me how relations in their own homes are emblematic of a more "rational form of social organization" than those experienced by their parents, and how the modern love they share with their husbands protects them in a new way from the sort of "arbitrary use of power" that they say their mothers might have experienced at their fathers' hands. But, although the stories my informants tell might sound like a chorus in some global hymn of modernity, the story I tell should not be read as part of that same project. First of all, the relationships these young men and women build together, though they certainly differ in important ways from those of their parents, are not becoming unbound by gender; the way these couples talk, share, pass the time, and make love are not only—as they might argue—the result of the fact that their individual preferences differ from their parents', or that they are somehow freer to form relationships according to these preferences. As with Collier's exploration of the shift to a more companionate model of marital relations in rural Spain, I too am "skeptical of narratives that portray recent history as a saga of loosening constraints."[52] The intimacy these young couples share (or at least hope to share) is shaped by the social and economic fabric of their lives: the architecture of their houses, the 1986 Immigration Reform and Control Act, historic declines in fertility and gains in longevity in Mexico over the past half-century, the simultaneity of the economic boom in the southeastern United States and the currency shocks in Mexico in the 1990s, and the arrival of satellite television in rural Mexico are only a few of the social factors that have shaped how these Mexican men and women build their families.

My point, though, is not that all of these social and economic changes are inevitably making these men and women more modern—because that would, of course, be exactly the sort of tale about the inevitability of the intertwining of social, economic, technological change, and progress, of modernization, which has so frequently beset research on changes in family life in the developing world.[53] That this is not a story about how gender identities and relations are inevitably transformed by social and economic change is evident for a number of reasons. First, although I do describe at length the changing social and economic conditions that shape the choices people make, I focus equally as much on why people make the choices they do. In other words, I explore the perceived desirability of these new relationship forms and look at how people deliberately seek them out, rather than taking the effects of structural change to be automatic.

My attention to individual agency, however, would not in itself be sufficient to justify my claim about taking a critical stance toward the project of modernity, since that could easily be interpreted to be, in Harvey's words, a depiction of "individuals working freely and creatively" to remake family life. The second criteria that sets this work apart is that I look beyond the perceived desirability of these modern relationships, refusing to take at face value my informants' claims that their new way of loving is inherently superior to their parents'. Rather than approach companionate marriage as a more "rational form of social organization," I explore the culturally specific rationality that makes it seem inherently superior to more traditional marriage. Although my informants' marital ideals are quite similar, in some ways, to my own, and this similarity complicates any effort to develop the distance necessary for a critical look at the changes they describe, I have endeavored to approach the shift to a more companionate marital ideal as change rather than progress, exploring both the gains *and* the losses associated with this perhaps more pleasurable, but certainly more fragile, model of intimate relations.

Third, the search for the "universal, eternal, and the immutable qualities of all humanity" implies a homogeneity that is hardly borne out in the pages that follow—nor do we see in this community a "desacralization of knowledge and social order." The changes I describe in Mexican families are evidence of vernacular modernities—a fragmentation of the idea of a globally homogenous ideal of modern life into a concept that directs us to look at the range of ways that people deliberately build what they perceive to be modern lives and relationships in very diverse social and cultural contexts.[54] Reflecting on what might be peculiar to the Mexican experience of modernity, I think in particular of Pilar, who has hardly been delivered through the "scientific domination of nature" to "freedom from scarcity, want, and the arbitrariness of natural calamity." The winter I spent in Degollado and El Fuerte followed hard on the heels of a severe drought, which meant very little work for Pilar's husband, a day laborer in El Fuerte; scarcely anyone needed help bringing in the meager harvest. Furthermore, the meagerness of that harvest meant little left over locally for home improvements, so her husband also had little luck finding work on the occasional construction project, as he might have in fatter years. Nor were Pilar's living conditions particularly modern; she lived, as had her mother when she married, in her father-in-law's house. Pilar and her husband were living out an affective modernity, not a material one; as they walked hand in hand through their town, what was new about their love was the centrality of its place in their marriage and Pilar's knowledge that she was her husband's best friend.

I did not set out to explore gendered modernity in Mexican families, and my research only shifted in this direction because of women's and men's insistent claims that they were not like their parents. In part, perhaps, they spoke of this to me because, as Collier found, "I was a representative of the modern whether I liked it or not."[55] Simply through being who I was—an American woman, married for five years with no children, a woman who wore pants in public and learned to drive at eighteen, a woman who would travel 1,000 miles from her husband, driven not by want but by curiosity—I was a lightning rod for comments about gender and change. As Gutmann also found in Mexico, however, the men and women I spoke with were already having these conversations when I arrived; my presence merely served as an additional stimulus and perhaps a new point of comparison for their reflections.[56] Having learned about these women's and men's particular local sense of what is modern, one of the questions with which this project ended is why being modern in this context is inextricably intertwined with the family—that is, why people seek to be modern husbands and wives and modern parents, rather than, say, modern workers or citizens. Although family relations were not the only way men and women demonstrated their modernity to me—

consumption practices, for example, were also critical—they were certainly the principal route. In the Conclusion, I explore a bit further why it might be that these men and women choose to remake themselves as modern subjects by reinventing gender.

THE TRANSNATIONAL PERSPECTIVE IN MIGRATION STUDIES

A Mexican transnational community is the specific ethnographic context in which I examine this trend toward companionate marriage. Anthropologists and sociologists studying migration have focused lately on the cross-border connections and mutually constituted identities of transnational communities.[57] The literature on transnationalism makes two major points. First, it presents evidence of migrants who feel and act both Mexican and American, thus serving as a corrective to earlier research's simplistic assumptions about identity and assimilation.[58] Second, transnationalism reframes migration by emphasizing the articulation of local communities with global processes of capitalism instead of explaining migration solely through reference to wage differentials between two countries or to individual or household choice.[59] Among those who study transnational communities, there is a growing recognition of the importance of examining the way gender structures and is in turn structured by transnational social ties.[60]

Very little work has been done by researchers working within the transnational perspective on how the regulation of gender, sexuality, and reproduction differs in these two geographically separate places that are part of the same social space. Hondagneu-Sotelo's *Gendered Transitions* (1994) is a landmark exploration of how gender at the micro- and macrolevel shapes the settlement experiences of Mexican immigrants to the United States; it makes clear that the immigrants themselves see differences between the United States and Mexico through the lens of gender, among other things, but she only worked with migrants on the U.S. side; here, I use participant observation on both sides of the border to explore these questions.[61] The women I interviewed in Atlanta shared many beliefs and ideals with their sisters and sisters-in-law in Mexico, but their economic and social contexts were very different. This study examines the consequences of those differences for how women think about and use their bodies.

The work presented here also speaks to research on gender and migration and in particular to the question of whether and how migration changes gender inequality. I argue throughout this study that it is hard to understand the changes that occur with migration without knowing more about how life in the sending community has been changing. Proponents of thinking about migration in transnational terms may talk about the way that both sending and receiving communities are tied into the same capitalist world system, but by making comparisons between life in the developed and the developing world we still run the risk of implying that people are moving from a more traditional society to a more modern one. Those women who stay in (or return to) the sending community share with their sisters in the North a new ideal of family relations. It is as important to understand how all of these young women's dreams may differ from their mothers' as it is to see why those women in the United States may have more power to achieve those dreams.

INTRODUCTION TO FIELD SITES

A brief description of the field sites suggests the kinds of differences that might exist between locations of this transnational community.

Atlanta

Statewide, 108,922 Hispanics or Latinos of any race were enumerated in Georgia in 1990, while 435,227 were counted ten years later.[62] As a proportion of the overall population, Georgia's Hispanic population increased from 1.7 percent of the population in 1990 to 5.3 percent in 2000. Maps 1.1 and 1.2 depict these increases in Hispanics as a percentage of the overall population. The rapid increase in Hispanic population occurred throughout the southeastern United States; in Alabama, South Carolina, and Tennessee the Hispanic population grew by more than 200 percent in the 1990s, and in North Carolina the Hispanic population grew by almost 400 percent. More ethnographically speaking, in the 1990s residents of small towns and large cities throughout the southeastern United States saw the opening of their town's first *taquería* (taco restaurant), the publication of the town's first Spanish-language local newspaper, and—as they spun through the AM dial—were surprised to find *rancheras* and *norteñas* in addition to country, bluegrass, or R & B.[63]

The ten-county Atlanta metropolitan area (Cherokee, Clayton, Cobb, DeKalb, Douglas, Fayette, Fulton, Gwinnett, Henry, and Rockdale Counties), which is home to some 3.4 million people, reflects these regional trends. Atlanta includes some of the fastest growing counties (in terms of population) in the United States, and much of this growth

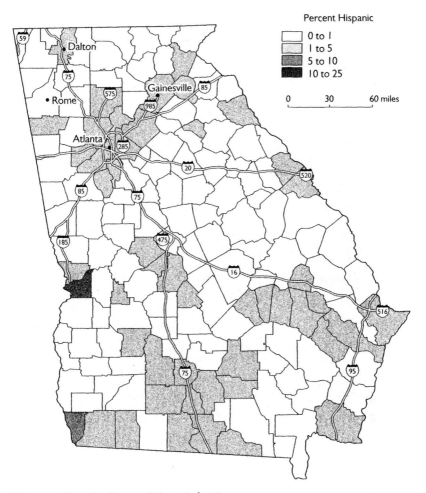

Map 1.1. Georgia, Percent Hispanic by County, 1990.

is due to increases in the Hispanic population. Maps 1.3 and 1.4 indicate the distribution of this growth throughout the metro area. The four most populous counties (Cobb, DeKalb, Fulton, and Gwinnett) alone reported a Hispanic population of 211,699 in 2000.[64]

Atlanta has had a Cuban-American community since the late 1960s, and Cuban Americans still make up a portion of the elite of the city's Hispanic community (that is, the boards of directors of the Latin American Association and other Hispanic business and social service organizations). The Hispanic—and in particular the Mexican—population began growing rapidly in the 1980s due to the strength of the local

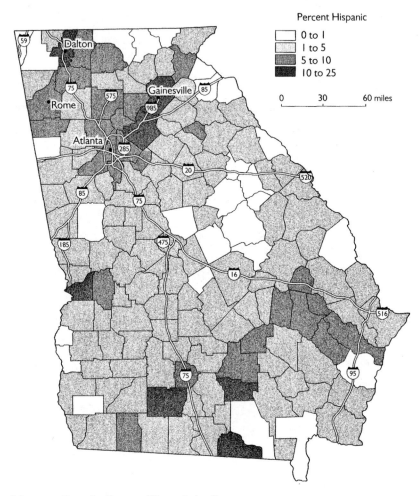

Map 1.2. Georgia, Percent Hispanic by County, 2000.

economy (and the consequent boom in commercial and residential construction) and the economic depression in California and Texas (both of
which have large Mexican-origin populations), among other factors.
Atlanta is also the home of the central Immigration and Naturalization
Service (INS) office for the southeastern United States, so Mexicans living from Florida to North Carolina traveled to Atlanta to make
arrangements for processing their papers under the 1986 amnesty law.
By the late 1990s, the community was large enough to support two
major and several minor newspapers, at least three radio stations, and
four soccer leagues, and Mexican immigration to Atlanta showed no
signs of slowing.[65]

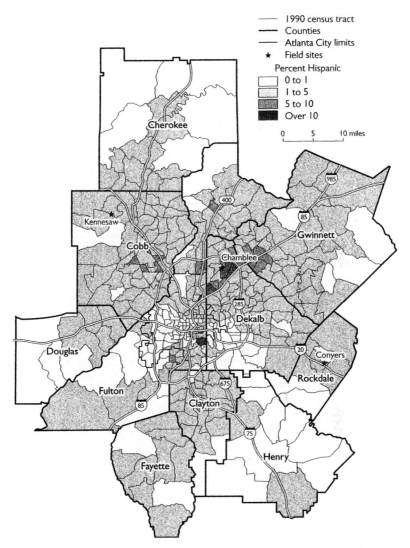

Map 1.3. Metropolitan Atlanta (10-County Region), Percent Hispanic by Census Tract, 1990.

Some of those interviewed lived in Chamblee, a neighborhood on the northeastern edge of the city that has been invigorated by the influx of Latino and Asian immigrants (see Photo 1.1).[66] Bustling stores in strip malls boast signs in Spanish, Korean, and Vietnamese. The Catholic Mission of Our Lady of the Americas—a church, shelter, and social service clearing house—is just off Buford Highway (the main road) in Chamblee, as are a number of Protestant Evangelical churches serving

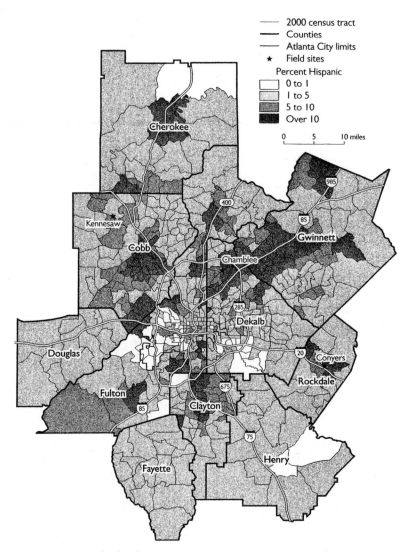

Map 1.4. Metropolital Atlanta (10-County Region), Percent Hispanic by
Census Tract, 2000.

the Spanish-speaking population. Two bus companies right on Buford
Highway offer direct bus service to towns throughout Mexico (see
Photo 1.2), and those looking for local transportation are well served
by the bus and metro lines that run through the neighborhood. Two
weekend flea markets mimic somewhat imperfectly the outdoor markets of small-town Mexico, selling herbal remedies, prickly pear cactus
leaves, and other gastronomic delicacies, as well as elaborate christen-

Photograph 1.1. Welcome Home. The demographic growth of Atlanta's Mexican community is part of the larger ethnic diversification that has occurred across the metro area. Here, a sign in English, Vietnamese, and Spanish located at an apartment complex on Buford Highway welcomes residents and visitors.

ing outfits, Mexican flags, and cassettes of music in Spanish (see Photo 1.3). Almost half the students in nearby Cross Keys High School come from families that speak Spanish at home. Since the completion of the fieldwork, several of the women interviewed have left these communities thick with recent immigrants for the plusher lawns of Norcross, moving into their own split-level suburban homes and, in one case, starting her own business.

The other life history informants lived in trailer parks outside the Perimeter (the highway that encircles the city). Those from El Fuerte, Michoacán, lived in a trailer park in Conyers, about 25 miles east of Atlanta. Rockdale County (where Conyers is located) is much more sparsely populated with Mexicans, and in fact many of those who lived here would drive to Chamblee occasionally to search for a special ingredient or a doctor who speaks Spanish. Although Conyers lacks public transportation and many of the conveniences of an urban community such as Chamblee, many of its residents said they prefer the quiet of their trailer park (which reminds them of the rancho) and the feeling that they may be more protected from the *migra* (the INS) in this less-obvious location.

The rest of the informants lived in or near Kennesaw, to the northwest of the city. A Civil War–era town, Kennesaw has gradually merged

Photograph 1.2. Departures to Mexico. The sign
at one of the bus terminals on Buford Highway
(just across from the flea market) offers
departures to Mexico, Texas, and the Carolinas.
Multiple buses leave daily for points south, and a
wallet-sized card printed in Spanish and available
at the bus station provides people with local
numbers to call throughout the southeastern
United States to inquire about schedules and
areas served.

with the rest of Atlanta's northern suburbs to create a vast expanse of
new residential housing interspersed with big-box superstores and car
dealerships, connected to downtown Atlanta via a six-lane highway.
Some from Degollado, Mexico, live in one of the few remaining trailer
parks in town, while others live in houses nearby. Kennesaw, like the
rest of Cobb County, has limited public transportation, but bus service
goes up and down U.S. 41, the old main highway, and those enterpris-
ing enough to walk the mile or so to the nearest bus stop do at least
have that option for their trips to K-Mart or the supermarket. Like
those in Conyers, those who live in Kennesaw prefer the quiet and feeling of protection from the migra. While INS raids in Chamblee are a
common occurrence (most recently in March 1998 the INS established

Photograph 1.3. Imagined Crossroads. This photo, taken inside the flea market on Buford Highway, shows the street signs that run throughout the building. These signs help the market's many small merchants who sell clothes, Mexican music, herbs, food, cowboy boots and hats made in Mexico, and elaborate dresses for baptisms and first communions locate themselves—but they also serve as a subtle reminder of how much more comfortable Mexican migrants feel strolling down these protected thoroughfares than they would at the actual intersection of Pharr Road and Peachtree Street, in the heart of Atlanta's wealthy Buckhead community.

a roadblock across Buford Highway at midday to check papers) they are less common in the wealthier northern suburbs.

Mexican Field Sites

Degollado is a large town in western Mexico (see Map 1.5) and offers many services to its inhabitants. The population was 9,299 in the 1990 census, and 10,217 in the 2000 count. The disparity between the male and female population, which was slight but not pronounced in 1990 (4,424 men and 4,875 women were enumerated, for a male-to-female

Map 1.5. Map of Mexico Showing Location of Field Sites and Other Locations Mentioned in the Text.

ratio of 0.907), was more marked in 2000, when the ratio fell to 0.856.[67] There are five government-run primary schools, though one-fifth of the approximately 2,400 children between six and fourteen are not in school. There are several government middle schools and one high school, as well as a private parochial school that offers classes through the end of middle school. Of the approximately 5,000 people older than fifteen years of age, 961 reported no formal schooling at all, but 1,432 had education beyond the sixth-grade (*primaria*) level, and the 1990 census reported only 608 of the more than 9,000 residents as illiterate.

Of the 1,764 dwellings counted by the census, all but one hundred or so had cement floors (as opposed to dirt), running water, and electricity. The streets in the ten square blocks around the plaza are mostly paved, but the land farther up and down the gentle hill on which the town is built features newer construction and dusty streets. There are very few adobe houses left in town, though many of the newer houses in the *colonia* are precariously constructed out of brick, cinderblock, or sheets of tin. The more elaborate houses, most of which are closer to the plaza, are built of brick and cinderblock, stuccoed, and painted. The fanciest feature carved sandstone ornaments in front. Phone service has been available for the past decade or so but is still a relative luxury, limited to the well-off and to those with relatives in the United States. Most people make their phone calls from one of the local *casetas* (phone services), all of which now also offer fax service. There is a central market just off the main plaza, and the streets around town are filled with small stores selling fruit, vegetables, sodas, beer, and candy; there are also stores selling dry goods, construction materials, electronics, and furniture, as well as several that rent videos and sell cassettes and compact disks. Other commercial establishments include a number of photo studios, some small restaurants, and numerous cantinas.

South of town, unprocessed sewage runs downhill into a large lake. On the north edge of town, on the top of the hill beyond a blue-green field of maguey cactuses, is a small white chapel with a cross on top; this chapel on private property opens once a year as the destination for the Good Friday procession acting out the Stations of the Cross. On the eastern edge of town, beyond the cemetery and the soccer field, is a flat expanse filled with brickworks, where men make bricks from mud, straw, and horse dung. On the western edge of town there is a long string of sandstone workshops, where men carve by hand the soft pink stone, making fountains, benches, and pillars to send to all of Mexico, and even sometimes abroad. Beyond that, the road to Guadalajara (two hours away by bus) stretches through the arid plain.

El Fuerte, Michoacán, is a small rural community next to the Lerma River, just off the main road between Degollado and the relatively large city (1990 population more than 80,000) of La Piedad, Michoacán. The population of El Fuerte, according to the 1990 census, was 645 people.[68] The fact that many who consider themselves residents of El Fuerte may not have been present to be enumerated is reflected by the disproportionate numbers of women and men: there were 381 women, and only 264 men. Of the approximately 400 people over age fifteen, almost one-quarter were unable to read, and only thirty-one were educated beyond the grade-school level. There is a grade school with both morning and afternoon sessions, but those seeking middle school travel down the dusty road that runs along the river to the next ranch over, San Juan del Fuerte, where the shared middle school is located. None of the ranchos in this area have high schools, so the few who continue their studies that far do so by taking the bus to La Piedad.

The 1990 census counted 124 dwellings in town, all of which had electricity and most of which had running water (of dubious potability). Though there were still some houses made of adobe, the riches brought back from the North by migrants have enabled most residents to lay down cement floors and cinderblock walls. Some of the more ambitious have even built two- and three-story houses topped by enormous parabolic antennas; these were the houses that seem most likely to be unoccupied except for brief periods during the year when their owners returned from Chicago, Los Angeles, or Atlanta. Only 27 of those 124 houses had an indoor toilet, but the refuse from even those indoor toilets was for the most part piped outside and then run (through open canals) directly into the Lerma River. Residential phone lines reached the community in the summer of 1997, and most of the families with relatives in the United States had a phone installed.

Every Sunday a priest comes from La Piedad to hear confession and perform Mass at one of the two chapels in El Fuerte. Outside one of the chapels is a large, flat public area with a bandstand in the middle, where people congregate before and after Mass on Sundays; games and rides are set up here during an annual fiesta. The other gathering places are several small stores that sell a variety of groceries, soda, and beer; usually when I passed by these stores, there was a small crowd of men standing outside socializing. Some women see each other every morning at the *molino*, the mill, where they take the corn that has been soaking overnight to be ground into *masa*, dough, to make fresh tortillas. Now there is a truck that comes through town, honking to announce that it sells machine-made tortillas, so fewer and fewer of those at the mill are young women. There is also bus service into La Piedad; every hour or so either the red or the blue school bus rushes through the narrow unpaved street, the driver pounding the horn to warn of his approach. Since there is no pharmacy, doctor, or butcher in El Fuerte, most women go into La Piedad at least once a week to shop and run errands.

Research Methods

Because this is a scholarly study rather than a journalistic essay or a work of fiction, researchers and students will certainly want to know exactly how I came to the conclusions I set out in the following chapters, and so they will bring a critical eye to my discussions of sampling, data collection, and data analysis. The lay reader might prefer just to skim these discussions, stopping only to linger on the section "Self-Presentation," where I explore some of the challenges of letting my informants get to know me as I simultaneously worked to get to know them; those pages provide a critical sense of context for the brief snippets of conversation I use as evidence throughout the book. At the close of this chapter, I outline the book's argument in order to orient both lay and academic readers.

My intent in presenting a detailed discussion of research methods is both to establish the validity of my conclusions and, more broadly, to present my work as an experiment in interdisciplinary communication, a piece of research designed to mediate two very different sets of epistemological assumptions. Whereas ethnographers frequently establish the validity of their conclusions primarily through the internal coherence of their narratives, in the public-health community—as in the broader world of applied social science research—methodological transparency is the cornerstone on which generalizability and validity rest. In the discussion of research methods that follows, I present the specific approaches to sampling, data collection, and analysis on which I relied in the construction of this study. Beyond discussing the specific methods, however, I also explore the different sorts of concerns that anthropologists and demographers (or applied researchers in general) have about the production of scientific knowledge.[69]

In spite of some moves toward collaboration from both sides, most demographers and cultural anthropologists are still quite far apart in the vocabulary they use to discuss issues of sampling, research design, and data analysis.[70] Furthermore, demographers and public-health researchers tend to treat these questions as purely methodological ones, whereas anthropologists approach them as theoretical and epistemological—specifically, as related to the politics of the production of scientific knowledge. In the tradition of applied research of which demography is a part, a sound research design is one that avoids various forms of bias; the implication here is that all sources of bias can actually be known and eradicated and that it is even possible for research to reflect the truth transparently. Many anthropologists, in contrast, start from the stance that all knowledge is a product of social relationships and thus reflects some partial truth about the knower as well as what is known.[71]

Any account of a culture or experience is necessarily partial (both in the sense of not being complete or whole and in the sense of not being impartial), and so the challenge is to strike a balance between this awareness that knowledge is socially constructed and the need to make a coherent argument for a particular point of view. Fortunately, there are options other than clinging to a theoretically naive positivism or rushing boldly into a postmodern hall of mirrors.[72] The conclusions I draw in the pages that follow are not the only ones possible, but neither does it seem necessary to give up altogether and say that all conclusions are equally valid. My goal in presenting the research methods is to describe the process through which I created this particular research project in a way that is transparent enough to be critically evaluated. I also take this opportunity to map out where the differences between these two research traditions are merely ones of vocabulary and where they are more fundamental.

The "Needle-in-the-Haystack" Method: Systematic Ethnographic Sampling

The life histories of a relatively small number of Mexican women may be richly evocative portraits of how some women have responded to the constraints and opportunities of their lives by making certain choices about sexuality and reproduction. To speak only of the richness of the data, however, begs the question of how these stories relate to the larger community of Mexican women in Atlanta, or to that in the sending community. Raising the issue of sampling is not just a concession to demographers; deciding whom to talk to is a crucial logistical and, ultimately, epistemological issue.

Furthermore, it is important to deal with generalizability because I am telling a story not just about a small group of Mexican women in Atlanta and Mexico, but about the minds and hearts of the largest group of foreign-born people in the United States. In 2000, the 9.2 million Mexicans born in Mexico who were enumerated by the census represented almost 30 percent of the total foreign-born population, as well as the single largest group of foreign-born persons in the country; the same trend was true in Georgia, where the 190,621 Mexican-born Hispanics enumerated accounted for 33 percent of the state's foreign-born.[73] Recent increases in the Mexican-origin population is one of the demographic factors driving the growth in the much broader category, used by the Census Bureau, "people of Hispanic Origin." In the decade between 1990 and 2000, the Hispanic population grew by 57.9 percent, compared to 13.2 percent for the overall United States population, and the 2000 census counted 20.6 million people of Mexican origin (which includes both U.S.- and foreign-born).[74] Immigration from Mexico drives some of the growth in the U.S. Hispanic population, but natural increase is also important. Hispanics have higher fertility rates than non-

Hispanics and consequently account for a growing percentage of all U.S. births. In spite of representing only 10.3 percent of the total population in 1995, Hispanics accounted for 18 percent of total births, 69 percent of which—or approximately 12 percent of all U.S. births—were to women of Mexican origin.[75] In Cobb, DeKalb, Fulton, and Gwinnett Counties, births to Hispanic mothers accounted for between 9 and 11.5 percent of births in 1998, up from 6.1 to 7.2 percent of births just three years earlier.[76] Many of these women, who are living well below the poverty line and giving birth to U.S. citizens, do not qualify for Medicaid-supported prenatal care because of their legal status, but if services are ever expanded to protect and promote Mexican-origin women's reproductive health, a good starting place might be to know more about what these women actually think about reproduction.

Anthropologists who wish to contribute to shaping the policies and programs that serve the populations with whom they work must address the generalizability of research based on nonrepresentative approaches to sampling. During the past decade, cultural anthropologists, informed by research on the sociology of knowledge, have struggled with a variety of solutions to the idea that ethnographic monographs are not objective reports on the facts of life in a particular social group, but rather are representations of the author's experience. One response has been to include multiple versions of a single event or issue, but emphasizing the existence of multiple truths undercuts the contributions an ethnographer can make to policy formation.[77]

Research that is already potentially perceived as soft because it is done with words rather than with hard numbers becomes useless in the policy arena if it is not constructed in such a way that its authors can argue that it is generalizable.[78] At the same time, I cannot in good conscience ignore recent ideas about the socially constructed nature of all (not just ethnographic) knowledge. The discussion that follows represents my attempt to pose a solution to these problems of epistemology.[79]

The ethnographic equivalent of what survey researchers call sampling has not received a great deal of attention. A sampling theory is fundamentally an epistemology. To extrapolate from information gathered from some reduced number of group members to the whole group, one must have a theory about the relationship between the group and the individual members. The intellectual traditions of ethnography and demography have distinct assumptions about that relationship. Demographic sampling is universalizing and individually oriented. To construct a sample for a demographic survey, one begins with certain a priori categories, such as race or ethnicity, sex, and age. For the purposes of a stratified survey sample, the thirty-five-year-old married white middle-class woman with three children who was chosen to be interviewed is as good as any other thirty-five-year-old woman of the same race, income, parity, and marital status. A statistician with recent census maps can draw up a sampling frame for a country he or she has never visited; but it is only by ignoring the local intricacies of social organization and making autonomous individuals their sampling unit that survey researchers can justify using the same sampling techniques all over the world. Where demographers are universal, ethnographers are particularistic in approach, so that in an ethnography the actual sampling method used depends both on a reasonable knowledge of the society studied and on the topic under study. In the case of Mexican migrants, the primary social networks are regional and familial, based in the sending communities in Mexico.[80] The ethnographic focus is on that very level of social organization that is generally invisible in individually oriented survey research—the idea is to study people embedded in social networks, instead of stripped from them.

The generalizability of survey data comes from using samples large enough to interpret the data with a certain level of confidence as representing the entire population. Ethnographic generalizability does not deal with the distribution of behaviors, but with their meaning. An ethnographic study is not useful for finding out what percentage of women rely on coitus interruptus to control their fertility. It is the only way, however, to learn that many newly married women may prefer the risk of unplanned conception to the perceived emotional risk a more effective method may pose to their marriage.[81] Similarly, at the end of the study it will not be possible to conclude what percentage of women are more or less powerful than their husbands. The very idea of dividing power into a categorical variable would make most anthropologists' hair stand on end. Anthropologists see power as more diffuse and thus tend to focus on the different types and sources of power wielded and resisted, rather than thinking of power as a quality that people simply do or do not possess. In-depth ethnographic research helps us find appropriate local measures of power; we can learn that for Mexican immigrant women in Atlanta, U.S.-born children, a driver's license, and consanguineal kin nearby are key sources of power.

This concern with representation suggests that more attention should be paid to a community's internal stratification. My response here is to represent types of people. For example, in a jar of five colors of marbles, the goal here is to select marbles of each color, not to discover what proportion of the marbles is which color.[82] Of course, women can be categorized in many different ways, depending on the criteria, and achieving diversity is complicated by the fact that only some of the categories are even visible to an outsider. Only after several months of fieldwork, for example, did it become clear that the exact location of a woman's parents' house in her hometown (that is, its distance and direction from the central plaza) was a reliable marker of social class, or that a driver's license is a hallmark of independence for migrant women.

Finally, ethnographic sampling is personal. There is no fiction here that the contacts with informants exist outside of other social relationships. Instead, they depend on these social relationships, because even in this more systematized version of the snowball method, the researcher is dependent on the good will of each informant to introduce her to other members of the community.[83]

There are sampling challenges specific to research with Mexican women on both sides of the border. Transnationalism obviously informed the research design, since the whole idea of matching women in two cross-border communities depended on the existence of continued social ties between those communities. The question remained, though, of how the small and socially diverse group selected may differ from the larger community of Mexican immigrants in Atlanta or from Mexicans in western Mexico who have family in the United States. I dealt with this during the slow process of actually selecting a sending community with which to do the research.

*Informal Demography: Finding a Community
and Selecting Life History Informants*

Atlanta's four Latino soccer leagues played a key part in the original plan to find a group of women. The teams are generally organized by a sending community in Mexico, and this method has been used successfully by male researchers looking at male migrants.[84] Once in the field, however, it became clear that I would need another strategy: the only gringas who hang around alone trying to meet people at soccer games are commercial sex workers. Moreover, in the summer of 1995 INS raids all over Atlanta including at several soccer games meant that the few women who did attend soccer games were particularly unlikely to want to talk to unknown North Americans. Making a virtue out of necessity, I focused instead on, borrowing from Cornelius, the Needle-in-the-Haystack method, in which finding a community is like looking for a needle in a haystack: by the time one finds the needle, one has learned all about the inside of the haystack.[85]

The initial exploration of Atlanta's Mexican community consisted of a series of informal interviews with Spanish-speaking health and social service workers, Catholic priests who give Mass in Spanish, and community leaders. I explored two questions: (1) What are the important social institutions in Mexican women's lives, and (2) What are their relationships to the Spanish speakers in these institutions?[86] After four and a half months, the names of three towns had come up repeatedly, and I finally settled on Degollado and the nearby rancho of El Fuerte. At the time of the fieldwork, there were at least fifty women in the Atlanta metro region from Degollado and El Fuerte.

The process followed in Phase I was an adequate, if imperfect, solution to the problem of how to find a group of women living in Atlanta who were all from the same place. The ideal would have been to work with a group of women whose husbands all play on the same regionally organized soccer team (a local or "emic" definition of what it means to be from the same place). There were also social distinctions within the communities selected that were not initially apparent to me as an outsider—so that in spite of my work to select people who belonged to one transnational community, the result has been instead three smaller transnational communities, spread over six locations.[87]

While collecting the information that led to the selection of the research communities, I learned about diversity within the communities in ways that would be useful for selecting the individual informants in the second phase of the sampling. By the time the communities were selected, enough women had been interviewed so that I knew what "colors of marbles" should be included in the final group of informants, in terms both of sociodemographic characteristics and of women's own measures of power and autonomy. Throughout Phase I, I had asked about factors that Mexican women see as making them more or less dependent on their husbands (since the study looked at bargaining power it was key to have diversity in this area). The more obvious sources of power are speaking English and having working papers, but knowing how to drive and owning a car, having consanguineal family in Atlanta, and having American-born children (so they could get Medicaid and WIC coupons) were also significant.

As I met more and more women from the selected community, I summarized what I knew about each woman on a matrix, which facilitated constructing a sample with maximum diversity by helping to compare the range of parity or time in the United States, for example, among the history informants. Women were chosen step by step (as opposed to all at once) as more was learned about the community and as contacts developed. After spending several months interviewing in Atlanta, I went to Degollado and El Fuerte in April 1996 for three months and worked there to "match" women to friends or relatives in Mexico. From the beginning women knew that I would be going to their hometown to interview their families there, and as we progressed toward the end of the six life history interviews they were asked to recommend a sister, sister-in-law, cousin, or friend who was very like them but who was still in their hometown.[88] Matching the life history informants ensured some socioeconomic similarity between the two groups of women interviewed. Further, the structural similarity of the two groups allows for a deeper exploration of other issues in migrant selectivity, such as the role played by personal goals, marital and other relationships, and stages of family formation.

Tables 1.1 and 1.2 give some sense of the socioeconomic and demographic diversity of the life history informants. Their educational backgrounds ranged from almost no formal education, in the cases of Mariana, Concha, and Norma, to college degrees for Patricia and Esperanza. Some grew up on the edge of penury, while at least one of them traveled to Disneyland as an adolescent tourist. These simple descriptive categories, to be sure, do not begin to convey the diversity of their personalities, which made the fieldwork such fun to conduct. From those I worked with in Atlanta, I remember with particular *cariño* (warmth, tenderness) María's pride in her hard-won successes in Atlanta, Mercedes's adventurousness in exploring her neighborhood, Guadalupe's good-natured helpfulness with introducing me to others from El Fuerte, Rosa's determination to prove her independence before marriage, and Mariana's economic resourcefulness, which allowed her to turn twenty years of migrant remittances into fairly large landholdings in her native El Fuerte. Some worked hard to expand their autonomy in obvious ways by learning English and getting drivers' licenses, while others, like Victoria, insisted that these steps toward self-sufficiency would only give their husbands an excuse to stop helping them. From the Mexican field sites, I recall warmly Josefina's irreverent sense of humor, Patricia's companionship and guidance with knitting, and the way that Concha could date her husband's trips to the United States by casting her eyes across her house to the improvements they had paid for through each successive journey. I also remember Perla's delight at finally having a

TABLE 1.1. DESCRIPTIVE INFORMATION, LIFE HISTORY INFORMANTS IN ATLANTA, GEORGIA

Pseudonym	Age	Marital Experience	Parity	Education	Work Experience	Family Background	Migration Experience
Beatriz	Mid-20s	Married for 5 years	1 (U.S.-born)	Primary school	No experience with formal employment	Family owns successful small business in Degollado (town), live in colonia	Returned to Degollado after fieldwork period, then back to Atlanta
Blanca	Early 20s	Engaged during fieldwork	0	High school degree	Full-time work in Degollado and in Atlanta	Prosperous family in Degollado (town, as opposed to poorer colonia)	Came to Atlanta with parents
Clara	Early 20s	Married for 5 years	2 (U.S.-born)	Primary school	Full time in Degollado prior to marriage; occasional informal employment in Atlanta	Large family in Degollado (town); father left them when she was young	Came to U.S. several years after her husband did
Diana	Early 20s	Married for 4 years	1	Primary school	Full time prior to her child's birth	From El Fuerte; father and brother are migrants	Came to U.S. with her husband immediately after marrying
Eva	Mid-30s	Married for almost 20 years	7 (all U.S.-born)	Middle school	Occasional part-time and full-time employment in U.S. and in Mexico	Family from Degollado (town); father was a migrant	Has moved back and forth many times
Guadalupe	Mid-30s	Married for more than 10 years	0	Primary school	Full-time employment both in El Fuerte and in Atlanta	Family owns a farm in El Fuerte; father and brothers also migrants	Came to Atlanta with her husband

Name	Age	Marriage	Children	Education	Work	Family background	Migration history
Lucha	Late 30s	Married for 10+ years to second husband	4 (U.S.-born)	Primary school	Working full time while interviewed	Large family in Degollado (colonia)	Came to U.S. after end of first marriage; here for 20+ years
Maria	Mid-20s	Married for almost a decade	3 (2 U.S.-born)	Primary school	Full-time work in Atlanta	Large family in Degollado (colonia)	Followed husband to Atlanta several months after they wed
Mariana	Mid-40s	Married for 25+ years	8 (all born in Mexico)	Can read	Farmed in El Fuerte and active as community organizer; runs at-home daycare in Atlanta	Saved migrant remittances from her husband to purchase land for each of her 8 children	Spent most of her marriage living in El Fuerte while husband was in U.S.
Mercedes	Late teens	Married for 4 years	1 (U.S.-born)	Primary school	Full time in Degollado; began paid employment in Atlanta after interviews	Large family in the colonia; father a migrant, mother worked full time	Followed husband to U.S. several months after they wed
Patricia	Mid-20s	Married for 3 years	1 (born in Atlanta)	College degree	Full time in Degollado; occasional part-time work in Atlanta	Prosperous family in Degollado (town)	Came to Atlanta with husband
Rosa	Mid-20s	Married for 3 years	1	High school	Full-time employment in U.S. prior to marriage; occasional part time since	From El Fuerte; father was a migrant laborer, as are her brothers	Came to U.S. as a single woman to work
Victoria	Late 30s	Married for 10+ years	3 (U.S.-born)	Primary school	Worked in U.S. prior to marriage; has not worked since	Father and older brothers are migrants	Has moved back and forth, but now quite settled in Atlanta

TABLE I.2. DESCRIPTIVE INFORMATION, LIFE HISTORY INFORMANTS
IN DEGOLLADO AND EL FUERTE

Pseudonym	Age	Marital Experience	Parity	Education	Work Experience	Family Background	Relationship to other LH1
Claudia	Early 30s	Married for 8 years	2	Primary school	No formal employment experience	Lives with her mother in El Fuerte; husband is a migrant in U.S., as was her father	Rosa's sister
Concha	Late 40s	Married for 30+ years	9	Can read and write	No formal employment since marriage; informal employment prior to marriage	Large family in Degollado's colonia; husband has worked as a migrant	Lucha's sister
Esperanza	Early 20s	Married for 2 years	0	College degree	Owns small business in Degollado	Prosperous family in Degollado (town)	Blanca's best friend
Isabel	Early 30s	Married for almost 10 years	3	High school degree	Owns small business in Degollado	Prosperous family in Degollado (town)	Patricia's sister
Josefina	Mid-30s	Married for 15 years	7	Primary school	Part-time informal employment	Large family in Degollado's colonia	Maria's sister
Juana	Early 30s	Married for 15 years	4	Primary school	Part-time informal employment	Father small-business owner in Degollado (town) and migrant; husband owns small business and has worked in U.S.	Eva's sister
Lourdes	Mid-teens	Married for more than 1 year	0	Primary school	No employment experience	Parents owned a successful small business in Degollado (town); grew up in colonia, married into a prosperous family there	Beatriz's sister

Name	Age	Marital status		Education	Work experience	Family background	Relationship
Magdalena	Late 20s	Married for 10+ years	3	Primary school	Full time prior to marriage	Large family in Degollado (town), father left them when they were young; husband is migrant	Clara's sister
Norma	Mid-40s	Married for 25 + years	8	Reads with difficulty	Agricultural work experience	Farmers in El Fuerte; brothers migrate to U.S.	Victoria's sister-in-law
Perla	Late teens	Married for 3 years	2	Primary school	Formal employment prior to marriage	Grew up in the colonia; husband has worked as a migrant	Mercedes's sister-in-law
Pilar	Early 20s	Married for 2 years	1	Primary school	Occasional part-time informal employment	Father is a migrant; she lives with her husband in El Fuerte	Diana's best friend
Soledad	Almost 50	Unmarried	1	Technical college	Full time, also owns small business	Prominent family in Degollado (town); father and brothers are migrants	Victoria's sister
Susana	Early 20s	Unmarried	0	Middle school	Full-time work in Atlanta, but no formal work experience in Mexico other than agriculture	Family owns a farm in El Fuerte; father and brothers also migrants	Guadalupe's sister

home of her own, Juana's off-color jokes, Soledad's and Norma's hospitality, and the interrupted dreams of Lourdes, Claudia, and Pilar.

There are categories of women whom it was impossible to include in the study: in Degollado, for example, there is a notorious lesbian who is said to "kidnap" young women and seduce them, but I did not feel that I could risk speaking either to her or to her "seducees" because it might have irrevocably marred my reputation as a decent woman. Similarly, one attraction of becoming a Jehovah's Witness may be the religion's slightly more open attitude about fertility control methods (and lack of confession), but conversion anxiety runs so high in the town that it seemed equally risky to demonstrate an interest in women of this religious minority.

This method of sampling increases ethnographic accountability by serving as a constant stimulus for diversity. The diversity is socioeconomic, including women from the pueblo, the colonia, and the rancho, but also goes beyond that: women interviewed included those who never miss Sunday Mass and those who say, "*Soy Católica porque me dicen*" (I am just Catholic because they tell me I am); women who ran away with their boyfriends and women who got married first like nice girls; women who tell dirty jokes in front of men and women who will not even tell them in front of other women. In the final analysis, the representation is still mine to create, but going through the process of systematically choosing women makes the story much more complete.[89]

Life History Interviews and Other Methods

The principal method of data collection was focused on life histories from thirteen women in each location. The classic life history method focuses on only one person, showing how he or she has experienced and understood wider social change on an individual level.[90] This modified life history method, which combines a focus on a small number of people with much wider interviewing, has been used effectively by other anthropologists.[91] As with the individual life histories, this method allows us to see how people struggle to find meaning and satisfaction in their lives instead of depicting them as automatons acting out a rigid set of cultural rules. This modified life history method, however, is less vulnerable to charges that it is overly influenced by one individual person's experience, since data are generated from a wider range of sources.

This method provided a structured method of creating relationships with women before asking them directly about very personal topics.

Also, since I started out wanting to learn about the range of factors that shape gender and sexuality, I needed a research method that would not constrain women unduly to predefined topics. Rather than being strictly chronological, the life histories were organized into six topical interviews: (1) childhood and family life; (2) social networks, migration, and differences between life in the United States and Mexico; (3) gender, earning and spending money, and the household division of labor; (4) menstruation, reproduction, and fertility control; (5) health, reproductive health, STDs, and infidelity; and (6) dating, marriage, and sexuality.[92] By the last interview, I had visited all of the life history informants at least eight times. I had not asked anyone to be a life history informant without at least one prior visit to introduce myself, and with every life history informant there was at least one visit in which I was not able to—or did not even try to—conduct a formal interview.

Every visit provided opportunities for informal conversation, and even when I did arrive at someone's house and found her ready and willing to do an interview, I would spend some time before and after just visiting. These other conversations were often just as or even more useful than the actual interviews. After the tape recorder was off, for example, women sometimes told me stories that they had not wished to have recorded. It was during these other conversations that women asked me about myself, about my marriage, my husband, my family.

For each interview I used an ethnographic field guide to ensure that I covered the same topics. These field guides changed as the research questions evolved. I initially asked women what sorts of games they liked to play as a child, hoping to elicit a sort of dolls-versus-trucks response about gendered play. However, many of the life history informants grew up without any toys at all, so I eventually came up with more relevant ways of asking about learning to be a girl, changing the question to one about who they would play with (girls or boys) and where they would play (inside the house or in the street), questions that touched on local categories about homo- versus heterosociality and the gendered nature of the social space. Over time I grew interested in how women used the words *respeto* and *confianza,* and as I asked and learned more about these concepts they became central organizing principles for my description of generational changes in marriage.

The initial research design included a plan to interview women's husbands, but this began to seem impossible once I was in the field: I had been unprepared for the extreme sex-segregation of everyday life in both the Mexican and U.S. field sites. Many of the men seemed unwilling to be in the same room with me, even with their wives present, and their presence made me acutely uncomfortable, so the feeling was mutual. So it seemed hard to imagine spending an hour alone with them in a closed room. (It would not have been possible to do the interviews in a public place because being seen talking alone with any of these men would have led to certain scandal, but at the same time it seemed even less possible to conduct an interview in the privacy of their homes.)

Eventually I did interview eight out of the twenty-two husbands who were eligible. (There were twenty-six life history informants, but only twenty-two possible husbands because two of the life history informants were not married and the husbands of two others were migrant workers who do not live in Atlanta and were not visiting in Mexico during the time I was there.) Half of the men interviewed are from the colonia and the other half from the pueblo. Five of the eight live in Degollado, and a sixth was living in Degollado at the time I met him, although now he is in Atlanta. The oldest of the men was in his midforties, and the youngest in his midtwenties. One of them has a college education, but none of the rest had finished middle school (*secundaria*). They were all from Degollado except for one, Oscar, who is from northern Mexico (he met and married his wife, Blanca, in Atlanta). None of the men from the rancho were willing to be interviewed formally, although I did meet most of them and spoke at some length with Norma and Guadalupe's husbands.[93]

Interviewing the men was very awkward. Being *recogida* (well behaved) as a woman means not talking to men to whom one is not related, so there was little social precedent during fieldwork for these relatively intimate conversations with men with whom I shared neither ties of blood nor of *compadrazgo* (a kinship practice in which one's children's godparents become one's own fictive kin; see note 16, Chapter 2). In this part of Mexico, there is almost no nonsexual social context for an unrelated man and woman to be alone together, so being alone with these men felt as if it had distinctly sexual overtones. In all the interviews, we spoke out of earshot of others, and in several cases the only place this was possible was in the bedroom (or, if it was a one-room house, as in the case of Pedro and Josefina's house, alone in the house with the family outside).

The interviews with the mothers, conducted late in the fieldwork, reflected my growing interest in generational changes in the social construction of gender, sexuality, and marriage. Many of the twenty-six life history informants were sisters, so there were fifteen possible mothers that I could have interviewed. That I only managed to interview nine of them reflects, more than anything, the fact that I perhaps started interviewing them too late in the fieldwork, and I could not change the date of my return home to Atlanta. With the exception of one who lives in Atlanta, all the rest live in Mexico. The nine whom I did interview were distributed among the different field sites in Mexico: four from the rancho, three from the pueblo, and two from the colonia.

Before beginning the life history interviews, I conducted a series of group drawing exercises to get a better sense of how women might understand the idea of having a life history and to ensure that the ethnographic field guides did not overlook any crucial topics. In all the field sites, I started the group drawing exercise by explaining to a group of women I had gathered together that I wanted to learn about their lives but was not sure what the important questions were. I requested that they help me by drawing the most important moments in their past, present, and future. To see how the women understood the idea of a life history, I tried to be quite vague as to my interests. I gave them colored markers and a large sheet of blank newsprint. Borrowing from ideas about participatory research, the drawings presented a way for women to define the critical moments in their life histories.[94] Most women were initially reluctant to draw, protesting their lack of artistic skill, but after some encouragement they produced wonderfully expressive drawings about their lives, relationships, accomplishments, and hopes for the future (some of which are included as illustrations in Chapters 2, 3, 4, 5, and 8).

In Atlanta, women frequently asked me to drive them to doctors' appointments, so we had hours of unstructured time to talk while waiting for the doctor. The women from Degollado gathered each Wednesday to say a rosary together in Spanish, and I went with them most Wednesdays, ostensibly to provide transportation since they knew I was not Catholic. In Mexico I spent most of every day visiting different families. Early on in the research, I decided to learn to knit, and the knitting store became one of my favorite locations for participant observation. Not more than 8 feet wide, the store is one of several in town that sells yarn for knitting and crocheting and thread for cross-stitch. It has four chairs, but women often just leaned in the wide doorway as they paused to talk after making their purchase. Men rarely entered—in fact, the only men I ever saw set foot in the store were either door-to-door salesmen or the husband and brothers of the store's owner. Even they never lingered.

Self-Presentation

I began to knit out of a fear that time might hang heavy on my hands while in Degollado, but I quickly saw that knitting would serve a number of other purposes.[95] I liked the dynamic of learning something from my informants, of being in the position of wanting to acquire a skill that many of them had learned as children.[96] Knitting was also an intentional performance of both gender and social ties. Moreover, I had no domestic responsibilities because I was renting a room from Evita Lujambio, a woman in Degollado who also cooked all the meals in the house and whose maid did all the washing and cleaning. I hoped that knitting would demonstrate to other women that even though I did not have a house and children to take care of, we still had something in common. My bag of knitting was also a handy symbol of the fact that I did in fact have a family: over the course of my fieldwork I made a scarf for my mother, a baby sweater for my sister-in-law's third child, an elaborate baby blanket for my goddaughter, a baby sweater for a friend who has had two children through in vitro fertilization, and a baby sweater for a childhood friend who had a baby with her boyfriend from Jamaica. Each piece of knitting represented a different set of social relationships that I could discuss with people; the knitting was literally a way of showing off the strings that tie me into a variety of social networks, as well as a useful conversation starter about the way that family relationships are the same or different in the United States and Mexico.

Knitting also reinforced what I told people about eventually wanting to have children. My lack of children after more than four years of marriage was a subject of constant discussion and speculation, and so knitting for other women's babies was one way of showing that I did care about babies. I would frequently tell people that I was learning how to knit so that when I had a baby of my own I would be able to knit things for it.[97] When I was not working on my knitting I was toting around a quilt square or two, which then also allowed me to show women in Mexico that even gringas do traditional crafts. Many of the women I met—including those who had spent time in the United States—thought that the American diet consisted exclusively of frozen or canned food, pizzas, or hamburgers, so I was constantly fielding questions as to what I might make my husband for dinner. Women commented constantly and approvingly on my knitting, and my more general interest in feminine arts did not go unnoticed.[98]

Issues of self-presentation included sexuality, social class, and national identity. While in the Mexican field sites, my behavior as a married woman far from her husband was under constant scrutiny. I eventually learned that the safest way to avoid provoking comments was to avoid talking to, or even looking at, men in the street. Most people in town know each other by sight if not by name, and women greet other women in the street with an "*adiós*" as they pass each other. Men do the same to each other, but most women avert their eyes at the approach of a man. A greeting from an unknown man should be read as a flirtatious sally, and a response is understood to be coquettish. Even inside people's houses, sex-segregation remains strong, and most women do not speak much to unrelated men.

Married women in Degollado and El Fuerte frequently spend months if not years apart from their spouses who are working in the United States, but in those cases it is the man who has left his house, not the woman. In the past a woman whose husband was away might live with her own parents, or her in-laws, so as to continue under the moral and physical protection of an adult man, and married women without children continue to do so. As a woman who was alone and who said she was married but (until my husband came to visit me) could offer no proof, the safest way to show that my intentions were beyond reproach was to live with a respectable family as if I were their daughter, so that is what I did. Even then, no sooner did I move in with Evita (who had one unmarried son, Alan), than the rumor flew through the town that Alan had kidnapped the gringa and taken her to his mother's house to live with him as his wife.

In both families with whom I lived, the unmarried sons living at home took on the role of my older brothers, remarking on my comings and goings and threatening to report any potential misbehavior to my husband. I learned to turn their protection to my advantage: one day I stopped by one of the restaurants facing the plaza to chat with the owner, a woman who was a friend of one of the life history informants in Atlanta. A man in the restaurant was rather clumsily trying to flirt with me, in spite of the fact that I rather curtly informed him that I was married and was in his town doing research, not looking for a husband. Finally I told him that if he did not leave me alone, I would have to tell Alan, the son of the woman I was living with, that he had shown me a lack of respect. He calmed down immediately and apologized.

Try as I might to present myself as a decent woman, I inevitably committed multiple infractions—sometimes out of not knowing better, and sometimes out of my own unwillingness to sacrifice custom and comfort to fit in. For example, I initially told the man from Degollado who picked me up at the airport that he should speak to me as *tú* instead of *usted*, since the formal case grated on my sense of democracy; only later did I learn that such a request could easily be read as an invitation to other kinds of social closeness. Eventually, I came to appreciate the distinction between the formal and informal terms of address and even to enjoy the way that addressing a man as usted implied a demand for reciprocal respect and distance.

After some weeks in the Mexican field sites it dawned on me that one reason people were repeatedly mistaking me for a *muchacha* (unmarried girl) as opposed to a *señora* (married woman) was that I was not dressing correctly. Mostly I wore either knee-length Bermuda shorts or long pants with a t-shirt or a blouse; while some younger married women dressed as I did, most wore skirts, blouses, and flat shoes. Although hardly immodest by American standards, my clothes were definitely those of a muchacha rather than a señora. Another thing I did that was unusual (though not unheard of) for a married woman was exercise; a local woman held aerobics classes in her living room several times a week, and I attended fairly regularly during my time in Degollado. Other married women in town told me that on occasion they had participated, but during my stay I was the only señora in a roomful of muchachas.

It was only after my husband came to visit me in January 1997 that people really believed that I was married. Unfortunately, it was toward the end of my fieldwork. Interestingly, after meeting him (or even hearing that he had visited), a number of older women whom I had always addressed as usted began to return the gesture of respect. His appearance meant that I really was a married woman. One even apologized to me for having earlier used the informal case with me.[99]

I tried to reflect on the persona I was creating in the field, but people constantly read meanings other than the intended ones into my behavior. I did not wear my diamond engagement ring while working in Atlanta, and I left it behind when I went to Mexico. In both cases, this was motivated by a desire to de-emphasize class differences between my informants and me. In both sites, women eventually asked me why my husband had not bought me some better piece of jewelry than the plain, thin gold band I wore as a wedding ring. Similarly, in Atlanta, the car that I drove at first was a 1986 Volkswagen Cabriolet, which we eventually traded in for a Ford pickup truck. I deliberately chose to drive these rather than our "good" car, a 1994 Honda Accord, for the same reason—to downplay differences in social circumstances between my informants and me. On occasion, however, I would need to drive a woman and her children to a local clinic, and so John and I would switch cars and I would show up in the Accord. Several times women commented that it was a much more appropriate car for me, and they found it equally curious that he would not strongly prefer to drive the truck. I had been thinking about the cars in terms of social class, but they read them as messages about gender.

I was (at least I think I was) somewhat more successful in communicating a distinct message about my identity as an American. Throughout the fieldwork, I consistently referred to myself as a gringa, rather than calling myself an *americana* or the more technically correct *estadounidense* (someone from Los Estados Unidos). People tended to laugh when I would do this. They asked me if gringa was not disrespectful, and I would say that I liked to use it because it was clearer than the term americana, since Mexicans are after all also "American," and easier to pronounce than estadounidense. I used the word deliberately, however, to poke fun at North American self-importance and to position myself critically in terms of power relations between Mexico and the United States. People clearly enjoyed the joke. There was another North American woman living in Degollado (she had married a local man who was living in Chicago and returned to his hometown with him to settle), and people frequently shared with me their opinion that she was *apretada* (uptight) to take offense at a word that had become for me a sort of affectionate nickname.

Trying to behave properly—which was both a deliberate decision on my part and a function of my personality (by nature, I like to follow the rules)—limited my access to certain social worlds. While in Degollado I felt that I had to be *recogida en mi casa* (back in the protection of my own house) by ten o'clock every night. Consequently, my only knowledge of who might be in the street past those hours or what they might be doing comes from asking the few men with whom I was comfortable talking. Alan Lujambio, for example, Evita's son, would shower and change almost every night around nine and go out *a la calle*. I sometimes asked him at breakfast where he had been and with whom, or even what it was that guys do in the street until two or three in the morning. He said that during the week they go visit their girlfriends, sit around and drink, and tell jokes, and the routine varies on Sundays to include going to the plaza and then later to the disco.

One of the limitations of being a woman visiting a gender-segregated society is that I was afforded only rare glimpses into male social worlds.

Perhaps if I had been less concerned about acting like a proper woman (knitting, trying to sit with my knees together and ankles primly crossed, being recogida en mi casa, not talking to men in the street or meeting their eyes), I could have gained entree into some of those places. I cannot, however, imagine a woman of any status (married, single, even a gringa who might not know better) really being a participant-observer in a group of men in western Mexico. I am certain, furthermore, that trying to gain access with men would have cost me my status as a respectable friend for my married female informants.

Differences in Relationships with Informants

Although I spent some time socializing with all of the women I formally interviewed, there were differences in the kinds of relationships I had with them. Most obviously, the relationships I had with women's mothers tended to be more formal than with the life history informants themselves; for example, I spoke to all of the mothers as usted, while by the end of the fieldwork I was on less formal (tú) terms with all of the life history informants. In addition to the obvious difference in sheer amount of time spent interviewing the daughters and their mothers, the logistics of repeated interviewing meant that I was able to ask the life history informants about the same topics several times; infidelity was discussed, for example, both in interview #3 (things that are intolerable in a marriage), interview #5 (infidelity and sexually transmitted diseases), and interview #6 (sexual relationships and what happens when partners are not sexually satisfied).

The differences in the type of relationships with the mothers and daughters have two implications. First, I felt that it would have been disrespectful on my part to ask the mothers directly about their sexual relationships with their husbands. Second, the difference in closeness made it less likely (though not impossible) that they would answer me honestly about painful subjects. One older woman, for example, told me that her husband had never, to her knowledge, been unfaithful, but I later learned from a female relative of hers that the woman and her husband had had terrible fights over the years due to his repeatedly infecting her with the STDs he had caught while working in the United States. Two of the mothers, however, were quite honest with me about their husbands' infidelity and other assorted cruelties.

Nor did I become equally friendly with all of the life history informants. Two of the women in Degollado, Isabel and Josefina, really became my friends. I enjoyed and looked forward to spending time with them, and they were the women I sought out when I was lonely or worried about something in particular. They also knew the most about me; by the end of the fieldwork I had stopped worrying about what impression I might be making with them and was answering their questions with candor. They asked me about a wide range of topics, including my past, my marriage, my religious practices and beliefs as a Jew, and my family.[100]

There were also differences in the fieldwork among the different field sites. In Atlanta my contacts with the women were friendly and certainly quite frequent, but much less intense. I was not dependent on them for company or to explain the local rules to me; rather, I was the one who was doing the explaining. They were grateful to me for the favors I did them, but if I had not given them rides and translated telephone and cable bills, letters from the INS, and instructions for new electronic equipment, they all certainly would have found someone else to do so. In Degollado, in contrast, I depended on the people I knew for company.

Finally, the specifics of participant observation in Degollado were different than in El Fuerte. While I lived in Degollado during my time there, I merely visited the rancho, usually once a week for a day or two. I stayed overnight with one of two families while I was there. Given that four of the thirteen life history informants lived in the rancho, I often thought that I should spend more time there, but logistics (such as lack of bus, taxi, and even telephone service) seemed to conspire against my doing so. In addition, life in the rancho was much less comfortable than life in Degollado, as people in both the rancho and Degollado acknowledged. Those in the rancho seemed constantly amazed that I would visit them at all, much less occasionally sleep over; they assumed that most gringas would be unable to tolerate the dust, lack of phones, strong smell of sewage, and intermittent electric power that were part of daily life. In fact, though hardly delicate in constitution, I frequently got sick from something I ate or drank while visiting the rancho. (In part, no doubt, this was because I did my best to eat enthusiastically whatever was offered to me, as part of my general effort to be pleasant and likeable.) In Degollado, similarly, people constantly commented on how adventurous I was to spend so much time in a rancho. Toward the end of my stay in Mexico, I was staying in the rancho for two or three days at a time each week, both to correct what I feared had been an imbalance in time allocation of participant observation and to complete the life history interviews.

Data Analysis

I used somewhat different analytic strategies for the chapters that describe broad currents of generational and migration-related social
change and the chapters that look more at the diversity of the life history informants. For the sake of clarity, I will discuss first the analysis
on which the chapters on dating, marriage, and migration are based,
then turn to the analysis on which the sexuality and fertility chapters
are based, and then return to some issues of style and writing common
to all chapters.

In Chapters 3 and 4, I compare what older and younger women say
about dating and marriage. For these chapters, the first stage of analysis involved compressing the interview data into a format in which it
would be possible to make a comparison. To do this, I extracted selec-
tions from the interviews with the life history informants and their
mothers (anywhere from a key phrase to a half-page interchange between myself and the interview subject) into files on the following topics: historical changes in gender; respeto; confianza; vergüenza; bodies
(comments women made about men trying to control their bodies in
various ways, including how they dressed); courtship; feelings (about
the emotional expectations women have from their relationships); fight
(about how and when couples fight); *mandar* (general comments about
power and decision making); money (about who earns money and how
they decide to spend it); *quehacer* (about housework and child care);
salir (about what they would do if they left their husbands, and why
they might leave them); and women's work (women's own and their
husband's feelings about women, work, and income generation). The
analysis of the interviews with men proceeded similarly; the interviews
were sorted directly into topical files on gender, marriage, limits (why a
man might leave his wife), *el mando* (power and decision making),
money, and violence.

All this work was preliminary to the actual analysis. (Of course, sort-
ing the data clearly involved making analytic choices; by choosing certain key words rather than others, I concentrated on some lines of inquiry and foreclosed others.) Next, I read through the topic files, taking
notes about patterns and themes in what became the outline of Chapters
2 and 3. Looking at courtship, for example, I noted what younger and
older women said about how courtship had changed in terms of things
like physical intimacy or the relationship between one's boyfriend and
one's parents. I also noted how women used words like respeto and

confianza in relation to courtship; this contrast seemed to crystallize many of the broader generational changes in intimate relationships. The topic files were not further subdivided, so the file on courtship contained examples that might support or contradict my argument about generational change. Leaving all of the examples relating to a specific topic together helped me see areas in which pieces of the data contradicted or complicated the argument I was trying to make. For example, although the younger women talked about confianza in courtship as a good thing, as opposed to their mothers who generally said that it was a bad thing, I also saw that they still valued respeto, as did their mothers. The chapters about generational changes in courtship and marriage focus more on the broad social change and less on individual diversity, and so there are a number of places where I talk about "most" women or "many" women without qualifying the differences between those who do feel some particular way and those who do not.

For the migration chapters, I drew more heavily on my own notes and observations. Chapter 2 begins with an extended description of Degollado and El Fuerte that is drawn from a letter I wrote, combined with notes I jotted down throughout the course of my stay. Although I did not do the same kind of narrative analysis for the migration sections that I did for Chapters 2 and 3, I was careful to check my conclusions in two ways. First, I began to distill my ideas about key social context differences between U.S. and Mexico locations for a poster I presented at several professional meetings in 1996 and 1997. Formulating some preliminary results while I was still in the field gave me the advantage of then being able to go back to my informants and discuss my findings with them. They agreed with me that the issues I had identified were in fact some of the key ways their lives had changed with migration. Second, I was invited to present my research on how women's lives change with migration to a support group for battered women at a Catholic Church in a heavily Mexican neighborhood of Atlanta. As I discuss in Chapter 6, this diverse group of Hispanic women strongly agreed with my conclusions.

In Chapters 7 and 8 I examine much more closely the diversity among the life history informants; rather than just trying to describe the majority experience, as is the goal in Chapters 2 and 3, the point is precisely to explore the way that culturally constructed ideologies, social context, and individual women's strategies combine to shape intimacy and fertility regulation practices. The primary analytic goal, therefore, was to tease out the social and cultural sources of behavioral and attitudinal differences among women. Both chapters draw principally on material from interview #6 (courtship and sexuality). A first reading generated topical themes, such as confianza, and sorted sections of narrative into separate files on sexual experiences, family planning ideas and experiences, menstrual regulation and abortion, and feelings about families without children. Data compression also involved the construction of several matrices. For Chapter 7, the matrix contained column headings to record women's comments about saying no to sex, initiating sex, being forced to have sex, orgasms and pleasure, and the relationship of sex to marriage. The two matrices for Chapter 8 looked at women's family ideals and at fertility regulation practices. The columns in the former included reasons to have children, delay a first birth, and limit subsequent births; communication with a spouse or anyone else about desired fertility; who should have the last word in disagreements; and the relationship between children and marriage. The fertility regulation matrix included knowledge of different contraceptive methods, experiences with methods, discussions/disagreements with husband about methods, discussions with others about method, religious issues, and abortion and menstrual regulation. For Chapter 8 I also made two tables with even more compressed information about women's fertility and contraceptive behavior, modified versions of which are included in the text of that chapter.

Having compressed the data so that they could be displayed and reviewed somewhat more manageably, I used the matrices, tables, and topical files to explore the variability within specific topics, looking at differences in what women said about the importance of sexual intimacy, or reasons why one might delay a first birth. A third level of analysis explored differences between the groups of women who shared a particular opinion or behavior and those who did not—looking, for example, at the differences between women who said that intimacy was the key to a successful marriage and those who said that it was less important than respectful behavior, or at differences between those who had tried to delay their first birth and those who had not. My goal in following this intricate process was to move beyond the sort of cultural determinism frequently found in qualitative research in public health by representing as accurately as possible the range of variability in the data and accounting for this variability through reference to social structure, individual strategy, and culturally constructed beliefs about bodies, sex, relationships, and gender.

Each interview averaged more than thirty pages in length once it was transcribed, so the combined length of the life history interviews and the interviews with mothers and husbands was somewhere between four and five thousand pages. While it might have been possible to analyze women's sexual and reproductive health practices simply by reading through the interviews and taking notes, it certainly would have been slow and unwieldy. Moreover, the analysis process here facilitated repeated reference back to what women actually said and did, without having to read through thousands of pages over again to confirm or disprove any suspected patterns. The combination of the matrices, the demographic groupings of informants, and the informal notes taken while reading through the interviews allowed me to explore the data and develop and test hypotheses systematically. For example, only by constructing a table that looked at contraceptive use and migration experience did I see that the women in Atlanta were much more likely than their matches in Mexico to use a technological method for birth spacing; having made that observation, I could refer back to their comments about the pros and cons of different methods to construct an explanation drawing on the different value of women's fertility as a resource in Mexico and in Atlanta.

The style in which quotations are presented also involves analytic choices. The quotations I used were drawn from both formal interviews (for which I have transcripts) and from participant observation (from which I have conversation fragments as recorded in my daily field notes). Of course, in the actual writing, not all of the relevant interview fragments are quoted or even cited; rather, I chose quotes that seemed both typical of the point I was trying to make and that I felt expressed the point clearly. I was careful, however, not to build any part of my argument on just one quote or one case, but instead to think about how generalizable whatever I was saying might be to the whole group of women. To reflect the conversations within which the data were generated and to give a sense of the context within which statements are made in the text, I include as many of my questions as possible in addition to women's and men's answers. Even those few lines of text take place in the larger context of the whole conversation, as well as in the context of the specific relationship I had with each informant.

Translation is the other issue in quoting fragments of interviews and conversations. All of the fieldwork was conducted in Spanish (though some of the women in Atlanta occasionally drop an English word into their Spanish). My field notes were written in a mix of English and Spanish, and the interviews were transcribed, read, and re-read in Spanish. Mexican Spanish, to a foreigner's ear, explodes with references to power and sexuality—not just in the echoes of rape and conquest in verbs such as *chingar* (to fuck or to beat), but even in quieter words such as *dejarse* (to let oneself be overpowered), which is the word women use when talking about how and when they resist their husbands' commands.[101]

In quoting from the interviews I have followed the lead of Gutmann, quoting primarily in English but including certain key words and phrases in the original Spanish. I would hardly argue that the subtle messages about gender and sexuality concentrated in certain words are untranslatable, since after all my goal here is precisely to translate and explain those subtleties of language and culture, nor would I want to limit readership to those already fluent in Mexican Spanish. I have, however, tried to preserve as much of the flavor as possible while not being exclusionary through using too much Spanish in the text. Equally important are the many *dichos* (sayings) that women and men use to refer to a universe of shared values and experiences about gender and sexuality, such as *"ojos que no ven, corazón que no siente"* (eyes that don't see, heart that doesn't feel; a common saying about dealing with men's inevitable infidelity). Many of the dichos rhyme or have a certain poetic rhythm that is lost in translation (at least in my inexpert translation), and so I have also generally included them in both languages.

Ethical Considerations

The fieldwork for this study was reviewed and approved by the Institutional Review Board at the Johns Hopkins School of Public Health, and I followed the IRB's recommendations for human subjects' protection. The main risk to participants was that I might reveal sensitive and possibly embarrassing information. Throughout, I tried to minimize this risk by protecting the identities of the women I interviewed from others in their community who might see writings based on the fieldwork; this is an issue for all of the women, not just those in the United States.[102] The IRB emphasized the importance of identifying women by pseudonyms in any publications resulting from the study (which I do), but the use of pseudonyms does not even begin to resolve the complexity of truly protecting women from identification by those who know them. While I never gave anyone a list of the life history informants, and while

I did occasionally visit women who were not life history informants, it still would have been fairly easy for any interested member of the community to guess whom I was interviewing.

The whole point of life history research on sexuality is to be able to put a woman's most intimate behavior in the context of many other aspects of her life—her migration experience, material and social resources, and family relationships, to name but a few—but paradoxically it is just this richness of information that makes the presentation of the findings ethically complicated. Those same biographical details that provide context could also make direct quotations identifiable. Some researchers have suggested inventing composite characters in situations where it is likely that biographical details could violate confidentiality, but this solution seems unworkable when the topic at hand is the relationship between a person's biographical details and her sexual and reproductive health practices, or even her ideas about gender.[103] If you are looking at how women's whole lives shape her sexuality, you need to be able to present their actual stories in a way that is complete enough to support an argument but not so complete as to violate confidentiality.

Some quotations—particularly in the sections about sexual intimacy—are not attributed or else the speaker is only vaguely described as "an older woman" or "a woman in Atlanta." Tables 1.1 and 1.2 give the reader some sense of these women's lives and circumstances, but in addition to using pseudonyms I have changed some details in every case. None of the photos in this book contain images of the women I interviewed. For the quotations that are attributed, the reader can refer back to the tables to get a clearer sense of the speaker. In dealing with especially sensitive information, I always made confidentiality a greater priority than transparency; it is important not to ask readers to take quotations out of the context of a certain speaker, but it is more important to protect the speakers themselves.

Outline of Argument

In the following chapter I describe some of the rhythms of daily life in Degollado and El Fuerte and the intense interconnectedness of people in these migrant-sending communities with their sisters, brothers, sons, and daughters living more than 1,000 miles away in the urban Southeast. My goal is both to give the reader a sense a place, a feeling for the sounds, smells, and sights of rural western Mexico, and to show how the texture and organization of social life have been transformed both by the web of cross-border social relations and by economic, demo-graphic, and social change in rural Mexico. In Chapter 3, I trace the ef-fects of these social changes on courtship patterns, arguing that genera-tional differences in the process of becoming married can show us a great deal about changes in gender and marriage. Chapter 4 expands on this theme by showing how younger women and men are creating mar-riages that are more companionate than were their parents' marriages. Newlyweds, though, may think a great deal about love, sex, and ro-mance, whereas couples with three or four decades may have less ro-mantic (or more realistic?) marital ideals, and so in Chapter 5 I discuss other recent findings from Mexican social history and anthropology and explore more generally how anthropologists can disentangle actual historical change from life course effects. Chapter 6 shows the second trajectory of change in this transnational community, describing how the generational changes in gender are further accelerated among some couples who migrate. In Chapter 7, I discuss the new meaning of sexual intimacy within these companionate marriages, and in Chapter 8, I show how these generational and migration-related changes in gender and sexuality come together to shape fertility behavior. In the final chapters, I connect the stories and analysis presented throughout to bodies of theoretical work mentioned in this introduction.

CHAPTER 2

"Here with Us"

*Introduction to a
Transnational Community*

When I arrived in April 1996, both Degollado and El Fuerte looked to me like little worlds unto themselves—sleepy places that could not be more different from the strip malls, trailer parks, and six-lane highways of suburban Atlanta. Over time I learned that the Mexican and U.S. field sites are intensely intertwined, and in fact some of those features that struck me as most strongly "Mexican" looking, such as the colonial-style sandstone details on the homes of some of the town's wealthier residents, date back not to Mexico's colonial past but rather to the more recent prosperity of migrant families. Migrant-sending communities in Mexico have been so profoundly transformed by migration that it is not possible to think about rural life in western Mexico without acknowledging the multiple interconnections with urban life in the United States. This chapter describes how individuals bridge the space that divides the two places to create a shared social life and gives some examples of how regional identity continues to be an organizing principle for Mexican women and men in Atlanta. I write in the present tense to give a sense of immediacy, but—as should become clear through the description itself—what follows is not a timeless portrait of life in Mexico but rather a snapshot taken at a particular historical moment.

I had been hearing about the fiestas since I first met women from this community in December 1995; people had been telling me all along how important it was that I be there to experience them, that the fiesta season is *cuando se pone más bonito el pueblo* (the time when the town is at its nicest). My description makes clear that what I mean by a transnational community (a phrase that has been used in various ways) is one that spans physically distinct locations but that is closely linked through the movement of people and information, and one in which there is a broader sense of membership in a community that transcends physical borders.

CONSTRUCTING A TRANSNATIONAL COMMUNITY: EXPERIENCES OF CONNECTION

When, toward the end of my stay in Degollado, several people asked me how long I had been doing research in their community, I would begin to calculate the number of months I had been in Mexico: "April through July makes three," I would say, "and then mid-October through February is another four." Inevitably, they corrected me, dating the start of my work with the community to December 1995, when I first began interviewing women from El Fuerte and Degollado in Atlanta. Being "here with us" meant to them being part of the larger community of Mexicans from Degollado or El Fuerte. The annual fiestas in Degollado provide a fine example of the intensity of these cross-border ties and of the implications of these ties for daily life in rural Mexico. These fiestas, which locals experience as the paradigmatic celebration of their Mexican identity, owe much in texture and timing to the changing patterns of temporary and permanent migration between Mexican sending communities and the United States.

FIESTAS IN A TRANSNATIONAL COMMUNITY

Since early November this whole western-central region of Mexico has been abuzz with the excitement of the approaching fiestas, and with them the returning norteños. Their return portends both a busy season for local merchants and the changing gender ratios that usher in the start of the courting and wedding season. The cars and trucks are one of the first signs, rumbling into town with placas gringas (U.S. plates). Most are from Illinois and California, but Oregon, Nevada, Texas, Alabama, Tennessee, the Carolinas, and Georgia are also well represented. Large, full-size vans are the most popular—how else to fit all the presents one must bring home for one's family? There is also a fair share of extended-cab pickup trucks, some with chrome detailing and extra lamps on top; these trucks could carry a bull, several pigs, or 2 tons of bricks (or a whole extended family seated on folding chairs to a picnic in *el cerro*, the hills). Some of the younger men, the single ones, drive low-slung red or black Camaros with neon underlighting and shaded windows. (Not everyone drives home from the United States—especially those families with children in school, who are likely to stay just a week or two and who will take a bus or, if they can afford it, a plane. There are direct buses from Atlanta to La Piedad, twenty minutes from Degollado.)

Suddenly, everyone has new clothes. T-shirts and baseball hats from the Bulls or the Rams are coveted gifts, but any sports team, U.S. city, tourist attraction, or even company logo is warmly welcomed and proudly worn. At Mass on Sundays you can look around and see all the shiny new shoes and handbags. The norteños themselves, of course, are splendid in their new clothes: the men's attire crisply ironed, the women perfectly made up. Everyone exclaims over how white they have become in the North. Their hair seems glossier, free of the split ends caused by dust and heat and hard water. The ones who had been too skinny have put on weight, and the ones who were already healthy looking have become even more *lleno/a* (fuller, that is, heavier). Altogether, everyone comes back looking more *compuesto/a* (fixed up).[1]

The taco wagons in the plaza multiply. During the rest of year they are only crowded on Sundays, but now there seems to be a throng around every wagon, every night. The *cenadurias*, tiny kitchens that sell sopes and pozole and fried tacos, spill their patrons out into the street.[2] In the sleepy summer months the only men in the plaza during the day are old men on benches outside the church, whose cowboy hats shade eyes that inspect every passerby, but suddenly—even during the day—the plaza is full of young men. They luxuriate in the weak winter sun, so much warmer than where they have come from, and in the freedom of being able to sit in public and talk with their friends—of being able to sit down at all without looking over their shoulders for la migra.

Commerce hums. The market runs out of meat if one does not go early—who buys meat every day but *los que traen dólares* (those who carry dollars)? The bricklayers on the edge of town work in a frenzy; not only is the rainy season around the corner, but everyone who comes back wants his (or her) house finished, so they can't make bricks fast enough. The construction workers have more work than they can possibly manage, and the building supply stores are full of people busily getting estimates and placing orders. The *mariachis* and *conjuntos* who the rest of the year stand for hours in the plaza, waiting for someone

rich enough or drunk enough to spend 50 pesos for a song, now never
sit still. The store just outside the market that sells *birria* (spicy goat
stew) opens every day instead of intermittently. The town's three travel
agencies do brisk business, arranging family package vacations to the
beach; later, in January and February, they will get even busier as people book their return trips.[3] And dollars are everywhere; "A cuanto está
el dólar?" (How much is the dollar at?) echoes not just at the bank and
the three *casas de cambio* but in stores throughout town, as men and
women pull out wads of dearly earned, proudly spent bills. Like their
families who cash money orders in increments of $50 or $100 the rest
of the year, they hope the dollar is up, giving them more pesos—but also
like their families they feel a touch of sadness or even a twinge of guilt
when it rises, knowing that there are some in the town with no money
orders or foreign checks to cash.

Even during the rest of the year, Sundays are different. Families ride
in, packed in the back of pickup trucks, from the surrounding ranchos,
to do their shopping and attend one of the five Masses offered that day
in the main church on the plaza, or one of the several at the two
churches in las colonias. Sunday morning the *tianguis* (flea market) sets
up on one of the streets bordering the plaza, offering stall after stall of
dishes, underwear, herbal remedies, clothes made in Mexico, America,
or Southeast Asia, needlework, makeup, shoes and sneakers, and tapes
and compact discs. Young girls invent errands, beg to take their grand-
mothers to Mass, or volunteer to go for the tortillas, desperate for an
excuse to visit the plaza and the flea market.

Even on a regular Sunday in the middle of summer, the air is heavy
with food smells, and people eat as they shop: sugar-coated peanuts;
churros (caramel-filled fried donuts); popcorn; small plastic bags
spilling over with chopped watermelon, cucumber, cantaloupe, mango,
and papaya, with a squeeze of lime and heavy sprinkle of salt and
ground chiles; hot dogs wrapped in bacon and fried, served on a bun
with ketchup, mustard, and *jalapeños* in vinegar; *tortas planchadas*
(grilled cheese and ham sandwiches). For families who can afford it,
Sunday morning is not a time to cook; those who would rather eat at
home scurry back with bags of steaming *tacos de cabeza* (tacos made
from head meat), goat stew (not cheap at 40 pesos the kilo), or *menudo*
(tripe and chile soup, excellent for taking the bite out of a hangover).

As midafternoon draws near, those from the ranchos tend to head
back, their shopping done and their Mass finished (the Mass at noon is
known as the *misa del rancho*). In spite of the exodus toward the ran-

chos, if anything the pace in town starts to pick up as dusk falls. The early evening Mass (at 7:30) is the *misa de adolescentes,* the teenagers' Mass.[4] As the 7:30 Mass lets out, young single people flood out into the plaza to sit on the benches or to *dar la vuelta* (promenade around the plaza). Women walk counterclockwise, men clockwise. The young women tend to link arms or hold hands; men walk in groups of two or three, but without touching each other. In the past, people say, young men let their intentions be known via an elaborately coded courtship language of real and artificial flowers and confetti-filled eggs, but now (they say because of *la crisis*) exchanges are immaterial, though no less significant: a glance, a smile, perhaps a few words as they pass.

The air fills with nighttime smells: cologne, roasting green garbanzos and ears of corn, *buñuelos* (another fried pastry), tacos, and more bacon-wrapped hot dogs. In between the ringing bells before each Mass, one hears the throb of disco music from that den of iniquity, the disco, which most of the year opens only on Sunday nights but during the twelve days of the annual fiestas of the Virgin of Guadalupe (December 1–12) is open nightly. The crowd in the plaza thickens at 9:30 when the last Mass ends. Now there are no spaces to be found on the benches, and the paving stones are thick with the green shells of roasted garbanzos. At ten o'clock the streets clear of families and the noise dies down. Now is the time for married women, good girls (las recogidas), and young children to be safely home. Men, whether married or single, may stay out later. Some bad girls do too, because the disco continues until 1 or 2 in the morning.

So if the streets brim with excitement on Sundays in May or June, when the crops are just coming in; in the Salinas Valley and construction, landscaping, and paving are at their peak in Georgia, imagine Sundays in the winter. The bandshell, silent all year, fills with a group of local musicians courtesy of the mayor's office (which pleads poverty during the summer months, but coughs up the money in the winter to please the returning migrants). During the summer months, the line going counterclockwise (girls) is several times thicker than the one going in the other direction. The few boys who come to promenade in the summer are noticeably younger than most of the girls—that is, still too young to go north—but in November and December the boys' line and the benches around the plaza fill with new faces. Most of them of course are actually familiar faces, but with new clothes, pockets bulging with dollars, and chins smooth after a carefully done, though barely needed, shave. In the girls' line one sees teenagers but also women in their twenties, thirties, and even forties. Because some men go north and marry Mexicans from other towns, Chicanas, or even gringas, there is a sizable group of adult, unmarried women in town.[5] Still technically muchachas, many of them put on heels and stockings and continue to optimistically dar la vuelta.

The return of these norteños ushers in courting season.[6] Many men come back hoping to find a girlfriend; they are looking for a nice girl, one who expects to be respected. If all goes well, they can spend several months courting, talk on the phone weekly after he goes back north in January or February, and then marry the following year. Young women dress with care for these crucial Sundays. Some wear the latest fashions from the United States (during my fieldwork, clunky black shoes, low-slung baggy pants, and midriff-baring tops), but it is not uncommon to see muchachas in off-the-shoulder, ankle-length velvet, taffeta, or sequined dresses. (A bridesmaid dress can live a long life in this part of the world.) The more sophisticated girls from the pueblo mock those in long dresses, choosing instead suits in printed rayon fabrics, copied from designs in K-Mart, Sears, and J.C. Penney catalogs sent from the other side.

November is also wedding season; young men who have worked hard all year come back prepared for a splendid wedding, with mariachis and *carnitas* (tender, deep-fried pork meat) and then a honeymoon at the beach.[7] Several times a day on Sundays in November, December, and January, a bride and groom brave a torrent of flying rice to leave the church. Sometimes the couple pauses for photos outside the church, interrupted by clapping and shouts of "*beso, beso*" (kiss) from the gathered crowd (they do not kiss in church in this part of Mexico; it would be disrespectful). Then the newlyweds hop into their heavily decorated wedding car and lead a parade of cars through the town streets, beeping their horns and driving in circles, until they can be sure that enough guests will have arrived at the party so they can make a grand entrance (see Photo 2.1). (Between wedding processions and norteños showing off their cars, traffic gets so heavy this time of year in Degollado that the police make several normally two-way streets one way, to lessen the possibility of serious accidents and relieve congestion.) Even couples who themselves do not go north often wait until November or December to marry or baptize, counting on the help of returning relatives as *padrinos* and thus cosponsors of the party—and many families who live in the United States baptize their children in Mexico, strengthening their and their children's ties to home by choosing *compadres* in their hometown.

Photograph 2.1. "Just Married." This minivan, sporting Georgia plates and a "Just Married" sign in English, was the car of choice for a couple from El Fuerte who married in La Piedad in January 1997 and left soon afterward for Atlanta. From November through January, a bride walks down the aisle at the main church in Degollado several times a day, and even the other chapels are sometimes fully booked.

People try to make it home by November 23, when there is live music and dancing in the plaza from dawn till dusk during the fiesta of Saint Cecilia, patron saint of musicians. Shortly thereafter begins the twelve days of the fiestas for the Virgin of Guadalupe, Mexico's beloved patron saint, culminating on December 12, the day she is said to have appeared in a vision to Juan Diego. The plaza fills with booths of games, a mechanical bull, and carnival rides offering the chance for young couples to get stuck on top of the Ferris wheel, forced to clutch each other in fright. The acrid sulfur smell and sharp crack of firecrackers accompany the bells that announce the early morning (6 A.M.) and afternoon (7 P.M.) processions through the town before the special daily Masses of the fiestas. Some go to the early Mass to show their love for the Virgin; others go because it provides a good excuse to linger in the plaza afterward, drinking coffee, eating hot donuts, and checking out the boys.

Photograph 2.2. La Peregrinación del los Hijos Ausentes/ The Procession of the Absent Sons. Men, women, and children stroll happily down the main street in Degollado, dressed in their best clothes, to line up for the religious procession sponsored by returned migrants.

Each of the twice-daily religious processions is organized by a different group: the sick; the stone cutters; inhabitants of the four "quarters" of town; those who have moved to Guadalajara; elementary and secondary schoolchildren and their teachers; and of course *los hijos ausentes* (the absent sons [and daughters]), those who have moved to the United States and are back to visit. The pilgrimage financed by los hijos ausentes is paid for by canvassing groups of migrants living in different cities in the United States during the year and is expected to be the most splendid: more firecrackers in the morning than on other days and actual fireworks at night; huge multicolored arches of helium balloons spreading over the main street; several groups of hired "Indian" dancers; and a number of marching bands and groups of mariachis.[8]

The biggest attraction of the *peregrinación de los hijos ausentes* (the religious procession sponsored by the town's absent sons) is, of course, the migrants themselves (see Photos 2.2 and 2.3). The men are

Photograph 2.3. La Peregrinación del los Hijos Ausentes/The Procession of the Absent Sons. On their procession down Degollado's main street, returned migrants carry a banner of the Virgin of Guadalupe, a Mexican flag, and an American flag. The parade also featured a banner that read "Los hijos ausentes agradecemos a Nuestra Madre de Guadalupe y a Degollado que nos reciben con los brazos abiertos" (The absent sons [and daughters] thank our mother of Guadalupe and Degollado, who welcomes us with open arms) and a truck with suitcases, representing the generosity and safe return of the town's *hijos ausentes*.

in suits and ties or in crisply ironed jeans with shiny boots, cowboy hats, and new belt buckles of brass, silver, or handwoven *piteado*.[9] Women shine in new dresses or tailored suits, some with matching hats, and children are on parade as well: little boys in suits and little girls in velvet dresses with tights and patent leather shoes. All the migrants carry candles, as one does in a pilgrimage, but they are the 30- or 40-peso kind, rather than the 20-peso version that their nonmigrant kin would buy. Many also carry video cameras; they will sell tapes of the parade to those back in the United States who were unable to make it this year. During the pilgrimage of los hijos ausentes, the return migrants march, grouped by U.S. state, under three flags: the banner of the Virgin, the Mexican flag, and the U.S. flag. The first float in this quintessentially "Mexican" parade is a pickup truck, its back piled high with suitcases representing the triumphant, gift-laden return of the migrant. The religious procession sponsored by los hijos ausentes highlights the way in which their whole trip home to Degollado is a kind of pilgrimage, a way of giving thanks for having survived and even prospered in el norte.

These fiestas, with the smells, tastes, and sounds of a communal street life, represent to migrants all the pleasures of life in Mexico, contrasted with the sacrifices of life in the North—but without the infusion of energy and money that the migrants bring, the fiestas would not be what they are. In years past the carnival rides left town on the 12th, the day the fiestas ended. Now they stay on—in 1996 nearly through the end of December—to take advantage of those migrants, home for school vacation with their young children, whose appetite for an authentically Mexican good time was not sated during the fiestas. The migrants' longing to replicate the smells, tastes, and sounds of their imagined pasts collides with their desire to help their town (and show how successful they have become) by renovating the church or the plaza or installing potable water and with the logistical constraints of their back-and-forth lives.[10] Migrants contribute to the creation of fiestas that are showier than in the past—more food, more fireworks, more souvenir stands and games— and that last the duration of school vacations in Chicago or Atlanta.[11]

Questions about Mexican authenticity hang in the air during this time. For example, on November 1, Evita called me from my breakfast to look outside our front door onto the main street at the passing parade. I was delighted to see a horde of kindergartners in black pants and shirts with paper bones pinned on, their faces painted as the traditional day of the dead skulls, carrying a large banner that read: "Mexicano, di no a Halloween—Festeja el día de los muertos" (Mexicans, say no to Halloween—Celebrate the Day of the Dead) (see Photo 2.4). During Christmas both in the rancho and in town people debated the most properly Mexican way to celebrate the holiday. The Three Kings (*los Reyes Magos*) had always brought Mexican children whose families could afford it a new dress, shoes, or a toy on Three Kings Day (January 6); children dreamed of breaking a *piñata* on Christmas Eve, then sitting down to a steaming bowl of pozole. Lately, however, a Santa Claus they see on TV and depicted on gifts from the United States has begun to appear in children's daydreams; Santa's visit on TV is followed by turkey and stuffing, rather than pozole and tamales. I asked one four-year-old boy who lives in El Fuerte with his mother and grandmother (his father is in Harvey, Illinois) what the Three Kings might bring him this year, and he told me with a serious face that it was Santa Claus who was going to bring him presents. When I stuck my foot in my mouth by saying rather insensitively, "No, Santa Claus lives in

Photograph 2.4. Protest against Halloween. Children marching in a 1996 parade to celebrate the Mexican holiday *día de los muertos* (The Day of the Dead) carry a sign that reads "Mexicans, say no to Halloween, Celebrate the Day of the Dead."

gringolandia (where the gringos live) near your father, and here in Mexico it is the Three Kings who bring little boys and girls presents," he got very worried and started to cry. His grandmother stepped in to save the day, telling him not to worry, that Santa Claus and the Three Kings would together make sure that he was not forgotten.

U.S.-MEXICO MIGRATION AND CHANGES IN THE SENDING COMMUNITIES

The fiesta season is framed with flags and pictures of the Virgin of Guadalupe as a celebration of all that which is *lo mexicano* (most Mexican), but this very sense of Mexican-ness makes sense only in implicit contrast to *lo gringo*—and the annual creation of the fiesta relies on resources to which residents of this town only have access because of their sojourns in the United States. In addition to the fiestas, transformations in architecture and residence patterns, the local economies, and markers of social status in El Fuerte and Degollado over the past generation are at least partially a result of the communities' growing links to migrant networks.

As the saying *la que se casa quiere casa* (she who marries wants a house) suggests, one consequence of the increasing integration of local Mexican economies into migrant circuits is that newly married couples are

Drawing 2.1. Finishing the House. This drawing, by a young
woman in Degollado, shows what she says is her most
important hope for the future: "In my future, I would like
for my house to be finished. Now my husband is in the
United States to finish the house, if God helps us."

much more likely to start off with their own houses (built before or soon
after marriage with money earned working in the United States) (see
Drawing 2.1 and Photo 2.5). As Inhorn concluded based on her fieldwork
with infertile couples in urban Egypt, neolocal residence forces a couple to
rely much more heavily on each other both socially and emotionally.[12]
Five out of the seven life history informants who live in Mexico and own
their own homes purchased or built them with money saved through their
husbands' trips north.[13]

Photograph 2.5. Construction Site in Degollado. Piles of rebar, stacks of bricks, cement pipes, and heaps of gravel—as well as a two-story house such as the one rising in the background—show how migration is transforming the appearance of small towns throughout Mexico.

The look of houses in this region has also changed. Twenty years ago, the typical house was a one-story brick or adobe house. The front wall was flush with the street, and the doors and windows were covered with decorative (but strong) wrought-iron bars. Inside, the room or rooms faced an inner courtyard full of flowering plants, where wash hung to dry, beans cooked over a wooden fire, and birds were kept. The roof was made of clay tiles, or large sheets of tin or fiberglass. The bathroom, if there was one, was shared by the whole family. Most of the rooms were multipurpose; during the day, people would sit, eat, and cook in rooms in which they would sleep at night. Siblings frequently shared a bed, but boys and girls slept in different rooms if possible, or at least in separate beds. One frequently walked through one room to get to another; no precious space was wasted on hallways.

As González and Pader have noted based on fieldwork in other Mexican towns with large migrant populations and as is illustrated by Photo 2.6, the influence of North American suburban architecture has become unmistakable.[14] The front wall has receded from the sidewalk, making the garden a floral showplace rather than a communal living area. Newer houses have living rooms, and the rich have both a living room and a family room, giving them the luxury of a room of wasted space

Photograph 2.6. New House. Newer homes reflect new needs, such as a garage for cars purchased through hard labor in the United States. The home pictured here integrates some traditional Mexican design elements (stucco, sandstone trim on the windows and along the roof, a tile roof, and the wrought-iron-and-glass decorative lamps), but also provides room for a two-car garage. The two-story design separates living areas into public and private in a way that is quite distinct from older homes.

and untouched furniture just like their North American neighbors. Bedrooms are set off from the rest of the house, often opening onto a shared hallway, and some houses now have multiple bathrooms. More houses are two-story, with the bedrooms upstairs and the common areas downstairs, and some also include room for off-street parking; a few even have pull-down garage doors. These new-style homes show not just that a family has money but that they have modern tastes. A person living in one of these new houses learns privacy through the closed doors, hallways, and multiple bathrooms; they learn to have more individual possessions that they can store in their closets (another innovation). Some of these new houses stand empty, yet they still perform an important function, marking a migrant's continued identity as a native daughter or son of their hometown. Many migrants live in cramped, rented quarters in the United States while sending as much as they can scrape together (often every other paycheck) to Mexico to build a splendid house in which they will never live, and only rarely visit.

During a quick walk through El Fuerte or the colonias of Degollado, it is easy to pick out those families in which either the husband or the whole family spends most of the year working for dollars: a pickup in front of the house or a large parabolic antenna are sure signs of norteños. As suggested by the transformation in domestic architecture, through decades of migration people have become accustomed to a whole range of status symbols that are attainable either with great difficulty or not at all to those who do not migrate. As far back as the 1920s, the store-bought clothes and radios accessible only to migrants were prized possessions, and now many other items distinguish those who have family in el norte from those who do not: cars, microwaves, video cameras, VCRs, and satellite dishes.[15] Extravagant weddings, baptisms, and *quinceañeras* (fifteenth-birthday celebrations) are another example of this migration-dependent system of marking social status; in order to finance the requisite mariachis, party favors, sartorial splendor, and food it is often necessary to involve multiple sets of padrinos who, as ritual godparents, cosponsor part of the party.[16] Videotapes have become an important component of the transnational sharing of these ritual moments; no celebration is complete without a video camera recording events for relatives in the United States who are not able to be present, and these tapes are eagerly awaited and viewed over and over by those on the other side.

Migrants continue to invest in maintaining a social identity in the sending community—as exemplified by the focus on building houses in one's hometown in Mexico. Migration is a strategy for local (that is, Mexican) social mobility for those who go north. This is true most obviously in terms of the possessions they accumulate to fill houses they barely visit, but even the very fact of having stepped on gringo soil can cast a halo of importance on people.[17]

The local economy has also been transformed, both by the influx of migrant dollars and by growing insertion into regional, national, and international markets.[18] The demand for housing has created local industries of brick making and construction work, and people credit post-NAFTA international competition in porciculture, combined with skyrocketing interest rates, for having driven many local pork producers either into debt or out of business. An *ejido* is a system of communal landownership developed after the Mexican Revolution's failed attempts at more wide-spread land reform.[19] Under former President Zedillo (1994–2000), all the ejidos were dissolved and land was parceled out to individual ownership. Since the ejido has been dissolved in Degollado (none of the land near El Fuerte was ever part of an ejido), land speculation (driven by migrants eager to invest their dollars locally) has begun; prices for land with irriga-tion have reportedly climbed to 20,000 pesos a hectare. Migration is not the only force that has changed rural ways; equally important have been increased regional integration due to the highway, the telephone, and the television, and, as I discuss in Chapter 5, the precipitous decline through-out the past several decades in the percentage of families engaged in agri-cultural work as their main source of support.

BUILDING THE TRANSNATIONAL COMMUNITY: STAYING IN TOUCH

Even when migrants do not physically return, they maintain an intense level of communication with family and friends in the sending commu-nity. People move back and forth in regular, seasonal patterns, facili-tated by the relative speed of air travel (see Photo 2.7) and even direct bus service, but even during the summer when most norteños are hard at work in the United States, the flow of information is nothing short of astonishing. María, who lives in Atlanta, joked to me that the speed with which information travels surpasses the accuracy: she had barely missed her first period in her last pregnancy, she told me, when her mother called her (collect) from home to say how happy she was to hear that her daughter was pregnant with twins!

In El Fuerte, individual phone service only became available in the summer of 1996; before that people had to line up to make and receive phone calls at the general store, which had a thriving business charging for phone calls. Even under those less-than-private circumstances, many spoke to husbands or children in the United States on a weekly basis. For most of the families I knew in the rancho, the cost (several hundred dollars) of a private phone was subsidized by relatives in the United States who wanted the convenience of being able to call at any hour of the day. In Degollado, the first individual phones were installed more than a decade ago, but many families do not have a private line. Several shops near the plaza have phone booths, and those who do have phones (especially in la colonia, where they are sparser) frequently receive calls for their neighbors. Fax service is also available, though generally less

Photograph 2.7. Travel Agency. This travel agency, one of several in Degollado, quoted prices in the winter of 1997 for travel between Guadalajara and some of the destinations to which people travel frequently. Residents of this region have been traveling for decades to places such as Chicago, San Francisco, Los Angeles, and Oakland; Atlanta and Nashville are more recent incorporations into migrant itineraries.

desirable for anything other than sending copies of documents (when people get married in the church in the United States, for example, they need to send parish records indicating that they were baptized and that they are not married in Mexico) because a fax is much less private.

Some also write letters, but it can take three to four weeks for a letter to travel from a U.S. city to El Fuerte or Degollado (see Photo 2.8). Consequently, those who write on either side tend to send their letters with someone who can deliver them personally. There is almost always someone heading either north or south, and it is not uncommon for people not to know a child or a spouse's mailing address; it is possible to stay in close touch without ever mailing a letter. Videotapes also play an important

Photograph 2.8. Mexico Express.
Mexico Express is one of a number of
businesses that have sprung up to take
advantage of people's intense desire to
maintain relationships across great
distances. Letters mailed between the
United States and Mexico can take up
to three or even four weeks to arrive,
but Mexico Express (which has out-
lets in Degollado and other migrant-
sending communities in Mexico) gets
letters and small packages to their
destination in about a week by sending them directly to southern California in a bus and then mailing them to
destinations throughout the United
States with an American stamp.

role; people watch these tapes over and over again, and minute details do
not escape notice: Susana, whose boyfriend is in Atlanta, told me that one
of their biggest fights started because he noticed her dancing with another
young man in a videotape of a wedding in El Fuerte that he saw in Atlanta.

For migrants to the United States, their identity as residents of El Fuerte or Degollado is a source of solace, reminding them that in Mexico they are valued members of a community in spite of the fact that they work in low-paying, low-status jobs in Atlanta. Men and women also use their connections to others from the same community to build their lives in America. The primary way that people hear about work opportunities is through relatives and friends from home. Migrants who arrive in Atlanta may start work within a day or two because a cousin or a sibling will have scouted out possibilities in advance. Recent migrants count on relatives and friends for information about apartments, medical services, and school enrollment for their children, and most socialize primarily with fellow townspeople.

As is typical of Mexican migrants, the men from El Fuerte have a soccer team in Atlanta composed primarily of fellow townspeople. Degollado has fielded soccer teams in Chicago and southern California, but the men are either too dispersed or else the migrant stream is not sufficiently established for a soccer team to have been organized (though some men play on other towns' teams). When the Mexican migrants join soccer teams in Atlanta or other U.S. cities, they are re-creating the weekly rhythm of their social lives in Mexico: in both Degollado and El Fuerte, soccer is as much of a Sunday ritual for many men as Mass is for their wives. The women from Degollado who live in a suburb north of Atlanta meet regularly on Wednesdays at a local church for a rosary in Spanish. Both single-sex social events like baby showers and mixed ones such as baptisms, weddings, and birthday parties are primarily attended by others from the same hometown, and in moments of crisis the local network springs into action, banding together.

IMAGINING THE FAMILY: LIVING-ROOM DECOR

A description of the photos and objects with which men and women on both sides of the border decorate their living spaces gives a bit of depth to one's understanding of how these families imagine themselves.[20] Living rooms in Mexico and the United States are decorated with one or two large, many-shelved pieces of furniture, a cross between bookshelves and stereo cabinets. These shelves are frequently the only piece of furniture in a room other than a bed, a couch, or a chair. Made of wood or formica, they display electronic equipment, crocheted doilies, party favors from weddings and baptisms, formal, posed family photos from a portrait studio, religious icons, and small, sentimental gifts that men may give to their wives or children to their mothers—a sort of altar to the family. These altars on both sides of the border have the same categories of items, yet there are subtle but important differences between them.

Prominently displayed on the shelves will be some combination of electronic equipment: a stereo, a television, a VCR, or a portable boom box (preferably one that plays CDs instead of tapes). Among Mexicans in the United States, the stereos and televisions tend to be of recent vintage and in good working order.[21] In Mexico the shelves will frequently contain electronic equipment that does not work (for example, three TVs, only one of which works or only one of which is in color and connected to the antenna). Nonfunctioning items are not discarded both because there is always the hope they can be fixed, and because, even if they do not actually work, they still do the symbolic work of representing connections with successful family members in el norte.

The second item gracing these pieces of furniture are crocheted doilies. As with the electronic equipment, the doilies have related but distinct meanings in Atlanta and in the sending communities. In both locations, they are a focal point for demonstrating feminine homemaking and attention to detail, visible proof of the emotional bonds between women. Heavily starched and ironed doilies also decorate wardrobes, couches, chairs, tables, and china cabinets (only the larger homes, of course, have china cabinets). In some homes, they seem to cover any available horizontal or vertical surface; they are tucked into wardrobe doors and drawers, and slipped beneath picture frames and ceramic figurines. Women and girls crochet doilies for each other as gifts or, less frequently, for themselves, weaving together families and homes with these elaborate needlework creations.[22] Part of a feminine currency of exchange, a set of doilies makes a well-received Mother's Day or Christmas gift.[23] I received several sets as Christmas gifts while in Degollado, and many women gave them to me as going-away gifts before I left. Concha, assuming that the doily style of decorating was universal, asked me if I had an eight-doily bookshelf in my living room or if we had the larger, twelve-doily style.

In Mexico most women crochet their own as gifts, or if they can afford to or do not know how (most women seemed to know how to crochet, though not all enjoyed it) they will pay someone else to make a set for them as a gift. Josefina, for example, made sets of doilies for other women. Women also give gifts of cross-stitch, either in the form of large (24″ × 24″) napkins used to wrap stacks of hot tortillas, pillowcases (which are not as private a gift as one might think, since most bedrooms double as sitting rooms during the day) or, most splendidly, large table-cloths.[24]

In Atlanta, in contrast, many Mexican women buy sets of doilies for their homes, usually from other women who have purchased them in Mexico specifically to bring to the United States and sell. Pilar, who lives outside Degollado in a small farming community, crochets doilies to sell to a woman for about 8 pesos (1 dollar each); the doilies might sell for several dollars at the Mexican flea market in the United States. Some continue to do needlework as they did in Mexico, but many say that between working outside their homes and the endless diversions offered by life in the United States there is no longer time to sit and crochet. Women continue to exchange sets of doilies as gifts, but less commonly than in Mexico. Doilies continue to have their place in the living room as a sign of a feminine, well-ordered home and of the threads of connection that build community, but they also become a symbol of consumption and of the changing value of women's time.

The party favors known as *recuerdos* (literally, memories) or as *arroces* (rices) are a less-gendered signifier of cross-border social ties. Arroces are small ceramic or plastic figures from wedding, baptisms, and quinceañeras, in the shape of a swan, a shoe, a bell, a couple, a heart, or perhaps a wedding ring. Decorated with glitter or bits of tulle, the ones from weddings may actually contain a small (symbolic) amount of rice, although rice-filled bags of tulle are given to the guests at a wedding so that the arroz can be saved as a souvenir. On them one reads the name of the couple, infant, or honored señorita (for example, "wedding of Juan and Guadalupe" or "baptism of Pedro Figueroa"), the date, and the name of the padrinos who contributed that particular recuerdo to the party. Many people in Degollado and El Fuerte plan a wedding or baptism around the December or January arrival of relatives from el norte, upon whom they know they can count for a level of generosity hard to match among those who earn in pesos. It is nearly impossible to refuse a request to be someone's padrino or *madrina* (godmother) without giving offense, so those who journey back count these sponsorships as one of the costs, and the pleasures, of showing how well they have done "on the other side." When it was time to head north again, Guadalupe's sister joked that she could not afford any more *compadrazgos*.

Mexicans who marry in the United States also have recuerdos; Isabela in Degollado made the arroces for her sister Blanca's wedding in Atlanta so late that she had to send them via DHL Second Day Air so they would arrive in time for the wedding. Whether displayed in Mexico or the United States, the recuerdos are both personal, glittery reminders of having been invited to, and attended, a party, and more generally a reminder to all that a new tie of compadrazgo has been created. But in Mexico they can also serve to note the munificence and prosperity of those who have been in el norte, while in Atlanta they are also physical evidence of how one continues to be thickly knit into a social network in the South.

On these living-room shelves one also sees photos of family. These are not the snapshots so common in American homes, though; film is expensive and a camera is a luxury—instead, one sees professional photos of large groups of relatives, taken for the most part at weddings. Also common are large-format, full-length wedding portraits; it is a point of pride for a woman to have gotten married in white rather than eloping, and so women eagerly display their wedding photos as a tangible reminder of their triumph. In Mexico, I also saw many old, handcolored studio portraits of people's parents and grandparents. These older photos are quite rare in Mexican houses in Atlanta; most of these studio portraits are the only photos people have of their now-deceased parents or grandparents and thus not something they are likely to give a child or spouse departing for what is hoped to be a temporary absence in el norte. Newer-looking portraits of nuclear families, arrayed against the mottled blue background used by American photo studios, are displayed on both sides of the border: the father, mother, and two or three children seem a typically North American grouping, and they are smiling, in sharp contrast to the serious demeanor of the older wedding pictures. Although I suspect the difference in emotional tone of the photos is due at least in part to fluoridated water and greater access to dentistry among Mexicans in the United States (part of what people do when they smile is show off shiny, straight white teeth), the intended message also seems distinct. The older photos suggest that the act of having one's picture taken is momentous and that one should face the camera directly in one's Sunday best—these are depictions of respectability, rather than charm. The newer photos, in contrast, show families grouped to convey warmth and happiness; the father's hand is on the mother's, and they stand close, touching each other and their children. They are still in their best dress, the women carefully made-up and every hair on the men's heads in place, so part of the message is prosperity and success, but the difference in emotional tone is striking, the focus on capturing happiness for all to see.

Decorative, sentimental gifts exchanged among family members, such as arrangements of plastic flowers or small ceramic figurines bearing messages such as "World's Best Mom" or "Te quiero, madre" (I love you, mother), also reflect this emphasis on emotion as constitutive of family ties. Men are less frequently on the receiving end of these gifts, and they never exchange them among themselves (for example, sons to fathers). Most typically, a son or a daughter gives them to a mother for her birthday or Mother's Day, but occasionally a husband who is particularly *detallista* (thoughtful) will give one to his wife for Valentine's Day; these spousal exchanges draw meaning from the trend toward companionate marriage.

The other images displayed on the shelves or the walls around them in homes on both sides of the border are religious ones: the dark-eyed, dark-skinned Virgin of Guadalupe is most common, but also popular is the Virgin of San Juan de Los Lagos, from the nearby town in Jalisco of the same name.[25] Crucifixes are also sometimes displayed on these shelves, but the most common place for a crucifix in a home is the bedroom. It is the rare home in the Bajio region of Mexico that does not have a crucifix hanging over the bed's headboard, and people frequently hang their rosary beads on the bedpost. Without putting too fine a point on it, the doleful countenance and bloody stigmata of *Nuestro Señor* (Our Father) serve as a constant reminder of the values that should be lived out in the marital bed. Although I did not enter the bedrooms of all the women I interviewed in the United States, at least several of the ones I saw lacked the crucifix. When I asked Blanca, recently married, why there was no crucifix above her bed in their little townhouse in a suburb north of Atlanta, she laughed enigmatically. Most Mexican women do not turn away from the church when they migrate, and for some women both their social relationship to the institutional church and their personal relationship with La Virgen de Guadalupe continued to be an important source of strength and support—but the missing crucifixes in some bedrooms in Atlanta hint at a private sphere beyond the reach of the confessional.[26]

People in the sending and receiving communities share a vision of the ideal family. These families value technological connection to modern sources of entertainment and the material success that these items represent. They also prize social connections, both the feminine ties embodied in multiple sets of doilies and the less-gendered ones symbolized by large collections of party favors. The sentimental gifts suggest another kind of tie, a tie based not on blood like the photos or exchange like the doilies and party favors but rather on emotion, and the family photos imply both the shared importance of blood ties and a subtle shift in how people understand what it is, exactly, that ties them together.

I saw many of those I met in Atlanta later in Mexico, and people I met in Mexico popped up constantly in Atlanta. The intensity of this movement complicates making comparisons between those who go and those who stay—those who go frequently return, and many of those who stay seem perpetually poised on the brink of leaving. Furthermore, people do not just move between places—some of them continue to own property and maintain an identity as residents of communities on both sides of the border, communities that depend on each other in integral ways. Both economically and culturally, Degollado and El Fuerte would not be what they are without the support of migrants. The migrant communities, it barely needs to be said, base their group identity on shared background, on the fact that they know each other's families *al otro lado* (on the other side). But in spite of these transnational social ties, there persist important differences between the two locations—differences that led men and women in Degollado, El Fuerte, and Atlanta to tell me that "in the United States, women give the orders." Before exploring those differences, however, it is important to look a little more carefully at how the influence of migration has combined with other social changes to reshape gender relations in the sending communities.

CHAPTER 3

From *Respeto* (Respect) to *Confianza* (Trust)

Changing Marital Ideals

In Mexican Spanish, the words *novio* and *novia* refer to boyfriend and girlfriend, respectively, but also to one's intended spouse; there is no separate term for a fiancé(e). For the older women in the Mexican field sites, the concepts were indistinguishable: the goal of a *noviazgo* (courtship) was to produce a marriage. These brief noviazgos, which were strictly controlled by the girls' parents, allowed for very little personal interaction between the future spouses. My use of the term "courtship" rather than "dating" as a translation for noviazgo, dated though it may sound, is deliberate. Courtship—and the implication of tightly controlled opportunities for interaction and a highly socially scripted process leading inevitably (it is hoped) to marriage—seems a much more appropriate translation.

Courtship, however, has changed radically over the last generation.[1] The desired outcome is still marriage, but courtship has also become an end in itself, a life stage to be savored for its pleasures rather than rushed through for its perils. Boyfriends and girlfriends place great emphasis on spending time together and on getting to know one another, and these relationships have become *una diversión* (entertainment or amusement). These generational transformations in the process through which young people choose a partner to marry demonstrate fundamental changes in marriage itself—a transition toward relationships in which the ties that bind are perceived to be primarily those of affection, rather than obligation.

The generational contrasts I draw are rather broad: the older women were over forty at the time of the fieldwork (born before 1955), while the younger were under forty (born after 1955). When I refer to older women, I include both the mothers of the life history informants and some of the older life history informants themselves, four of whom were born before 1955. While forty is hardly old in any absolute sense, for the most part the experiences and ideas of these older informants were more similar to those of the mothers than to the rest of the life history informants. When I say "mothers," I am generally referring to the life history informants' mothers, although most of the life history informants have children and so are themselves mothers.

HISTORICAL CONTEXT:
WHAT HAS CHANGED IN THE PAST THIRTY YEARS?

Three recent developments have had an important impact on Mexican sexual culture: mass media, schooling and a resulting rising age at marriage, and migration. Mass media received through satellite TV transmission, videocassette recorders, and pop music has increased the influence of national and international popular culture on small towns and ranchos. Satellite television arrived in Degollado and El Fuerte in the mid-1980s, changing TV viewing from a nightly battle with erratic, static-filled pictures to a reliably clear, easily audible, and extremely beguiling nonstop stream of *telenovelas* (soap operas), variety shows, and U.S.-made movies dubbed in Spanish. VCRs increased access to U.S.-made movies in general and to pornography in particular: a surprising number of the life history informants told me they had snuck over to a friend's house during the day at least once to learn about *que hacen los casados* (what married people do) by popping a porn movie into the VCR. TV variety shows promote popular songs about sex and love through a brazen reliance on barely dressed women, which stands in strong contrast to more traditional ideas about modesty.

These examples of how the mass media shape sexuality are meant to show the intertwining of cultural influences with structural change: the images available on television would be irrelevant if these girls' families did not have televisions and (for many) satellite dishes, and that they do is largely due to migrant remittances. Furthermore, the possibility of being able to turn on the TV depends as well on the availability of electricity, which in rural Mexico has frequently been provided to communities on a patronage basis by the former ruling party, the PRI, in exchange for support in the voting booth. Finally, even if people have televisions and electricity, they also need leisure time in which to view them (and in some cases to do so unsupervised), so the influence of media also depends on the social changes that have created situations in which girls might be at home alone, without pigs to feed or corn to grind into masa for tortillas.

Education has been an important influence in a number of ways. In the rural area that includes El Fuerte, the percentage of the population over age fifteen who is illiterate fell from 48 percent in the 1960 census to 24 percent in the 1990 census.[2] In Degollado, illiteracy in the adult population declined from 32 to 11 percent during the same time period.[3] Rising literacy means that women with access to printed materials can seek out information about their bodies, sex, and reproduction, as a number of the younger life history informants recounted doing. Second, in the 1960s a national education reform movement revised the sixth-grade textbooks used throughout the country to include basic information about reproduction.[4] Since then, the federal government has had an official policy of encouraging the teaching of sex education, although the form these programs take varies widely according to local politics.[5] The older women grew up with the idea that sex and reproduction were topics about which respectable people did not speak in public, whereas all of the younger life history informants were exposed to some kind of information about reproduction in primary school. Whatever else their daughters may have learned in school about how babies were made, the very fact that the teacher would have discussed these topics is an important message about the social value of knowledge about one's body.

A related demographic trend has been the rising age at marriage. Data from one survey, for example, indicate that among women who were aged 15–29 in the 1970s (a little bit younger than most of the life history informants' mothers), the median age at marriage was 18.8 years. For the cohorts born two decades later, who were between the ages of 15 and 29 in 1994, the median age at marriage was 21.2 years.[6] In the past it was not uncommon for women in Degollado and El Fuerte to marry as early as 15 or 16. Some still do so, but marriage at 15 is increasingly cause for comment or even criticism. During the time of my fieldwork, for example, a 15-year-old woman I knew in Degollado ran away with her boyfriend; her sister in Atlanta repeatedly referred to her sister and brother-in-law in Degollado as *"un pinche par de crias"* (a pair of damn kids).

Third, the increasing integration of the two sending communities into migrant circuits during the past generation has had cultural and social implications for courtship and marriage. As growing numbers of married and single women have migrated north throughout the past decade, slipping off to el norte has become firmly established as an option for women whose behavior does not conform to community standards. Female return-migrants parade their superior status as norteñas by dressing less modestly, smoking in public, driving, and in general going out of their way to show townspeople how things are done al otro lado. A generation ago hand-holding was a stain on an unmarried woman's honor, but it is now widely regarded as innocuous. Women insist on sticking to all the old customs at their peril: most of the year there are many fewer young men than women in the town, and in fact the town is full of *quedadas* (literally, leftover women) in their thirties and forties.

The transformation in courtship is due in part to the cultural and economic aspects of Mexico's relationship with its northern neighbor and in part to inherently Mexican social processes. The prominence of migration as an individual strategy for economic security and mobility has been shaped by Mexican strategies for national development (remittances represent a major portion of Mexico's GDP and were estimated at between five and six billion dollars in 1997) as well as by the U.S. demand for cheap labor.[7] Furthermore, the most widely watched television programs are not *Baywatch* or *Magnum PI* but rather the Mexican telenovelas, which express ideas about gender, sexuality, and social class that suggest a new *Mexican* sexuality, rather than a simple mimicking of North American modes of thought. Changing courtship patterns in rural Mexico cannot be understood in isolation from international influences—but neither are those changes solely a product of those influences. As Parker argues in *Beneath the Equator,* when we explore local variation in sexuality, we should acknowledge the intertwining of the local and global, rather than trying to isolate one from the other.[8]

Courtship begins, of course, with choosing (or being chosen). Once a choice is made, the question arises of how to see one's beloved. But once a time and a place are agreed on, the most crucial questions remain still unanswered: What will they talk about? Will he try to kiss her? Will she let him? In the final part of this chapter, I review the rules for stealing kisses in the dark.

COURTSHIP: CHOOSING AND BEING CHOSEN IN NOVIAZGO

Matrimonio y mortaja, del cielo baja.

Marriage and funeral shrouds come down from above.

Mexican saying

Casarse bien (to marry properly or well) does not have the connotation it does in English of making a good match. Rather the implication is of conducting oneself properly through the process, of getting married decently like a good girl. Having one's daughters marry properly is an achievement for a mother. There are two paths to marriage (both of which have changed over time): getting married "properly" (casarse bien), and eloping or running off together (*irse*). In the first, the novio and the novia would decide to marry, and the novio would ask his parents to send a representative to the girl's parents to ask for her hand. This would usually be either the priest or some other locally respected person, along with a relative of the young man (his parents if they dared), but never the young man himself (this would have been disrespectful). The novia, meanwhile, might have warned her parents so they would not be caught unawares by the visit. Girls were asked if they really wanted to marry the young man; if the answer was yes, either the couple or the parents would decide on the *plazo*, which was the formal engagement, during which time either the novia or the novio had the right to call it off (supposedly) with no loss of face.

Now, when couples marry "properly" it is frequently the young man himself who comes to ask the girl's parents for their permission, or at most the young man's parents. The times are long gone when people were afraid that the girl's father would be so outraged that anyone would dare approach him that he would respond by drawing a loaded gun on the visitors (that is, people used to ask the priest to accompany them to emphasize that it was a respectful visit, and because no one would have dared assault a priest). Nowadays parents are so pleased that their daughters even care about getting married properly (as opposed to running away) that they are much more willing to accept a visit even from the bridegroom himself. The plazo is much shorter than in the past: parents worry that young couples will not be able to resist the temptation to run away together, even though they are engaged. (I heard of a number of cases in Degollado where couples who were engaged to be married ran off together, so apparently this fear is justified.)

When a couple elopes, they arrange beforehand for the girl to spend the night out of her house. In the past, this meant sneaking her out of her parents' house and leaving her for the night with a well-respected family in the community. Having spent the night outside her parents' house ruined her reputation, and so forced her parents to allow her to marry. She would remain in *una casa de respeto* (a respectable house) until they had been married in a church ceremony. Being in a respectable house made it publicly clear that although the couple had disobeyed the girl's parents (that is, shown them a lack of respect, *una falta de respeto*), the boy had not shown a lack of respect to the girl herself. In an alternate version of this scenario, the young man would take her home to his own house, but she would sleep in bed with his mother rather than with him until they were married. Now when couples elope it just means that the girl spends the night with the boy anywhere outside her own home; this could mean in a hotel, in his car, or in his bedroom in his parents' house. Sometimes they have sexual intercourse right away and sometimes they decide between themselves to wait until they have been married in a civil ceremony. (Rebhun found an identical set of formal and informal paths to marriage in northeastern Brazil.)[9]

Couples elope (*se van*) for a number of reasons. Most obviously, running away together means not having to wait for the girl's parents permission, so they frequently do it in cases where they fear encountering opposition (for example, if the girl is fifteen or younger or if they know that the parents do not approve of the match). A number of the life history informants began their conjugal life in this way. Usually they get married in a civil ceremony immediately afterward and in a church ceremony as soon as they can afford to. The life history informants who came from wealthier families were much more likely to have gotten married properly than were the women from poorer ones.

The local church has tried to discourage people from running off together rather than beginning their married life with the blessing of the sacrament. In the past, young men who had run off first were required to walk to their wedding Mass from the edge of town (downhill from the church) carrying a large wooden cross on their backs as a symbol of their shame. I was told that priests stopped making them do this when one young man stopped in a bar, cross and all, for a drink before the Mass. Girls, for their part, were forbidden to wear white to the Mass. Now couples who run off together are only allowed to be wed in a 6

A.M. Mass, not an ideal hour for those planning a large celebration. Even the prohibition against wearing white seems to be weakening: one of the life history informants who eloped when she was fourteen has their wedding photo proudly displayed in her living room in Atlanta, and in it she is wearing a tiara and a long white sequined gown.

With all of these changes, older and younger women talk differently about the process of choosing and being chosen in courtship. Older women talk about marriage as a question of destiny, an issue determined by divine will rather than by individual action. Younger women pay lip service to the idea that women are the prize rather than the seekers, but between the lines they admit to a much more active role in choosing among novios. Regardless of the difference in how they tell their courtship stories, both older and younger women played some role in choosing their husbands, but the generational difference in discourse suggests a real cleavage in gender ideology. Furthermore, older women said that, to the extent that one could choose, it was important to focus on finding a man who could fulfill his obligations as a husband, while younger women want a man who is both a good provider and a good companion.

The older women in Degollado and El Fuerte told me stories about the rough times, a generation ago, when men in the ranchos would carry women off at gunpoint.[10] In the 1950s and 1960s, when these older women courted, young women felt vulnerable to being kidnapped whenever they were outside their homes, away from the moral and physical protection of their families (for example, when they went to the river to bathe and do laundry). The kidnapping involved abducting a woman, perhaps with the aid of several friends, and raping her so that she would be forced to marry to save the family's honor. In some cases the men would reportedly break into women's homes, particularly if the father and brothers were away. The seven who spent their dating years in ranchos (the youngest of whom was married in 1968) all knew stories about women their age who had been kidnapped.

Kidnapping did not deprive women of any control over courtship. None of the life history informants' mothers, after all, were kidnapped, and even those women who were could still resist the union—but the possibility of violence made courtship a dangerous time, limiting the extent to which some women were able to decide freely. Two of the life history informants' mothers thought about changing their minds after they were engaged, only to have their fiancés send word that they would kidnap them anyway. Both women said that they decided it was more important to protect their parents from the public humiliation of having daughters who had not followed the ideal path to marriage. Doña Luisa, though, did change her mind, in spite of a threatened kidnapping. She told me how her novio "sent word...that [she] was not going to escape him," but every time she saw him she would run and lock herself in her house. She went on to marry a man of whom she was quite fond.

Although the violence in many cases was quite real, the way women return again and again to kidnapping suggests that they also use violence as a metaphor, as discursive support for an ideal of female passivity. Their insistent depictions of themselves as without agency reveals an underlying generational difference: the older women emphasize the choice less because for them it was not the crucial element of a successful marriage. Rather, as suggested by the saying that marriage and death are determined in heaven, they talk about marriage in terms of destiny, in terms of marrying *el que te toca* (the one for whom you are destined). For a marriage to be successful, what mattered was to know how to sacrifice and suffer, how to bend oneself to one's husband's will, not to know how to choose.

Some older women certainly loved their husbands and felt emotionally close to them. Mariana, for example, talked about how she accepted her husband because "I grew fond of him, I had a lot a fondness for him, and I liked him and I, I don't know, we really liked each other" (*yo lo quise*). One broke into tears talking about how much she missed her husband, who had been away working for four months in the United States, and Doña Luisa (who chose her husband because he was "*amable*" [so nice]) started to cry when remembering him.

These older women were not passive during the courtship process; most of the mothers, after all, said that they chose their husbands themselves. Norma admitted that she was the one who suggested to her husband that they run away together rather than wait to ask her father's permission. Doña Luisa noted, "We had agreed that he would ask for permission to marry me," and Rosalia reminded me that up to the last minute before the church ceremony, women are free to change their minds because, "She's asked for, but she's not given away."

The generational difference lies in how women choose to tell their stories. The older women deliberately frame their experiences in terms of their own passivity because Mexican women in the past derived a certain amount of power from marrying *el que le tocó* (he for whom you are destined). Their power lay in knowing how to *saberse llevar* (to know how to get along). In some cases, this was the power of martyr-dom, but it was a power nonetheless. Saying that marriage "*es una cruz*" (is a cross) implies that the goal is endurance, not pleasure or in-timacy; the issue is not how one feels about the cross, but rather that one have the strength to endure its weight, to *aguantar* (to suffer or to endure). Similarly, the saying that marriage "*es un albur*" (is a riddle, or a dirty joke) implies that there is no point to choosing, because what one chooses always turns out to be something other than what it ap-peared. Choosing a good husband was beside the point; the goals were to get married without tarnishing one's good name and family repu-tation, and then to have the strength to *aguantar*, to endure whatever lay ahead.[11]

Although they depicted their courtships as ones in which they were chosen, older women also suggested that—if one did have any con-trol—there were certainly some qualities one might prefer in a spouse. Older women told me that a good husband was "one who would not drink so much," a man who was "serious" and "not a scoundrel." Oth-ers recalled how handsome their husbands were as young men.[12] Al-though one or two of the women mentioned hoping for someone with whom it would be easy to get along, or a man with a gentle manner, it was hardly a major emphasis, and none talked about looking for a companion or a friend. They decided based on whether he was respect-ful toward them, on whether he wanted to get married properly or run away with them, and on his family's reputation. The emphasis on a man's family casts light on a finer distinction: the older women did not emphasize the necessity of getting to know a young man because they already knew what they needed to about him by knowing what sort of family he came from, whereas younger women were concerned with in-dividual compatibility and personality. Older women spoke of rejecting suitors because they came from families with bad reputations, either with fathers who drank and did not work or mothers who were less than respectable. This idea of seeing whether someone comes from good stock was among the most powerful criteria for choosing a mate: the saying in Spanish is *hijo de tigre sale pintito* (the son of the tiger turns out striped), and over and over again in interviews and conversa-tions older women told me that the best way of really knowing some-one was through knowledge of his family. One informant, who lives with her husband in Atlanta, said her mother "always told us to pay at-tention to their roots" (*que nos fijemos en la raíz*). Family reputation still enters into young women's concerns (and their mother's advice), but some young women challenge their mother's advice with another saying, about how not all five fingers on the hand are the same.

Younger Women

For younger women, in contrast, marital success depended on their skill at choosing a mate, rather than in adapting to their destiny. The ideal of female passivity has been transformed into a sort of "passive agency" in which nice girls can encourage pursuit, although the younger women take pains to distinguish between their indications of willingness to be pursued and a more active role. Young women frame their behavior not as true pursuit but rather as letting that special someone know that they are willing to be pursued. Blanca, for example, described how a courtship begins: a young woman sees "someone to whom you are attracted [*que te guste*]...and you give him a little look [*le eches el ojito*], and he gives you a little look back and that is how it starts,...then he goes up to you and he talks to you and you begin to talk." She emphatically distinguished that sort of "little look" from actually initiating a relationship. When I questioned her further ("But can you also go up to him?"), she said, "No, just the man approaches the woman." She described women who would actually approach a man as *aventadas* (very wild), *ingratas* (disagreeable), and *rogonas* (women who beg for it). The same game of exchanging looks and smiles was mentioned by many other women; in spite of repeated assertions that "they seek you out," women just as often admit that "when they go by and you look at them, you smile."

There is a limit beyond which flirtatiousness becomes transgression, and the younger women were eager to distinguish between giving little looks and smiles and being a rogona. They did this by telling stories about women who crossed the line, about bad girls who pursued men. One of the young women even admitted with mild dismay that she had come close to actually pursuing her boyfriend. They had broken up, but she was still interested in him. Just as she was going to send a message that she wanted to talk to him, their intermediary came up to her and told her that he wanted to talk to her. Reflecting back, she says, "I was ashamed, I thought to myself, how is it possible for me? Because I am a woman, and supposedly it is the man's job—later they would have said that I am a rogona."

The young women laughed when I asked if they knew anyone who had been kidnapped; although their mothers still warn them not to ruin

Drawing 3.1. Friends and Boyfriends. This drawing, by a married woman in Degollado, depicts today's more drawn-out courtships. In the first frame she shows herself pleasantly chatting with a suitor; the physical distance between the two of them suggests that this relationship is characterized more by respect than by *confianza*. The caption reads "Conociendo Amigos" (getting to know male friends). In the second frame, a different fellow kneels down and offers some flowers; she coyly leans away while simultaneously reaching out toward him. The caption to this one is "Mi Noviazgo" (my courtship).

their lives with a premarital pregnancy, clearly the danger of irreparably staining the family's honor has diminished, even though the time spent courting has grown (see Drawing 3.1). Whereas several of the twenty-six life history informants married their first boyfriend, most of them had broken off with at least one novio before choosing a husband; one even deliberately broke up with her boyfriend (who was quite eager to marry her) several times because she did not want to marry without having had other boyfriends.

Some of the younger women also talked, retrospectively, about balancing between their noviazgos and their other life plans. Isabel, for example, stressed that she had chosen her boyfriend from among several suitors ("I had the opportunity to choose, and I chose him") because she wanted time to do her homework: he was the only one who was studying out of town rather than locally and thus the only one who would not be around to pester her during the week. "I said to myself, 'If I choose one of the others they are going to want to see me during the week, at least every two or three days, *and I said no, I am in school and I have to do my homework, I have to study.* So ... it was better to choose the one who would come see me every two weeks'" (emphasis added). Rosa, who now lives with her husband in Atlanta, showed this same focus on achieving a goal. Her boyfriend courted her for years, first in her *ranchito* and later long distance when she was living and working in Chicago and he was in Atlanta. He asked her to marry him many times, but she put him off until she had accomplished what she set out to do before getting married: finishing high school, working for a time in Mexico in the profession in which she had been trained (accounting), and living in the United States as a single woman and earning money to send back to her mother. Then, she said, she was ready to marry. (That Rosa included supporting her mother—a task that had primarily fallen on her brothers—among her goals reinforces the idea that this transformation in the ideal life course has more complex causes than simply the diffusion of American ideals. It seems likely that many American women would see the provision of economic support for a parent as a burden rather than an achievement or an indication of gender equity.)

The generational contrast also stands out in what the younger women said they sought in a future husband. Younger women focused more on individual personality than on family character, individual attractiveness, or a man's perceived quality as a worker. Susana, who had lived in Atlanta but who when interviewed was back in El Fuerte, talked about paying attention to appearances (*lo físico*) with her first boyfriend, but then said that she learned with time to focus on other criteria. With her next boyfriend, she recalled, "I didn't pay so much attention to the physical but rather in his feelings [*los sentimientos*] and now what's more important are feelings, not appearances. If I broke up with him, what I would look for in another would be the feelings too, I wouldn't pay attention to the physical." With the exception of one of the younger women, who is discussed below, all gave some considerations to a man's potential ability to support a family—but for none of the women who had been married for less than ten years was this the outstanding factor.[13]

What stands out in the younger women's narratives is their focus on the quality of the emotional tie developed during courtship. Mercedes, for example, talked about the importance of a man's ability and willingness to communicate. She said that men and women look for the same thing in their partner—sincerity—and when I asked her to expand, she said, "He is sincere, he's frank, ... as if he were opening up his heart to me so that I could see all that has happened to him." Blanca, who was engaged during the interviews, responded to a question about what men look for in a girlfriend by talking about how courtships change over time. She said: "You get to an age in which you begin to think of things more seriously. You say, 'How are we going to live, how are we going to get along?' You are more centered...you choose a boyfriend at first just for attraction, but later, when you want a stable relationship, you start to think about...whether you have a good relationship, [if he is...] a companion, a friend. As they say, courtship is a lovely time, but you have to know how to choose,...to talk about things, to have a lot of trust and communication." Susana, still single in her early twenties and living with her parents in the rancho, responded easily to the question about what one wants from a boyfriend by saying, "What I want is that he love me and respect me." When I asked her why she thought her current boyfriend would make a good husband, she said she could tell by "the way he is and how he treats me, that is that he treats me as if I am everything to him."

This generational difference in what women look for in a husband reflects an underlying shift in how women conceive of the purpose and potential of marriage. Women's own economic resources may have something to do with this change: the only woman interviewed who said she thought *only* of the affective dimension of her marriage was also the only woman whose father left her a large (for Mexico) inheritance. When I asked her what she expected from a boyfriend, she answered: "I wanted someone like that...guy who spoke so sweetly to my friend....I wanted someone very loving. I think because of how my childhood was—there were so many problems and I was so distanced from my mother—I wanted someone very sweet, thoughtful.... *I never thought to have a husband that didn't smoke, that wasn't a drunk, that was a hard worker, I never thought of that. I think I was lucky, because I got carried away with him and what if he had been lazy or a drunk? I think, 'Jeez, what I could have gotten stuck with'*" (emphasis added).

If this change were only found among women who had access to paying jobs (or inheritances), one might conclude that women's entrance into the labor force transforms marriage from a primarily economic to a primarily affective partnership. However, it was two young women from the rancho who spoke most compellingly about this vision of marriage as an affectionate partnership. Neither has more than a sixth-grade education and neither comes from a family with any significant material resources. Interestingly, both of their fathers were absent for much of their own childhoods, working in the United States to support the family. One of the things women repeatedly talk about when they discuss the decision to migrate with their husbands is that they do not want their children to grow up the way they did, barely knowing their own fathers.

Claudia and her husband spent six years as novios. At first they courted through the closed door of her house and later they stood next to each other (but never touching), just outside that door. When I asked her what she liked about him, she talked about how he had been respectful: he was punctual and he did not dance with other girls before dancing with her, did not try to kiss her or to convince her to elope instead of getting married the right way. The quality she held dearest, however, was the trust they had, the confianza. She described this trust as allowing them "to talk very deeply about everything, so that he tells me about his life and I tell him about mine. [We shared] his thoughts, his way of thinking, what I liked and what I don't like, and my way of thinking."

Pilar, in El Fuerte, was in her early twenties and had been married for about two years. She talked about the moral support her husband (then boyfriend) gave her during her mother's illness: "I cried a lot when I saw my mother so sick, but he really helped me.... Sometimes, after seeing her so sick, I ran and told him everything, and then it's as if I felt calmer.... Everything that happened to me, I would go talk to him and he would give me advice.... He really helped me a lot." She trusted him enough to borrow money in secret when her father's checks from the United States were late, so that she would be able to buy food or her mother's medication. Pilar described how, after they had courted for two and half years, he couched the marriage proposal in emotional terms, telling her that he "felt really lonely." Although she said she felt young and unprepared for marriage, she accepted his proposal because "I liked the way he is. He was not crazy, he kept to himself all the time. I liked that he never told other people what I said to him.... I liked his personality [su modo]." After this lengthy description of the importance she gave to the emotional content of their relationship, Pilar closed that section of the interview by summarizing formulaically her requirements for a husband: "trabajador, serio, que me respetará" (a hard worker, serious, and that he will respect me). Her use of this refrain—which just as easily could have come from her mother—reminds us of the importance of respect across generations. Looking for a man who respects you—whether that respect is demonstrated in stolen, momentary conversations through a stone wall or during daily, half-hour visits—is seen by all the women as a key predictor of a successful marriage. As Mercedes said, "A man who respects, cares for you seriously... if he doesn't respect you as a girlfriend, will he respect you as a wife?" Younger and older women's use of the same word, however, is somewhat misleading, since respectful behavior from a boyfriend can mean anything from never touching even a woman's hand to not trying to touch below her waist while kissing her. Having examined the steps of the courtship dance, I turn now to what I call the changing social geography of courtship: the gendered distinction between the house and the street, the symbolic nature of front doors, and the hidden-ness of what lies in plain sight.

THE SOCIAL GEOGRAPHY OF COURTSHIP

J[14]: And were there girls who get pregnant without being married *(fracasaban)*?

C: Yes, all of our lives there have been.

J: And how [is that possible], if their families had them so closely supervised (recogidas)?

C: Exactly, it's incredible but yes, there have always been girls like that. There's a joke about the plaza, you know how they sit so close together so that they look just like one person, you don't see two bodies. So an old woman goes by and she says, "Ay, look, how shameless [*desvergonzadas*] they are, and the darkness is so nice at night in the cornfield!" The point is, you do the same thing in the cornfield as there in the plaza, but the cornfield is nicer and there in the plaza, it seemed to her—well that's why I say that there have always been [girls who get in trouble].

The decreasing hiddenness of courtship in Degollado and El Fuerte speaks to a loosening of parental control and an increasing ownership of their bodies by young women; their sexuality has not ceased to be a marker of family honor, but it has also become a vehicle for their individual entertainment and pleasure. Below I sketch out the changing logistics of courtship and discuss what it means that young lovers embrace on benches in the plaza rather than meeting discreetly when the corn is high.

The space in which people choose to perform sexual acts gives meaning to those acts by implying a particular set of intentions and relationships; a flirtatious sally over the watercooler is subject to a different set of social (and legal) regulations than over a beer in a bar. In the case of heterosexual intercourse, one imagines specific implications about risk, transgression, and relationships depending on whether the setting is a parked car, an airplane bathroom, the kitchen table, or a bedroom with locked doors. The American cultural insider immediately recognizes that "bedroom sex" refers to a different moment in married life than "kitchen table sex."[15] Sexual behavior is spatially organized, and people can resist this organization or try to transform it by engaging in sexual behavior in ways that contradict accepted ideas.[16] This discussion of sex as something that is observed by others and that draws meaning from being observed, rather than just a private way of communicating between two (or more) people, calls attention to the ways in which personal milestones such as a first kiss also have important social (that is, public and shared) meaning.[17]

People in Degollado told me over and over again how couples have become shameless about kissing and embracing in the plaza, and several shared with me a story about a couple who were discovered in broad daylight having sex in the plaza, on the grass behind some trees. Supposedly the police did come, and they put the young couple in the back of their truck and drove them around town naked with their underwear flying from the truck's antenna. While I could find no eyewitnesses to this (probably apocryphal) event, shortly before I arrived all the trees in the center of the plaza were cut down, grass was planted, and signs were erected forbidding people to walk on the grass.

All of the older women say that they conducted their noviazgos *a escondidas* (in secret, or literally, in hiding). They talked through a chink in the wall, but their mothers never gave them much chance to slip off unsupervised. Some Sundays they did not talk at all because a respectful boyfriend would not dare approach the house if the girl's father, uncles, or older brothers were in sight. Even when older women did see their novios in the street during the week, modesty did not permit more than a restrained exchange of "*buenos días.*" On Sundays, a girl would bathe and put on her good dress and shoes (if she had them) and go to Mass, either in the little chapel in the rancho or in the plaza in town; this was her big opportunity to be seen by potential suitors. In town, girls would perhaps be allowed to dar la vuelta, a slow promenade around the plaza (girls counterclockwise, boys clockwise) with an aunt, older sister, or female cousin. A boy would not approach a girl if she were with her parents—that would show them a lack of respect—but if she were with someone other than her parents he might break an egg filled with confetti on her head, or give her a flower.

Where and for how long unmarried girls can see their suitors have changed, in part because their mothers have allowed them to. Many of the younger life history informants talk about how their mothers let them have boyfriends, but tried to keep it out of sight of their fathers. Arrangements varied, but generally a girl's mother would give her permission to visit with her boyfriend outside the house for half an hour, or every other night for an hour. Girls nowadays have many more excuses to be outside of their houses, whether they are in school or not; they run out to the store to get soda, a kilo of tortillas, or a bag of tomatoes for their mothers, they go to the plaza with their friends to sit on the benches and eat roasted chickpeas or fruit ices, or visit the post office to see if any letters have arrived from the United States.[18] On Sundays in Degollado they go to the flea market in the morning and to the Mass specifically for teenagers at night. Afterward, they congregate in the plaza, sitting on the outer benches or promenading, or they move to the inside benches, where the novios kiss while pretending they are invisible. In the disco, unmarried people from Degollado and the surrounding ranchos gather to dance, or to slip into a dark corner to kiss; the disco is a new setting, neither private and protected like the home nor public (and thus under the community's vigilance) like the plaza. Even in the rancho, where girls' movements are still more tightly controlled by their parents than in the town, they go to Mass on Sundays and gather afterward around the taco wagon and the little grocery store, where boys come to flirt and buy them sodas.

These logistical changes speak to more profound changes in the social control of sexuality. The changes in the social spaces in which courtships take place reflect a loosening of paternal control of young women's sexuality. To understand the import of women seeing their boyfriends in the disco instead of talking through a stone wall, or of mothers discussing inviting the future boyfriends of their prepubescent daughters to visit them in their houses, some context about the spatial organization of sexuality is necessary, in particular, about the idea that seeing is knowing and about the gendered division of space between the house and the street.

To See Is to Know

One of the life history informant's mothers told me that her father was vigilant about keeping her sisters and her enclosed in the house and unseen; he would tell them that *"santo que no es visto, no es adorado"* (the saint who is unseen will not be worshiped). To be seen is to exist; observing one's neighbors is a popular activity in small-town life. Appearances matter as much as the actual intention of one's behavior, as I was taught by my informants in Mexico who cautioned me *"no hagas cosas buenas que parecen cosas malas"* (do not do good things that look like bad things). This saying was invoked, for example, to explain to me why it was not proper to stop and talk to a man in the street—regardless of what one might actually say, any interchange more prolonged than "buenos días" between a woman and man who are not closely related by blood or marriage provokes suspicion by all who see it.

In small-town Mexico, a communal gaze monitors the dress, comportment, and speech of all members of the community. The final proof of sexual wrongdoing is visual. For example, in terms of infidelity women distinguish between what they hear about how their husbands behave and what is "thrown in their faces"; they maintain that what they do not see cannot be true and thus cannot hurt them.[19] What is seen is what counts: when people talk about a woman having *fracasada* (failed), they do not mean that she has had sex without being married but that she has gotten pregnant without being married.[20] It is the leaking of private (that is, sexual) behavior into the public sphere (via the visibility of a pregnancy) that is a contaminating social failure.

When older women say that they conducted their noviazgos in secret, they do not mean literally that their parents did not know. Rather, they mean that they took great care to help their parents avoid seeing them with their boyfriends, which would have forced them to acknowledge the relationship. It was not a lack of respect to have a boyfriend, but it would have been a serious lack of respect if the boyfriend did not run away the minute his lookout told him that his future father-in-law was rounding the corner. In some families any brother or uncle would demand this same respect by insisting that the suitor run away at his approach.

The older women also talked about how, as unmarried girls, they sought to hide any visual evidence of their developing sexuality. As their bodies started to develop, for example, they would cover their growing hips and breasts with a *rebozo* (large shawl) to show their modesty. Respecting one's parents in the home involved not only hiding one's sexuality from them, but also not seeing theirs. One life history informant, noting how the atmosphere in her home was *"muy respetuoso,"* said that this included her parents never touching each other in front of the children.[21] Respect is a code for marking and acknowledging hierarchy; to talk about sex, or to acknowledge it, is to ignore or even attack that hierarchy. Women say, for example, that they refrained from asking their mothers about sex, or even about menstruation, out of respect; similarly, women told me that members of their family never told *dobles sentidos* (Mexican puns that frequently play on sexual double meanings of words) because everyone was very respectful. Family lines of authority were marked by the management of sexuality.

The House and the Street

As others have found throughout Latin America, the street (*la calle*) and the house (*la casa*) are gendered spaces.[22] The street belongs to men; it is an appropriate place for them to sit, stand, talk, and take up space. A man does not invite criticism if he says that he has been in the street; the fact that he likes to be in the street (*le gusta andar en la calle*) may frustrate his wife (who does not know where he is) and may even imply bad behavior such as drinking or infidelity, but it is a range of motion granted to men as men, based on their gendered responsibility to support their families.[23] When men go out into the street in Degollado and El Fuerte, they never ask their wives' permission, and only sometimes do they tell them where they are going. Women's freedom of movement through the streets of Degollado and El Fuerte, in contrast, is a key arena for testing the domestic balance of power. In the Mexican field sites some women ask permission ("*¿Me dejas ir?*" [Will you let me go?]), and almost all let their husbands know if they plan to leave the house during the day, though this changes with some couples when they migrate to the United States. Women sometimes smile mischievously or apologetically when saying that they have been in the street; they almost always justify it immediately with reference to their domestic responsibilities (having to buy food, take a child to a doctor, or mail a letter to the United States). For a woman to say that she likes being in the street is to admit to being *callejera* (street-er), a word I never heard in the masculine (*callejero*). For a woman, to like being in the street is at best to admit to being a gossip, to liking to *comadrear* (gossip with one's comadres), and at worst to imply sexual wrongdoings. The worst, of course, is to be a woman *of* the street, *una mujer de la calle* (a prostitute) and the symbolic opposite of *la mujer de la casa* (the wife).

From a young age, boys are allowed to roam the streets in rural small-town Mexico with much greater freedom than their sisters. When a girl asks her mother why, she is told *el hombre no pierde nada, la mujer pierde todo* (men have nothing to lose, women have everything); too much exposure could tarnish a girl's reputation irreparably. Girls today are frequently sent on errands (though they rarely go alone), but parents keep much closer track of their daughters' movements outside the house than they do their sons'. Furthermore, two adjectives frequently used to praise or criticize an unmarried woman's behavior have to do with how she moves through the gendered space of house and street: a good girl is said to be recogida, which literally means protected or gathered in (but also refers to a female prison inmate!). It also has a sense of being tucked in; on Sunday nights, after the intense excitement of the plaza, all the good girls are safely home, recogidas en sus casas, by 10 P.M. A girl who is *volada* (the past participle of the verb *volar*, to fly) is one who is wild, who is often seen in the street, who talks too much or flirts too openly with men.

The house, in contrast, symbolizes ordered and managed sexuality as opposed to the sexual danger and ferment of the street. It is a female space, the place where a woman belongs; when a friend asks what one has been doing, and one replies, "Nothing, I have been here at home," the response is not a statement about inactivity but an assertion of properly gendered behavior. Houses are extensions of a particular man's physical presence—the father provides a structure that shelters and protects his family when he is not physically present, a border within which they are supposedly safe. Within this sexually safe space, a girl's virginity is protected just as she is protected from being seen by men who are not in the family.[24] In this context, the way that married women used to cover their heads with a rebozo whenever they left the house takes on a new meaning; like the veil in other societies, the shawl was a symbolic extension of the house, indicating modesty and covering a woman with the protective respect that married women deserve.[25]

The house, however, is more than a symbolically female space: it is also supposed to be a sexually neutral space for members of the immediate family. (The "desexualized" space at home implies that girls are automatically safe from incest with the men in their family, although of course this is not true. Two of the life history informants were sexually abused by men who, as close relatives of the family, had free access to their houses.) Girls are taught from a very young age to hide their genitals, whereas it is not unusual to see little boys run around naked between diaper changes. This connects back to how seeing is knowing: an element of vergüenza (modesty, shame) is to protect oneself from the potentially incestuous gaze of one's brothers.[26] Modesty is a more important code for women to master than it is for men. Demonstrations of shame are ultimately demonstrations of a woman's respectability.

Front doors are the passage between male and female, the house and the street. The closed front door was alluded to by many of my informants as symbolic of a girl's virginity. The front of people's houses is a place to burnish the family's public image; before the daily sweeping and mopping of the inside of their houses, women sweep and then wash down the street in front of their house. The front door is the prototypical liminal space—guarding the front door becomes a stand-in for guarding other entrances to the body.[27] Several times women joked with me about front and back doors when I was asking them about anal sex, saying that they insisted that their husbands enter "*por la puerta de adelante*" (through the front door). In the most traditional families, a young man was not permitted to cross the threshold until he did so as a son-in-law. In more modern families, the young man is allowed to enter once he and the family's daughter are formally engaged. In the only case where the boyfriend had been permitted to sit and talk with his girlfriend in the parlor, it was widely assumed that the couple had had premarital sex.

As the transition point between the protected house and the dangerous street, front doors have become an important backdrop for the daily dramas of noviazgo. Perhaps having given up on the idea that courtships would be altogether invisible, mothers of adolescent girls now make permission to talk with a suitor conditional on their standing on the doorstep, where they are under the moral protection of the house. The upper portion of most front doors in small-town western Mexico is made of frosted glass, covered with elaborate wrought-iron bars; one girl's mother insisted that her daughter actually stand directly in front of the door while being courted, so that she could see from within if her daughter's boyfriend tried to kiss her. [28]

Changing Scenes, Challenging Ownership

All the younger women had permission from their mothers to have boyfriends, and some boyfriends dared speak directly to a girl's mother, or even to her father.[29] This unwillingness to hide oneself seems like a challenge to a young man's future father-in-law, an assertion of some sort of right to court his daughters (assuming that it is done with respect). For the parents, a willingness to see a daughter's boyfriend implies both an acknowledgment that it is no longer possible to control their daughters' movements as tightly as in past (to have them so recogida) and, perhaps only slightly, a growing desire on the part of some parents to have some contact with their future son-in-law in order to assess his character as an individual (rather than inferring it from his family's reputation). On the part of a daughter, the reluctance to hide her courtships signifies a potential separation of a girl's interests from her family's, the desire to manage her noviazgos in accordance with her own short- or long-term goals.

In the course of a generation, the spatial arrangements for courtship in the Mexican sending communities have moved from talking across a physical barrier to talking in front of the house and then finally to talk-ing in the plaza or in the disco.[30] (This may be a question more of ap-pearances than of actual behavior; the joke about the cornfield at the beginning of this section reminds us that even in the past young couples found a way to sneak in moments of intimacy.) Nonetheless, the change in what is concealed and what is revealed is striking: while the Sunday promenade continues along the outer perimeter of the plaza, benches along paths leading to the bandstand in the middle are filled with young couples kissing and hugging. In a park in a large city, the lovers' privacy would stem from their actual anonymity, but everybody in the town knows each other by sight, if not by name, so privacy is based on the pretense of not being seen and not seeing. Although the girl's parents may be sitting 100 yards away on an outer bench, they pretend not to know that she is sitting on her boyfriend's lap within shouting distance.

These public kisses represent a challenge to parental—particularly pa-ternal—control over young women's sexuality. They are an assertion of a young woman's ownership of her body, of her right to enjoy the risks and pleasures of courtship rather than being so closely guarded by her parents for the sake of the family's good name. The new staging of courtship presents to the local audience a resonant and (to some) a trou-bling public performance of female desire; throughout the course of my fieldwork women complained over and over again to me about those *sinvergüenzas* (shameless girls) who make out with their boyfriends in the plaza. For the young lovers, the very fact that they are in public may allow them to kiss with such abandon, because there is a limit to how far beyond kisses and caresses they can go. (It is easier to resist a boy's re-quest to let him *"probar el pastel"* [taste the cake] before buying it, for example, on a park bench than it would be in the backseat of a car.) Part of the strength of people's reaction seems to originate in how difficult it becomes to preserve the idea of sexual interaction as something that men seek and women withhold when the plaza is full of young women who are obviously being kissed voluntarily—who are even kissing back.

INTIMACY, RESPECT, AND TRUST:
WOMEN'S EXPERIENCES OF THEIR NOVIAZGOS

In addition to the larger social meanings of standing in public locked in a passionate embrace, these kisses have a subjective, intensely personal, meaning. As the saying *el hombre llega hasta donde la mujer quiere* (men go as far as women want them to) indicates, women have been the policers of desire, but now both the amount of physical contact and the extent to which women articulate their own desire have changed. All of the women told me repeatedly that they have to be the ones in charge of how "far" men go, but as respect has been redefined to include some physical intimacy between unmarried couples, and as trust or emotional intimacy has moved front and center as a goal, the ideal courtship has shifted from a paradigm of enforced distance to one of managed closeness. Confianza has both verbal and sexual aspects (although of course trusting a boyfriend enough to tell him one's deepest secrets is related to trusting him enough to kiss him).

Together, the staging of courtship, which emphasizes the family's changing regulation of sexuality, and young women's increasing acceptance of physical intimacy within courtship due to a more general valorization of heterosexual sexual and emotional intimacy reflect part of the larger story. The external "look" of courtship has changed, but there have always been some couples who exchanged more than love letters. It is important to listen critically to what the women say; their words tell us both about their town's sexual culture and about how they see themselves fitting in. In the same way women talk simultaneously about giving little looks to their boyfriends and about how some girls today are voladas and rogonas, women's repeated criticism of the couples in the plaza serves to legitimate their own discreet kisses.

Young couples have much more time to talk, and what they talk about has changed. Blanca, for example, joked with her fiancé about being a jumpy sleeper and how they would share the bed on their wedding night. Her mother, in contrast, told of promenading around the plaza, escorted by her older sister-in-law; every time that she passed her boyfriend they would stop and exchange a few words, taking care not to talk for long enough that her parents would notice the delay. Another woman (now in her midthirties) got up the courage with some difficulty to ask her husband just days before they married if he planned to treat her as badly as his father had treated his mother (drinking, publicly going around with another woman); although this may not seem like a radical act, it is compared to her mother who says that in her time "*ni siquiera platicaba uno*" (one didn't even talk to him). One of the older informants talked about valuing a boyfriend who would not bring up embarrassing (that is, sexual) subjects, while several of the younger ones spoke proudly about having the confianza to mention their menstrual cramps to a boyfriend. Several of the life history informants discussed with their future husbands how many children they would like to have and when, whereas the mothers were uniformly shocked at the idea that an unmarried couple would have the confianza to discuss fertility control.

"Before, We Did Not Have That Confianza"

The older women told me that it was important to avoid having too much confianza during courtship. Catalina, a woman in her midforties on the rancho, said she didn't like today's noviazgos because "they have so much confianza. I tell them that before we did not have that trust. You would never have seen someone sit down next to their boyfriend, and now sometimes they go around even holding hands, as if they were married. I've never seen my daughters—but you do see a lot of girls, and I don't like that because...holding hands or kissing implies bigger things sometimes. In one of those times they'll fall." Older women invoke respect as the opposite of confianza and as the reason that a novio would never have asked to hold his girlfriend's hand or give her a kiss. They say that respect meant not trying to steal a kiss, or even to hold hands.

Preventing physical intimacy during courtship kept a woman's options open, so that if she wanted to break off with one boyfriend she would not be seen as *quemada* (literally, burned—having spoiled her reputation). As one of the older women said, the danger of permitting physical intimacy was that "later if that man did not marry that woman, that man would go around saying, 'No, I already kissed her, she's already been kissed,' and then nobody would want her." Being quemada relates not to the behavior itself but rather to public knowledge of that behavior.

Some of the younger life history informants continue to see physical distance as a way of keeping one's options open. Susana, for example, talked about how it was more important to think about her long-term goal (finding a good husband) than it was about her short-term desires:

> J: And when you were talking with him, he never asked you if he could hold your hand or if you would give him a kiss?

S: Well, sometimes, he would hold my hand, but to want to kiss me or something, no. One time he did ask me if I would give him a kiss, and I just gave him a look and he said, "Well, fine," but he never went on about it.

J: And you never gave him a kiss?

S: Just one time.

J: And how was it that you gave it to him? Did he ask you for it?

S: It was when I was about to go back [to Mexico]. He said to me that we had already [been going out for] two years, and he asked if after all that time I wasn't going to give in and I just looked at him. I said to him, "Well, just one." It was just...to say goodbye, but that was all.

J: But you never wanted to kiss him, to know what it would be like?

S: Yes, but—how should I say it—that is, I didn't dare because sometimes you break up and then they go around telling afterward. So, because of that I said, if I kiss him, he might go around talking about it but I hope not. So just that one time.

Others echoed this concern for their reputation. As Isabel recounted her grandmother telling her, "*La mujer es como un vaso de vidrio que con cualquier vaporcito se empaña y asi es una muchacha aquí*" (a woman is like a glass—with just a breath of air she gets fogged up—that's how girls are here). This delicate balance, where the young man asks and the young woman declines, is predicated on the assumption that women are more able to master their desire. Women's mastery draws strength from fear rather than from some ascetic impulse. Since they are the ones who stand to lose from having been kissed, it is up to them to keep saying no.

A woman has been the one who risks more through sexual intimacy during courtship, both in terms of her ability to attract other suitors and in terms of the respect she can demand from her current suitor if they do marry. Any sexual contact during noviazgo opens the door to future accusations of infidelity (*Si lo hiciste conmigo, ¿con cuántos no?* [If you did it with me, then with how many others did you do it?]) and so a woman sees strategic advantage in being respetada throughout a courtship. Some young women, however, are striking a new balance between trust and respect; they use the emotional trust built during courtship to lessen the risk that intimacy now means less respect later.

Negotiating Respect

When women reject physical advances, they are demanding respect. Respect is a more general term connoting social status in the community.[31]

Men, for example, can be referred to as *un hombre de respeto* with no sexual connotation; the phrase means someone is a valued member of the community, a serious person who deserves respect. Respect indicates both public image and power; the more important and higher status you are, the more respect people owe you. Respect also comes into play among equals: to demand respect is to assert equality.

For women, being respected has a distinctly sexual overtone; a woman can demand respect by declaring her body off-limits, by acting respectably (that is, beyond reproach for sexual misdoings). The saying that "el hombre no pierde nada, la mujer pierde todo" means that men do not lose any respect through their sexual behavior (although people can lose respect for them for other reasons) whereas women lose everything because their reputation is primarily based on a publicly respectable sexuality.

Men show respect for women by acknowledging their social status (for example, speaking to an unknown woman as usted rather than using the more familiar tú). More explicitly sexual, a man shows a lack of respect to a woman when he forces unwanted sexual intimacy, or even makes an inappropriate advance. Forcing sexual intimacy of any sort, whether kisses or intercourse, also indicates a lack of respect: when women talked about observing a short period of postpartum abstinence (usually forty days), or not having sex while they are menstruating, they said, "He respected me," and they used the same phrase to describe a man's willingness to wait to have sex when a couple has eloped but not yet been formally married.

The language of respect remains a crucial discourse through which people describe and regulate social relationships between unrelated men and women. Indeed, it is so common that the word respeto is sometimes omitted: when people want to know if someone has behaved badly, all they say is "*¿te faltó?*" (Did he show you a lack?). Ideas about appropriate sexual behavior are interwoven in multiple ways with the concept of respect: sex implies a lack of respect when it is seen by those who should not see it, or when it is forced on those who do not want it.

Seen in this light, the negotiation of physical intimacy is just that—an explicit negotiation, which women see as an opportunity to show the strength of their willpower and to insist on respect. These negotiations, which take place in the early phases of modern noviazgos, depend on a young woman's ability to put aside at least temporarily her own desire; her power rests on how well she can convince her boyfriend that she does not want to be kissed.[32] Isabel, for example, talked about how her mother had instructed her to "demand his respect, not let myself be grabbed, make myself valued—to show him that he could not just do what he pleased with me." On the one hand, this is only a temporary demonstration of power, derived from a woman's virginity and her physical innocence, from her "glass" not having been "fogged." On the other hand, these negotiations mean that a relationship begins with a young woman showing suitors the force of her will and testing the extent to which her right to say no will be respected, which certainly has more general implications.[33] Later, as married women, few see any strategic benefit in pretending to be passionless.

In response to a question about how one can tell a good boyfriend from a bad one, Pilar told me with pride about slapping a young man who had tried to kiss her against her will:

> You can tell right away...those who just want to pass the time with you....One day Javier came [to my house] and we talked nicely, but I told him not to come because I had a boyfriend. So he said, "That doesn't matter,"...and then the next moment he asked me for a kiss. I said no and he wanted to kiss me by force, he grabbed me really hard. I gave him a big slap—I didn't let him. I sure did give him a big slap. I told him, "Look, if you just want to be with me to see how far you can get, well, you are really wrong. Go look for another girl who likes that because I don't."

I asked her if she hadn't been just a little curious to know what it was like to kiss someone, and she responded by saying that later she had kissed her husband several times after they were engaged, but that "without love, no, I did not think it would be nice." In other words, before admitting to having desire, young women seek to establish an emotional context and to have extracted proof of being respected.

Women always interpreted questions about respect in courtship as having to do with sexual advances. Juana told me about how she demanded respect from her boyfriends:

> JH: And what would you do so that your boyfriend would respect you?
>
> J: Like so that he wouldn't touch me? Well, not a single one touched me. They wanted to kiss me and I [wouldn't let them]. No, we would break up.
>
> JH: If they asked you for a kiss you would break off with them right away?
>
> J: Yes, because I said, "We've barely been going out even two days and he's already asking me for a kiss?"

Now young women can have it both ways, assuming that they do not say yes until after they have said no for a sufficiently long period of time to establish that they are *muchachas de respeto* (respectable girls). All but two of the women who had been married for less than ten years shared a kiss (or more) with their boyfriends; several of the women among the older cohort had kissed their boyfriends, but physical intimacy seems to have gone from something that is the exception (or at least something which everyone says is the exception) to the rule.

Kisses and Confianza

One woman told me how, after fighting off her boyfriend's entreaties and her own desire for long enough, once she finally kissed him it was hard to stop: "One time I even broke up with him, because he asked me for a kiss and for me a kiss was a dishonor. Then later, after I gave him the first one, wow, I even asked him for them [laughs], no that's not true." Young women talk about abandoning their concern with appearances once they finally kissed—or even touched—their boyfriends: Mercedes, recounting how she danced with her boyfriend for the first time at the town festival, said, "We were in the plaza, it's a dance for everybody, all the people come. So we were talking a lot, just the two of us. And I had never—he also told me that he had never kept holding someone's hand after a dance, he never held on to a girl's hand after dancing with her, but with me he did. He put his arm around my waist, and *I felt so nice that I didn't care if they could see me or not*" (emphasis added). Some of the younger women even abandon the pretense that kisses are something for which a man begs and a woman doles out sparingly. Patricia, for example, emphasized her own participation: "It was both of us, as much from him as from me. It wasn't that he wanted to give it to me and I said no, or that I wanted to kiss him and he didn't. No, it was both of us."

Some couples go further, as evidenced by cautionary sayings such as *empiezan con la mano, y siguen con el pie* (they start with your hand, and then they continue with your foot). The word *faje*, which refers to everything between a kiss and intercourse, implies two aspects of this petting: that lovers stand or sit with their arms wrapped around each other, and that the lovers only touch each other above the belt.[34] There are couples, though, who go beyond a little *faje* and, as the saying goes, *se comen la torta antes del recreo* (they eat their sandwich before lunchtime). The town and (to a lesser extent) the rancho are full of couples whose first baby was born six or seven months after the wedding. These babies are called, with a wink, *sietemesinos* (literally, seven monthers), although gestational prematurity is widely understood not to be involved. The shame of premarital sex is erased to some extent by subsequent marriage, although at least one of the life history informants insisted to me that the couple remains marked (*queda tachada*). There is still the fact of losing one's virginity before marriage to contend with; as Susana said, "It is an insult to Jesus and the Virgin to stand up there in your white dress without being a virgin." Premarital sex is not uncommon among young couples in Degollado, but when it does occur it seems most likely after couples have been dating for several years, or after an engagement but before the wedding.

For younger women, premarital physical intimacy has a fundamentally different meaning than it did for their mothers. In one woman's story, part of the setting is that they had been novios for nine months the night they stood together on the street: "It was September 16th [Mexican Independence Day] and fireworks and it was really chilly" when "he gave me a kiss, and wow, what a kiss. . . . We didn't say anything but afterwards my lips felt really strange, and I said to myself I'm going to go inside and my aunt is going to know that I kissed him because my mouth felt really strange. And he says that he also felt, like, wow. . . . It was the first kiss that he gave me—he was always very respectful, he always gave me my place but he gave me my first kiss." She refers in her description both to the authentic and (she fears) plainly visible evidence of her passion and to her boyfriend's abiding respect for her because this first kiss is a moment of transition in the relationship from respect to confianza. All of the women who eventually kissed their boyfriends talked exhaustively first (both in the interviews and presumably with their boyfriends) about respect; they make sure that they are respected, and they demand that he demonstrate this respect by acknowledging that their will not to be kissed trumps (at least initially) his desire to kiss them. For these negotiations to make sense logically, of course, their own desire has to be totally submerged, since any hint of it weakens their position. Once respect has been established (which can take anywhere from several months to several years), the young women talk about having enough confianza, enough trust, to become physically intimate. In this context, a kiss becomes a bodily symbol not of conquest but of confianza—not of something that men give to or take from women, but of something shared in the knowledge that it is private.

When I asked women about confianza in a nonsexual context (in the second interview, as part of a question about their social networks), they said that having confianza with someone meant knowing that secrets could be shared with no fear that others would know. With no prompting on my part, they also tended to bring the discussion of confianza back around to sexual topics by indicating that confianza was to some degree a measure of one's comfort in talking about sex or telling sexual jokes in front of someone. When women of the same generation gather socially, it is common for them to engage in some sexual joking as a performance of friendship and social equality. Whereas respect deals fundamentally with what is public (particularly what is seen), a key element of confianza is privacy, the idea that knowledge of what passes between two people, whether verbal or physical, will not go beyond those two people.

Blanca made this point repeatedly in her description of her noviazgo with Oscar, placing their physical intimacy in the context of their growing emotional intimacy: "As we got to know each other we had more confianza, and he would hold my hand." She continued, "*As we went on he took my hand with more confianza.* We would be going to the store and he would embrace me.... And little by little, [we had] more confianza in the evenings. Every night when he was saying goodbye, he would ask for a kiss, and then later when he would come pick me up a kiss and when he would leave another kiss. That is, it was really nice because as we got to know each other, he increased our kisses" (emphasis added). When I asked her if she felt that she still had to keep saying no to him, she said:

> No. That is, he knows when and where and at what time and all.... Sometimes for example I say to him, "Give me another kiss, come on," or "Enough,...now I'm going inside," [and he says] "Aren't you going to give me a hug or a kiss?"...and I am also like that, I say, "O, love, won't you give me a kiss? Ay, give me a kiss," or when we are at a stoplight, both of us with a lot of confianza but very pure [*muy simple*].... And yes, sometimes I ask him, if I feel like it [*yo tengo ganas*] or sometimes he does.... It's something which is normal in novios, in the couple.

A generation ago, of course, this open sharing of physical affection was anything but the norm among novios. Whereas for their mothers respect meant that their suitors would never ask for a kiss, for the daughters it is more likely to mean that they do not ask too soon. The younger generation has not rejected their mothers' ideas; rather, they have remade them to fit better into an ideal image of dating (and, ultimately, marriage) that combines elements of both respect and intimacy.

The changes in noviazgo are important in their own right and for the light they shed on marriage. The goal of noviazgo has changed: no longer just a hopeful step to a respectable marriage with a respectful husband, noviazgo is now both una diversión and a time to get to know a young man *como compañero* (as a companion). Younger women, in contrast to their mothers and older sisters, increasingly emphasized both that they chose their partners (as opposed to being chosen by them) and that, in choosing, they looked deliberately for romance, responsibility, or sometimes even a soul mate. What women say they were looking for speaks to the range of possible marital ideals—respectful compliance with a gendered division of labor, or union bonded by passion and physical attraction, or companionate marriage.

That they choose at all, however, is perhaps the more significant change. Women no longer say that marriage is a cross or a riddle, just as they no longer talk about marrying the one for whom they are destined (*el que te toca*). This new view of courtship as a deliberate and pleasurable process of choosing a mate is expressed by the new social geography of noviazgo, which facilitates a focus on how the novios interact as individuals and on how they feel about each other. Changes in the staging and audience of courtship reflect that individual desires have begun to nudge family honor off center stage; to challenge the importance of respecting a girl's father suggests that a young woman, rather than her family, might hold a majority stake in her body. Preserving the respectability of one's family name is not unimportant, but the older value shares the scene with a newer one: pursuing happiness with one's spouse. This shifting emphasis from respeto to confianza is part of a larger generational change: the development of the Mexican companionate marriage.

CHAPTER 4

"Ya No Somos Como Nuestros Papas" (We Are Not Like Our Parents)

Companionate Marriage in a Mexican Migrant Community

En México, el hombre siempre tiene la ultima palabra. ¿Sabes cual es? "Si amor."

In Mexico, men always have the last word. You know what it is? "Yes, dear."

Analyses of marriage as a site for the reproduction of gender inequality have focused primarily on power and labor. Feminist social scientists have developed a language to describe and analyze domestic struggles for power, but our theoretical tools have failed to incorporate a paradox with which many of us are intimately familiar: marriage can be simultaneously a site for the negotiation and reproduction of gender inequality and a relationship of mutual assistance, emotional support, and shared pleasure.[1] To understand the social context and lived experience of marriage in this migrant community—simultaneously a site for hierarchy and intimacy—we need a framework that incorporates emotion in addition to power. Here, the three categories that Connell uses to describe different aspects of the social organization of gender—labor, power, and emotion—provide a useful framework for my discussion of generational changes in marriage, which focuses on differences between marriages of respeto and those of confianza.[2] By describing this generational change in marital ideals, I do not mean to imply that all of the young women's marriages are more egalitarian or companionate than were their mothers', or that all of the older women were as *dejada* (easily pushed around) as their daughters make them out to be. Rather, the change in marriage should be understood as a shift in the cultural center of gravity, as a change in ideals, although considerable diversity exists within each cohort. These ideals certainly do not dictate behavior, but they do shape the parameters within which people negotiate.

This companionate model of intimate relations is a core ideology of modernity, related to the transformation of households from sites of production to consumption, to falling fertility and increased life spans, and to modern notions of personhood. I am not, however, describing a global cultural convergence: the companionate marriage for which Mexicans strive is quite different than that for which Cambodian immigrants in Massachusetts yearn, and both differ from related ideals in southern Italy, Papua New Guinea, Pakistan, China, Spain, Brazil, and Nigeria.[3] Each of these marital ideals is informed by the same global ideology and influenced by similar economic and social transformations; the ethnographic challenge is to explore the locally specific ways in which people use and transform this global ideology of modernity.

GENERATIONAL CHANGE IN MARRIAGE

J: And to finish, you were telling me that your grandmother told you not to answer back, that whatever kind of mood the man comes home in you should not talk back to him, and that the woman has to keep herself from fighting back in order to get along, but I don't see you as so submissive, so easily walked upon, and I know your daughters pretty well, and they don't let themselves be taken advantage of for anything.

L: No, look, that's why I was sometimes embarrassed there with Lucha, because he would say one thing to her and she would respond with two or three. I said to her, "No, no." I said to them, "You act like no one taught you better [*ustedes no tienen madre*], you can't keep your mouths shut." I told them to keep quiet. Or sometimes we would go to Mass, and they would be going along, fighting with them. I would tell her not to answer back, that he is a good guy. María would also sass back to her husband—don't think that she would just let things go either. But I'm telling you, they just don't have the pull with their husbands—do you think that the men would let themselves get pushed around? In the end the women know that they are the ones who stand to lose after all, with the man.... You just can't win with them. Like now, if you wanted to boss [your husband] around, you couldn't. Well, by getting on his good side [*por las buenas*] yes, you can. You tell him, look, "this or that," but sweetly, but the bad way, no. If you want to insist on getting your way you can't, with men it's not possible, well, there [in the United States] they say it is.... I'm telling you that the man always has to be the boss in his home.

J: Why?

L: Because the man is the man. He has to be the boss. As a woman, one can give orders, but not to him, that's what I'm trying to explain to you. One can't order them around. If you to force them to do this or that, and you say, "I order you"—no, they would say, "I'm not going to let myself get pushed around."

J: So here with your husband, was he the boss in everything, or did you give orders too in some things?

L: No, I did too, and as I told you, through his soft side [*por la buena*]. I would say to him, "Look, this or that," [and he would say] "Oh, well, ok, yes."...There is a saying that many men use, "I am the only one in this house who wears pants," but now you don't even know anymore who wears the pants.

Women and men refer to these questions of domestic decision making in terms of *quien manda*.[4] (The literal translation of this common phrase might be "who commands" or "who gives the orders." It could also be translated, more colloquially, as "who is the boss" or "who wears the pants" [*quien trae los pantalones*].) Old and young, women and men—when asked about gender, they respond by placing themselves on a continuum of change: the level of defiance audible in a young woman's refusal to bring her husband a beer registers much more strongly in contrast with her mother's words than it does in a historical vacuum.[5] (This older generation, who courted and married in the 1950s and 1960s, was the younger generation when compared to their own parents; they represent not a timeless traditional past but rather a generation that also came of age under specific historical circumstances.)[6]

Some of the younger women perhaps exaggerated the extent to which they have cooperative decision-making processes with their husbands, or even the extent to which they would dare talk back to them, but this does not take away from the fact that they were trying to create themselves, in my eyes, as modern and powerful. The older women wanted to teach me, as a gringa (perhaps well intentioned but clueless enough to have left her husband to care for himself), that they were decent women who knew how to respect and be respected by their husbands. They were deliberately sharing with me the central narrative of their era, *el hombre tiene que mandar,* showing that they were experts in both the official story and its private complexities. Acknowledging that each group shaped its story for me does not leave us in a postmodern hall of mirrors. Rather, it only serves to underline the point that their idea of what a good impression is has changed. The younger women's intense desire to convince me that they were not *dejadas* (women who let others push them around—*dejar* means to let, to leave, but in these conversations it means "to let [others dominate you]") led me to wonder about their eagerness to show me that they were modern and about their choice of a discourse of gender as a means to do so. They emphasized specific aspects of their stories in order to impress me with the fact that they were not like their mothers (*"ya no somos como las de antes"* was a constant refrain): they wanted me to understand that things are changing in Mexico and among Mexicans in the United States.

"IN THE PAST WOMEN WERE VERY SUBMISSIVE"

> J: And what did you think you would have to do to be a good wife?
>
> C: Well, to obey all of his—I did all the things I had to do....In the past women were very submissive, they did what their husbands said, whether it was right or wrong, you just had to do it. Now I see that things are different.

When I asked the life history informants' mothers about what made for a good marriage, they always brought up the question of who should give the orders before I did. They framed their comments with explanations that "this is the way things are here" or "in my time, but now things are different"; their words reveal both a suspicion on their part that things might be different for me as a gringa and also the knowledge that their daughters were trying to strike a different kind of bargain with their own husbands.

All of the life history informants' mothers said that when they married they expected their husbands to be the arbiter of when they could leave the house, what they could wear, when they would have sex. Women said that he had the right to hit her if she gave him reason to (*si le daba motivo*) by answering back. In short, her body belonged to him. The woman's job was to wash, mend, and iron clothes; keep the house and children clean; cook food and serve a hot meal to her husband in the morning and in the afternoon; raise the children to be polite (*bien educados*), God-fearing, and respectful of their elders; and make sure that however much money her husband gave her to buy food lasted for the whole week.[7] In return, he was responsible for providing her and their children with food, clothes, and shelter as best he could. This bare bones descriptions of rights and responsibilities should under no circumstances be taken as a generalization about the actual conditions of most marriages contracted in the 1950s and 1960s. Rather, it is a description of the extreme of what was theoretically inherent in the phrase "el hombre tiene que mandar."

Just because men could enforce a despotic rule did not mean that they did. Most of the older women said that they felt free to go to a neighbor's house, to see their mothers, or to go to the market or to church without asking permission—but they did tell their husbands where they were going and when they would return. For journeys farther afield (out of town, anywhere after dark, or involving social events at which unmarried daughters might speak with men) women needed to *pedirle permiso* (ask formal permission), though this was one of the many rules that got bent when women's husbands were in the United States. Some men would seek their wives' opinion about financial decisions such as buying a piece of land or selling an animal; older women referred to this as "taking her into account" or "asking her opinion," and they clearly derived satisfaction from this more cooperative approach.[8]

Rather than wield direct challenges, older women gained a certain amount of leverage by complying scrupulously with behavioral expectations.[9] They generally wore knee- to calf-length skirts; some still wear a rebozo to cover their heads when they go out in the street, and I saw only two of all the mothers ever wear pants. Of these two, one lives in the United States, and the other, a widow, only wears pants at home (never in the street). To wear pants in the street would be interpreted by others not as a sign of female autonomy but rather as an improper display of her body to the eyes of other men and a sign that she was trying to "wear the pants" in her own home.[10]

Similarly, older women implied that there was little to be gained by directly challenging men's sexual rights to their bodies. I did not have the confianza to ask the mothers directly about marital rape, but when I asked about the things that women should do to have a good marriage, a number noted that a woman should *cumplir como esposa* (meet her obligations as wife). The word *cumplir* means to meet any sort of obligation, but when used in this way it clearly refers to a woman's obligation to be sexually available to her husband: men, for example, will sometimes talk about feeling entitled to look for sex elsewhere *si no me cumple* (if she does not comply). Within this logic, sex exists to satisfy men (so they will not look elsewhere) and to produce children. (None of the older women mentioned a husband's responsibility to satisfy his wife, perhaps because they thought it unlikely that she could want to have sex more frequently than her husband.) For a woman, irreproachable compliance with her duties was a useful strategy to pressure her husband into treating her respectfully.

Women were not powerless to defend themselves. They could use the gendered code of behavior implied in respect, as well as their own or even their husband's families, their relationships with other women, the church, or even local authorities, to protect themselves. As one woman said, "Even though they are men, they still have to show respect for their wives." Women characterized it as una falta de respeto, a lack of respect, when a man engaged in flagrant infidelity, raised his voice, used unjustified and unprovoked violence or bad words (*groserías*), grabbed a woman in public or spoke publicly about having sex with his wife, or when a man forced his wife to have sex. It is not really clear how much of a resource these shared ideas about respect were—women could take the moral upper hand neither to the bank nor to the police station—but still, at least it was clear to men who cared about their neighbors' and in-laws' opinions that certain behaviors were not socially valued.

Furthermore, only in fairy tales is the mother-in-law always evil; women told stories of mothers-in-law intervening to protect their daughters-in-law.[11] In one case, for example, a man who infected his wife with a sexually transmitted disease was told by his mother that his behavior was unacceptable and that while they lived under her roof he must treat his wife more respectfully. Women also turned to the church, with varying success. In one instance, a priest told a woman whose husband drank and was abusive and unfaithful that "if you don't want to leave, that's ok, but tell him, well, that it's all over, that now it's as if you were not married." (In other words, she was no longer obligated to have sex with him.) Much more frequently, however, priests would tell women that they should be patient, that they should pray, and finally that they should just accept their suffering, that marriage *es una cruz* (it's a cross [to bear]).

The older women seemed not to expect any intervention from their own families. I was struck, if anything, by women's vehemence about *not* asking their own families for help. They suggested that their parents would see it as a slap in the face and that it would tarnish their parents' reputation if it were known that their daughter's marriage was unsuccessful. It was seen as being especially painful for mothers—since a well-married daughter is a mother's achievement, the revelation that her daughter is either unhappy or unable to bear the suffering indicates a failure on her part. Some even expressed doubt as to whether their parents would have taken them back. One said she thought her parents would have told her *"te lo buscaste pues ahora friégate"* (you sought him out, so now you suffer). As one woman said, "I always tell my girls, you have to be smart, that's what counts. Because look, if what you want is, as they say, to win a pissing contest [*si uno quiere como dicen que no más mis chicharrones truenen*], I really don't think that's the best way.... There are other ways of getting to them, but you have to use your smarts. For me, as they say, there's more noise than nuts [*como dicen es más el ruido que las nueces*]."[12] When the woman quoted here drew a picture of her married life, she said she should choose purple for suffering, but she said she never would have considered leaving her husband. His difficult behavior was not cause for marital failure; rather, it was her responsibility to make the marriage work no matter what. Another of the older women, Catalina, talked about the importance of *reinforcing* men's higher status; she said that if one *darles su lugar* (gives them their place), it makes them feel important as men, and they will hold the reins of power much more loosely. Giving a man his place involves knowing his dislikes and working within them. I ended the interview with her by asking about how things really worked in her marriage:

> J: Well...who do you think is really the boss?
>
> C: Look, in many things, you give them their place. Like, if...he says something to you, you have to do it, right? And well, in my case, how should I describe it? I am not very afraid of him. That is, as we have gotten to know each other, I wouldn't say he's very touchy. He knows my personality and I know his, and if he went crazy now, well, I wouldn't really pay much attention to him, after all this time. Up until now I—but it depends what your husband is like, because if you get one who is really demanding, who insists on a lot of things, who has his ways, you could even be afraid of him, no? And if you do something he doesn't like, you know he's going to get mad.

She went on at length about other women whose husbands forbade them to ever leave the house. She told me proudly that she, in contrast, never asked permission to go see her own mother in the rancho. Whenever she went out, however, she was always careful to leave him lunch already cooked so that he could just heat it up. I questioned her further on how one "gives a man his place":

> C: That is, you know already more or less what he doesn't like—
>
> J: And so you get more room to move around?
>
> C: Exactly. He's never liked that I—there must be something to eat,... and when I am going out I like to leave the house tidy, I don't like to leave it like a pigsty, so I get up really early or if I am going to leave

early I clean up the night before, and then the next day I just make breakfast. That's what he doesn't like either, that I would leave the house messy, that's why I never got used to leaving it messy. But if he liked me to leave it messy, [I would say] "Oh well, he won't say anything." That's how we are—the more you see that they don't fight, the more you push them, the more you start to get a little bit of confianza with them.

She describes how a woman can expand (or preserve) freedom of movement by attending carefully to the chores about which her husband cares most. This is part of the strategic technique known as managing one's husband "*por las buenas*." Women also call this getting to them through "*el lado débil*" (their weak side).

Whatever a woman's strategy, and regardless of her husband's idiosyncrasies, these older women told me that women have the final responsibility for making sure the married couple gets along. When I asked one woman why she thought some men were unfaithful, she said first that they did it to act macho, but then she continued, saying that actually she really thought it was the wife's fault: "I don't know, maybe I am very old fashioned, but in my house they always said that as a woman one was responsible for 99 percent of the marriage, that you were the one who was responsible, that you had to be very capable for everything, for the husband, for the children, for the house." For an older woman, being good at her job—doing a good job of being a wife, a housekeeper, and a mother—was her best defense against her husband's power.

"*With a Man, a Woman Can Never Win*"

Men's power derives in part from the possibility of violence. Women admitted, when pressed, that women sometimes did fight back physically when their husbands hit them, but they also countered with the saying "*con el hombre, la mujer nunca va a poder*" (with a man, a woman is never going to be able [to win]). Men are seen as inherently capable of greater violence, as able to inflict more serious physical harm on their wives than their wives are on them. Several of the older women described their marriages as good by saying that their husbands had never lifted a finger against them.

Women also suggested that men's power is rooted in women's dependence on men to provide them with respect and social status. Even younger women told me that "men bring respect to a home." Unmarried women, widows, and single mothers can earn the respect of others in the community by ongoing demonstrations of seriousness and modesty in public, but attachment to a man (even a man who is of unknown or dubious respectability himself) promotes a woman to a level of respect that she could only earn on her own through years of effort. The respect that a man confers on his household extends to the children as well, and several women talked about how the desire that their children be respected keeps many women in difficult marriages. Paulina, who suffered for years from her husband's violence until he finally left her, maintained that had she been the one to leave, it would have seriously harmed her children:

> Well, it always seems sad to me that people get divorced, that they leave, and then you have those little kids that don't live with their father or mother any more. As I lived through that in my own flesh and blood with my children, it doesn't appeal to me at all. *For me it's better to stick it out, to suffer a little bit more, than to see the sadness of those poor children who don't have their father* [emphasis added].
>
> It's like now, the women of today don't want to suffer. They fight over anything, and it's over. . . . As for me, well, if he hadn't gone, I would not have left him. Why? For my children, principally. Look, afterward if they don't have a father, here in this town they really humiliate them. They start in school, saying, "Ay, you don't have a father, your father doesn't love you," and those children suffer. . . . Also, maybe it's because of the poverty, . . . that women [here] can't find a good job to make it on their own, . . . so that because of that they really suffer without a man.

Running through all of the interviews was the idea that earning money gives men the right to command in their families—and thus that when the support of the family is shared jointly, the power should be shared too. As Concepción (who had worked most of her married life running a sewing workshop and even accompanied her husband to Chicago, where she worked seven days a week in a factory for several years) said:

> C: Let's think about it this way: here, before, there was no work, nothing. The man was always the one who worked, the one who brought home the money to support the family, the one who protected the family, he was the head of the house [*el jefe de la casa*], so that's why he should have the most authority.
>
> J: But you say that he should have the power because he is the one bringing in the money, but what if they both bring in the money?
>
> C: Well, to some extent then they both have the right. Let's say they both work hard and the woman feels like going on an outing, to get out of the house, he should [inaudible], because she also gets tired.

She explains that men are the head of the house because of their greater ability to support a family *and* because of the moral and physical protection—the respect—that a man's social status lends to his family. Women's assertions that a man ought to be solely responsible for the financial support of the family do not reflect their actual experiences. Six of the eight mothers interviewed had worked at least intermittently (sewing, knitting, selling food, or factory and agricultural work in the United States). While all of these women would no doubt say that they did work merely to supplement their husbands' income, there seem to have been stretches of time in which they were in fact the major source of support for their families.[13]

Of course, women's actual experiences varied widely. The two who cried, talking about how they missed their husbands (one had passed away, the other was in the United States), said they felt lucky in comparison to other women. Their husbands had been good providers and kind and loving fathers and husbands; they asked their opinions about major decisions, did not drink or run around with other women, and permitted them a great deal of freedom of movement—in short, marriages full of both respeto and a certain confianza. Both of these women pointed out, in fact, that they thought they had much happier marriages than their daughters. Other women suffered a great deal of physical and verbal abuse. All of the women describe their marriages, though, as a question of "the luck for which they were destined." They all, of course, may have contributed to the tenor of daily life through their individual ability (or inability) to get along, to *dejarse*, to bend to another's will. Whatever the quality of the actual relationships, all these women shared a level of vulnerability; their fate was in their husbands' hands. Small wonder, then, that they all talk about how as teenagers they prayed for God to send them a good husband.

"Women Do Not Know How to Suffer Anymore"

The older women were generally quite critical of young women who openly struggle for power with their husbands. Constantina, for example, said, "I don't like families where they see the man as nothing special," and Luisa saw her daughters' talking back as bad manners and bad strategy; they should be more skilled at managing their husbands por las buenas. Concepción said she found women who went around talking about how they could boss their husbands around to be quite distasteful, and Paulina found it unthinkable that a woman might put her own welfare before that of her children by leaving her husband. Even Catalina, the youngest of the mothers interviewed, did not let her daughters study beyond sixth grade (she wanted them to learn to do housework properly before they got married and she did not want them out in the street where their virtue might be at risk). She also held back on indulging them with toys and pretty clothes as small girls, fearing that spoiling them would make them unfit to bear whatever suffering lay ahead for them as wives.

At the same time, older women did not uniformly condemn their daughters for trying to strike a different bargain. Rosalia mentioned that her sons-in-law were very helpful around the house. When asked what she thought of that, she said:

> Well,...it seems good to me, because I see that they [the men] help them [the women]....My son-in-law helps [my daughter] a lot, washing and also...with the housework. The other day when they were here,...I said, "Hey, leave that [broom] there, it's a shame with so many women in the house and you are grabbing the broom, leave it there," but it's like he's already used to it. I don't know...but *here* you're not used to having them help you. Maybe they are rude and inconsiderate, though, because they never give you a hand with anything....They get used to us being the one to do all the housework, you have to do it all, they never worry about washing and helping you, you have to do everything. And there... the men know that the women work too, and so they have to help them out.

Doña Constantina, though critical of women who treat their husbands as nothing special, acknowledged that her daughters have options that she did not. If they were having problems she said she would first make sure that her daughters were fulfilling all of their marital duties, but if she did not see that they were provoking their husbands in any way, she would say, "Look, daughter, you shouldn't submit on that point, just because it happened to me. You have some rights, don't let him push you around just because you are a woman." All acknowledged that for some women of the younger generation, the rules have changed.

"We Both Are the Boss"

A number of the younger life history informants responded to the question of who gives the orders by saying first that their husbands do, but then qualifying that to suggest situations in which they would be the primary decision maker. In talking about *quién manda*, women used examples about budgeting and money management, selling animals, making large purchases for the home, women's physical autonomy, control over children, and the sharing of housecleaning, cooking, and childcare. To give orders meant that they made decisions concerning themselves and their children, but they still mostly stopped short of saying that they had a right to control their husbands' behavior. Pilar went to so far as to suggest, however, that she has the same degree of control over her husband's movements outside the house as he does of hers. Asked about their decision-making arrangements, she said:

> P: From the beginning—and maybe it is that I do not like for him to tell me what to do, that he should be the one to give orders—I told him here we are both in charge. He asked me why, and I said to him that when just the man gives the orders, they get really bossy with their wives. So [I told him] that here we are going to do what both of us say. Yes, in terms of being the boss, the man is the boss, but I do not let myself get pushed around. We both are the boss.
>
> J: But do you say he is the boss because it sounds better?
>
> P: Well, yes.

Assertions of joint decision making can be interpreted as aspersions on a man's masculinity.[14] As much as some women push for equal access to their family's resources and control over their own movement, men's respectability in the community continues to be related to public perceptions of their autonomy. If self-determination is a cornerstone of masculinity, and women derive some status from having a husband who is *un hombre de respeto* in the community, it is not to their benefit to have their husband publicly perceived as a *mandilón* (apron wearer). A woman may submit to her husband's will in public both to placate him and to demonstrate her mastery of gendered codes of behavior—being *dejada* in public may gain a woman some negotiating room in private.

After saying that they both were the boss but that her husband was "really the boss," Pilar continued her narrative with a story about how he asks her for permission to go out:

> J: And you said to me the other day that when he is going somewhere, he asks you for permission, and that sometimes you tell him not to go and he doesn't go?
>
> P: Yes, because there was a fiesta...over that way, and he asked me if I would let him go. I said "No, I won't, don't go...because it's far and I am going to be worried." So he said, "That's ok, I won't go." His

friends laughed at him, "Ay, well, your wife bosses you around" [*ay
pues te manda la mujer*], and I said to them, "It's not that I boss him,
but it's really far, and what would he do there anyway, he has his
family here."…So we went inside, and he put a movie on [the VCR],
and it was really cozy. I said to him, "You see [how nice this is], and
if [you went] you'd just be wandering around there, God knows how
you would be wandering around," and he just laughed.

J: But how do you do it so that he does not feel less manly, or that you
are bossing him around?

P: Look, sometimes in front of other people I do what he tells me, so
that people won't think—so that if he asks me to take him
something,…I do take it to him.…But sometimes when we are here
[at home] he says to me, "Bring me this" and I say to him "Ay, can't
you see that I am busy with the kid, pick it up yourself, you can
more easily than I." He doesn't answer me back anything, he just
goes and picks it up.

J: But you wouldn't say it in front of other people?

P: No, because it looks bad. They say, "Ay, how badly you treat him in
front of other people." So, no, I say to him we must pretend in front
of others.

J: That is, if you were to do it in front of others it would be like an insult for him?

P: Yes.

J: But when you are alone?

P: No, because when we are alone who's going to hear us? But…in
front of other people no, because right away they would criticize
him.

Pilar and her husband collude in the construction of public gender identities, conducting their renegotiation of who gives the orders behind
closed doors.

De-Gendering Housework

Just like their mothers, most of the life history informants consider
cooking and cleaning to be solely their responsibility, which means for
the most part that they do it all themselves, perhaps delegating some
chores to their female children, but a significant minority (several in
Mexico and several in Atlanta) either received some cooperation from
their husbands with housework or else felt that they ought to receive
such help.[15] The generational change is reflected in the redefinition of
ideal roles, so that a task that was once strictly gendered (sweeping,

cooking, washing clothes) becomes less so. This contribution to household management is framed both by younger women and their husbands as "helping," just as when women take paid jobs outside the home they call it "helping" (*ayudando*) their husbands. In response to my question, Juana explained how she had maneuvered her husband into helping her:

J.H.: And does your husband do some of the housework or help you?

J: He never helped me before. Lately he helps me make the beds [laughs].

J.H.: Why do you laugh?

J: Because he had never helped me [before].

J.H.: And he suddenly felt the urge to help you, or what did you do to him?

J: No, it's that sometimes he sees that I do not have enough time [*que no alcanzo*], like sometimes that he does not go to work, he's here in the house and he sees that I am running all over the place, [so] he gives me a hand. Or he'll make breakfast. [He asks me] "What are you going to make?" or I tell him I'm going to make them this, and he helps me. Before, no, even if I was running around like a dog in the sun, he would sit there, reading a magazine.

J.H.: And would you get mad?

J: Yes, I would, but I didn't say anything to him. I just said, "Wait until I am done if you want me to make you breakfast, let me just hurry to finish up here."

J.H.: Why didn't you say anything to him?

J: Because if I said to him "Do that," he would say I was bossing him around and then on purpose he wouldn't help me. You know how men are if you tell them something.... Now he sees—I think he himself is seeing that I don't have enough time, and he helps me.

Juana used the same word to justify her husband picking up a broom that a man might use to explain why his wife takes in washing or sells fruit from a cart on the street: *alcanzar* means to have enough, usually of time or money. Rather than ask for help, she simply makes it clear that if he wants to eat breakfast sooner rather than later, then he will have to pitch in and help make it (or, alternatively, that if she wants all the kids to have new shoes this year, she will have to help buy them). This tactic does not call into question the gendered division of labor, but rather suggests that if a woman makes a good faith effort and just "doesn't have enough time" then neither her femininity nor her husband's masculinity is imperiled by a little cooperation.

A New Way of Talking

Even Lourdes, who was living in la colonia in Degollado and who did
not question that her husband would be the one to give the orders, insisted on the right to be spoken to politely:

> L: Yes, he gives orders for things, but [he is not] bossy and demanding,
> no. When he demands something like that, very exacting, I say to
> him, "Tell me nicely, or I won't bring you anything," and he has to
> tell me nicely, or else he has to get up himself and get his things.
>
> J: What do you mean, por las buenas, that he ask you in a different
> way, more nicely?
>
> L: In a better way, more softly.
>
> J: That is, that he says please?
>
> L: Yes.
>
> J: And have you actually stayed sitting down, so that he...
>
> L: Yes.
>
> J: That is, you don't let him push you around?
>
> L: No, no.
>
> J: Like in what way do you stand up to him, apart from what you just
> said?
>
> L: Well, just in that way. Or when he scolds me and it wasn't my fault,
> [I say] "Don't give me any of that scolding."

A number of other women voiced a similar insistence that their husbands ask them nicely. This hardly seems like a radical request, but their
mothers might have preferred to keep quiet and let the men thunder,
then later go ahead and get what they wanted por las buenas, by working through the men's good side.

  The larger change in communication is one of substance, not style: as
suggested by their quest for confianza in courtship, the younger women
voice a desire for emotional intimacy, as illustrated in Drawing 4.1,
based on talking. Emotional (and sexual) intimacy is perceived to lay
the foundation for a strong marriage. Beatriz, interviewed in Atlanta,
complained about how frustrated she felt that her husband had no pet
names for her, and Victoria, also in Atlanta, acknowledged that her husband was hardworking, responsible, and a good father, but said she
wished he would seek her out immediately on arriving home and greet
her warmly. Lucha said that she did not mind spending all her free time
in the kitchen cooking for her family but wished that her husband
would get up from the sofa and the television to ask her how she was
doing or what she was preparing. Pilar talked about all the cards and

Drawing 4.1. "When I Was Courting." This drawing, in which Juana shows her courtship with Sergio and their marriage, suggests both the excitement of courtship and the dream of marital intimacy. Note especially the smile on her face as she and Sergio dance; the way they gaze into one another's eyes as they stand beneath an image of the Virgin of Guadalupe; and Juana's floor-length veil and gown.

letters her husband had sent her when they were courting and about how she wished he had not stopped giving her those cards when they got married. All of these cravings for a certain kind of talk suggest that for some couples communication has begun to take on a very different role in relationship building. Rather than evaluate speech in terms of respect, these younger women focus on the extent to which they and their husbands use speech to create emotional intimacy.

In summary, the younger women differ from women of their mothers' generation in terms of their ideas about marriage. In response to questions about who gives the orders, they talked about shared decision making, being able to speak their mind, cooperating in production and social reproduction, and seeking a binding emotional closeness that—although not unimportant to their mothers—was certainly less of a central issue in the past. Every marriage, of course, is made up of two parties, so to understand more about the modern Mexican marriage it is necessary to turn to their husbands, to explore what men say about sharing their *mando*.

First these
literally
articles
indeed
perfect

MEN, MARRIAGE, AND MASCULINITY

> J: And, well, who would you say is the boss in your house?
>
> F [Francisco,
> Perla's husband,
> in Atlanta, Georgia]: Nobody. That is, we agree and in some things we go with what she says and in other things what I say...
>
> J: What is her area and what is yours?
>
> F: None. That is, we go with whoever has the best idea. We say that whoever is right [decides]. That is, it's not that "here we are going to do what I say and this that and the other," no, I don't think so. [laughs].
>
> J: Why do you laugh?
>
> F: Because that is like, well, for a macho.
>
> J: You mean, you would not consider yourself macho.
>
> F: No.
>
> J: What would be, for you, a macho?
>
> F: A person that wants to say, I am the boss, and here you are going to do what I say and if you don't like it, too bad. That's how machos are, that's how I think they are, and hitting women. The macho and the man [el hombre] are very different things.
>
> J: What are they like?
>
> F: Well, a man is one who tries to give his wife and kids all that they deserve, and the macho is the guy who just goes around looking for women to satisfy himself and later hits them, and talks about them, later does all kinds of things, well that's a macho.

Men were aware that they could choose to act like a man in different ways and, for all of them, explaining their marriage meant describing their choices about how to be a man.[16] Others have discussed how the idea of machismo has taken on a life of its own in the social science literature—a life that bears strikingly little resemblance to the lived experiences of men in Mexico.[17] Francisco, above, was not alone in framing his comments either explicitly or implicitly in reference to this negative ideal of machismo. Although I never used the word unless the person I was interviewing brought it up first, five of the men told me directly that they were not *machista,* or else they spoke negatively of typically machista behaviors such as excessive drinking, violence toward women, and unwillingness to listen to others.

What Men Say about Quién Manda

It would be naive to understand their replies to my question of "Who gives the orders in your house?" as a simple reflection of actual power processes in their houses. Rather, their replies should be read as representations about the way power *ought* to work at home, as signposts pointing toward an ideal masculinity. Just as the difference between what the mothers and the daughters said about power needs to be interpreted in light of what they thought would impress me, so too do the men's comments need to be understood as deliberate constructions of a Mexican male identity for a young, white-skinned, educated gringa— but still, men tried to impress me in different ways. Miguel and Humberto wanted to make their absolute power clear to me, while the other men were making a different point about masculinity.

Only two men said that they alone were the ones to give orders. Miguel, Concha's husband, a forty-five-year-old man in la colonia, was quick to respond that his word was law, but when I followed up by asking about what they do when they disagree, he responded, "Well, we don't do anything, if there's not an agreement, well, no." Concha takes great pains to be a good wife. She makes sure that she is home when he gets home from work, keeps the house clean under trying conditions (five kids under age ten, intermittent running water), and does her best to stretch his small salary (most of which he gives her to administer) so that they all eat at least one full meal per day and there is money left to eat on the day before payday. When I last saw him, he suffered from a chronic illness that kept him in almost constant pain and so he was serious and slow to smile. Concha told me, however, that before his illness he would take her out for tacos occasionally and that he often sought out her company, even inviting her to go with him when his work took him to a neighboring town. She was beyond reproach in every way—modest, hardworking, thrifty, and quiet—and so Miguel's answer seemed to indicate that within the paradigm of "the man must be the boss" there was significant room for cooperative and caring relationships.

That cooperation, of course, was predicated on the man's authority remaining unchallenged, which was not the case for Humberto. During the time of my fieldwork, Humberto was engaged in an ongoing struggle with his wife, Isabel, about the small store she ran, which generated sufficient profit to buy the family's food and clothe herself and her children. He told me that he did not like her financial independence, nor did he like that she was out of the house most of the day; what seemed to bother him most was that her financial and physical autonomy weakened his control over her. In spite of his statement that when he objects to something he does not permit it (*"cuando yo veo que algo no es bueno no doy el permiso"*), he had not been able to force her to stop working. He admitted that, as part of his campaign against her working, he had stopped giving her any money at all for household expenses and had ignored her requests to take her to restock the store when inventory was low (she does not drive). When I left Degollado in February 1997 they were in a standoff, and when I returned the following January to visit she had somehow managed to restock. I suspected that in spite of his boasting about his professional skills he did not actually earn enough to pay all the bills that Isabel covered with her profits from the store, so though he tried to show her his power by making her wait longer than she would like, he eventually—albeit grudgingly—broke down and helped her.

For the remaining men, answers ranged from Mario's answer that "both of them" shared the power but that he had the last word to Pedro's comment that it was both but that "many people might say that it was actually her." Joint decision making reflects a certain style of masculinity, so men choose whether to share power (or not, and in what situations) based on what kind of man they want to be. Several men mentioned rights (*derechos*) in the context of marriage (that is, a man's right to drink a beer or two once in a while with his friends, a woman's right to ask a man to lower his voice and not yell at her), but most framed joint decision making as the product of their individual magnanimity rather than as a response to some larger moral framework.

Both men and women said that how they make decisions at home is nobody's business, which is ironic, of course, in light of the fact that I was interviewing them on precisely this topic. The fact that this change in power management within the families is supposedly a private one gives couples a certain amount of flexibility to work around traditional paradigms, but it also leaves women without any recourse at all if they do not like the way things are working. Men, like women, distinguished between how they actually make decisions with their wives and the public perception they seek to create. Francisco, for example, told me that just as he does not like his wife to go places without discussing it with him first, he also does not go out without first telling her. I responded by asking him if his friends didn't accuse him of letting his wife push him around, and he said, "No, I don't like to talk with my friends, saying, you know what, 'I ask her permission.' If I can't go [with them] because I need to take her somewhere, I just say to them 'I can't go.' I don't have to give any explanation, that is, one's life is private." Private renegotiation has important effects both on the lives of specific couples and on what their children learn about how families operate (it would be interesting, for example, to talk with these men's sons about masculinity). Also, even though the bargains these couples strike are ostensibly "private," frequently they have public consequences—such as whether a man goes out drinking with his friends or not—so they should hardly be considered irrelevant to whether and how people reformulate shared representations of gender. By being officially private, however, these assertions of shared decision making fall short of a full-fledged attack on the ideological connections between masculinity and domestic power. For these couples, a woman's access to power depends primarily on her husband's magnanimity. An alternative would be the case of Oscar and Blanca, where he and she both say that she has certain "rights" that must be respected.[18]

"We Talk about Everything"

In contrast to Miguel and Humberto's proclamation that "what I say goes," the other men said that both partners should be free to express their opinions in terms of spending money, leisure-time activities, child raising, and correcting a spouse's behavior. Sergio gave a verbal portrait of how he and Juana talk together: "Between her and me, we talk about everything. If we want to go somewhere, we discuss it, 'Hey, I want to do this,' and she [talks] as much as I do, or sometimes one makes excuses, 'You know what, not like that.' I don't think there is a power to give orders, not on her side or on mine." Several of the other men responded in this same way, quoting to me a back-and-forth discussion style (that is, "I say this, and then she says that") to represent their decision-making processes. Pedro, Josefina's husband, described to me how—in spite of the fact that he does not like the harshness with which she physically disciplines their children—he generally defers to her opinion on child-rearing issues: "I'll tell you what—here neither one of us is the boss. That is, whatever she says is ok—just that sometimes I'll say, 'No, that's not ok,' but all the same I give her the last word, because she is the one who spends the whole day with the kids, not me." A marriage with space for multiple voices suggests a profoundly different concept of respect than the one implied by the notion that under no circumstances should women answer back to their husbands. When I asked Juan how women show a lack of respect for their husbands, he said:

> For example, for me personally, if I tell Mercedes, "This needs to get done now, there are things which are not being done right, think about where you are in your things, there are things that are behind and are not getting done well," she should say to me, "Yes, I'll take care of it, I'll try to get everything done at the right time, like you say." I don't like that she would say, "I'm not going to do it, I won't do it because I don't feel like it"—that is not getting along well. That's respect, so then the day that she needs me to do something, or that she says, "Juan you are doing that wrong, that's not right," if I see that I made a mistake, I'll say, "I accept that, she is right." That's the way to get along and mutually respect each other, that she respect my decision and I respect hers, that she doesn't yell at me, nor that I yell at her. If we get angry we are not going to accomplish anything, she is very touchy and so am I.

In saying that both partners should talk and listen, these men are redefining respect so that a woman's independent thought is not perceived to be an assault on a man's masculinity. This is reflected also in what women say; it lends meaning to the pride I heard in their voices when they told me that at home, with their husbands, they also have opinions about domestic matters.

In their discussions of power and marital decision making, men frequently brought up the question of spending time together. I did not understand why, when asked about power, some men responded by talking about leisure time—until I realized that they were implicitly comparing themselves to men who measure their power by the amount of time they can spend away from their wives and families. Sergio responded to the question of who gives orders by saying:

> S: I don't believe that there is a boss, not on one side or the other....I don't know, but many people might even say that she is the boss. We go around together almost daily, I almost never go [anywhere] by myself, and people will sometimes say, "No, well she keeps you on a short leash," and all that.
>
> J: That is, when one goes around with a woman, they say that she is the boss?

S: Not in my way of thinking.... That is, when I go out, I don't go up [to la colonia] or to the plaza alone, no, I don't go alone. During the day yes, because I am working and all that, but that I would be tempted to go the plaza alone, no, really I wouldn't see any point to that.

J: And so how do you answer them when they say that she keeps you on a short leash or bosses you around?

S: I say to them, "No, think about it, how is it better, to have a woman mad, or to have her happy?"

When I asked Oscar about wanting to spend time with his wife, he said, "I married for that, to be with her, not to go around alone, in that case I wouldn't have gotten married, that's why one marries, to live with, to exchange feelings with one's spouse." By saying that he would rather be with his family, a man implies that he does not feel a need to prove that he has the power to control his own movements.

Sometimes men go even further, and admit that in fact they do not have this power. When I asked Pedro why it is such a serious insult to say that the woman is the boss, that *la mujer te manda,* he said:

P: Sometimes there are times that they'll say to me, "Let's have a couple beers," [and I'll say] "No, I'm not in the mood [*no traigo ganas*]." [They'll say] "Oh, does your wife hit you?" [and I'll say] "Well, yes, it's that my lioness is very fierce."

J: That's how you answer them?

P: Sometimes. Sometimes I say to them, "Well, what do you want me to do to her?" It's tough.

This is an interesting counterpart to the much more frequent way that women use their husbands' will as a substitute for their own in explaining why they "must" do something. Maybe Pedro himself, faced with this choice, would actually rather go home and be with his family, but by crediting Josefina with the power to make him go home he is calling into question basic assumptions about what it means to act like a man. Both he and his friends know that sharing a beer could easily lead (as it has in the past) to his spending an entire paycheck on an all-night binge, coming home drunk, beating up Josefina, leaving the whole family without money to eat for the week, and forcing Josefina to go around yet again to the local stores to find someone who will sell to her on credit.[19]

Pedro's refusal to be shamed into having to act "like a man" takes on greater importance in light of comments such as one that Paulina made about her own marriage: "The first step is booze, and their friends, paying attention to their friends. Here it's very common that they say, 'Oh, you're not drinking because your wife rules you, no well, she will hit you with her slippers.' That's how it is here, and so to get in good with their friends they'll do anything." Men can resist pressure to act like a certain kind of man by selecting companions who share their ideas. Oscar, for example, talked about avoiding his own brothers (who also live in Atlanta) because he does not think they understand or approve of the intimacy he seeks to share with his wife. Francisco also talks about constructing a social network that supports his vision of himself as a family man: "There are some that are more macho, and there are some that are like me, or maybe even better. I always think that the person who talks with a lot of machismo, I don't like that guy because I feel that he's not what he says he is, that he's all talk, so he starts to irritate me, and I push him aside, and start not to talk to him. And there are others, that you say, well, 'Let's get our families together, or let's all go somewhere together'—that is, right away, you can tell a family man." Mirandé has discussed how Latinos in California perceived this same distinction between a negative masculinity associated with an irresponsible use of power and a more positive ideal of the family man whose power derives from his ability to take care of his family.[20] When men share el mando, they demonstrate a vision of masculinity in which some degree of autonomy on the part of their wives is not read as an attack on their manhood. Sharing the mando is a crack in the ideology of separate spheres, in which categories of male and female exist in opposition to each other in a way that is written into the social division of space.

"When You Start to Burn Up": Violence and Power

Men were much more forthcoming about the appropriate uses of violence than were women, and their comments about the situations in which violence is appropriate give a telling picture of the kind of man they imagine themselves to be, and the way they do (or do not) conceive of women as physically autonomous.[21] All of the men spoke disdainfully of men who beat their wives without a justification. Men distinguish between *una cachetada* (a slap) and *un golpe* (a blow), and all of the men—even those who did not take pains to distinguish themselves as not macho—said that there was no justification for un golpe.[22] They classified men who hit their wives with a closed fist as irresponsible, as machos, as men who get drunk and lose control of themselves.

A number of the men, however, did mention situations in which they thought it justifiable to slap their wives, but there is no simple relationship between what men said about quién manda and their attitudes toward violence. Neither of the two who claimed all the power to give orders said he would hit his wife in anger or to discipline her, while several who professed more egalitarian modes of decision making said they had slapped or could imagine slapping their wives "to calm them down." The stories that Juan, Pedro, and Sergio shared with me all show different aspects of men's experience with violence. Perhaps the most striking comment any of the men made about violence was Juan's, who said—in response to my question about what it meant to respect his wife—that men should not force their wives to have sex: "For example, the way one respects one's wife is that you give them their place. For example, when you want to have relations with her, we should both be in agreement, not just one of us. To do it violently, that's what one has to be careful of—one shouldn't be violent with one's wife, or force her. That's the key thing for me, that she has her will, that is, to talk with them, to get along, in that intimate way." He notes here both her right to say no and her right to say yes.[23] However, Juan saw no contradiction in an occasional slap to show her who's boss. He talked about how violence serves to reestablish hierarchy—perhaps even more of an issue when women might imagine that they are equal partners.

The way that Sergio and Pedro responded to my questions about violence suggests that we can understand it best when we look both at ideas about masculinity and at material factors. Sergio, who lives in Degollado, told me that now he would never hit her, but that he did strike her in anger and frustration when they were first married. He told me:

> When I was recently married, I did hit her—what's more, I felt desperate. I said to myself, "Why did I get married?" You see no way out, you don't know what to do. Maybe it's that many of us need some advice. I did get some, [a friend] told me, "Every time you hit your wife and leave the house, you left her there beaten up or whatever, but tell me what state of mind you are in, how you feel. Do you feel strong and brave after having hit her?" And I said to him, "But sometimes they yell so much, don't they deserve it?" He said, "Wouldn't it be better not to judge her, but just to leave the house?"

His friend encouraged him to cool down emotionally and talk things out later. Sergio said that in addition to this initial advice, his friend continued:

And how are you going to show your face again afterward?...Next time you start to argue with your wife, [say to her] "If you don't like this house, there's the door for you to leave, or fix my suitcases. Why should we stay here and fight, why should we be here beating each other up?" That's the easiest way to avoid trouble, because if you fight, then you'll be in the judge's office, explaining the case and everything, everyone will find out, some will tell you what a fool you are, others will tell you not to put up with it, and finally they will make your head spin because you can't figure out who to listen to.

Sergio's threat to leave Juana might silence her in a way that a slap could not. His friend is instructing him to use his power in a more modern, more sophisticated way—that rather than show himself to be weak by losing control and striking out, he should just remind her how hard it would be to live without him.

His mother, however, told him he needed to show his wife more directly that he would not let her push him around. When he went to her for counsel after a fight with his young bride, she told him that "you need to be careful, because as a woman I know how women are." She continued, he recounted, "It's as if the man is a wild colt, as long as he is not saddled he'll keep being wild, and if they saddle him, he's broken, and that's how women are, they are just waiting to tame the animal, to put the saddle on." Although men say that domestic violence and the question of quién manda are private issues, they obviously do not form their ideas in isolation. Not all men push their friends toward macho performances, nor do all women automatically disapprove of violence.

Pedro and Josefina disagreed about who really made the decisions (he said that she did, and she told me that he always had the last word because he was strong enough to make her shut up), but they did agree that he had hit her several times over the course of their marriage. His violence seems less a considered demonstration of power and more a product of desperation and poverty. The first time he hit her was just shortly after they were married, and he has hit her several times since then but "just a light touch because I've never dared hit her hard." He explained why he had hit her with an anguished torrent of words:

> I'll tell you, that sometimes there are strong reasons, that sometimes there are these reasons—you have been angry for days and you get home and you see all that mess, and then just because you say to her, "Just look at how the room is," she gets mad too, and says things to you. That's when you start to burn up, like I'm telling you. I don't say that I haven't because I have hit her, but always with a soft hand, not even making a fist,

> because,...I don't know, I don't like to hit her. That's why, when I have
> given it to her, I don't do it hard, I just tap her that's all.

I felt very fond of Josefina and Pedro and had been charmed by his story
of how he had fallen in love with her at first sight and worked to win her
away from her first boyfriend. It is hard for me to understand why he hit
her, and I do not wish to apologize for Pedro's violence by making him
out to be just a victim of their poverty or by suggesting that he is any less
in control of his behavior than the other men. Gutmann, however, has
argued that violence against women has worsened as a result of the recent economic crisis in Mexico.[24] Traditionally, a central component of
successful masculinity, he suggests, is a man's ability to support his family, and in cases where structural conditions make it harder for men to
succeed as *hombres familiares* (good family men who provide well), men
are more likely to express their anger and frustration by acting out violently, to show that they still have at least some power left at home.

Pedro had one of the largest families of any of the men interviewed,
and one of the smallest salaries. None of their children were old enough
to contribute significantly to supporting the family, although they both
hoped things would ease somewhat once their oldest son graduated
from grade school that June and could work. Every day, Josefina had
her hands full: cook breakfast, walk the children to school, dress and
feed the others, walk back to school with breakfast for her kids in
school, do some needlework or go wash the dishes down the street (as
an act of charity, a neighbor paid her 20 pesos [$3] a week to wash her
breakfast dishes), and get home to start making lunch. (And that was if
there was still something to cook. If not, she had to screw up her
courage to ask, yet again, for credit from a local grocery. The frequency
with which she had done this, she said, had numbed her to the humiliation, but she described poignantly how she shakes with rage when she
sees her better-off neighbors pass by with overflowing bags from the
market.) As Josefina herself told me, the woman who sweeps and does
not pick up the garbage is not a real woman—just as to be a man one
must adequately support one's family. Neither she nor Pedro was doing
a particularly good job of fulfilling their gendered responsibilities to the
family, but they were each doing the best they could under the circumstances. To see Pedro's violence toward her only as a product of gender
inequality is to miss the ways in which structural violence delineates the
conditions within which they struck their marital bargain. The occasional violent outbursts seem a sign of the war in which she and Pedro

were stuck due to their grinding poverty and consequent failure to meet the other's (and their own) expectations. Pedro certainly felt bad after hitting her—but still, she is the one who bears the bruises of their joint desperation.

Beyond the total level of family income, another crucial factor may be the disparity in income between the two partners. At any level of income, there is some evidence that women who earn much less than their partners are more likely to suffer from violence, and the likelihood that their partners will hit them rises even more when they have children to support.[25] There is no one factor that determined that Pedro would hit Josefina—but Pedro earned more than three times what she did, they had seven children, her father was dead, and the difficult relationships she had with her mother and brothers made it unlikely that they would intervene in the even more unlikely event that she would turn to them.

Economic explanations of violence, however, cannot fully explain why some men hit their wives and others do not. While Mercedes does not work, neither does her sister-in-law Perla, and Perla's husband, Francisco, says he would never hit her. The fact that Eva and Josefina, both of whom had been hit by their husbands, had very large families and limited income of their own might suggest that these factors make women vulnerable to men's violence, but I spoke with other women in similar situations (such as Mariana and Norma) whose husbands had never lifted a hand against them. In addition, an alternative explanation seems to make the most sense in cases such as that of María, who probably earns more than her husband: he slaps her occasionally *because* of her independent access to resources. But in the case of Blanca who has the same or more earning power as Oscar—she has papers and he does not, and she has the added advantages of more education and nearby kin—it seems unlikely that he would hit her because it is ideologically repellent to him. Esperanza, by contrast, has many of the same resources that her best friend, Blanca, has, but I could imagine Mario hitting her in a burst of anger even though she owns her own business and manages their joint finances—or perhaps because of these things. Although Pilar has none of Blanca and Esperanza's material advantages (she lives in El Fuerte and has never worked outside the home), it seems unlikely that her husband, who described her as "his friend, his wife, his lover—everything," would use violence to enforce his will.

In some cases, it seems that men hit their wives when they do not earn enough to feel they are filling the male role as providers, while in others it seems that they hit them because they earn enough to have power over them. These contradictions suggest that explanations of violence should integrate micro- and macrolevel factors with attention to ideologies of gendered behavior—and in particular to masculinity. The men who said that they would not hit their wives frequently framed their position in terms of the kind of men they are, or want to be: that is, they did not want to lay claim to a power grounded in violence. Women whose husbands strive to be "family men" seem much less likely to suffer violence at the hands of their husbands, regardless of their relative economic resources and regardless of whether they are men in their twenties striving to be modern or men in their fifties striving to be responsible patriarchs. All the men in this community, younger and older, whether in Mexico or the United States, have access to the structural and cultural privileges of being a man (mediated, of course, by their actual social position); men's masculinity ideals explain at least in part why some choose to resolve disputes through violence, while others do so through verbal negotiation.

Local Theories of Gender and Power

> *Juan:* The man has to wear the pants at home, because he is the one who has to support his wife and kids.

Men portrayed machos as a caricature of masculinity, as men who take (and abuse) power without earning it by fulfilling their responsibilities. As Francisco said, "Well, a man is one who tries to give his wife and children everything they deserve, and the macho is one who just goes around looking for women to satisfy himself, and later hits them."[26] When I asked Oscar who was the head of their family, he hesitated: "Well, I am, because—well she is too, but—well, I am a little bit more than she is." When I pushed him on what it means to be the head of the house, he said:

> *O:* Well, for example, now she's working, and as they say she is supporting herself but after the baby is born, she won't work anymore, so I'll be the one supporting the family. I have to work for both of them, to buy a house or whatever.
>
> *J:* She's never going to work again?
>
> *O:* It depends how she feels, my obligation is to support her and the child, and if she doesn't want to work again, that's her decision.

Francisco, Juan, and Sergio all made the same point: women's wages can be a welcome contribution, but the real responsibility for the family's economic security must be shouldered by the man alone.[27] Similarly, most of the men said that they had helped their wives with housework on occasion, but none of them suggested that the couple held joint responsibility for domestic work.

Juan said that he is always happy to help Mercedes when she is tired, or the baby is sick, and that when he sees she needs help he does not wait for her to ask, but normally he does not volunteer to do housework when not asked. (He does, however, clear his own plate when he is done eating, something his father never did and told them not to do.) Oscar also touched on this point, saying that not only did his father never wash a dish but that he reprimanded his sons if they tried to, telling them that they should leave that work for their sisters. These men's own sons, presumably, will grow up learning that men can clear their own plates and help make the beds, when asked. Both in Mexico and Atlanta, men talked about being happy to help with the domestic chores in order to occasionally lighten their wives' burden, but none of them suggested it was in fact their burden as well. Similarly, women's income is seen as extra.[28] Men may be willing to share some power in the interest of increased marital harmony, but this sharing of the mando should hardly be interpreted as a wholesale bid for egalitarian relationships.

"To Live and to Exchange Feelings with Your Partner"

J: And how do you see your marriage, in comparison with that of your parents?

O: Well, I see that my father has been harder with my mother. He would go out to bars.... My mother would be there at home with us little ones and my father out drinking in town—so he didn't give much freedom to my mother so that they could go out together and I do with my wife, Blanca, we go here and there. Wherever I go, she goes with me.

J: And did you say to yourself since you were little that you wanted something different when you had your own family?

O: I never thought about it. It just comes out naturally, the way that I do things just comes from how I am.

J: But don't your brothers say to you, or your friends, "Oh, your wife bosses you around," because you are always with her?

O: I have seen that—like,...they say, "Oscar just got married and now his wife doesn't let him do anything." But no—I got married for that, to be with her, not to go around alone. In that case I shouldn't have gotten married. That's why you get married, to live and to exchange feelings with your partner [yo me casé por eso, para estar

> con ella, no para andar solo, en ese caso no me hubiera casado, por
> eso se casó uno para vivir, intercambiar sentimientos con su pareja].

Oscar was not alone in suggesting that sentiment lies at the core of
the marital bond. Ultimately, what men themselves seemed to find most
remarkable about their marriages was neither the softening of gendered
work boundaries nor the occasionally cooperative nature of their decision making; rather, what stands out for them is the nature of this emotional bond with their spouses.

Looking for a Wife: The Ideal Woman

A minority of men talked primarily about marrying for love, noting
only secondarily what they observed about their future wife's potential
as a homemaker. Pedro, for example, talked about *el flechazo* (cupid's
arrow strike) when he first saw Josefina. The moment he saw her at a
dance, "ever since I saw her, it was love at first sight." He said he barely
thought about anything else. When I asked him what made him think
that she would be a good wife, he said, "Right away she was very deep
in my heart."[29]

Oscar, in Atlanta, also fell fast: he said, "I loved her when I saw her"
(*yo me enamoré de ella cuando yo la vi*). When I asked him what made
such a strong impression in that first moment, he said, "She was not
crazy, like those girls who like to run around here and there," but more
than anything he talked about her character: "She's calm, it looked like
we could be good friends, and I noticed her because she is always smiling, and she talks a lot—that is, more than anything, the way she is, her
personality." Talking about the courtship, he said that day by day, "it
was like our hearts were developing more trust." When I asked what he
was looking for in a wife, he said "that I felt like I couldn't be happy
without her. When I was at home [in Atlanta] and my mother came to
visit from Mexico, she said, 'Son, why aren't you spending any time at
home with me, if I came all this way to see you.' 'Oh, mother,' I said to
her, 'I'm going out, I'll be home later.' I felt better with her [Blanca], there
in her house." He continued: "When you are in love you want to be with
her all day, with your girlfriend, to go out, to have fun, to play, more
than anything just to be together." Neither Pedro nor Oscar talked about
marrying the one for whom they were destined, as the older women did;
the convention of marrying "he for whom you are destined" is only used
to describe women's experience. Even the men who fell in love at first

sight are still the action-heroes of their own narratives, persistently pursuing the object of their affections until she consents.

Sergio also focused more heavily on personal characteristics than on respectability or domestic skills, saying that he initially liked Juana because she was not afraid to disagree with him. Other girls, when he asked them what kind of marriage they would like to have, would say: "Don't ask me, whatever you say." He explained, "But I don't like that, because, no, *supposedly you get married with a partner, not just to look for someone to be bossing around in everything,* what I like is to live together, that she also makes her own decisions, has her own opinions. That's what I didn't like about the other girls, that if I said to them, let's go there, then we went there, they never said no to me" (emphasis added). When I asked him, as I asked all the men, what behavior he could not pardon in his wife, he responded by saying that what he could not bear would be "if I wanted to succeed in something and she made fun of my wanting to get ahead, that would be like pushing me back"; he was looking for someone who would support him in his dreams.

It is one thing for a man to say he fell in love with his wife because of her personality and strong opinions and quite another for him to react well when she asserts that personality. Yet what these three men said about how they chose their spouses is reflected at least partially in their current evaluation of what it means to be a good husband. Although they had only been married for just over a year at the time of the interview, Oscar did seem to have followed through on his initial desire for a friend by approaching his wife as his companion and his equal. Sergio and Pedro had both been married for much longer (almost fifteen years), and each had struggled with difficult times in his marriage. Pedro and Josefina were separated for a time after about five years of marriage, and Sergio earlier described his anguished feeling that he had made a mistake in marrying Juana. Both of them had hit their wives, and Pedro occasionally still did. Yet they maintained their companionate ideals. When asked what it meant to him to be a good husband, Sergio kept returning to the idea of *convivencia* (spending time together) as the key. He did not deny his responsibility to support her, but he noted this only after talking about companionship and joint decision making. He even said, "I think I even get a little angry when my children come in because they take up so much time." Although Pedro talked about wanting a woman who is "a homemaker" and who can take care of him and of their children, when asked for his general philosophy of marriage after fifteen years, he said, "For me, marriage should be a harmonious thing, where you talk between the two of you. Dialogue, respect, and understanding are the three foundations of marriage."

Most of the men, however, courted with the clear idea of finding a woman who could reliably fit more traditional criteria: Juan, Humberto, and Francisco talked about wanting to marry a virgin, and Francisco added that what he most wanted was a woman who would give him children. What he said specifically was that "the Mexican man looks for a person who wants to give him children, because that's a Mexican man's dream, to have children, and that's the first thing you look for, is that a woman is disposed to have children." In spite of the oft-reported deep ties between machismo and the quest for paternity, he was the only man to mention a woman's willingness to have children, though other men did talk with pride and love of their children. Miguel and Juan both mentioned looking for a woman who was a hard worker (Miguel said he knew she was a hard worker because he had watched her help her father strip corn kernels from the cob after the harvest). Mario touched on a theme noted by Juan, Humberto, Francisco, and Miguel when he said that it was important to him to marry someone from a good family, a family that had respeto, which men may see as their best guarantee of a woman's future fidelity.

Juan and Francisco contrasted the women of their hometown with the muchachas *libertinas* (loose girls) they knew in the United States, saying that returning home to marry was the only way to find a woman who would share their values. It was also, of course, the only way to marry someone whose family history they could examine for evidence of sinvergüenza (shameless) behavior. After dating women in the United States who were willing to spend the night with him, Juan was charmed to date a woman who would not ride with him in his car for fear of damage to her reputation. Francisco was similarly taken with his future wife's innocence. Part of the appeal, they suggest, is the feeling of conquering (literally) virgin territory. When I asked Francisco if he ever thought of marrying one of the women he had dated in the United States, he said, "There are times that you share something fast, and like that, you don't get—you don't become fond of the person the way you do when it takes a while to get somewhere. You get very attached, because...if you get something easily you don't appreciate it and if you fight to have it you will want to keep it with you all the time." Francisco's wife, Perla, however, talked about how women encourage men's pursuit through smiles and little looks; these descriptions of men as pursuers and women as pursued are not actual descriptions of male activ-

ity and female passivity, but rather reports confirming that the participants have mastered a gendered code of sexual conduct.

Even these men, who sought a hardworking woman from a good
family, mentioned their desire for a certain kind of emotional bond. The
focus on confianza does not suggest a rejection of other ideas, but rather
the superimposition of a new, modern dimension. Francisco, for example, talks about wanting someone "who knows how to listen to you,
what you are discussing, and understands you, because some women,
you just start to tell them something about what is going on with you
and they say, 'I don't need your problems, I have enough with my
own.'" Similarly, Juan spoke about the importance of talk in a marriage. Comparing the confianza of marriage to the initial, tenuous intimacy of courtship, he said, "Now it's a more intimate trust, deeper, because you know that you have to live the rest of your life together. That
is, that your partner is yours for the rest of her life, and you know that
you need to trust them with any personal thing, to say, 'I have this problem.' It's being together and getting along. The way to have a happy
home is to talk about what's going on with you, and what's going on
with her.... Many people can't talk like that about intimate things."
Juan said that when looking for a partner he sought a woman who was
hogareña (a homemaker), but that did not mean she should necessarily
be stuck at home all the time (he thinks it is cute how she has learned to
ride the bus by herself in Atlanta), nor should she let him order her
around unfairly: "Whenever you're rude to them [women], of course
they have to be that way too, they can't just let themselves get pushed
around all the time. If I say to her 'do this' rudely, in a bad mood, she
has the right to say to me, 'Lower your voice, you're all worked up,
don't boss me around as if I were nobody, I have my feelings too, don't
treat me that way.' If you behave badly with them, they will act the
same way with you. I don't think they should be too submissive." He
sees his responsibilities first and foremost as supporting her, but then
adds that one of the many ways of being *cumplido* (the traditional word
for a good provider) is "to come home and say to your wife, 'What's
new?' 'How are you?' 'Is everything ok?' to come home joyfully, with
tenderness." Just as women are redefining respect to give themselves
more room to negotiate, men are also redefining key words such as
cumplido, which denotes gendered categories of behavior, to indicate a
new, more intimate vision of marriage.

Mario displays this same coupling of companionship and hierarchy
when he talks about his marital goals. Although he was looking for a

pretty, well-behaved girl from a good family, he was also quite insistent that he wanted a relationship in which they would have sufficient trust: "Well, so that she tells me everything, that I trust her [to talk about] everything that happens, whether it's in her family or whatever, the trust to talk to each other." The point of marriage is to enjoy life together: "As I have told Esperanza, my idea is that if you're going to live badly, it's no longer important that you're married, the whole thing is finished, your life together, because I don't see any point just because you're married to spend your whole life together." When I asked him what it meant to him to get along well, he said, "Well, not having problems, that you get home and they give you lunch." I asked him if that meant being *bien atendido* (well cared for) and he said that it was not just a question of cooking and washing and ironing: "Independently of women's work, that is, that you see that she treats you well." Taking good care of one's husband (*atender bien al marido*), Mario suggested, includes a smile and a kind word in addition to a hot meal and clean, well-pressed clothes (there is also a strong sexual implication to being "well taken care of"). Sergio said the same thing: that the point of marriage is to be happy together, and that if they are not happy they should separate. This transformation in marriage entices women with the promise of intimacy, but there is risk involved as well: men encourage women to speak and have opinions, but too much speaking, or the wrong kind of speaking, could lead to that dreaded unhappiness that now becomes justification for dissolving the union.

This new discourse on marital companionship as something that must be carefully tended through discussion and time spent together does not mean that happiness was not important to couples in the past, or that "modern" couples are in fact any happier. Miguel, the oldest man interviewed (he was forty-five at the time), told me that when he sought a wife, he was just looking for "one who would cook for me and that would make me happy, that's all." He wanted to be happy, and in fact would say that he is happy—the difference between him and the other informants is that happiness is achieved not through direct pursuit of it but rather through each person carefully completing his or her assigned tasks. Concha did feel tenderness (cariño) for him, but she showed it by keeping a clean home, raising their children to be respectful, making sure he always had a hot meal waiting for him at midday, and standing to heat his tortillas while he ate. They did not talk about sharing their feelings. Furthermore, public displays of sentiment or affection embarrassed Concha; she said she sees no point in couples walking around holding hands to show others how well they get along. Miguel and Concha saw their love as an automatic result of each person knowing how to respect the other and carrying out his or her individual responsibilities, rather than as part of a complex relationship that must be maintained through emotional work.

"So That You Feel Both Tenderness and Respect"

> *J.H.:* And what is your parents' marriage like?...Would you like your marriage to be different from theirs, from the model that you had at home?
>
> *J:* Well, I would like it to be better. My parents have always been happy, but it's as if they are very different. I have never seen my father kiss my mother—and I'm not saying on the mouth, I mean even on her cheek. In a celebration or a birthday, I have never seen them kiss, they are very private, very distant, that's how people were.
>
> *J.H.:* Too respectful?
>
> *J:* Too distant...I've never seen them kiss, or even hug. They're very private.
>
> *J.H.:* So your idea of marriage is very...
>
> *J:* Closer so that the children really know you love each other, that you feel both tenderness and respect and everything, and that they also learn to value having parents who love each other, so that they can learn something good from you, because if you spend your whole time fighting—well, it's better to get along.

Men such as Juan are consciously crafting relationships that are different than the family relationships they saw as children. When they talked about sharing el mando (the power to make decisions), not being machista, and helping their wives sweep, their words were in constant dialogue with a (perhaps exaggerated) vision of the past as a time when men were different. Some seem to be reacting to their fathers' negative example—certainly no one talked about aspiring to be the kind of man his father was, and several talked about clearing dishes, cooking, and helping with child care in spite of their fathers' admonitions to the contrary.[30] When I asked them about how they would like their marriages to be different than their parents', they emphasized feelings and closeness. Mario, for example, said that his parents spent more time worrying about their kids than paying attention to each other, and Juan launched into the narrative above about closeness and intimacy. Oscar spoke openly and disapprovingly of how his father had treated his mother, going off to drink in town and leaving her alone rather than being her companion. Humberto, who seemed pained to recall hiding behind his brothers so as not to have to greet the stranger arriving from el norte who they told him was his father, is demonstrative and even somewhat indulgent of his own children, in spite of his stern face.

Men did not, however, connect their affective goals to power-sharing. Most will say in one breath that they should be equal and intimate companions and in the next that they (the men) should have the last word. This reformulation of el mando into a new, more flexible hierarchy with more room for cooperation and intimacy is a key characteristic of these Mexican companionate marriages. Men are trying to redefine marriage and masculinity to allow more room for closeness and emotional satisfaction for both partners, but without relinquishing power. Only Oscar, and to some extent Sergio, connects the pursuit of intimacy with the issue of equality. For the most part, these men are trying to craft warm, affectionate marriages, but not egalitarian relationships. They may be seeking to redefine masculinity so that a less harsh mando leaves room for more intimacy, but as the saying goes, "*el que paga, manda*" (he who pays the piper calls the tune).

Marriages characterized by cariño and confianza certainly seem more appealing on the surface both to men and to women. And yet, if that cariño and occasional joint decision making depend primarily on men's vision of masculinity, then women's experience in marriage continues to depend primarily—as it did for their mothers—on the preferences of "he for whom you are destined." Women's experience of marriage is not wholly determined by their husbands, but men's desires are a crucial parameter within which women negotiate, and a man's vision of masculinity (and consequent ideas about quién manda) determines the style with which his wife will negotiate—whether, for example, she will disagree directly or (as her mother may have done) try to get what she wants by being nice.

Why Do People Want to Be Modern?

Toward the end of my fieldwork in Mexico, I was interviewing Pilar, who lived with her husband (a day laborer), their young child, and her father-in-law in El Fuerte. Work was scarce for young men in the rancho and money was tight; she was anguished as the annual fiesta approached and she would yet again have to go without a new dress for the *baile*. The returning norteños bring new clothes for their wives, and now they are increasingly joined by women who return with clothes they have purchased with their own hard-earned wages, so she felt as if she were one of the only women in town without something new. Her husband, who had found a half-day's work that would at least buy them some food, walked in the door as we were talking, looking for his uniform so he could go practice with the rancho's soccer team. When he asked Pilar where his socks were, she said that she did not know and that he would have to find them himself, as she was in the middle of talking to me and could not be interrupted. Unfazed, he kept looking, finally found them, and left for soccer practice. For older women, providing men with clean clothes and cooked food meant actually serving the hot food and handing a man his clean clothes as he steps out of the shower. Why, I wondered, was Pilar's husband so willing *not* to be waited on by her? And why was it so important to her to show me that she could refuse to do so?

Modernization (understood as technological, economic, and social change) does not automatically remake relationships; here I focus on the advantages men and women may perceive in adopting this modern style of intimate relations.[31] We need to ask *why* men and women in Mexico seek to build more modern gender identities through these companionate marriages, because in doing so they are moving toward a relationship ideal shared by the author and, presumably, many of the readers of this book; by not asking about the relative advantages and disadvantages of companionate marriage we run the risk of naturalizing it, of implying that people desire this particular style of intimate relationship because it is inherently superior.

At first glance, companionate marriage seems full of benefits for women. Women talk about the pleasures of emotional intimacy, and the (self-perceived) lucky ones talk about how their husbands provide material evidence of this closeness by being detallista. A thoughtful man marks a couple's wedding anniversary, Valentine's Day, her birthday, and Mother's Day with a card, flowers, or an invitation to dinner. Women talk not about the monetary value of these gifts but about their personal-ness; Beatriz, for example, was quite disappointed with the dozen roses her husband brought her for Valentine's Day—an expensive proposition in Atlanta—because he failed to write a sweet message or even sign his name to the card that accompanied them.[32]

Women see these intimacy-oriented relationships as offering a path to power and marital security. Those who felt that they had a good amount of input in matters pertaining to their family (whether economic or social) told me proudly that "I have opinions" (that is, opinions that count), or else "He takes me into account" (*me toma en cuenta*). Women hope that these bonds of love will force men to acknowledge that they have tastes, desires, even longings and that they have a right to expect some degree of satisfaction in these intangible areas. (This issue of the increased social legitimacy of satisfying individual whims recurs in women's discussions of reasons to limit their fertility—they talk about wanting fewer children so that they will be able to satisfy their wants and not just their needs. This parallel suggests that these changes in marital strategies reflect an underlying shift in ideas about personhood.) Companionate marriage can— though it does not always—give women a moral language with which to define the limits of acceptable behavior rather differently than it was defined for their mothers. For example, women talk about "having a right" (*tener el derecho*) to visit female relatives or friends as long as they do not neglect their other duties. Their mothers, in contrast, spoke of "getting permission." Visiting is not trivial; in their visits with each other women gather information, trade secrets, and build relationships in ways that can make them less exclusively dependent on their husbands. Josefina's husband frequently criticized her for spending time out visiting neighbors and running errands, time that could better be spent cleaning their house, washing, or minding their children, but from her point of view, visiting was a valuable, productive activity, as it knit her more firmly into a network of help and obligation. The daughters may not actually visit any more than their mothers did, but their movement through the streets as individuals who have the *right* to be outside their house has a different meaning to them.

Women also talk about rights in terms of the right to work; a few spoke about the right to "develop themselves as people" (*realizarse como persona*), or even just to earn some money for themselves. By working outside the home, or even just by spending more time outside the home— both of which women may potentially do more of in companionate marriages—women gain access to financial and social resources they might not otherwise have and thus to a sense of self-sufficiency. When they do work, whether in Atlanta or in Mexico, they gain much more than an income. They talk about the knowledge that one can *valerse por sí mismo* (make it on one's own or count on oneself) as one of the reasons to work. Having worked once, they know that in case of divorce or widowhood they could take care of themselves.

Third, women hope that these strong emotional ties make a marriage more likely to endure, so women maintain these affective bonds as a way to strengthen their marriages. They call it, among other things, *hacerle cosquillas al marido* (knowing how to tickle one's husband). The feminine equivalent of being detallista (though women can also be detallista), it implies knowing how to make them feel good, important, how to make them feel loved and valuable. Tickling one's husband could cover a range of public and private behaviors, from not contradicting him in front of his friends to physically pleasing him in other ways in private. Women do these things, no doubt, out of love, but they also talk explicitly of how they function to affirm the marital bond. A saying that several women shared with me, *"permiso y perdón se pide en la cama"* (one asks for permission and pardon in bed), underlines the strategic nature of sexual intimacy. (Although these strategies may work for individual women, the suggestion that intimacy strengthens these marriages is also ironic because the emphasis on the importance of satisfying emotional intimacy makes these companionate marriages in many ways fundamentally weaker than more traditional unions.)

Fourth, some women use this new marital ideal to justify migration and working outside the home, framing things that have individual benefits for them in terms of doing what is best for the couple. Their mothers may or may not have largely been content to stay in Mexico while their husbands journeyed north on the annual pilgrimage, but they rarely questioned the arrangement. Young women, though, make migration and marital togetherness an explicit negotiation point during courtship. Before they marry, they tell their boyfriends that if they are planning to go north they should save or borrow to pay the coyote for both of them, because *"no me voy a casar para estar sola"* (I am not getting married to be alone). The ideology of companionate marriage lends weight to women's desire to participate in the previously largely male adventure of migration. Women do the same with work: they talk about the importance of helping their husbands and of sacrificing for their families.

But I wondered, on that sunny winter day, if Pilar felt emboldened by my presence to act in a way she did not dare to otherwise. I asked her about this, and she said that no, that she goes out of her way not to wait on him too much. She did not, she said, want him to become *atenido* (spoiled), too used to relying on her for every little thing. I still think that she may have been showing off for my benefit, making sure that I knew that she was not a woman who was overly dominated by her husband—but by his reaction, or lack thereof, her husband was also showing me something about the kind of man he was. By de-emphasizing (though not altogether abandoning) hierarchy within marriage, proponents of the companionate ideal facilitate an intimacy, a *cariño*, which is its own reward. For men, the benefits of a marriage of *confianza* are emotional; men gain access to a certain kind of relatedness, an intimacy, which their fathers sacrificed as part of the cost of being *respetados*.

These men's derisive comments about machismo are also an assertion of a competent, modern masculinity. That they see the macho as backwards, ignorant, unaware that his old strengths are useless in the modern world is no accident, of course, since they are surrounded by Mexican-produced images communicating this message. Ignacio, for example, was the evil lead character in the recent telenovela *Te Sigo Amando* (I Still Love You), featured on Mexican TV in the winter of 1996, and on the U.S.-affiliate (in Spanish) later that spring. Darkly handsome and mustachioed, Ignacio owned a beautiful old hacienda somewhere in the fictitious heart of Mexico; he was rich, fearsome, and absolutely powerful in his own domain—but he was also confined to a wheelchair, unable either to walk or to consummate his marriage to the beautiful, sad Yulissa, due to a recent fall from a horse. Blond Yulissa, meanwhile, was sad because, while forced into an engagement with Ignacio, she had secretly fallen in love with a handsome, blond doctor from Mexico City, to whom, in a moment of passion, she had lost her virginity. In the sort of twist of fate inevitable in Mexican soap operas, the doctor was the only paralysis specialist in all of Mexico who could cure Ignacio, rendering him once again able to walk and to perform his manly duties.

By turning on the TV, easily available to all since the arrival of the parabolic antenna more than a decade ago in this part of Mexico, we learn that the old masculinity is impotent in this new world, that education and technology are man's salvation, and that the man who wins the prize—in which a woman's virginity still symbolizes her true love—is the one who seeks it with tenderness and soft words, rather than through cruelty and domination. (Yulissa's story also suggests that changes in Mexican gender ideologies may be more a question of style than substance; even in a world where a cell phone trumps a pistol, a woman's relationship with a man may still be a primary determinant of her security and social status.)

Mass media's presentation of modern masculinity as more prestigious, however, does not by itself explain men's interest in this new style of intimacy; people do not indiscriminately mimic everything they see on television (and most men do not watch novelas anyway). For men who migrate (as did all but three of the twenty-four spouses in the study) there are strategic advantages to even a temporary adoption of this alternative masculinity while in the United States. As Rouse has pointed out, Mexican men in the United States do not own the street in the same way that they do in Mexico, so choosing sneakers over cowboy boots and a baseball cap over a sombrero may serve as camouflage.[33] Men may also perceive social mobility advantages to this change in style; while some Mexican men in Atlanta work for their brothers and fathers, more commonly they work for gringos who own landscaping, Sheetrocking, or roofing companies, and they may think that emulating a more gringo style will serve them well in the local labor force. There are, furthermore, a number of other ways that migration reshapes gender, including expanding women's access to higher-earning jobs and increasing their physical mobility.

In addition to seeing these gendered transformations as self-protective, men who have worked in the United States say that their sojourns—during which they were forced to cook, clean, and wash their own clothes—forced them to see certain tasks as less strongly gendered. Although this may be true, it is not sufficient as an explanation; after all, similar journeys did not have that effect on these men's fathers. Mexican migrant men may also lean toward this modern masculinity as a response to the ways that migration feels disempowering to them as men. Adopting what they see as a more modern style of being a man is akin to changing the terms of the debate. Given that they no longer feel free to sit in the plaza and visit with their friends, that they may not speak the language, that if they are in the United States illegally every policeman represents a potential threat to their autonomy, and that they face daily the multiple small humiliations and large hurdles confronted by Mexican immigrant men in Atlanta, they instead choose to carry a cell phone—or, at the very least, *un beeper*—as a symbol of modern power and prestige.[34]

Mexican migrants in Atlanta have enthusiastically adopted these new communication technologies. On my visits to La Misión Catolica, the church in Chamblee that serves as social center to northeastern Atlanta's Mexican community, I frequently saw manual laborers with beepers on their belt loops or cell phones in hand. This may be due to practical considerations: for a population in which men live crowded together in apartments and move frequently, these mobile technologies offer a means to stay in touch with the kin and compadres from one's hometown who are a crucial source of security and social capital. In addition to their practical function, however, beepers and cell phones are also potent symbols of modernity—as evidenced by the fact that I met a number of Mexican men who sheepishly admitted that the cell phones or pagers they were wearing did not work or had been disconnected for nonpayment of bills. In Degollado and El Fuerte, men dangle large key chains from the pockets of their pants.[35] In Atlanta, cell phones and pagers have displaced key chains as tokens of masculine power.

It is less immediately clear why men who live in Degollado or El Fuerte should see any advantages other than emotional ones to rejecting Ignacio's style in favor of the doctor's—after all, their social world seems much closer to Ignacio's hacienda than to the doctor's sparkling clinic in the heart of Mexico City. Yet, depending on what kind of job they have, the demands placed on them to act like a certain kind of man can be more or less intense. A manual laborer, Pedro is routinely invited out drinking by his colleagues, who tease that *la mujer te manda* (his wife is the boss) when he declines to join them. Sergio, by contrast, owns his own small business. Although he may or may not have to curry favor with clients to ensure their business, there is no one he works with directly who is in a position to tease him about his preference for spending time with his wife instead of with his *cuates* (buddies).[36] In fact, Sergio routinely took Juana with him on day trips to visit local clients, and they both noted to me how they enjoyed spending the time together.

Education (or perhaps social class, for which higher education is a good marker) shapes men's ideas, but does not determine them. Pepe, an engineer with a degree from an elite university in Guadalajara who had his own business selling cellular phones and parabolic antennas, was the prototypical local example of this modern manhood. He was the son of the woman I lived with, and I got to know him fairly well over the course of my seven months in Degollado. He and his wife (who works full time in a managerial position) cooperated in the cooking, and even his style of dressing seemed to reflect these modern ideas about masculinity: he was much more likely to show up for lunch in loafers and a baseball cap than in boots and a cowboy hat. The one time we all went to their house for lunch, he and his wife were bustling around making cheeseburgers for the assembled crowd. By contrast, Humberto, who has a college degree in veterinary medicine and prides himself on his modern interests—he talked to me, for example, about wanting to hire a private tutor to teach his children English and computer skills—was the most insistent of all the men I spoke with in Mexico that el hombre tiene que mandar. In the exclusively male world of livestock and farming, a certain style of manliness continues to be advantageous. Advocacy of being *un hombre familiar* involves issues of social mobility, but does not map neatly onto social class: Pilar's husband in the rancho, who barely finished sixth grade, explained to a neighbor that the reason he and his wife hold hands in public is that she is "his friend, his wife, his lover—that she is everything to him."

For men and women in Mexico, asserting a modern masculinity can be one way of keeping up, of being modern *without* migrating. This makes particular sense when bearing in mind the way migration almost automatically increases a person's social status in the Mexican sending community. Those who do not migrate frequently remark on whether or not returning migrants *presumen del norte* (show off about having been in the United States).[37] When I returned in the summer of 1999 to visit Doña Evita, the woman I had lived with throughout my fieldwork in Mexico, she was doing a brisk business selling phone cards for people to use in their cell phones, but the vast majority of her clients were the families of migrants. (In rural Mexico, people buy phone cards, which they then use to allot time for use of their phone. Access to credit is limited and mail is unpredictable, so this eliminates the problem of billing and keeps people from making calls for which they cannot pay.) A cell phone—or any phone at all—is a luxury out of reach for those without family in the North. Women in both Atlanta and Mexico field sites joked about the way telenovelas would start on the Mexican networks several months ahead of when they were broadcast in the United States; they suggested that network programmers did this so that Mexican women in Mexico would have at least something to hold over the heads of their sisters in the United States.

For both men and women in Mexico, telling me and each other and themselves that they were no longer like their parents could be a strategy *para no quedarse átras* (to not get left behind). This quest to be modern could be read as part of the "northernization" of Mexican sending communities, through which the changes in these communities contribute to the production of more disciplined workers, but it could also be a response to the fact that nonmigrants are at a permanent disadvantage in terms of social status in this transnational community.[38] Those who do not migrate participate in a shared community of meaning that forever casts them as the country bumpkins, and gendered assertions of modernity are a strategic response to this problem. Cell phones and beepers may be expensive, but *abrazos* (hugs) and *cariños* (tenderness) are free.

The different ways that men and women in the United States and Mexico have access to these totems of modernity lead to a more general point about gender, identity, and social status in transnational communities. Both Mahler and Pessar have noted in their work how women and men in transnational communities use a gendered discourse to locate themselves in time (traditional or modern) and space (sending and receiving), and Rebhun notes a similar phenomena among rural-to-urban migrants in northeastern Brazil.[39] In Mahler's case, she describes how Salvadoran transmigrants on Long Island communicate to community members the ways they have or have not changed and make claims about where they belong through dress and sexual behavior, and how young men in the rural Salvadoran sending community do the same. Similarly, Pessar reports how Guatemalan women in Mexican refugee camps frame shifts in the household division of labor in terms of their own relative modernity. Gender, in these transnational communities, is a key discourse of identity that people use in different ways: people in receiving communities use gendered dress and speech to talk about belonging and difference, while those in sending countries use these same symbolic languages to assert that they have not been left behind.

The generational paradigm shift from marriages of respect to those of confianza mirrors the different aspirations for marriage suggested by changes in courtship practices. These marriages are part and parcel of women's marital goals, which are intertwined with their other goals (such as ensuring economic security, or developing and presenting a particular kind of social identity), but they are also ends in and of themselves. Through their discussions about how they make decisions, and whether men do or do not choose to use violence as a trump card, as well as their acknowledgments of slight shifts in the household division of labor and much greater generational changes in ideas about marital intimacy and companionship, men's and women's words demonstrate their commitment to gendered ideals of modernity. Migrant experience may also push men toward this reconstruction of masculinity, and the behavioral demands of the nonagricultural workplace (especially in the United States) are another influential factor. Ultimately men's hesitant embrace of this alternative masculinity seems due to a combination of influences, including family history, age, and situational factors that make it feel advantageous. It is a strategy for social mobility and self-protection, but it also feels good.

Understanding these connections between gender and social status helps us see what might motivate men in this community to reconstruct gender. In urban Mexico, Gutmann describes the cultural creativity with which women in Mexico City use their individual and collective social and economic power to press men for more personal autonomy and more egalitarian relationships.[40] In the social context of rural Mexico, where women are still quite dependent on men for economic resources and moral shelter, men's perception of the way gender and social status are interwoven can be another engine for gender change in Mexico. At the same time, however, internal contradictions in what men say about gender and power—such as when Juan said that he would never rape his wife but that he might slap her to remind her who's boss—should remind us that men's claims about intimacy and companionship are made in a context in which marital style is still largely their choice. Mexican men may use gendered discourse to claim membership in a larger, even perhaps global, community of meaning in which people use gender to talk about modernity and belonging—but it is still a community riven by inequality. Equal access to intimate companionship is not the same as equal access to power.

CHAPTER 5

Representing Change

A Methodological Pause to Reflect

Eloquent though they were, the stories men and women told me about courtship, love, and marriage do not speak for themselves. Differences in how the two groups of women compared here—women born in the 1920s, 1930s, and 1940s, and women born in the 1950s and 1960s—depict their intimate lives may be shaped by the fact that they are at different stages in their lives and marriages: given several decades of shared experience the younger couples may come to argue, as their parents do, that what truly holds a marriage together is work shared and obligations fulfilled, rather than sweet words and passionate kisses. A demographer might describe this methodological problem as one of trying to infer cohort change (that is, actual historical change) from cross-sectional data (which does not follow people over time but instead tries to see how the past differs from the present by taking people of different ages in the present to represent different generational experiences). Arland Thornton has called this the problem of "reading history sideways."[1]

I start at the most microlevel, working within the data and exploring how attention to issues of discourse and representation can substantiate these young women's insistent claims that they are not as easily pushed around as women of the past. Second, using what ethnographers refer to as "triangulation," I discuss how the things I actually saw people do fit in with these stories about gender and change.[2] Third, I review the evidence of demographic, economic, and social change in the field sites;

the rapidity of the change over the past several decades makes it clear that it would be surprising if we did not see shifts in how people view marriage and gender. Fourth, I am hardly the first to notice that the lives of young women in Mexico are in some ways quite different from their mothers'; although the causes to which these changes are ascribed vary, many others working across Mexico have noted similar transformations in gender and sexuality. Finally, I review some of the research that suggests that, around the globe, there has been a trend toward a more companionate model of marital relations. Reference to similar gendered social transformations in very different circumstances might seem an odd strategy when my goal is to construct an argument about change in Mexico, but the global trend toward companionate marriage lends credence to my argument that in Mexico, as in these other locations, social and economic change have reshaped gendered opportunity structures and interwoven gender and modernity at the symbolic level in ways that have important implications for love, kinship, and the modern family.

FROM BEING CARRIED OFF AT GUNPOINT TO "GIVING HIM A LITTLE LOOK"

Although the idea that courtship is a process through which one acquires a spouse remains constant across generations, the older women's brief and distant courtships were structured by an underlying concern with family honor, whereas the younger women's stories are organized around the idea of courtship as a time to build enough emotional and physical intimacy with a partner and to see if a marriage might work. Through their emphasis on the dangers of being kidnapped (though none of them were), women implied two key ideas: (1) that, as Jane Austen said in *Northanger Abbey*, "man has the advantage of choice, woman only the power of refusal"; and (2) that in fact even that power was much less important than a young woman's ability to go from muchacha to señora without damaging her family's reputation and, once a señora, to bear up under whatever suffering might be her destiny.[3] By using sayings such as "marriage is a cross" and "marriage is a pun" (literally, an *albur*, in which a phrase laced with double meanings turns out to have an aggressive sexual content), older women depicted marriage as a woman's own personal calvary, but even those women whose marriages had not taken them through the stations of the cross credited this to their own ability to comply with a man's wishes, and perhaps to his good character, not to some meeting of true minds.[4] To the extent that older women talked at all about choosing a mate, they concentrated on family characteristics, not emotional compatibility.

Although the younger women were careful to distinguish themselves from rogonas, girls who go looking for it, they communicated their interest and agency in subtle (and not so subtle) ways both to their suitors, and to me in their retelling of these adventures. The younger women—both those in seemingly satisfying relationships and those in marriages characterized by conflict and even violence—depicted their courtships as a time when they actively chose a partner. It may have been an ill-considered or even downright bad choice, but it was theirs nonetheless. This focus on individual choice and interpersonal compatibility suggests that these factors matter, that they make the difference between a good and a bad marriage. The differences in how older and younger women told their stories are deeper than merely the surface content; they reflect different underlying assumptions about what women and men bring to a courtship and what they should get out of it.

Furthermore, there do seem to be a set of concrete differences in the logistics of courtship—how long people spend courting, where and how they see their novios—which, although perhaps subject to some exaggeration as women recall them, are unlikely to be entirely imaginary. Mirroring the rising age at first marriage, most older women married their first suitor while still in their early teens, while the younger women married in their late teens or even older, and several of the younger women discussed the importance of having more than one boyfriend just for the experience. The generational difference in the amount of premarital physical intimacy to which women would admit does not necessarily mean that none of the older women "ate their sandwich before lunchtime," but it does suggest that it has become increasingly acceptable to admit to premarital contact.

Women clearly shape their words for their audience—that is, a gringa researcher—thus expressing their ideas about what I might most want to hear, or most need to know. Their narratives are not "facts" in the sense that they might correspond exactly to some objectively discernible reality; rather, they are representations of experiences, distorted by their desire to communicate something in particular and to be perceived in a specific way. Acknowledging that people's words are, at least in part, deliberate fictions does not render them uninterpretable; it merely reinforces the necessity of reflecting on the ways that their stories are shaped by both spoken and unspoken assumptions about who I am and what I represent and by people's strategic self-representation (which is why the Introduction included a brief discussion of how I tried to manage the issue of representing myself during the fieldwork). This book, though, is not about me and how they perceived me—it is about men and women from Degollado and El Fuerte and their complicated individual lives and relationships, which they build at a particular juncture of social and historical circumstances. Their perceptions of me are only significant insofar as that can help us interpret their words through a more appropriately critical lens.

People would not have seen me as an emissary from a place where women's lives are different if they did not already have some awareness of gender as socially constructed (although of course they would not put it exactly this way). As Gutmann also found in his work in Mexico, when they spoke to me about how gender was changing, they were including me in ongoing conversations about the social transformation of gender: the phrases "we are not as easily pushed around as women in the past," "in the United States, women give the orders," and "young people today do not have any respect" were not coined in conversation with me, nor, I am sure, were these interviews the only instances in which people discussed generational and migration-related changes in gender and marriage.[5] The men who told me without prompting that they were "not macho," the women who insisted to me that they were not like their mothers, and the women who told me, like Doña Luisa, that her own girls are so rude to their husbands that *no tienen madre* (they act like they have no mother) all already have consciously articulated gender identities, a sense that through choice and deliberate action they are crafting their lives through being a certain kind of woman or man. So, clearly, one frame through which people's words must be interpreted is the fact that when they spoke to me, they were trying to communicate where they place themselves as individuals in this gendered continuum of social change.

Obviously what women and men present about their marriages is idealized. Both older and younger men may have been trying deliberately to create an impression by answering questions a certain way, but their ideas about what might impress a gringa researcher were clearly different: older men strove to prove that they exercised control over their wives and were the last word on all matters, while younger men made a point of how they believed in joint decision making and domestic cooperation. Similarly, among the women there was a generational difference in the direction in which they exaggerated: older women were demonstrating to me their mastery of a gendered system of respect, while younger women were trying to show mastery of a gendered idiom of modernity. For a survey researcher, all of these ways informants deliberately shape their words might fall into the category of "biases," but for our purposes—that is, investigating changing gender ideals—it is these "biases" themselves that are at least partially the focus of our inquiry. Furthermore, some of the couples who professed these more companionate ideals had been married for more than a decade, so presumably their words reflect some of the wisdom of experience, rather than just the tender dreams of newlyweds.

GENERATIONAL DIFFERENCES IN MARITAL PRACTICES

Younger couples did things that they said their parents had never done, and their parents concurred: I saw younger men, but not older ones, clearing their plates from the table and standing to get themselves a glass of water rather than asking for one. Perhaps a more profound example is the way in which I saw young spouses spend time together, both in and out of the house. I accompanied Esperanza and Mario, who was an avid breeder of fighting cocks, when they went once to a cockfight, which they regularly did together (his choice, to be sure, not hers, but she happily accompanied him rather than having him go out without her). I joined Isabel and Humberto several times for their regular Sunday evening promenade around the plaza. Pilar talked about how cozy it was to curl up on the couch and watch a movie with her husband, Juan Carlos. Sergio mentioned how he would take Juana with him on day trips for business whenever he could, and Magdalena told me when agreeing to do the interviews that we would need to complete them before her husband arrived from Atlanta, because once he arrived she would be too busy going on *paseos* (excursions) to talk with me. After he arrived, I saw them pass by many times in his car, on their way to spend the day at their family farm in the rancho with their children. I spent several lazy Sundays with Pedro and Josefina, picnicking under a tree on the hill north of town. This same heterosociality was evident among the Mexicans I interviewed in Atlanta, though the activities were different: they took trips to the mall, went together on the weekly grocery run or out dancing at a local country-and-western club, or took the occasional family excursion to the zoo or to a water park in the summer.

Among the older couples I visited, in contrast, the men tended to spend Sundays out of the house (in the street, en la calle). Some of them may have been drinking (one, I remember, was still drunk from a bender when I showed up to interview his wife on a Tuesday), but they may equally as well have been quietly sharing a game of dominos or feeding their pigs. The point is, wherever they were, it was not with their wives, and no one found this to be at all remarkable. The younger women, though, would rail if their husbands dared disappear for a whole day of leisure time without them. I remember how Esperanza complained bitterly one Sunday about Mario going to play soccer and not coming back until the evening.

The generational difference in how women deal with unhappy marriages provides even stronger evidence that this change is real. Some older women had kind and loving husbands, but others suffered the worst kinds of marital misfortune: regular beatings, abandonment, drinking sprees that would run through the week's food money, infection with sexually transmitted diseases acquired while in the United States, and incapacitating illnesses that left men unable to support the family. Among the life history informants' mothers—not just those interviewed, but all of them, since all of the women I interviewed at length told me about their parents' marriage—not a single one left her husband. In contrast, several of the younger women (Victoria, Josefina, Eva, María, and Juana) had been separated from their husbands for a time, and one (Lucha) actually left her first husband because, as she said, he treated her so badly that it was obvious that "he did not want to be married." Doña Evita's comment that women nowadays leave their husbands because they are unsatisfied sexually was perhaps uncharitable, but in a sense she was right: women now leave their husbands (if mostly only temporarily) because they expect marriage to make them happy. As Paulina said, "Women today do not know how to suffer."

Women also demonstrated this generational difference in how they see themselves in relation to the world around them through the drawings they shared with me. Before beginning the extended life history interviews in Atlanta, Degollado, and El Fuerte, I conducted a series of drawing exercises with women, asking them to represent the most important moments in their life in the past, present, and future. Without exception, the older women (including the older of the life history informants) responded by drawing a single frame in which they portrayed their house, sometimes including some farm animals and frequently including an antenna or satellite dish on top of the house (see Drawing 5.1). Admittedly (as anyone who ever tried it will recall), human figures are hard to draw—but still it is striking that women chose to represent themselves through a picture of their house. The older women's drawings suggest not

Drawing 5.1. House with Antenna. This drawing by a woman in El Fuerte is typical of those that older women made when asked to depict the most important moments in their past, present, and future. That it shows a house in which the husband is a migrant is made clear by the antenna on top of the house (a luxury unaffordable to families without someone in the United States).

only that these houses are the embodiment of their dreams and their identities, but also that their identity is inextricable from their family membership and that their story is about individual experiences and desires.

The younger women, in contrast, depicted themselves as the central character of a story, and, as in Drawing 5.2, the young women's drawings brim with events seen as important because of their significance to these women as individuals: first communions, quinceañeras, graduation from school, a first job, a first boyfriend, a first child. Whereas the older women's drawings are static, the younger women's drawings suggest a very different sort of an individual life course. The younger women's drawings also depict their quest for modern symbols of social status: they show houses with electric lights, parties with mariachis, driveways with cars, and longed-for trips across the border.

SOCIAL AND DEMOGRAPHIC CHANGES

Evita would frequently sigh to me over breakfast, making comments like "the whole town is disappearing. Alan and I might as well go pack our bags with all the others, and move to Atlanta." Her perception that more and more young people were choosing migration is substantiated by a quick look at how the sex ratios in the sending communities have

Drawing 5.2. Isabel's Life. In this drawing, Isabel depicts the important moments of her past, present, and future. *Left to right, top to bottom,* she shows herself at her first communion, having a mariachi band and a picnic on a bus as part of the grand celebration of her *quinceañera,* receiving her diploma from high school, marrying Humberto, and then with her first, second, and third children. The prosperity and mobility for which she hopes are represented by the two cars parked outside her dream house.

changed in the past forty years. In the 1960 census in Degollado (taken at the height of the Bracero program), there were 993 men in the town of Degollado for every 1,000 women—hardly a striking imbalance. Thirty years later, there were 907 men for every 1,000 women. After another decade, the number had fallen even lower, to 856 men for every 1,000 women. Data on men ages twenty to twenty-four for the whole county in which Degollado is located give an even more startling figure of 689 men per 1,000 women.[6] Similarly, the observation a woman made to me in El Fuerte that "the ranchos are going to disappear" seems, if not totally accurate in the short term, a real possibility in the long term. In 1960, El Fuerte counted 981 men for every 1,000 women. Thirty years later, there were 693.

Immigration, by itself, does not explain this generational paradigm shift in marital ideals, although the economic and cultural influence of migrants could certainly have contributed to it. The most obvious form of cultural influence (migrants having seen a more companionate ideal in the United States and desiring to copy it in their own families) actually seems fairly unlikely; for most of the Mexicans I knew in Atlanta, I was the only gringo with whom they had ever spoken at length about personal topics—nor did most of them watch TV or movies in English. Migration may contribute in more subtle ways, however, by encouraging people to present more modern gender identities so as not to get "left behind." An argument could certainly be made that the sex ratios created by migration have been one of the forces behind young women's increasing acceptance of premarital intimacy: a girl who finds a good catch might go further than she wants (or be more easily convinced to do what she really wants to anyway) to avoid being one of the *quedadas* (leftover women) still circling the plaza in her late thirties.

It is not necessary, though, to try to explain these changes through immigration alone, since there have been other striking demographic transformations: at a national level, women born in Mexico in the 1930s (as were the mothers of the life history informants) had a life expectancy of less than forty years (of course, all of the ones with whom I spoke lived a great deal longer than that, or they would not have been around to speak with me). Those born in the 1960s, like their daughters, could expect to live between sixty and sixty-five years. The life history informants' own daughters, born in the 1990s, join a cohort who can expect to live, on average, almost seventy-five years.[7] In Michoacán, the total fertility rate, which is a measure of how many children a woman might have if she passed through her fertile years experiencing current age-specific rates, declined from 7.6 in 1960 to 2.9 in 1997; in Jalisco, the decline was from 7.3 to 2.9 during the same period of time.[8]

There were economic changes as well: in Degollado in 1960, more than 90 percent of the employed population was engaged in some sort of agricultural pursuit. By 1990, this had fallen to just under 25 percent. Growth had occurred in the industrial sector (mining, extraction of oil and gas, manufacturing, electricity, water, and construction), which accounted for 38 percent of the employed population. The most prominent feature of the local industrial sector would be the *cantera*, stone-carving businesses, which have become a major source of employment in Degollado, and the industries associated with residential construction. The commercial and service sectors (commerce, transportation, communications, and services) have also grown in relative importance, employing 32 percent of those working locally. This would include all of those running the many small stores that survive on the spending of those families regularly receiving migrant remittances.

The material conditions of daily life have been transformed. In Degollado, the percentage of the population older than age fifteen who are illiterate dropped from 32 percent in 1960 to only 11 percent in 1990. During that same period, the percentage of homes with running water increased from 12 to 92 percent, and those with interior plumbing to carry away wastewater increased from 2.9 to 93 percent (that does not mean that the water was carried away to somewhere where it was treated properly, but that is a story for another day). In 1960, just above 18 percent of the population had a radio in their home (which means they may have had electricity too), and just under 4 percent reported using either electricity or propane (rather than wood, coal, or petroleum) as a cooking fuel. Thirty years later, 97 percent of homes report electricity. (Data from the 1960 census from the state of Michoacán present only the barest of data below the *municipio* [county] level, and the county where El Fuerte lies includes the very large city of La Piedad, so those data are not useful illustrations of these same trends.)

Life in rural Mexico has changed rapidly during the past several decades. The cohort into the which younger women were born was likely to marry later and with more education, to have fewer children, to have access to mass media through books, television, and radio, and to spend many years with their husbands after the last of their two or three children has left the house. Given these demographic, social, and economic changes, it is not surprising that people have begun to reimagine the meaning of marriage. It would be surprising if they did not.

OTHER RESEARCH ON CHANGES IN GENDER IN MEXICO

A great deal of recent research on gender and the family in Central/ Western Mexico reports similar social transformations in courtship and marriage. From Oaxaca to Veracruz, ethnographers and social historians have noted changes in adolescent relationships similar to the ones described in El Fuerte and Degollado. Mummert, for example, in an article entitled "Changes in Family Formation Among Rural Western Families," writes:

> Faced by the pressures of economic, social and cultural processes, patterns of courtship, nuptiality, postmarital residence, and procreation of children are being modified.... The emigration of adult men, a very deeply rooted practice with a history of almost a century in some communities, has become a mass phenomenon in the region in the past three decades....

From the mid-1980s, the men's departures have been accompanied by a
notable increase in family and female migration. This entry of women and
children into migrant flows has meant that in the community of origin people observe, compare and make judgments about new standards of behavior in relation to courtship and marriage, especially in terms of gender and
intergenerational relations and the intervention of the State in family matters. (Translation mine.)[9]

Mummert goes on to note other demographic changes in the region's
demographic profile: new marital patterns, characterized by later ages
at first marriage, and increases in exogamy and neolocal residence; new
patterns and levels of fertility, measured by increased access to and use
of contraceptive methods, longer intervals between births, and lower
overall fertility; and profound changes throughout women's life course:
increases in daughters' premarital economic contributions to family
support, women's migration, women's participation in wage labor, and
the percentage of women who, because of falling sex ratios and marital
exogamy, remain single throughout their lives. Mummert found these
changes in her ethnographic research as well; her work in a small agricultural community in Michoacán describes behavioral changes—new
courtship patterns, rising age at first union, declining family size, and
increased neolocality—which are strikingly reminiscent of those seen in
Degollado and El Fuerte. In a paragraph that could just as easily describe Degollado or El Fuerte, she writes:

Courting patterns in Quiringüicharo have become much more open:
couples now have ample opportunities to meet and get to know one
another. They may meet in the plaza and talk at the gate to the girl's home.
Dances and parties are daily occurrences at year's end, when the migrants
return and matches are made and cemented in marriage. Although fathers
seem to be having a difficult time accepting the new mores, mothers tend
to consider such openness preferable to the surreptitious meetings of their
own courting days and the frequent elopements necessary to circumvent
parental disapproval. Mothers also see the increased communication with
their daughters on matters of sexuality as a positive change.[10]

She continues, describing marriage and gender:

As for the power relations underlying gender roles, there is increased
participation of wives and daughters in family decision making.... Middle-
aged women compare their daughters' more equitable relationships with
their spouses with their own sense of powerlessness in the early days of
marriage: the mistreatment and humiliation by the in-laws, the need to
pressure the husband to found an independent household in which they
could make decisions without the extended family's constant interference.

Clearly, most young wives today are not willing to adopt a submissive role when faced with physical abuse or adultery on the part of their husbands. Young girls are adamant in their views, and they reject being victimized: "I don't think like my mother did that one must put up with whatever kind of husband one might happen to marry."[11]

Mummert explains these changes through reference to women's incorporation into wage labor in Mexico and to increased migration from this region to the United States, which, she suggests, has operated both through the cultural influence of return migrants and through the increased autonomy experienced by women whose husbands migrate, leaving them alone to manage the household. Grimes, who conducted ethnographic research in a migrant-sending community in Putla, Oaxaca (in southern Mexico), also found much discussion in her community regarding changes in gender roles; she notes, "Many Putlecan women are becoming less tolerant of macho ideals." She ascribes these changes primarily to migration, though she also notes the importance of women's access to education, wage labor, and fertility.[12]

The fact that similar transformations have been observed in urban and rural settings across Mexico, not just in states with strong traditions of U.S.-Mexico migration, suggests that migration may not be as singularly important a factor in these gendered transformations as Mummert and Grimes make it out to be. Working in Xalatlalco in the state of Mexico (where migration to the United States is uncommon, in part because of the proximity of Mexico City), González-Montes reported that by the early 1990s, people talked about "courtship and betrothal as a socially acceptable stage. Even during the 1970s couples found in the act of courtship were physically punished and some were forced to marry. Today young people can back up their wishes with the income they receive from jobs away from their parents' lands. They have earned more individual decision-making power over their own lives."[13] Similarly, in Pajapan, Veracruz, Vásquez-García describes the recent development of the practice of "extended courtships."[14] Working in three locations—in a Zapotec community outside of Oaxaca City, Oaxaca, an urban neighborhood in Mexico City, and a rural village about 20 kilometers from the hillside town of San Miguel de Allende in Guanajuato—Amuchástegui found young men and women deliberately crafting what they perceived to be modern sexual relationships; her finely grained exploration of the ways in which young people negotiate between discourses about pleasure and individual choice and the reality that in certain circumstances young women still need their bodies—and their virginity—as a resource captures a key aspect of the perils of modern Mexican courtships.[15] All of these works seem to describe the same generational difference in courtship practices I have discussed.

Researchers in field sites across Mexico have also found generational differences in people's experiences of marriage. Drawing on interviews with middle-class couples in Uruapan, Michoacán, Hubbell notes that especially among some well-educated couples, men and women "express the principle of equal power in family decisions....Definite changes in areas like acceptance of married women in the workplace, sharing domestic labor, fertility control, and equality between spouses in family decision making have begun to appear."[16] Similarly, in Cuernavaca, LeVine, Sunderland, and Tapia Uribe found that "despite the persistence of a double standard of sexual morality, younger urban women with more formal education and access to contraception are beginning to challenge traditional norms of husband-wife relations rather than endure infidelity, physical violence, and other forms of abuse."[17] Younger women, LeVine and her colleagues note, have greater emotional expectations from their marriages than did their mothers; they talk more about emotional closeness than do older women, and they articulate a strong preference not to know if their husbands have other sexual partners.[18] Among the younger women, confianza is a widely shared goal, albeit a sometimes unattainable one. Chant, exploring the impact of the economic crisis of the mid-1990s in León, Querétaro, and Puerto Vallarta, saw similar changes: "some democratization of household decision making, and an apparent relaxation of the sexual and moral mores which have so often forced women into early and ill-fated marriages."[19]

Not very far away geographically, but at the furthest possible remove in terms of social distance, Martínez-Vásquez writes that among elite women holding executive positions in Mexico City, "intimate relationships tend to be more egalitarian and to have greater levels of satisfaction and communication than those found among the traditional family" (translation mine).[20] Rodríguez-Dorantes, conducting research on how women became household heads, found that these ideas about love and marriage are not limited to women whose marriages have endured; many, though not all of them, spoke about unhappiness with the emotional aspect of their relationship or problems with sex as the precipitating factors in the breakup.[21] González-Montes, whose work in Xalatlalco is mentioned above, found that although as recently as 1974 the proportion of households that was female headed was negligible, the 1990 census reported that 10 percent of households were female headed. "The most common reason separated women gave for not returning to their husbands," she explains, "was that the husbands continued to live in an extended family with their parents, a conflictive situation which they were no longer willing to accept. The second most frequent cause for separations was that the husband did not fulfill his obligation to support the household, was an alcoholic, and/or beat his wife. The appearance of such a modern cause as incompatibility of character is very significant."[22] Across Mexico, female-headed households are an increasingly important demographic phenomenon; between 1976 and 1990, female-headship in Mexico increased from 13.5 percent of households to 17.3 percent, though the increase was more marked in urban areas than in rural.[23] These data on increases in female headship, together with the types of reasons women provide, serve both to suggest that belief in the importance of emotional compatibility in marriage is increasingly widespread and to remind us that bonds of affection may be quite fragile in comparison with those of respect and obligation.

Perhaps the most important recent work in English on changes in gender in Mexico, Gutmann's *The Meanings of Macho* (1996), also found that family relationships have been transformed as gender is de- and reconstructed in urban Mexico. Gutmann, in his fieldwork in Colonia Santo Domingo, found Mexican men and women to be articulate observers of shifts in gendered practices and ideologies; he writes not just about changes in what men and women do, but also about the tensions and contradictions in his informants' own critical analyses of the changing social construction of gender in Mexico. Just as Francisco, quoted in the previous chapter, insisted to me that a "macho" was a man who takes advantage of his wife, rather than taking care of her, many of the men with whom Gutmann spoke told him that they were men, not machos. Gutmann also found, as I did, that certain aspects of men's and women's relationships with each other (he cites alcohol use and housework) have become "degendered," less firmly seen as something men either must or must not do in their pursuit of a masculine identity.[24]

Most reports of generational changes in gender relations that are not drawn from research in migrant-sending communities argue that economic change is the key force behind these social transformations. The arguments tracing the effects of economic transformation on the social construction of gender vary in complexity. At the most basic level, some explore the implications of increases in women's labor force participation for domestic power relations, looking at the effects of women's income on decision-making power at home and on men's contributions to domestic work.[25] Gutmann focuses on the juncture between economic and social change and individual consciousness, looking at the "cultural creativity" with which men and women are reinventing gender. His work attends to social factors other than women's wage labor:

> In the 1970s and 1980s, the role of women in autonomous movements to obtain housing, jobs and many social services in Colonia Santo Domingo, together with the struggles concerning broader issues of gender equality, gay and lesbian rights, and other factors like the widespread availability and use of contraception, have combined to provide the seeds and soil of self-reliant opposition to dominant gender meanings and practices in Mexico.... The falling numbers of births, the higher educational levels reached by young women, and the higher rates of women's paid employment in Mexico City than elsewhere in the country do not indicate that gender roles and relations have automatically followed suit or will do so, no matter how structurally significant these changes may be. But such factors as employment, birth [control] and education, while not determinant, can both reflect larger cultural shifts under way and in some instances precipitate them.[26]

Degollado and El Fuerte, though affected by some of these changes such as higher educational levels and access to birth control, were relatively insulated from others: the women's and gay rights movements have not reached deep into the heart of rural Mexico, and women in my two field sites did not have access to the same opportunities for economic self-sufficiency (albeit under sometimes exploitative conditions) that have been found by others such as Gutmann, Tiano, Mummert, and Chant.[27]

Others look more broadly at the effects of economic change, exploring how industrialization has reshaped Mexican kinship systems and tracing the gender implications of those changes. González-Montes, for example, describes how an enormous shift away from agriculture over a relatively short period of time reshaped family formation patterns in rural Xalatlalco; in the town in which she worked, the percentage of the labor force engaged in economic activity declined from 90 percent in 1960 to less then 50 percent only twenty years later. The shift toward wage work meant that young people no longer worked for their parents, or had to wait for their land (or their blessing) to marry. Furthermore, wage work facilitated exogamy (marriage to partners outside the immediate community), which then further weakened the older generations' control of the younger. In the 1990 census, she found four new residential patterns: more men living with their in-laws (quite a switch from the more traditional pattern of patrilocal residence), more single mothers, more female heads of households, and more divorced women who had returned to their paternal homes. In her reading of these social changes, the development of extended courtships and the rise in divorce are part of the same phenomenon: a wider transformation in kinship systems, away from strong extended families. Chant, in her work on female-headed households in Mexico, makes a similar point about how the spread of wage labor has contributed to a new diversity of family forms in Mexico.[28] Chant and González-Montes are essentially describing different aspects of a larger phenomenon: increases in divorce are an essential element of the rise of companionate marriage.

Working in several locations (the town of Amacueca, two ranchos in the Sierra del Tigre, and the provincial city of Ciudad Guzman in southern Jalisco), de la Peña describes how the change from a mercantile-agrarian to an agro-industrial system made possible a more intimacy-oriented model of family relations. In his microhistory of the fortunes of several peasant, entrepreneur, and ranchero families from 1930 to 1980, he explores the way that agricultural production supported gender inequality in various strata of society. His discussion of life among peasant families up until the middle of the century is an apt description of how economic forces shape the families described by older women in Degollado and El Fuerte:

> For the peasants themselves, the family was a context in which labor resources were pooled to generate the food, money and services necessary to survive and be minimally happy. This context implied 1) the consolidation of a residential unit (the household), either neolocal or patrilocal, composed of a man, his wife and their offspring; 2) the emergence of patterns of cooperation, within and among households united by patrilateral ties, over a span of three generations; 3) the recognition of a hierarchy of authority whereby the senior married male (usually the father) could demand absolute compliance from other household members...and 4) the segregation of roles by sex and age. Men worked in the fields, did the strenuous orchard tasks, and undertook casual and seasonal wage labor; women were in charge of all other tasks within the orchard, cared for household animals, and performed domestic chores.[29]

From midcentury on, towns throughout Jalisco became more and more tightly knit into international migrant circuits. At the same time, he writes, the industrialization of agriculture "displaced [families] from fields and orchards. Lack of access to productive land and massive emigration...resulted in the emergence of households of varied composition. Wage labor and the absence of men have decreased the importance of cooperation among households and of male authority."[30] In the lifetimes of the older women interviewed in Degollado and El Fuerte, similar economic transformations occurred in the Mexican field sites. Safa sums up this line of argument by saying that, in looking at how economic change shapes gender in Mexico, it is a question not just of women's gains but of men's losses—in other words, it is not just that wage work has increased women's bargaining power, but also that economic transformation has cut away at the traditional sources of men's domestic power.[31] In summary, then, research from across Mexico has found changes in courtship and marital practices. Some have tried to explain these changes by looking primarily at local economic or social factors, such as women's increased access to wage labor or migration, while others have taken a broader view of potential causal factors. Whatever the explanation, though, the research cited here provides good evidence that the differences between the lives of older and younger women in this community go beyond the style in which women choose to tell their stories, to encompass the very substance of women's and men's lives.

Mexican cultural critics (as opposed to social scientists drawing on a specific set of empirical evidence) have also described broad transformations in gendered ideologies and practices in ways that are quite reminiscent of the changes portrayed in Degollado and El Fuerte. Teresita de Barbieri, in a widely cited article, describes generational changes in gender in the following way:

> Parent-daughter relations have become less authoritarian, in terms of permission to leave the house, choice of a spouse, and language (Rosado 1987). Other changes have occurred between spouses, principally in putting in check the production of children, outings from home to spend time together, socializing, and participation in paid labor. Women's bargaining power has increased. And in the extreme—irresponsibility [*desobligación*], ongoing beatings, alcoholism—women have become the abandoners of the conjugal household, taking their young children with them.[32]

Further echoing the changes described by others, de Barbieri notes that especially in households in which women work outside the home, "The traditional rigid division of labor within the household has eroded."[33] De Barbieri ascribes these changes to a variety of macrosocial processes, including women's entrance into the labor force, rural-urban migration, decreases in patrilocal marriage, increasing education, access to mass media, women's higher education, government-sponsored family planning programs, the explicit questioning of gender norms by the feminist and gay liberation movements, and the lack of strong resistance to these changes on the part of the Mexican Catholic Church. These changes, she notes, are not entirely to women's benefit (she cites work by Arias, for example, on how women's integration into the labor market may limit women's opportunities to invest in developing networks of assistance with other women).[34]

De Barbieri writes that these changes have been embraced more by women (and in particular by women who work outside the home) than by men, and Montesinos-Carrera takes this issue up in an article entitled "Cultural Change and Crisis in Masculine Identity" in the magazine *El Cotidiano*. He writes that Mexican men have essentially been dragged kicking and screaming into the new world, and—saying the opposite of what de Barbieri argues—that public transformations of gender (such as increases in women's schooling and participation in the labor market) are more marked than those in the private domestic sphere, where men have been largely unwilling to let go of their privileges. His list of causal factors is quite similar to de Barbieri's (he credits wage labor, family planning, and mass media), but he also casts his eye northward, looking back to the 1960s, when both the influence of the Mexican feminist movement and news of the sexual revolution in the United States presented the idea of deliberately transforming gender culture as a marker of modernity: "Our collective imagination," he writes, "becomes seduced by the behaviors that we see projected from outside, that present us with the new, the modern" (translation mine).[35] Although the weight of the evidence presented here counters his assertion that there have not been significant changes in gendered practices in the domestic sphere, his reminder that households continue to be the site for the negotiation and in some cases the production of gendered inequalities is a useful one. Furthermore, the issue he raises of the symbolic intertwining of gender and modernity is intriguing; he suggests that as women's entrance into the labor market has made the sexual division of labor less useful as an organizing concept for gender differences, people have had to rethink its meaning in their lives. This is the connection to "the modern"—that people start to think of gender as an identity, and to self-consciously craft a gender identity to locate themselves in the world, even though they are not really as free from the gendered division of labor as they would like to be. Gender, in other words, has become a lifestyle choice in Mexico. Gutmann places great emphasis on the power of women in Colonia Santo Domingo to push men toward a less hierarchical and more cooperative model of family relations. In Degollado and El Fuerte, women did not have the social movement experience that he argues was so crucial in his field site as a source of their increased power. Montesinos-Carrera's argument, then, is useful here because it lends support to my argument for why Juan

Carlos was so willing to let Pilar tell him to find his own socks. Montesinos-Carrera says that men are less interested in these restructured gender relations than women—but by gesturing toward the intertwining of gender identities and the lure of modernity, he also gives us a reason why their interest might grow. Without denying the importance of the macrosocial processes listed above, another factor to which less attention has been paid is the prestige of modern masculinity.

COMPANIONATE MARRIAGE AROUND THE WORLD

Finally, abundant ethnographic evidence suggests that around the world men and women have begun to think about marriage in terms of companionship and emotional intimacy. Smith, for example, draws on his fieldwork among the Igbo in southeastern Nigeria to argue that:

> Patterns of courtship and the growing symbolic importance of Christian wedding ceremonies mark significant changes in Igbo conceptions of what a marriage is. Marriage relationships themselves have also changed. Polygyny, once fairly common, is exceedingly rare among the younger generation. Within monogamous marriages, the strength of the conjugal relationship has grown vis-à-vis other family and community relationships. Young couples are far more likely than their parents to share one bedroom, eat together, and maintain a single household budget, and [to] live in town away from the compound of the husband's family, which is the traditional place of residence. The quality of a young couple's relationship, including the degree of emotional intimacy and sexual compatibility, is more likely to figure in their private assessments of the state of their marriage than was the case with their parents.[36]

Among the Huli in Papua New Guinea, Wardlow writes of how young people draw strategically on a "notion of love...discursively embedded in a Christian framework...in their attempts to form modern marriages." However, she also notes that although "in many cases, young people now succeed in choosing their own marriage partners based on sexual attraction and emotional intimacy,...there are other discourses and practices that militate against the success of these marriages."[37] Among these, she includes both the continued practice of patrilocal marriage and older Huli ideologies about gender and love. Chan, comparing older and younger women in Hong Kong and Singapore, found that "the changing pattern of consuming and [exchanging] jewelry shows the weakening of patriarchal control [and] the strengthening of conjugal ties."[38] Among the older women, gifts of jewelry given to them at their wedding by their natal family were one way of gaining respect from their husband's family, while gifts given by their new kin indicated approval of the marriage. Among the younger women, however, these gifts from extended kin have declined in symbolic importance; Chan even describes how some of the younger women melted down gold jewelry received from a husband's distant kin—in one case, to buy a computer, and in another to purchase jewelry more to her taste. For the older women, Chan says, this disrespect, as well as this emphasis on individual preferences, would have been unimaginable. Moreover, younger couples have begun to exchange wedding rings, and younger women discuss expecting regular gifts of jewelry from their husbands as a "durable means to consolidate conjugal ties."[39] As these examples suggest, this shift toward an emphasis on the importance of emotional intimacy and sexual attraction for the conjugal bond has been found in a wide variety of social contexts.[40] As I noted in the Introduction, similar transformations occurred from the late nineteenth through the mid–twentieth century in Europe and North America.[41]

The ideological power of a model of companionate relations can even be seen, others have argued, in contexts in which people either form relationships that express resistance to the intertwining of ideas about love, marriage, and pleasure, or, because of poverty, are unable to achieve their companionate ideals. In a shantytown in northeastern Brazil, for example, Gregg found that some women reject ideas about love and marriage, choosing instead a single life in which they can "use their sexuality as a form of protest."[42] These women argue that it is better to be single and that "I won't ever let a man make me suffer the way my father made her [my mother] suffer," in a context within which "political corruption, unfair land practices, and an unstable economy that privileges the wealthy have all contributed to a situation in which men cannot support their wives and in which the scarcity of male employment encourages male mobility and makes transitory sexual relationships...the norm."[43] Given the material conditions of their lives—that is, that they can eke out a living on their own and that men's economic contributions are meager and unreliable—women who choose *liberdade* (Portugese: freedom) over marriage prefer being able to live on their own, rather than accepting the same "patriarchal burden" into which their mothers entered.[44] Although Gregg's work seems to imply that, in one way, marriage has changed little in northeastern Brazil, the fact that she found a group of women who choose to live outside marriage because "we refuse to be beneath them" certainly suggests the development of a potent ideological critique of more traditional forms of marriage. Similarly, Erikson, working with Latina teen mothers in East Los Angeles, found that after the first flush of adolescent passion burned down, many of the young women yearned to have a "companionate style of love—a shared partnership" with the fathers of their children. In this community, though, like in the Brazilian *favelas*, "although most held companionate marriage as an ideal, their lack of economic resources and emotional maturity tended to undermine this desire for all but a few who had good jobs or whose families were particularly supportive."[45] Finally, Junge has argued that debates in the American gay press about the politics of gay marriage and barebacking (gay sex without a condom) are shaped discursively by ideas about companionate marriage:

> Struggles over which sexual and companionate model should be pursued for gay men are structured by elements of a model—the legitimate couple model—which produced the modern homosexual in the first place. Interestingly, the struggle over ideals of coupling among gay men leaves little room for multiple subjects. That is to say, the debates tend to be articulated in terms of pro-marriage versus anti-marriage, rather than in terms of a plurality of normative models.... Evident in the debates [about barebacking and gay marriage] is the thinly veiled valuation that men who pursue multiple sexual encounters (or, to use the pejorative label, men who are *promiscuous*) are morally deficient, sad creatures. In this configuration, promiscuity is deviant because it opposes monogamy.[46]

Junge suggests here that ideas about the moral superiority of sexual intimacy in the service of monogamous relationships—a cornerstone of companionate ideals in both Latin America and the United States—have even shaped the way people think about homosexual relationships.

To be sure, the companionate relationships longed for by Indian *hijras* (eunuch-transvestites) in Hyderabad are quite different in many respects from the relationships of which young girls in Mexico dream.[47] The variation in how people deploy ideas about companionate relations is as interesting—and as theoretically significant—as is the increasing frequency with which these ideas have been documented. In Uganda and Papua New Guinea, for example, second and higher-order wives are much more likely to be love matches, whereas in Nigeria proponents of companionate ideals roundly condemn polygyny.[48] In some places people see companionate marriage as a way to marry for love, whereas in others people believe that it means having a marriage that is held together by love. Mutually pleasurable marital sexuality, which in

Mexican conceptualizations of the successful companionate marriage seem to serve as a kind of marital glue to hold together an otherwise fragile relationship, has a much lower profile in Vietnamese, Nigerian, and Huli ideas about how to sustain these relationships. Among Mexican couples, these ideas about love and sexuality seem related to a desire to delay the first birth, whereas in China the rise of affective conjugality has been linked to shorter intervals between marriage and the first birth.[49] In Nigeria and New Guinea, companionate marital ideologies are intertwined with religion, so that converts to Christianity are much more likely to express companionate ideals. In many places, companionate relations are seen as markers of modernity, but in other places they are seen to be the expression of cultural continuities.[50] Nowhere have these companionate models of relations entirely erased previously widely held ideas about gender, sexuality, and relationships; rather, people weave together the traditional and the modern in a way that is as complex as it is deliberate.

The belief, expressed by Humberto, that good sex is "half of what makes a marriage," is not limited to Mexico; there does seem to be a particularly Latin American (or even Mediterranean) version of companionate marriage. In these marriages, as in those described by Rebhun in northeast Brazil and Collier in rural Spain, the focus on affectivity almost entirely silences any discussion of power. There are other particularly Latin American characteristics such as the ongoing distinction between women of the house and of the street, the way that sexuality is framed through terms of respect and trust, and the continuing power of images of female shame and modesty.

There are, however, some significant continuities across regions in how people think about companionate marital relationships. Individual, as opposed to family, selection of one's spouse frequently characterizes these companionate relations, as does some form of "modern" courtship. Increases in neolocal residence and an increased focus on the social and emotional aspects of the conjugal bond are also common. Women often perceive these relationships to be especially beneficial, frequently mentioning how women have more power within companionate relations than in more traditional marriages, but—as Collier discusses and I have shown here—companionate marriage coexists in complex ways with persistent gender inequality, and could even be interpreted to be an ideological expression of that very inequality.[51]

The authors cited above list a variety of factors that have promoted a companionate ideal, including cultural (Christian missionizing, access to mass media, local ethnic tensions), economic (decreases in men's economic power and increases in women's economic power, capitalist industrialization, the transformation of the household from primarily a site of production to primarily a site of consumption, increases in neolocal residence due to a rising standard of living), social (increased access to education), and demographic (rising age at first union, longevity gains, fertility decline) changes. The similarities and differences both in local ideals about companionate marriage and in factors promoting the development of those ideals are intriguing, and in future work I will address this issue of cross-cultural comparisons of the companionate ideal more systematically.[52] My brief exploration of this literature here makes two points. First, the striking similarities in how recent ethnographic research has depicted changes in marital ideals across the globe support my argument about a generational shift in Mexican marital ideals. Second, the differences across sites in how people think of companionate marriage remind us that this is a story about how people deliberately produce modern lives, and not a story about modernization. If people's lives were only subject to the same relentlessly homogenizing structural forces everywhere, then love in Nigeria would be much like love in Nepal. That it is not reminds us that existing local conditions (cultural, social, and economic), along with the minds and hearts of those living in those diverse conditions, have played an important role in the development, around the world, of the intertwining of love, companionship, gender, and modernity.

CHAPTER 6

"En el Norte la Mujer Manda" (In the North, the Woman Gives the Orders)

How Migration Changes Marriage

What are the differences in the social constructions of gender between two locations of a transnational community? The first generation of studies examining questions of gender and migration in the Mexican, Caribbean, and Central American contexts looked at whether women who migrate to the United States gain power, relative to their sisters who stay behind. Most found that in fact women are more powerful in the United States, primarily because of the social and economic effects of women's participation in wage labor. These studies, however, assumed for the most part that gender in the sending communities was a static set of patriarchal norms, taking these communities to represent the past, the traditional, in contrast to the present or the modern that was found in the United States. Furthermore, these studies failed to represent the extreme fluidity of some women's residential patterns in these transnational communities—that is, just as I did initially, they compared women who left to women who stayed, avoiding the fact that many will move back and forth several times over the course of their lives.[1] Studies of gender and migration have also generally neglected how men's lives change with migration; they have looked at how economic and social context affects women's resources and bargaining power, without examining how the dreams and resources of those with whom they bargain might also shift with the journey north.[2]

Migration studies that focus on transnational communities, in contrast, have accurately depicted the intensity of social ties between linked

communities on different sides of international borders, but have perhaps underemphasized the extent to which—in spite of shared values
and identities—material conditions in different locations are quite distinct, and physical borders are often more easily crossed by anthropologists than by their informants.[3] Here, I draw on both the gender and
the transnationalism traditions in migration research, examining how
the social construction of gender differs between the two locations I
studied in spite of shared culture.

The question of whether and how migration affects the gendered
balance of power in Mexican families cannot be reduced to a simple answer—there is not one story about gender, power, and migration, but
rather several. As is discussed by Cole in her study of Portuguese fishing
women, Collier in her study of families in a rural Spanish village, and
González de la Rocha in the urban slums of Guadalajara, the benefits to
women of nuclearization of the family and of industrialization are
equivocal: although some women may gain from being able to generate
an independent income, there are also losses in terms of reduced female
social networks (and thus possible increased dependence on a spouse)
and domestic isolation.[4] One should not underestimate the autonomy
and decision-making power of women in de facto woman-headed
households in which the men are seasonal labor migrants.[5]

For some women in this transnational community, migration may
mean that they are likely to live in a cramped trailer out of reach of public transportation in a country where they do not speak the language and
have no one to turn to for help. Their mothers, in contrast, may have
spent eleven out of twelve months a year independently administering
the family's resources, caring for their children in the company of their
own mothers and other female relatives, and moving about the rancho
as they pleased. For other migrant women, their legal status, nearby kin,
physical mobility, and command of English mean that they can fulfill the
commonplace truth that in the North, women do have more power.[6]

COMPARING THOSE WHO GO TO THOSE WHO STAY

The distinction between those who go and those who stay turned out to
be less clear-cut than I had initially thought. The lives of even those
women who have never left Mexico have been profoundly affected by
migration.[7] Short visits back and forth are most practicable for those in
Atlanta whose legal status ensures an easy return to the United States or
for those in Mexico whose economic position gives them greater likeli-

hood of receiving a visitor's visa to the United States. It is not unheard of, however, for Mexicans without papers to return to Mexico (whether in a family emergency or to enjoy las fiestas) with no guarantee of an easy return passage. Beatriz, for example, has made repeated trips between Atlanta and Degollado, although each time she goes north it is with a coyote.

The phenomenon of migrant selectivity further complicates any comparison between those who go and those who stay. Migrants are likely to differ in unknown ways from nonmigrants, so any claims about migration causing differences between groups should be met with the suspicion that the reverse is true. Interviews and participant observation with migrants and nonmigrants allow us to see what can be learned ethnographically about factors that make women more likely to migrate. My exploration of risk factors for migration looks both at actual migration and future potential for migration, as I examine why thirteen life history informants migrated and their "matches" did not and why some of the women in the sending communities may still migrate north.

Based on interviews and observations, there are two types of factors that seem to affect the likelihood of migration: conditions that root women or families more firmly to the sending communities, and therefore impede migration, and those that lower the costs of migration and therefore facilitate it. Social and economic status in the sending community and stage in family formation are key factors in the former category. Access to legal U.S. residence papers and a woman's natal and consanguineal family migration histories are among the key factors in the latter group.

Migration is a route to status improvement in the sending communities, so those already in a privileged economic and social position are unlikely to feel the North's pull as strongly as those with fewer resources. Many of the nonmigrant sisters had individual or family resources in Mexico (such as a small business, or a home they owned) that insulated them from the pressures that force others to migrate. Women in the sending communities who enjoyed a social status they would be loathe to trade for the anonymity and marginality that can be the migrant's lot seemed even less likely to migrate. Esperanza, for example, said she would like to go the United States someday—as a tourist, preferably to visit Disneyland, but not to live.

Women who have many dependent children are unlikely to migrate illegally or leave their children behind. Concha, for example, had ten children, five of whom still lived at home and did not work. Her husband had made several trips to the United States, but she merely laughed at the idea that she might have accompanied him. Some women do go north, leaving one or two children with a sister, aunt, or mother, but five is too many to leave with someone else. Norma, in El Fuerte, waited patiently for her papers rather than joining her husband in Atlanta for the same reason.

When Isabel's parents left Degollado suddenly in the winter of 1995, they took their three unmarried adolescent children with them (all of whom promptly got jobs in Atlanta) and were joined as well by their married (but childless) daughter Patricia and her husband. Isabel, however, stayed behind. The fact that she stayed while her sisters left cannot be explained solely by the status incentives not to go, since her sisters had enjoyed all the privileges she had. She and Humberto, however, had three children in grade school, making it considerably more complicated to head north. Especially in cases where a man's migration is part of a short-term strategy for capital accumulation and neither the man nor the woman has a green card (as was the case with Concha's husband), it is uncommon for his wife to accompany him if they have more than one or two children. In cases where the spouse does follow, such as Perla who with her two children recently joined Francisco in Atlanta, the woman's move northward signifies the conversion of what was initially a short-term strategy into a longer-term one. Initially Francisco talked about going to Atlanta to save money for a house in Degollado, but shortly after his family arrived he bought a trailer—a move that suggests fairly long-term, if not permanent, plans to stay in el norte.

Obtaining legal residence papers is another determinant of the likelihood of women's migration to the United States. Some women wait to migrate until they have papers, which they receive either as daughters or wives via the family reunification provision of U.S. immigration law. Other women go north illegally and then manage to regularize their situation, either under the family reunification provision or under the 1986 amnesty law, using their work history to qualify. Some women do migrate, of course, with little or no hope of ever qualifying for a green card; several of the women interviewed were in this situation.

A final factor that encourages migration is a woman's husband's family history regarding migration.[8] The impact of a woman's own family history, of course, is not measurable in this study since most of the pairs of women were from the same family or related by marriage. A man's family influences his life course by emphasizing the already common idea that the journey north is an important rite of manhood, an expected step, as well as by facilitating that step by giving men a strong kin tie on which they can count for help finding a job and a place to live.

These factors are not, of course, the only determinants of whether a woman migrates or not. Recent feminist scholarship has cautioned against conflating individual and household strategies—that is, against assuming that women's individual interests are given equal weight in decisions that are described as part of a household strategy, as family migration frequently is.[9] The characteristics predisposing or impeding migration should not be understood as final determinants of migration, but rather as a starting point. The ultimate outcome is a product of negotiations between women and their husbands or, if they are not married, their families of origin.

In the cases represented here, there are certainly examples of ways that women see migration to be in their individual best interests. Most obviously, when Victoria and Lucha moved to Los Angeles to make it on their own as single mothers, they were acting for themselves (although family honor and their children's future economic security were also at issue). María and Rosa spoke openly about the economic bargaining power they gained as individuals through working outside the home, but others (though they enjoy those same benefits) may choose to frame them in terms of how much better a life it is for their children. Mercedes, for example, was always talking about sacrificing for her son, although she seemed to delight in many aspects of her life in Atlanta. Making an analytically useful distinction between individual and family interests rests on the assumption that this distinction is meaningful for the women in question, and the issue becomes confusing when women tend to justify what they want to do in terms of helping their husbands or children.

Couples often disagreed about whether it is best to live in Mexico or the United States—just because a woman's husband longs to go north does not mean that she necessarily does. I never heard of a woman convincing her husband to go north against his will, but it is hard to know if that means men are always willing to go or simply unwilling to admit that they would rather not. Similarly, some women did convince their husbands to help them go north without papers. There are other cases in which a married woman migrated against her wishes in order to be with her husband. Both Mariana and Diana (both of whom live in Atlanta) would have preferred to be in the rancho, if only they could have convinced their husbands to return there with them. Magdalena was still in Degollado at the end of my fieldwork, but she will likely end up in the United States when her papers come through. She said she would rather not go, but at the same time she and her daughters missed her husband and wanted to see him more than one month out of the year. Nor is migration a decision involving solely the marital dyad. Perla was eager to follow her husband from the minute he snuck across the border, but her mother-in-law (all of whose sons have ended up living scattered around the United States) convinced Francisco that he would be better off having her stay in Degollado so he could save money to build a house there. Eventually, though, Perla convinced him otherwise, and nearly a year after his initial departure she joined him. His extended family criticized her for placing more value on being with him than on helping him save money.

DIFFERENCES AMONG MIGRANT WOMEN

Not all migrant women in Atlanta are equally positioned to take advantage of the greater leverage that life in the United States potentially affords them. Women who do not have residence papers, or whose husbands will not let them work, are much more isolated and dependent on their husbands than they would be if they had remained in Mexico. Comparisons between women's experiences on either side of the border should not obscure the heterogeneity among women, either in Atlanta or in the Mexican field sites.

One of the most important divisions among Mexican women (and men) in Atlanta is legal status. Possession of papers, either permanent resident status, or, as is increasingly common, citizenship, opens the door to legal personhood in the United States: a social security number, a bank account, a driver's license, and a credit history.[10] Jorge Durand argues that the experiences of those who have papers and those who do not are so different that they can be regarded as two separate social classes.[11] Papers give migrants access to a wider range of better-paid, physically less demanding work. Women and men frequently purchase false papers to show a prospective employer; although these often work for the purposes of employment, they are less useful in contact with government agencies. The lion's share of immigrants who were in the United States before the 1986 Immigration Reform and Control Act (IRCA) and who are now in the process of applying for legal residence for their families are men, and so men are frequently in the powerful position of applying (or not) for papers for the rest of the family.[12] When a man has legal residence and his wife does not, she is particularly dependent on her husband. These same women tend to have arrived more recently in the United States than their husbands, and so they are also less likely to have learned some English, mastered public transportation, and developed their own social networks on which they can rely. In couples such as this, women depend on their husbands for access to precisely those resources that would make it possible for them at some point to survive on their own. Women do, of course, also work in the formal sector with false papers.

Family networks also structure women's and men's experiences and opportunities in the United States. It is rare for a migrant to have no relatives at all in the receiving community—but women do not see all relatives as equally valuable. As Hondagneu-Sotelo also found, they regard relatives by marriage in quite a different light than their own (natal) family.[13] When I asked women *"¿Con quién puedes contar?"* (Who can you rely on?), they most frequently answered their own sisters. Women who live near their own sisters in Atlanta tend to socialize with them frequently and to use them unhesitatingly for emergency child care. To a lesser extent, the same is true of other female relatives: mothers (though it is a rarity to have one's mother in the United States), nieces, aunts, and cousins. Leaving children in child care in order to work is considered by most to be a necessary evil of life in el norte, but one that is greatly ameliorated if they are left in the care of a blood relative; women think their relatives are both less likely to mistreat the child and less likely to criticize them (than, for example, a sister-in-law might be) for not staying home. Even without fractious relations with their husband's family, women tend to be wary of relying too heavily on their husband's wider kin networks, knowing that a request for help is also an admission of vulnerability.[14]

The third axis of distinction among Mexican women living in Atlanta is the point in their family formation at which they migrated. Given the symbolic moral value of being under one's parents' roof when single, it is complicated and risky for single women to go north. The life history informants who did migrate as single women did so in three kinds of situations. Some, like Blanca, accompany their family. Those who go without their parents tend to arrive by prior arrangement with male relatives who provide a sort of satellite version of remaining under the moral protection of being at home. This was the case with Victoria and Rosa, each of whom spent time working in Chicago while single. These young women are likely to be as closely supervised while in Chicago and Atlanta as they might have been in Mexico, or even more so, given the perception of greater danger. Finally, women migrate alone when pregnant and unmarried or separated.

Once married, it is increasingly common for young couples to head north together immediately. Frequently they will have negotiated travel plans while courting. Most young women today are emphatically not interested in living (as their mothers did) separated from their husbands for eleven months a year.[15] Beatriz, for example, traveled north at dawn the day after her wedding. Never having lived apart from her parents or even spent the night away from them, she said she doubted her ability to actually say good-bye, so she and her husband left directly for the border from the hotel where they spent their wedding night. In María's and Mercedes's case, their husbands left for the United States immediately after the wedding, and they both followed several months later. María said she had told her husband she would give him three months to save money and send for her. When he arrived back in town to get her he was just in the nick of time—she had already sold their furniture and was preparing to go find him on her own.

Women go north when recently married because it is easier to travel (especially illegally) without children. Beginning their family in the United States rather than in Mexico has a variety of implications for women's lives. First, their children will be citizens and will most likely grow up in the United States. Although these women may dream of returning to Mexico in their old age, it is unlikely that they will do so, as a lifetime of child rearing and work creates a network of social ties and obligations too dense to break off.[16] Second, those who start childbearing in the United States have different patterns of contraceptive use and fertility than those who migrate later in their marriages. Migrating early in marriage has implications for the negotiation of gender as well as for demographic change: those women who begin their married lives in the United States do not have to contend with an established pattern of how things were in Mexico (for example, in terms of the gendered division of labor).

A fourth factor that contributes to diversity of experience among the women in Atlanta is the difficult to measure but nonetheless important question of a woman's character. Guadalupe and Lucha, for example, had all of the legal requirements for a driver's license but both said they were afraid to learn. (They also both had the good fortune of living near their younger sisters who had gotten their licenses and were willing to give them rides without charging them.) María had actually gotten a driver's license without having all the legal prerequisites and then had purchased a car before ever having driven on the expressway. Mercedes resembled María; she lived more than 1 mile from the nearest bus stop, but had become adept at calling for taxis in English so that she could go out during the day and had learned to get around on the bus so that she could travel farther afield less expensively. Beatriz, who had barely ever gone outside during her previous months in Atlanta, was delighted to find a friend bolder than she was. With Mercedes as the leader, together they told me proudly of the time they took the bus all the way to the mall. Women's character also contributes to the risks they are willing to take in terms of working without the correct papers. Several have purchased green cards, while others said they did not dare take the risk of working without papers.

A final element that shapes a woman's experiences is her marriage, particularly the extent to which a man wishes to limit his wife's autonomy by controlling whether or not she works and the extent to which she can leave the house. Beatriz and Clara, neither of whom worked outside the home in Atlanta, had both been forbidden to do so by their husbands. Since power and control are squarely among the issues that are being examined here for how they *change* with migration, it may seem odd to include them as well among a list of the influences on that very experience. Yet both among women in Atlanta and among those in the sending communities, a man's preferences are among the most important constraints shaping women's experiences. Especially in situations where women have few resources of their own (like papers) and are even more socially and economically dependent on their husbands than they might otherwise be, men's wishes cannot be ignored.[17]

Migration does affect women's lives, but the specific ways in which it does so depends on a woman's legal status and that of her husband, the availability of consanguineal family, the stage at the family cycle when she migrated, her personality, and her marriage. A discussion of how migration paths are gendered and of the social organization of gender among Mexican migrants provides more detail on how these factors play out in women's lives.

"EN EL NORTE LA MUJER MANDA": GENDER AND THE SOCIAL ORGANIZATION OF MIGRATION

Doña Elena had spent several months with her daughters in Atlanta. When she criticized María and her sisters for answering back to their husbands and not taking care of them properly, she told me that María had explained to her: "María said, 'No, mom, here the woman is the boss, it's not like back in Mexico where the men are the boss.... No, here they don't hit you.... Here, the men are the ones who stand to lose.'" Comments such as this can be read as attempts to tell a reassuring tale about Mexico as a refuge of tradition and respeto in contrast with the godless, dollar-driven individualism of life in the United States. For men in Mexico, in particular, such statements can be interpreted either as denials that Mexico has changed or as justifications for not permitting their wives to accompany them north. María's comment also directs our attention to real differences between various locations of the same transnational community.

The very act of migration is shaped by gender.[18] Up until the mid-1980s, the preponderance of Mexican migrants were men, and their journeys north were understood to be necessary extensions of men's responsibility to support their families.[19] Single men talk about migration as a quicker, more reliable means to save the money necessary to marry (that is, enough for a man to pay for a wedding and to build a house or to return north with his bride). For both married and single men a trip to el norte offers other attractions: the possibility of adventure, a test of one's manhood and one's wits against la migra and workplaces ruled by the time clock, the sexual lure of easily available gringas and Chicanas, and the increased social status of arriving back in one's hometown with new clothes, a new stereo, or maybe even a car. During the Bracero era, it was not seen as "necessary" for women to accompany their husbands; women did not gain the same status that men did through the public display of their earnings, and they exposed themselves to the possible loss of reputation associated with unsupervised time anywhere outside their town and especially in the United States. Many families, of course, moved together or in stages to California and Chicago and settled there, but the ones who stayed behind frequently explained their choice in terms of the moral superiority of Mexican gender norms.

The exception in terms of women's migration has been for single women who get pregnant—las fracasadas. *Fracasar* means to fail; these women have failed themselves and their families by being publicly exposed as sexual, unmarried women. (It is not the sex outside of marriage by itself that is the grave moral sin, in spite of the lip service all pay to the importance of virginity; rather, it is the fact that the situation was not rectified through the boyfriend's correct, honorable response [*responder*], which is to marry her and make her an honest woman.) The United States has been a refuge for las fracasadas, because if women leave early enough in their pregnancy, they can spare their families the

shame by keeping it at least a partial secret. Of course, information networks being as efficient as they are, it will not *really* be a secret, but
women spare their families some of the shame—and show that in spite
of their indiscretion they know enough to be ashamed—by hiding their
pregnant bodies from public sight. (This harkens back to the connections mentioned earlier between seeing, knowing, and sexuality.) Pregnant women who migrate north may still choose to live under the moral
protection of their extended families, but they will not need their economic support in the same way that they might in semirural Mexico.
Although the single mother's life is not an easy or luxurious one in the
United States, the possibilities for financial independence are much
greater in the United States than in Mexico.

Furthermore, although they will most likely settle in the United
States in a community of people from their hometown, single motherhood is perceived to be less humiliating in the United States than it
would be at home in Mexico. This is why, historically, relatively few
single women who are not "in trouble" have been permitted the journey north; the same lack of moral pressure that might make life easier for their fracasada sisters makes it too dangerous for single
women.[20] The gradual loosening of this tighter control on single
women is a key way in which the gendered patterns of migration are
changing. The few women over thirty in these communities who
worked in the United States before marriage all comment on the unusual circumstances surrounding their trips north and the intense vigilance with which their male relatives guarded their honor while so
far from home. Victoria remembers that while she was in Chicago her
brothers kept a much closer watch on her than her parents had at
home; they never let her leave the house alone, insisted that she come
directly home from work, and monitored her dress, forbidding short
skirts and revealing necklines. Now it is more common to find
women in their late teens and twenties who journey north, and the
way these women explain their decision has changed as well: rather
than justify it by talking about their family's extreme poverty or some
other familial extenuating circumstance, they talk about individual
desires for adventure and expanded opportunities for consumption
and about their curiosity to see if they are tough enough to survive al
otro lado (on the other side).

Although the United States continues to be seen by Mexicans as a
land of moral peril, women are increasingly responding to the siren

song that has been ringing in their husbands' and brothers' ears since the 1920s.[21] In part this seems due to IRCA, which encouraged many men who had been temporary migrants to bring their families north to live with them. It is also, no doubt, partly due to the repeated waves of crisis that have rocked the Mexican middle and working classes since the 1980s.[22] As more women return to their pueblos on vacation with new clothes and jewelry, arms full of gifts, and speech full of strange new words in English, it becomes increasingly imaginable to all who see them that decent, God-fearing Mexican women can raise their families in the north. Whatever the cause, young couples are much more likely to head North together several weeks after their wedding, rather than to wait for the first pregnancy and then bid each other good-bye as the new husband and father-to-be slips away to shoulder his growing responsibility. It is also more and more common for young women to head North on their own, in spite of the real and imagined dangers a woman without a man might face.

Just as their mothers' lives were characterized by a migration pattern shaped by specific political and economic forces, so too do the younger life history informants experience marriage and migration at a specific historical moment in the development of their transnational community. Doña Lupe, who owned a small store in El Fuerte, told me several times, nodding her head sadly, that *se van a acabar los ranchos* (the ranchos are going to disappear). Descriptions of villages in Michoacán and Jalisco where married women hold together households full of school-age children and aging grandparents while the men send remittances from the United States may slowly give way to tales of villages where, except during the summer months and Christmas holidays, there are fewer and fewer children.[23] Some families have moved to large towns like Degollado, while others have gone to the United States. Their children, in turn, may grow up with fond memories of vacations spent playing with the chickens in grandma's yard, but no matter how fond their memories it seems unlikely that they would trade paved roads and proximity to the K-Mart for the dust and tranquility of rural Mexican life. Larger towns like Degollado are unlikely to be wiped out, at least in the short term, by the combined forces of migration and regional urbanization, but they will certainly continue to change. The ways that gender is transformed with migration right now can be generalized to other communities at this same phase in a historical process, but it is unlikely that they will apply a generation from now.

PRIVACY, WOMEN'S MOBILITY, AND THE SOCIAL MARKING
OF SPACE INTO "CALLE" AND "CASA"

> *J:* And what happens to gossip here [in Atlanta]?
>
> *P:* No, well, here it's a totally different life. Nobody knows you. Here
> you can go wherever you want, with whoever you want, and nobody
> knows you, nobody sees you. And there no—there in the town, in
> Degollado where we live, everyone knows each other,...everyone
> knows whose daughter you are, and whose granddaughter, and who
> are your friends, everyone. It's like the whole town knows each other,
> so the whole town [would say], "Did you see Fulano's daughter
> going around with that guy's son? And I saw them in the store, they
> were all over each other, and then in the plaza they were making out
> so heavily, they looked like one person instead of two!"
>
> And no—here, who cares about those things? You can go around
> in a store, just suppose—I could go around in a store with another
> man, at least if I didn't see anyone I knew. If people saw me, who
> would say, "Look, who she's with"? No one, because no one knows
> you.... There, gee, they would excommunicate you just for walking
> around with a guy, for example if they saw a married woman with
> someone, that's the worst.

The buses that leave from the plaza in Degollado and arrive in Atlanta fill with single men and women. In January 1997, one young
woman, knowing that her mother would not give her permission, said
that she was just stepping out on *un mandado* (an errand), and then
nonchalantly strolled down to the plaza and snuck on the bus, carrying
in her hand a small bundle with a change of clothes, money for the coyote, and the address of her destination in the North. Once in Atlanta,
she likely found what so many other women—both single and married—have found on arriving: that in many ways, some blatant and
others subtle, Mexican women's lives are different in the United States.

One of the most notable differences is in the way social space is organized, and in the amount of privacy that urban life provides. The
American street is a less intensely gendered stage than the calle in Mexico. This creates new pressures for men and new opportunities for
women. The plaza in Degollado and the street (particularly the areas
outside the stores) are public spaces where people walk and stop to visit
with one another. In Atlanta, where public transportation is quite limited and those with cars drive everywhere, there is little opportunity
among the middle class for unscheduled social contact with one's neighbors in the course of a normal day. (This may be moderately less true

Photograph 6.1. Nobody Is Illegal. This photo, taken inside
the Catholic Mission of Our Lady of the Americas in Chamblee, shows an immigrants' rights poster that reads: "Rights
without Borders: Nobody Is Illegal." The scuffed linoleum
halls of the Catholic Mission perform some of the same func-
tions as the plaza would in a small town in Mexico: migrants
feel safe socializing and participating in group activities
regardless of their legal status, and the complex—which offers
a job bank, computer training, limited health services, a food
pantry, prescriptions for Medicaid, and a domestic violence
prevention program and is conveniently located next to a
metro stop—hums with activity from morning until night.

among the poor, who lack the cars and air-conditioning that keep their
better-off neighbors from rubbing shoulders with each other.) The design of the few public parks (Grant Park, Piedmont Park, Kennesaw
Mountain State Park) promotes individual or small-group relaxation
and appreciation of green spaces; this is quite distinct from the concentrated social interaction that seems to be the design goal of the benches
and the promenade around the central plaza in Degollado. (In Atlanta,
the crowded halls of the Catholic Mission of Our Lady of the Americas
[see Photo 6.1] serve as the "plaza" of the local immigrant community,
providing those who enter with a rare sense of security.) Some of the
large gathering spaces in Atlanta are commercial (and expensive) such
as amusement parks and the zoo; others are free of charge (such as indoor malls) but are designed to limit lingering without shopping. To

some extent this is more a product of urban-rural migration than it is of migration from Mexico to the United States, but it is particularly pronounced in the move to Atlanta. Migrants to Guadalajara or Mexico City, for example, find cities that certainly have problems of their own but do not lack open spaces created solely for walking, talking, and watching other people do the same.

A combination of political and economic factors makes men less comfortable on the street in Atlanta, and women more so. Displays of masculine prerogatives such as public drinking or fighting are just those behaviors most likely to catch the attention of the migra, but Mexican men and women in Atlanta worry even about routine traffic stops. Others have discussed how Mexican men, rather than "owning" the street as they do in Mexico, are well aware they are just visiting.[24] Because of their legal vulnerability, the street becomes as full of actual danger for men as it had been full of moral danger, previously, for women. A dutiful husband, one who goes *de su trabajo a la casa* (straight home from his job, that is, who does not waste time/money in the street) has become the same as a man who knows how to protect himself in the North.

Women's widespread participation in the formal labor market in Atlanta further neutralizes the gendered aspects of the street. Working outside the home gives women as much justification as men to be outside, and women in Atlanta have much more physical mobility than they do in the sending communities. They also use the ideology of family progress (*salir adelante como familia*—making it as a family) to justify entry into the labor force and access to other previously masculine privileges of physical mobility such as driving and owning a car. In Degollado and El Fuerte only women from the wealthiest families drive at all, and it is extremely rare for a woman to own her own car. During the time of the fieldwork, only four of the thirteen life history informants in Atlanta drove (though at least one has learned since); the others either were not brave enough to learn or else did not have the necessary papers to get a Georgia driver's license.[25] The Mexican women in Atlanta who do drive never tire of the thrill of freedom, of being able to go wherever they want without having to ask, of their new mastery of the street.

Furthermore—and this is crucial not just for men but for women as well—the audience in the street is not the same as in small-town Mexico. The constant vigilance of all public behavior (characteristic not just of Mexican communities but perhaps of any small town) is lost in the urban United States. Most of the people who see these immigrants do not know them, nor do they know their families, nor even most likely whether they are from Jalisco or Guanajuato. One of the biggest changes people experience in the North is the feeling of freedom that accompanies the realization that *aquí nadie te conoce* (here no one knows you).

For men, the physical diffuseness of the community in Atlanta lessens the social and economic pressures to participate in a certain style of masculine leisure-time activities: many Mexicans in Atlanta work for gringo bosses who care more about whether they show up on time and work hard than whether they are suspect as homosexuals because they refuse to go drinking.[26] For men who do choose to be "family men," the lack of one public, central social space such as the plaza, and the consequently increased privacy of socializing, makes it easier to pick friends who share their masculinity ideals and avoid those who will push them to perform in other ways.

Women in Atlanta relax the sort of resolute appearance management they display in Mexico, dressing more for comfort than for modesty or to express social status. In the field sites in Mexico, some women put on stockings and hairspray to walk two blocks to the market to buy tortillas for lunch. In Atlanta, Doña Elena, an older woman whose husband never would have let her wear slacks (much less jeans) in Mexico, goes out in sweatpants without asking permission. On returning to Mexico after a year living with her older sister in Atlanta, one unmarried woman left behind all the Bermuda shorts she had bought in Atlanta; she knew without asking that her father would never let her wear them in the rancho. It is not that women in Atlanta stop caring about clothes or their appearance—they still dress up to go out at night with their husbands, or for parties (see, for example, the nicely turned-out couple in Photo 6.2)—but on a day-to-day basis, they feel almost invisible and thus freed from some of gender's performative demands.

Women delight in the relatively low prices and wide selection in U.S. stores, but rather than wear their treasures they stockpile them for visits to Mexico. In Mexico, all but the richest in town would wear a new dress perhaps once a year, on the last day of the fiestas in Degollado (December 12) or during the fiesta in El Fuerte (February 10). In the United States, in contrast, wearing something new is so common as to be almost unworthy of notice—so they wait to do it somewhere it *will* be noticed. This invisibility is expressed as well in other ways. In Mexico women sweep outside their front doors first thing in the morning and sometimes again in the afternoon, but I never in all my visiting in Atlanta (sometimes quite early in the morning) saw anyone sweeping

Photograph 6.2. Religious Procession for
the Virgin of Guadalupe, Atlanta. A couple,
the man holding their young daughter in
her holiday finery, chats with his wife in
the parking lot of a Chamblee apartment
complex while waiting for the procession
in honor of the Virgin of Guadalupe to
begin. The parade featured folk dancers,
flowers, and balloons, just like the one in
Degollado—but unlike in Mexico, the
midday procession was sparsely attended,
since December 12 (the day of the Virgin)
fell on a workday in 2001. The dawn and
evening Masses held at the Catholic
Mission that day in the Virgin's honor,
however, were standing room only.

outside her door. In fact, many Mexicans expressed a preference for living near Americans, because they say they keep their front yards neater.
Women hinted at other ways in which privacy, the lack of social vigilance, and their newfound physical mobility together expand the range of
the possible. They joked about how easy it would be to take a lover
here—all you would need to do would be to hop on the bus, or get in
your car, and go meet him. You could walk around a mall holding hands
with him and no one who sees you would know whether he is your husband or not. You could even get in a car with him; whereas to be seen riding in a car with an unknown man in Degollado would at best need some
serious explaining, in all likelihood it would pass completely unnoticed
amid Atlanta's urban anonymity. The absence of an audience that con-

stantly monitors gendered behavior as an indicator of social prestige increases the possibilities for experimentation (and transgression).

Finally, the confessional does not reach into women's sexual lives in Atlanta in the same way that it does in Mexican sending communities. Although even in Mexico the Catholic Church is certainly a heterogeneous institution, the region of Mexico these women are from, El Bajio, continues to be home to an extremely conservative, strongly pronatalist strain of Catholicism. Couples who marry are still routinely (though not always) asked if they will accept "*todos los hijos que Dios les mande*" (all the children God sends them). Women and their husbands are scolded in confession (the priests ask them directly) for using any but the Billings method of contraception.[27] The authority of the confessional seems absolute; women say that lying in confession is a mortal sin, perhaps even worse than the initial sin of nonprocreative sex. In Atlanta, in contrast, some priests ask about contraception and some do not, and women can cannily choose their confessor. (Also, more practically, it may be easier to selectively reveal information to a priest in Atlanta, who knows women as isolated individuals, than to do so with a priest in Mexico, who knows women's whole extended families.) Some women—especially those who do not drive and live far from public transportation—sidestep the question altogether by no longer attending Mass. Others drift toward other Christian sects such as Southern Baptist or Jehovah's Witnesses.[28]

MIGRATION AND DOMESTIC VIOLENCE

I heard about domestic violence among couples in all the field sites, but location inflects the meaning of violence. Men explained to me that one of the two reasons that women have so much more power in the North is that their husbands can't hit them (they ascribe the general breakdown in family lines of authority to this cause as well, saying that it is no longer possible to discipline children properly once they go to kindergarten and learn to dial 911). In contrast to Mexico, where police are reluctant to intervene in cases of men's violence toward their wives or parents' toward their children, Mexicans—whether or not they live in the United States—know that in the United States help is literally a phone call away. They talk about how much more responsive the police are toward claims of domestic violence in the United States than they are in Mexico. The way that the state intervenes to protect individuals against violence, both men and women say, is a crucial force in destabilizing the family.

It is of course a myth that men's violence against women does not exist in the United States, just as it is untrue that there are no social controls against men's violence in Mexico. But domestic violence does take on new meanings in the United States, and the U.S. legal system—combined with the legal vulnerability of many Mexicans who live in fear of deportation—gives women a different sort of leverage on the issue of domestic violence. Eva and Pancho, for example, were fighting constantly during the time I was getting to know her. Although I never met him, her reports of their fights suggested that they both really tried to hurt the other person physically, and from what she said, they seemed on the brink of divorce. But she said she could get him to calm down by threatening to "call her lawyer." It was never exactly clear to me who her lawyer was, or even if it was really a lawyer rather than a domestic violence counselor, but the function of having a lawyer was clear; she and he both knew that if things got bad enough she could get a restraining order to throw him out of the house. Furthermore, since they were both legal immigrants (hence he works under his real name, address, and social security number) she reminded him that in the event of a divorce the mandatory child support he would have to pay for their six children would leave him barely enough to support himself.[29]

Some women do call the police, but there are significant reasons why women might choose not to involve the authorities. Juan, like Pancho, had been working in the United States since before he turned twenty. In his early thirties, he was a citizen. He and his wife, Mercedes, had one son, born in Atlanta. Juan spoke movingly about the emotional texture of their relationship, of Mercedes's right to have her own opinions, even to correct him, and of wanting to create a family bonded by warmth and physical affection rather than the respectful reserve his parents showed each other. The most important way a man respects his wife, he said, was in not forcing her to have sex against her will; intimacy should always be mutual and voluntary. And yet Juan reserved the right to slap his wife "to get her to calm down" and to remind her that he is ultimately the boss. He is not just showing her her place—he is making sure that it is the same place that she occupied in Mexico. By not dialing 911 she allows him to continue to believe that he really has the last word, that being in the United States has not led her astray from what she learned as a girl about how to get along por las buenas (by being nice). By asserting that domestic violence is a private issue, men essentially argue that they have a right to choose whether to hit their wives. To make it an issue of state regulation, and of the right of individuals to assert the protection of the state for their bodies, is a direct and profound challenge to the ideology implied in the phrase *"mi mujer."*

Clara told me that her husband, Alfonso, had beaten her up several times, but she insisted that it was no one else's business if she chose to endure it. Of all the women I interviewed in Atlanta, she was perhaps the most isolated: not even twenty, she had two children under age three and though she had a sister nearby she saw her infrequently, because neither of them knew how to drive. She did not have residence papers and had never worked for money. Reporting her husband's violence would in her eyes almost certainly mean the end of their marriage, and she would face a hard road alone. Although she could count on her sister for emotional support, it was unlikely she could expect much more than that from her: Clara's sister was married to one of Alfonso's brothers, making them unlikely to take her in on a long-term basis. Unable to avail herself of the options offered to some women by life in el norte, Clara suffered with her husband's occasional violence in much the same way that her mother suffered in Degollado a generation ago.

Under these conditions, direct resistance to domestic violence is rife with culturally loaded meanings. Even women who at first glance might seem less vulnerable to violence because of their individual resources and the protections of the American legal system are still faced with a range of hard choices; just because a woman lives in a country in which the police will respond to her call for help does not make it easy to pick up the phone. This may explain at least in part why a woman like María, who had been in the United States for a decade, drove her own car, spoke English, and earned more than her husband, did not call the police when he slapped her. By enduring the violence, she allowed him to reassert his power; he made her pay for her mobility and economic success with bruises.[30] It may be, then, that the violence that does occur between couples is an indication that the balance of power *has* changed and that the man is struggling against that change. Neither structural inequality nor the way women's employment challenges received ideas about gender can explain all the cases of violence among migrant couples—a certain amount of theoretical eclecticism is necessary to explain why violence occurs in some marriages and not in others. However, in spite of the fact that some migrant men in Atlanta use physical force against their wives, and do so deliberately to remind them of an unchanged gender order, it remains true on a wider scale that the possibility of state intervention makes many women feel more protected in the United States than in the sending communities.

MIGRATION, EL MANDO, AND WOMEN'S
WORK OUTSIDE THE HOME

The other reason Mexican women have more power in the United States than in Mexico, men say, is that they work. El mando, the power to give the orders, is an economically earned right. Women's labor force participation in the United States encroaches on men's sole right to el mando, but this is hardly just a case of women's incomes translating directly into domestic power. Leaving aside the obvious point that social reproduction is work as well, albeit unpaid and undervalued, women also work in Mexico. Three of the thirteen women I interviewed intensively in Mexico had their own businesses, and another five occasionally earned some cash by selling cheese, needlework, or livestock, or doing housecleaning and ironing. The life history informants' mothers were economically active as well. Doña Chuyita, for example, was only available to talk on Wednesday afternoons because in addition to running a grocery store out of her house she cooked for and managed her son's restaurant (he lives in the United States), which only closed on Wednesdays. Mercedes's mother also worked for many years, owning a sewing workshop that did piecework for a factory in a large town nearby, and a number of older women had accompanied their husbands north at least once, to try their hands at factory or fieldwork.

Women's labor in the United States, however, brings them much closer to economic independence than do their sisters' efforts south of the border. In Atlanta it is possible for a woman to live comfortably (where a standard of comfort is defined by Mexican working-class standards, not American middle-class ones) and to support her children earning just above the minimum wage. This is especially true if she has only a few children, or if they are U.S. citizens (and hence qualify for access to Medicaid), or if she has family nearby with whom she could live. In Degollado, there are few jobs available to women of limited education that pay even half the minimum wage (about 300 pesos/week [not quite $40] at the time of my fieldwork). A housekeeper who worked from 8 in the morning until 3 in the afternoon, for example, earned 70 pesos (a little over $9) a week; by taking in washing and ironing it might be possible to earn another 70. This is not sufficient to feed a family of four (which would be a small family) even the barest twice-daily meals of beans, tortillas, and chiles, much less provide for housing, clothes, shoes, schoolbooks, and the occasional medical emergency.

Furthermore, as Grassmuck and Pessar have pointed out, women's entrance into the formal wage labor market reverberates beyond their access to cash and increased participation in domestic financial decision making.[31] Though women may justify taking a job in terms of their commitment to sacrificing for their family, the workplace—and their coworkers—may teach a woman unexpected lessons about her ability to be self-reliant. María, for example, spoke glowingly about how she felt after learning how to make decorative fruit arrangements when she worked doing food preparation in the catering department of a large hotel:

> I liked it because we made these fruit displays, and you arrange the fruit, you make designs, like for Thanksgiving you do a turkey or a scarecrow, and it would come out so nice that I would feel excited to see it....I was so impressed, I had never seen anything like it, just imagine,...it would come out so nice, I couldn't even believe that I'd done it....Later, when more people came to work there, I was the one who knew how to do it, I was the boss there,...because then the chef said to me, "you know how to do it, tell them what they need to do."...
>
> And I really enjoyed it, as I got to know the people, I don't know, I really appreciated all the people who worked there. And after my day off, when I came back, my work companions, everyone would say "We missed you yesterday, when you weren't here." And you know, all that makes you feel good.

Beatriz, whose husband never allowed her to work outside the home while they were living in Atlanta (they have since moved back to Degollado), said that it was not the money she missed, since she lacked for nothing, so much as the proof that she could take care of herself. She had gone from being supported by her father to being taken care of by her husband, who has never let her work.[32] Before they had a child, he told her he wanted her at home to take care of the house and have a hot meal ready for him when he got home, and after their son was born he insisted that a child needs to be taken care of by his mother. Beatriz calls this an excuse (*un pretexto*), saying:

> He just doesn't want me to work. He said it looks bad that women who have someone to support them go around looking for work that they don't need. So he is just telling me the same story that my father told me. And I feel a little bad, oppressed [*agobiada*], that I always have to be dependent on others. I'd like to know what it is like to take care of myself economically, to see my own worth [*saberme valer por mi misma*], because I've never known what it is like to have the obligation of going to work, that is outside [the house], I've never had a responsibility like that, and here in the house, well, the days I feel like it, I do housework, and the days I don't, I just don't.

Women talk about knowing they could *valerse por si misma* (make it on one's own or count on oneself) as one of the reasons to work.

In spite of the limited opportunities for women's wage labor in the sending communities, women in Degollado and El Fuerte talk about this same self-confidence. Magdalena, for example, who helped her mother support their family by sewing from when she was twelve years old, told me confidently that if something happened to her husband she could just return to the sewing machine—that if she could help support a family of eight as a young teenager, she could certainly support a family of three on her own as an adult. Magdalena's comments suggest that being able to valerse por si misma is related both to an intangible confidence in oneself and to a concrete set of marketable skills.

Women also benefit from the workplace relationships. María introduced me to her current boss, the manager at the restaurant where she works, by putting her arm around her and saying that her boss had been like a mother to her. Her boss responded in kind, talking about what a good person and hard worker María is and how close they had become. Lucha, María's sister, said that the baby shower her coworkers had organized for her when she was separated from her first husband and pregnant was the nicest thing anyone had ever done for her. When she was single in Degollado, Beatriz said she longed to work in one of the sewing workshops "not so much to work and sew but rather for the atmosphere that there was among the girls there....Though they were sewing, they had lots of fun together." The social benefits of work are more limited for women who work as domestics or provide in-home day care, the majority of whom choose these jobs because they do not have the papers required for jobs in the formal sector. These jobs, though, still justify leaving the house and still help them gain the sense that if necessary they could support themselves.

GENERALIZING BEYOND THE LIFE HISTORY INFORMANTS

The net effect of all these differences is that some women do not need men in the same way in Atlanta as they do in the sending communities. Economically, they can take care of themselves in a pinch. Socially, a single mother can be respetada (respected) in a way that would be difficult in Mexico without a man. A discussion I had with a group of battered women suggests that women migrants are well aware of these differences in the social construction of gender. One evening in the autumn of 1997 after finishing my fieldwork I was invited to visit a support group for Hispanic battered women organized by Mercy Mobile Health Care in Atlanta. The program organizers had heard me present results from this study, and they thought that a brief, simple overview of the kinds of generational and geographic changes I found in the families studied would be an interesting stimulus for discussion. It was also an excellent opportunity to test the broader generalizability of the results in a group of women who came from farther afield in Mexico or even from other Central American countries.

At first, battered women seem an unlikely group to confirm assertions about how living in the United States gives Mexican women social and economic leverage that they do not have at home—that is, women who have been hit by their husbands are perhaps not a group that springs to mind as an example of women's empowerment. Yet many of these women had left or were in the process of planning to leave their husbands—a move that they vociferously argued they would not have been able to make if they were back in Mexico, Guatemala, Honduras, or Nicaragua. They spoke about how, with the support of social workers, they had learned to use the law to defend themselves through restraining orders, court-mandated child support, and mandatory batterers' programs for their husbands. One woman recounted how just the week before she had made a plan with the police to come protect her while she and her children moved out of their apartment; she had packed in secret and said nothing to her husband until the men in uniform showed up at their door. When her husband tried to plead with her not to go, that he would not hit her again, the police told him not to speak to her or threaten her or they would arrest him.

Both those who had left their husbands and those who had not ascribed the difference in their experiences in the United States to the combination of legal protection and women's economic opportunities in the United States. One woman noted that in Honduras there are also domestic violence laws, as well as domestic violence prevention and support programs. She said that last time she was back in her country she even thought about volunteering for the program and perhaps speaking publicly about her own experiences. She decided not to, though, since women who do not have professional training have extremely limited options for supporting themselves. Here in Atlanta, she said, you can work eight hours and earn $40; there you could work all month without earning that much—so talking about domestic violence laws in that economic context is just a lot of "blah, blah, blah." Another woman agreed, noting that for women without higher education or job skills, leaving one's husband in Mexico meant returning to live with one's parents, sacrificing the adult status and freedom of one's own house (or apartment) for the economic and social protection of going back to being *una hija de familia* (a girl who lives at home with her parents). In Atlanta, they said emphatically, it is much easier to valerse por si misma (to be valuable on your own)—that is, to support oneself.

Women talked about how the privacy of urban life in Atlanta facilitated a decision to leave one's husband. First, they said, in a small town your husband will easily be able to find you and thus beg or threaten you to take him back. Second, here in Atlanta, *nadie se mete contigo* (nobody gets in your business). I asked if this meant that women who had their own families here (parents, siblings, cousins) did not feel that they could provide a measure of social support. Women were divided on this. Some said that no matter what, everyone is alone in the United States and that furthermore, *la familia es tu peor enemigo* (the family is your worst enemy); several women clarified this statement by talking about how fathers would say, *"tú te lo buscaste, ahora aguantate"* (you wanted him, now suffer) or brothers would pressure them to take back estranged husbands. One young woman, however, noted how the freedom of privacy also has a cost. In Atlanta, she said, she is able to prove that she can support herself and her children, that not only can she wear the pants but that they fit her well (*aquí traigo los pantalones, y bien puestos*), but in her town in Guatemala she could turn to her father, who would never let her husband beat her up.

Women in Mexico continue to depend on men for economic support and social status in ways that their peers in the United States do not. Both in the field sites in Mexico and in Atlanta women share dreams of intimate partnership with their husbands. In Atlanta, however, the narrative about love is woven together—at least for some women—with the power to push a bit harder for an equal say.

A TALE OF THREE SISTERS

Several years ago in Atlanta, María's husband began staying out all night drinking. In the mornings, he refused to drive her to work. He stopped giving her any of his paycheck, and she suspected he was running around with other women. She threatened to buy her own car and learn to drive, but he just laughed—so she took her savings, called a friend, and bought a car. Once she could drive, she threw him out. She told him she did not need his nonsense—"*mejor sola que mal acom-*

pañada" (it's better to be alone than in bad company)—and that he should not come home until he had decided to be a more responsible husband and a better father to his two children. Several weeks later he was back, asking for forgiveness. María told me, laughing, that his sisters had tired of doing his laundry; apparently he expected (incorrectly) that though his wife might have changed after she migrated, his sisters would still take care of him in the old way. María and her husband still have occasional difficulties, but María says that for the most part he has settled down (*se ha aplacado*) and they live well together.

In Degollado, Josefina and Pedro were also separated for a time. While on a drinking binge he became involved with another woman and simply stopped coming home. Unable to support herself and their four children on the meager amount she earned crocheting doilies, she moved back in with her parents. During the year they spent apart, she says she was very happy, in spite of how her brothers criticized her for her failed marriage. Pedro eventually reconsidered, saying that if she did not take him back he would drink himself to death, and his brothers began trying to reunite the couple. She wavered, saying that she was quite content, had not missed having a husband, and that her parents at least provided enough for her and her kids to eat well, which Pedro had never done.

Finally, she sought her father's counsel; he told her that if she went back to him the suffering would be hers and so the choice was hers, that she was always welcome in his house but that he feared that eventually she would need to be with a man and he would not permit her to misbehave while in his house. Testing Pedro's good faith, she told him to build her a room so they would have some place to live other than with his parents. He did so, and she returned to him. They get along much better now; both of them give much of the credit to their participation in the church's Movimiento Familiar, a family support program. Yet Pedro was the one to leave Josefina, and she still lives with the possibility that if he chose to he could do so again. Now that her father has died she would feel less welcome returning to her mother's home; she says her mother favors her brothers and their wives and would begrudge her the room and the support. Josefina told me many times that, like her sisters in the North, women of her generation were different than their mothers: "*ya no somos tan dejadas*," now women do not let themselves get pushed around like their mothers. But although she may share her sisters' dreams, the structural conditions in which she lives are all too similar to those faced by her mother.

María and Josefina have another sister, Lucha. Married (in both civil and religious ceremonies) soon after she was fifteen to Roberto, she spent the early years of their marriage living with him in a room in his mother's house in Degollado, putting up with his verbal abuse, drunkenness, and infidelity. At one point even his mother scolded him, Lucha recounted, saying that if Roberto were going to live in her house, he must treat his wife with more respect. Finally, pregnant and humiliated, Lucha gathered up her few belongings, went home to her parents' house to ask for help, and left for Los Angeles to begin again as one of the many fracasadas in East Los Angeles. They procured a civil divorce, though a religious divorce was beyond reach for people of their limited means.

But Lucha still loved Roberto, and eventually he followed her to California where he convinced her to take him back. They lived together, albeit stormily. She worked and he earned occasional money through a variety of shady activities. But they still fought, and she still suspected his continued infidelity: "He did not want to be married," she recalled. Finally, to her relief, he was picked up by the police and deported, charged with a felony, and forbidden to reenter the country. Lucha, who by then had two children with Roberto, continued to support herself by working in a factory. The women she worked with became her friends; she said she was never in her life so touched as when they organized a surprise baby shower for her. She says she went a little crazy during this period in her life, but eventually she tired of being alone. She said she started to feel that even in Los Angeles she would never have the same kind of respect without a man. One day she met Jose. Quiet but steady, he seemed everything Roberto had not been, and they moved in together quickly. They had two children together, moving then to Atlanta where her sisters lived, housing was more affordable, and work easier to find. Although many Mexicans moved to escape the reach of la migra in the late 1980s, this was not a concern for them because they both had residence papers from the amnesty.

Her relationship with Jose was a constant struggle. Looking back, at one point she said that she thinks she was just looking for a man to shelter her. She complained to me about their lack of communication. If she were in the kitchen, he would just sit on the sofa, silently watching TV, never asking her what she was doing or if she would like him to keep her company. He worked hard, did not drink or run around with other women, and always provided for the children, but she missed having cariño. She said she couldn't bear it that he would just lie there at night without reaching out to hold her. Eventually, she said, she couldn't bear it when he did touch her, so estranged did she feel. She tried to convince Jose to go to a therapist with her, but he would not even consider it.

Finally, she saved up her money, bought a lot, and built a house in Degollado next to Josefina. Back in Mexico visiting her family, her path crossed Roberto's. He was living with another woman, but he told her he still loved her, that he wanted her back. Just being near him, she said, made her feel covered with goose bumps. He paid her compliments and made her laugh. She went back to Atlanta, biding her time, telling him to leave his girlfriend first and she would think about it. They wrote back and forth, secret letters carried not in the mail but by traveling accomplices.

Finally, she left Atlanta. Telling Jose only that she was going to Mexico for summer vacation, she packed up their children, some clothes, and got on the bus in Atlanta that goes directly to La Piedad, twenty minutes away from Degollado. I asked her how she felt before leaving: scared, she said, but also excited. She hoped it was the right thing to do, but if things didn't work out, she could always go back to the United States and start again alone. "*Al cabo, estoy arreglada*" (After all, I have my working papers).

Lucha's working papers were a kind of insurance policy, a guarantee that if Roberto turned out not to have changed (opinion in town was divided on this subject) she would not have to depend on him. Once in Degollado, she planned to not work, to have him support her, and to keep house for him, but she was only free to follow her heart rather than her head, to choose love rather than security, because she had supported herself and knew she could do so again, in el norte. This vision of Lucha, living with few luxuries but happily ensconced in her freshly painted house with her husband, walking to the market every day to buy hot tortillas to make lunch for her husband, may seem an odd end to a tale of women's power. She reminded me, though, that "in the eyes of God, and of the town, he is still my husband." And, with her passport and *mica* (green card) carefully tucked away in a safe spot, perhaps she chose the ultimate luxury, a luxury unthinkable to her mother and unavailable to her sister Josefina: a partner who promised love and pleasure rather than economic security. Lucha's story suggests that, though we can see how migration can expand women's opportunities, we should be cautious about sweeping predictions about what women may want to do with their new bargaining power.

Whether in Mexico or Atlanta, women and men from Degollado and El Fuerte build their families and their social lives within a network of social and economic links that tie them together in spite of the distance. Through the photos and recuerdos on their walls, they show themselves and each other that the community of which they are a part stretches across the border, that even when they are thousands of miles apart they can in some way still remain *aquí con nosotros* (here with us).[33]

Shared values about the family, however, do not mean identical experiences in the United States and Mexico. There is considerable heterogeneity to women's experiences both in Mexico and in the United States. For some women, the older pattern of migration in which women stayed behind created situations in which they had a great deal of autonomy and decision-making power, *el poder de la ausencia* (the power of absence), as González de la Rocha calls it.[34] Under the new patterns of migration, those women in Atlanta with access to certain resources (for example, kin, working papers, English-speaking ability) might have power and autonomy that their mothers never could have hoped to—but not all Mexican women in Atlanta are so fortunate. Second, the observations about structural diversity among women on both sides of the border should not overshadow the more general differences between the U.S. and Mexican locations in terms of the social organization of gender. That is, although not all women are equally well positioned to mandar, to give the orders, in the United States, the differences in privacy and the organization of social space, domestic violence, and economic opportunities do translate into real gains in power for women as a group.

The vocabulary of bargaining theory—goals, strategies, negotiations, resources—has implicitly framed much of this discussion of migration and changes in women's lives. In particular, I have highlighted the ways in which migration is shaped by, and in turn shapes, women's resources—that is, how the presence or absence of certain resources makes women more or less likely to migrate, and similarly how their access to other resources affects the likelihood that they will be able to take advantage of some of the structural advantages offered by life in el norte. To a lesser extent I have alluded to women's goals—the goal of having a house, of living with one's husband as opposed to seeing him only one month per year, of having a certain kind of family. Women's goals, and in particular women's and men's values about marriage, have undergone a major generational change. The question of gender and migration, then, is not only whether or not Mexican values are preserved in transnational communities. Mexico is a moving target, and those very values that are so often cast as traditional, in contrast to the modern United States, are in fact highly contested and in the process of profound transformation.

CHAPTER 7

Sexual Intimacy in Mexican Companionate Marriages

J: And what do you see as the role of the sexual relationship in marriage?

V: Yes, it's very important, it's half [of marriage].

J: And what's the other half?

V: The other half is getting along well, but sex is one of the most important things. For me personally, I think that the intimacy I have with [my husband] was worth a lot, to carry us through the big problems we have had.

J: To strengthen the relationship?

V: Yes, it was the thing that really helped the most. Perhaps it was not so much that we cared for each other, that we loved each other, not even the kids, as it was the sexual relationship that we have.

J: And why do you think it was so important, how did that work?

V: I don't know, because we enjoy it. I see that both of us enjoy it a lot. I sometimes ask myself, does everyone enjoy it so much? I ask myself that, because I really do enjoy it.[1]

Marital sexuality has been transformed from a relationship that produces social ties primarily through reproduction to one that is understood to produce conjugal ties directly. To a lesser extent, migration-related differences reveal themselves in what women said about their sexual relationships. I emphasize here the fluidity of cultural constructions of sexuality, drawing attention to the socially and historically constructed emotional content of relationships. The theoretical approach to

sexuality is that it is not a static cultural construction that dictates behavior or an attribute that people possess but rather a set of shared ideas,
values, and symbols that people *use* to build relationships and to construct social identities. In the interests of a strong marriage and a satisfying life, the younger women have worked to develop different sorts of
sexual relationships with their husbands than their mothers had.[2]

When Parker writes about Brazilians' delight in *sacanagem* (a trans-
gressive, no-holds-barred sexual interaction), or when the Schneiders
describe southern Italian couples' pride in their ability to control fertility through the physical discipline of coitus interruptus, they remind us
of the importance of the subjective, affective dimensions of sexual relationships—and of the way that people's most intimate emotions and
experiences are shaped by historical and social context. Women's words
implied some behavioral differences between the cohorts of women, for
example, the "normal" sexual repertoire has widened to include oral
sex and erotic lingerie, but my focus here is much more on the generational differences in sexual meanings.

The younger life history informants (particularly those with more
than a sixth-grade education) and the preponderance of those in the
United States shared an understanding of the purpose of marital sexual
intimacy that was sharply distinct in some ways from the attitudes of
the older women, some of the less-educated women, and the life history
informants' mothers. For the older women, the marital bargain entailed
mutual respect and an exchange of a woman's best efforts at social reproduction for her husband's productive efforts. For the younger
women, in contrast, the exchange included the somewhat less tangible—though no less real—sharing of pleasure and sentiment. The
younger couples asserted that the confianza that allows men and
women to set aside concerns of hierarchy and respectability and to
share pleasure and affection served as the foundation of a successful
marriage. Some women, in fact, asserted that *only* bonds of pleasure
and sentiment unite the couple, that there was no material element to
their marriage.

Rather than revealing two absolutely distinct groups, women's responses to questions about sex indicated that they fall along a spectrum
regarding the overriding purposes of marital sexuality. At one end of the
spectrum lies the idea that the mutual pleasure and emotional closeness
shared during sexual intimacy create the bonds that unite a couple. At
the other pole is the understanding that sex creates children, which are
what make a "real" family, and that men and women form lasting con-

nections through the production of children. Of the twenty-four married life history informants, fifteen clustered more toward the pole that could be called modern intimacy while the other nine issued responses more typical of a reproductively oriented sexuality. The clearest division between the two groups of women's attitudes toward marital sexuality was in how they responded to the question on the relationship between sex and marriage. Cohort differences emerged as well in their responses to questions about initiating and refusing sex, pleasure, sexual activities other than vaginal intercourse, and styles of communication between spouses. There were clear patterns in women's responses: those women who said they did not ever refuse to have sex with their husbands were also those most likely to say that they would never initiate it themselves, whether out of lack of desire or vergüenza. Similarly, they were the same women who, when I asked them about the role of the sexual relationship in marriage, responded by talking about the danger of an unsatisfied husband straying, rather than about how sexual intimacy strengthens the marital union.

One reason to say that women fall along a spectrum, rather than in two absolutely separate categories, is that some women shared aspects of both understandings. To call these two complexes of ideas about sexual relationships "constructions" exaggerates the extent to which they are separate. One woman in Degollado, for example, married for about ten years, was eloquent on the way that trust and sexual closeness were the foundation of a good marriage, but she still said that she would never refuse to have sex with her husband. Women also drew on both strategies when they talked about consent, saying in one breath that sex should be about mutual desire and pleasure, and in the next breath that *hay que cumplir* (you have to do your duty). Almost all of the women, furthermore, invoked the distinction between decent women and mujeres de la calle, those who have no shame. They may draw the line differently—with more traditional women suggesting that a decent woman's sexual repertoire is limited to vaginal intercourse initiated by her husband and more modern ones arguing that a woman loses nothing by incorporating a certain amount of variety into her sexual relationship with her husband, assuming that it is in the service of the marriage and not just for sheer pleasure, but they all use the distinction. Furthermore, most of the women, old and young, saw nothing shameful or indecent in a married woman's sexual pleasure. One older woman from the rancho, for example, who was so uncomfortable discussing the topic at all that most of her responses were either nervous giggles or monosyllables, responded to my question about who enjoys sex more, the man or the woman, by saying, "I think it's for both of them, no?" A younger woman in Degollado was a bit more expansive, saying, "The point is also for her to be left happy—if not, well, just them and not us—no, the thing has to be fair."

Unsure what term women might use for orgasm, I asked in a number of ways about women's sexual pleasure. First, I would ask if women had any physically intense response at the end of sexual intercourse, like men do.[3] Many of the women clearly understood what I was getting at; some responded by saying that women also have orgasms, though not always, and that they need time and foreplay to be physiologically and mentally ready. I also asked women if they and their spouses talk and touch each other before having sex, or if they just immediately proceed to vaginal intercourse. One young woman in Degollado responded as follows: "Sometimes [he just wants to skip the foreplay] and it makes me angry. I say, 'No, get off me,' and he'll say, 'Please, come on.' I say, 'No, I don't like it like that,' and he begs, 'Oh, just for today'—but I say, 'You always say that.' I think it's just how they are. I know I need a bit more of him touching me and kissing me, things like that, but he can just look at me and 'let's go.' So it's like a tug of war, then I'll say to him, 'Don't you want to make me feel good?' And he says ok." Women referred to both women's and men's orgasms as *terminar* (to finish) (though several of the more educated women were also familiar with the Spanish cognate of the English word, *orgasmo*), so in the later interviews I asked the life history informants if women finished too, or just men. One answered my question about whether she had ever "finished" by saying, "Of course, if not, what would be the point of doing it without feeling?" and she continued, "I really do, and if I feel a lot of desire then [I'll come] five times and if not, then just once, but if I am turned on I'll come over and over again, it really lasts. Why deny it? I feel like a woman, and so I feel it, and I don't know why many women say they don't feel anything." A few women seemed not to enjoy sex at all. One of them was young and very recently married; she expressed indifference to sex, saying that she never cared whether they had sex or not, much less what position they used. Another young woman told me that it always hurt her to have sex, but that it also felt good; it was harder to know what to make of that. A third, who had been married for more than a decade, said that she never liked having sex, that she was always trying to come up with excuses not to do it. She was painfully uncomfortable throughout the interview—fidgeting, looking

away, answering in much shorter sentences than in other interviews—
and she said afterward that the only other person with whom she had
ever discussed sex so directly was her priest.

The generational difference lies in the meaning women ascribe to
sexual pleasure, not in whether or not they experience it. Among the
older women, it was icing on the cake if a woman happened to marry a
man who cared that she enjoyed the sexual relationship—but if not, her
dissatisfaction was a private matter, hardly reason to leave an otherwise
perfectly good mate. The younger women, in contrast, asserted that a
mutually satisfying sexual relationship forms the foundation for a good
and happy marriage. There is widespread recognition of the new importance of sexual intimacy in marriage, though opinions vary on
whether or not this is a good thing: one day Evita, the woman I lived
with in Degollado, was bemoaning the egotism of young women who
pick up and leave their husbands just because they are unhappy. When
I asked why she thought these women left their husbands, she said that
it was purely sexual, that these selfish young women—who must not
feel sexually satisfied by their husbands—were not willing to live without that satisfaction, even if meant their children might suffer.

The most striking difference between the two ways of understanding
sexual relationships was revealed in women's responses to a question
about the role of sexuality in marriage. As demonstrated by the woman
in her thirties who said "sex is one of the most important things" in
marriage, younger women spoke of the ways that sexual intimacy produces a stronger marriage. When I asked a woman in one of the Mexican field sites about the role of sex in marriage, she responded: "Well,
it's what keeps us going, no? If you feel good in terms of intimacy, you
will feel good in [the rest of] your life. Because you are happy in one
way with your spouse,...because when you come [*cuando terminas*]—
I think that when you end up happy, you get up in the morning happy,
you have energy for things—I think it's what helps keep us going."
Younger women talked about mutual sexual satisfaction as a source of
union. Women who emphasized a more reproductively oriented understanding of sexuality tended to answer the question more negatively,
saying that if a man were not satisfied sexually he would look for another woman.

The language women use to talk about sex reflects the shift to a paradigm of mutual desire. Many of the older women—even those who
seem to have shared a pleasurable intimacy with their partners—employed the word *usar* (to use) to describe vaginal intercourse; for exam-

ple, they might say "*cuando el me usa*" (when he "uses" me) to describe sexual relations. Usar is a mechanical, instrumental word, describing the utilization of an inanimate object—the word one might employ to talk about an iron, or a plow. Younger women describe intercourse using words like *hacer el amor* (making love) or *estar juntos* (being together) or *tener relaciones* (having relations).

Some information about the respondents' mothers' subjective experiences of sex can be gleaned from their responses to a question that I had intended to be about gender roles in marriage. When asked what they expected from marriage, the older women all responded by saying that they knew nothing beforehand. In the words of one who lived in the rancho: "You went in blind, because in that time there was no television, when there was no television we didn't know anything." Another said, "We went in blind, and we were afraid." Their words hint at the fear and pain of a wedding night, when they had no idea what to expect and no one to ask.[4] More information about sexuality is available to younger, unmarried women, but decent unmarried women can also *admit* to knowing more. The message in the older women's words is that in their youth a good girl did not admit to knowing about sex; their protestations about not having known are also claims that they were correctly brought up.[5]

Their daughters, by contrast, study sexuality intently in preparation for marriage. Most have at least some practice kissing and petting by the time they are married, so their wedding night is hardly their first moment of physical intimacy. Furthermore, most received rudimentary biological information on reproduction in the final year of grade school. More than anything, however, media in the form of books, the television, and especially the videocassette recorder play an important role in their education about sexuality. Many had seen pornographic films as teenagers (either watching them on cable TV or renting one, during a moment after school when they knew the house would be empty), and discussing the relationship between "the way they do it in movies" and one's own imagined wedding night seemed to be a major concern of adolescent girls. Whereas their mothers prepared for marriage by learning how to cook, clean, iron, and wash, girls today learn all this but also how to be their husbands' lovers.

All of those younger women who share this new attitude talked about the importance of developing trust with their husbands over time, so that they would not feel ashamed to enjoy sexual intimacy. Vergüenza is a quality that all well-brought-up girls should know enough to display; showing shame early in marriage is a deliberate performance of being a good girl. They talk about gradually—for some women it was a matter of days, for others months or years—developing a trust, a confianza, that allows them to dispense with these deliberate performances of modesty and lack of desire.

Once confianza had been established, the younger women said, it became possible for a woman to initiate sexual intimacy, or even to engage in a variety of forms of sexual experimentation, including the purchase of lingerie, watching erotic films, and anal or oral sex. There was a tension in this part of our conversation, between their desires to satisfy their husbands and their fear of crossing a line and acting like a woman of the calle as opposed to one of the casa. As one woman said, discussing her reluctance to have anal sex with her husband, "*somos de amor, no somos de pago*" (we are the ones [who do it for] love, we are not [those who do it] for money).

One day in the knitting store I was privy to a conversation in which one woman was telling the others gathered there to knit and chat about having had oral sex with her husband (that is, she did it to him—no mention of him returning the favor). The other women asked animatedly: "Did it hurt you?" "Did you swallow the semen?" "Was it disgusting?" "Did you make him wash beforehand?" She reminded them of the importance of keeping one's husband from getting bored by not doing "the same every day" and then said that "after all, he's my husband," implying that the sexual intimacy and privileged social bond of marriage justify a certain amount of mutual, consenting exploration in the interest of pleasure. Another woman, in response to my question about whether having sex was supposed to be physically uncomfortable for women, said:

> Look, I knew someone in Mexico, someone with whom I had a lot of confianza, who said to me that whenever her husband asked her for it, she nearly screamed up to the heavens, because it hurt all the time. They already had five kids, and she asked me, "How is it that some women like to have sex so much?" For her it was a huge pain. So I said to her, "You need to know how to do it, and what you like, and then it's not a pain at all. *There's something to knowing how to do it.* It's like a toy, you need to know how to play with it so that it pleases you.... When I was recently married I said, 'Ay, no,' but with time you open your eyes a bit and you start to like sex a little better."
>
> But she said, "No, but then there's also the issue of our religion." There are people that are really Catholic, really religious, who can't have a very open relation [*una relación muy abierta*] with their husbands because, ay,

they think it would be such a big sin to enjoy it like a woman of the street
[*uno disfrute como una de la calle*]. You know that those women on the
street, whores, of course they are going to please a man, that's what they
do, *so you also have to have a little bit of experience, to keep your husband
happy, so they don't go looking in the* [street]. (Emphasis added.)

Women balance between the idea that by knowing how to "play with
the toy" one is revealed to be a woman of the street and the idea that a
woman's sexual adventurousness is part of being a good wife.

When I asked one young woman in Atlanta if her husband ever suggested sexual activities to her other than vaginal intercourse, she said,
"everything that he likes, I do." The phrase *alcabo es mi marido* (after
all, he's my husband) echoed through several women's discussions
about oral sex. Very few admitted to having had oral or anal sex. Many
said that they had heard of other people doing it but that they personally found it unappealing or even disgusting—but they also said to me
that it was the sort of thing that they would not admit to having done,
even if they had. For these women, to be an enthusiastic and open-
minded sexual partner is to do the work of intimacy, to build a strong
marriage.[6]

Some younger women rejected this emphasis on the importance of
sexual intimacy and indicated that a man's request for sexual variety
necessarily implied a lack of respect. Those who do not share this new
concept of marital sexuality define women's sexual responsibilities
within marriage much more narrowly, as the obligation to cumplir, to
be willing to have sex. One woman, for example, talked about sex as *la
obligación,* but she was extremely clear that this obligation did not extend beyond vaginal intercourse. She said that she had heard about oral
sex, but that the only women who would consent to it, as far as she
knew, were "those whores." Her husband had pushed her on the issue,
as she recounted:

One of his brothers had a VCR, and he would bring it to where they
worked, and they would watch those movies, so he would get home all
fired up to feel that same way.... So one day I said, in front of my mother-
in-law, "Hey, would you believe what he's been asking me to do?" And I
told her, so she said [to him], "Where have you seen that kind of thing?"
He said she shouldn't believe me, that I was just talking, but I said, "Yes,
it's true, and the other day he brought home a magazine, so that I would do
like it showed in the magazine. What does he think—I'm not a whore to
act like that one in the magazine. If I were, and I were paid, I assure you I
would do like he was trying to force me, just to earn something, but as I
am not...." And my mother-in-law yelled at him.

too normative?

The saga continued: apparently he was not sufficiently shamed by his mother's scolding, and so the next time he raised the issue his wife decided it would also be necessary to humiliate him in front of his coworkers. She went down to where they were watching the movies and demanded that he let her see as well, saying, "Let me go in and see, I have never seen one of those movies, so I can know how they do it." He yelled at her and told her to go home, but she went back to report to his mother, confirming that he had in fact been watching pornographic movies, and so his mother yelled at him again. She said that since then he has not asked her again.

Sex, however, continues to be an arena of conflict in their marriage. Although she does not deny the theoretical possibility that it might be pleasurable, she says that her husband wants to have sex so frequently that he does not allow her any time to build up an interest on her own. For example, after a long separation, she said that she did enjoy sex the first few times after they were reunited, but that she quickly shifted back to her former aversion. Yet it was not at all clear to me that the frequency of her husband's demands was really the central issue. She said to me a number of times, looking down lovingly at her youngest, still an infant, that she could hardly believe that "something so lovely could come from something so disgusting"—that is, from sex. She told me how she discouraged her husband's multiple attempts to create a more satisfying sexual relationship: after criticizing him for wanting to have intercourse with no thought for whether she was in the mood, he tried to caress her and help her become sexually excited, only to be told by her to hurry up and get it over with—that she "did not know what the hell he was doing trying to touch her all over, as he knew damn well where he could find what he was looking for." Finally, she recounted, he complained to her that "there is no way to make you happy." And, it seems, he was right; he was trying to create a sexual relationship of confianza, while she was insisting on the primacy of ideas about respect.

The woman described above, however, is the exception among younger women. Most of her peers, who do embrace the role of sexual pleasure in strengthening the marital relationship, demonstrated a certain deliberateness to how they talk about their sexual relationships with their husbands, an assumption that mutually satisfying marital sexual relationships are a goal for which to strive. The edge of anxiety in how they talked about preparing for marriage is quite different than the fear of the unknown at which their mothers hint; the younger generation seems to fear instead that they will not measure up, that they will fail to hold their husband's interest, and thus that a certain amount of study and preparation is necessary.

MEN'S PERSPECTIVES ON
SEXUAL INTIMACY AND AFFECTIVITY

The younger men, like their wives, talked about sexual intimacy as the foundation for a successful marriage. For Humberto, for example, sexual compatibility and social companionship were the two ways that a man and woman could express being the other person's "other half"; he talked about his desire that his wife would fit her work schedule around his:

> H: ...so that the times that I am free, she is also free, in case we want to go out, or go have fun or something, we could all go together, because if each one of us is going to go out alone, I have never approved of that.
>
> J: That is, you wanted someone who could be a companion in your free time?
>
> H: Well, the idea of marriage is that the companion should be your other half.
>
> J: Well, there are lots of ideas about what marriage is.
>
> H: Well, supposedly she's the other half, the complement, and for her to be the complement, you need to fit together, not just sexually but in life, in everything.

For Humberto's father, who spent much of Humberto's childhood as a migrant laborer in the United States, ideas about marital complementarity may have been expressed instead in terms of men's responsibilities for production and women's for reproduction. Intimacy, however, does not obviate hierarchy; it never seems to have occurred to Humberto that he could shape his much more flexible work schedule around his wife's. Clearly he and Isabel had spoken about these ideas about marriage, because she quoted his theory of sexual and social complementarity to me almost verbatim: "Since we were dating, Humberto told me that we had to really trust each other, that is, that a good understanding is half of marriage and the other half is sex. If the trust doesn't work then the sex doesn't work, and if the sexual side is not going well, the other is also not going to go well. Both aspects have to work for things to function well." The idea that sexual intimacy strengthens the emotional bonds of marriage runs as a theme through many other men's comments.

Some of what men think about sexuality can be inferred from their comments about infidelity. All of the men said that women's infidelity was unforgivable. Some see their partner's infidelity as a lack of respect, whereas others see it as a betrayal of trust. Making infidelity into a question of confianza de-genders it; men and women are understood to be equally vulnerable to having their feelings hurt. Sergio, for example, said that infidelity on the part of either partner "is the same thing" and that it would effectively end a marriage: "It's better just to split up, because when you lose trust there's no longer any point. In a marriage where there has been a betrayal, things are never the same again." Reflecting the idea that it is men's, as well as women's, responsibility to satisfy a partner, he noted that ultimately the source of sexual dissatisfaction in marriage is bad communication. When asked his opinion of men's infidelity, he said, "Well, it's bad, because really, if they are not finding satisfaction with their wife, I think it's better that they talk. Why go looking for trouble?"

Sergio implies here not just that a sexual relationship can be improved by talking about it, but that it is something about which people can actually talk. One of the key differences between marriages of respeto and those of confianza is that in the latter sex is considered an appropriate topic for direct discussion and in the former it is not. This different understanding of infidelity reflects back on a redefined masculinity and, by implication, on a new meaning of respect. Sergio went on to tell me that he loses respect for the man who has sex with a woman who is not his wife "because that man does not know how to respect himself." Redefining masculinity to mean the man who is capable of managing an affective relationship to his own satisfaction, he said, "In my way of seeing things, I would say that he is showing a lack of respect for himself *because he is not man enough to say what he feels.* If he is going to get involved with another woman, whether it's from foolishness or whatever, no one knows what he is going to lose along the way. Look, I am not saying I am an angel, like I told you I am an old rooster, but there's always been something different in what we share. We are always looking for something different, and I think that for other men, it just gets to be routine."[7] Since their marriage, he said they have deliberately worked at creating a varied and mutually fulfilling sexual intimacy. Men who turn to other women, he said, do so out of a lack of manhood, not a surfeit. Several other men made similar comments. Oscar, who defines a lack of respect within marriage so broadly as to include either partner making social plans without first consulting with his or her spouse, said that men who run around with other women "humiliate their wives." Criticizing the idea that it is their right as men, he said, "Well, I think that's machismo, it's a machismo on the part of those guys, to think that just because they are men they can have any woman they want. That's not true."

Other men noted that while infidelity on the part of men and women might be equally egregious in theory, it is often not received the same way in practice. In other words, while many couples privately frame infidelity in terms of intimacy and betrayal, it still publicly resonates with issues of male privilege. Mario echoed Sergio's comment that infidelity shows a lack of respect both for oneself and one's partner and that "it's the same for both." However, he said, women are much more likely to tolerate it than men out of fear and limited options. Miguel concurred, saying that he would leave his wife if he saw her with another man. He condemned even men who are unfaithful during long separations as migrant workers from their wives, but he did say that in practice it is much more likely that the woman will have to tolerate it (aguantarlo). Humberto said infidelity presented a breach of trust, a risk of disease (he was the only one to mention this), and a violation of the sacrament of marriage for both partners. Juan also said that his power as a man does not give him a right to infidelity. He said that if men love their wives, they should feel no need to be with another woman; furthermore, a man who is unfaithful may provoke his wife to seek revenge in the same way. And yet, although he said that men *ought* to hold themselves to the same standard as their wives, he said that the man who is faithful to his wife during the long months in the United States is a rare one. In the many years he worked in the United States before marrying her he had ample time to see how married men from his hometown became "friends" with women in the United States.[8] He framed these men's betrayals, like Sergio, as questions of love and masculinity: "Usually, when one sees the opportunity, it can happen, if he doesn't really love his wife—but he who has his pants on right can be [faithful], and so yes, there are [men] who are [faithful]." His use of the word *pantalones* (pants) echoes the question of there being only one person to wear the pants at home, but it also suggests that part of the power of those pants derives from them being worn properly—that is, with the fly zipped up.

Men's understanding of infidelity reflects their ideas about manhood, about the proper relationship between a man and his body, and about the source of sexual desire. Nencel, writing about men's sexuality and

infidelity in Peru, talks about this in terms of the relative "fragmentation" or "de-fragmentation" of desire.[9] Those men who experience
their desire as fragmented talk about sexual intercourse as a physical release (descargo) unrelated to sentiment; other men talk about a differently socialized bodily experience in which sexuality is qualitatively better in the context of a relationship. Along these same lines, Mario
asserted, for example, that men cannot resist naked women: "We are
weak" (somos debiles), and both Pedro and Francisco asserted that men
physically need sex. Pedro said he was taught in school that men need
sex as a release (desahogo), which women do not need in the same way
because menstruation is their release; infidelity, he suggested, is not
great but it can help prevent marital discord (presumably, marital rape)
in situations where the man has a greater desire for sex than his wife
and she does not satisfy him (no le cumple). Francisco also said, "If I am
denied at home, I wouldn't need to leave her, I would just look for it in
the street." Saying that he would look for it in the street implies that in
fact he would find the same thing in the street as he might in his house—
that is, that sex with all women is equivalent.[10]

Francisco continued, saying that it is precisely to prevent this sort of
situation that men do not want their wives to work outside the home:
"Since the time when you are courting, what you look for is a wife who
will have food and everything ready for you when you come home.
That's the idea, that you don't have your wife working at anything, so
that she can take good care of you [que lo atiendan a uno bien], and
baby you." This is quite distinct from Sergio's and Juan's assertions that
men are in fact able to control their bodies and that real manhood is
demonstrated through this control, this socializing of male sexuality.
Furthermore, Francisco's idea that sex falls under the general paradigm
of women taking care of men contrasts strikingly with Sergio's, Humberto's, and Juan's descriptions of sexual intimacy as a product of mutual desire and a means for mutual satisfaction.[11]

NEW WINE IN OLD BOTTLES? SAYING NO TO SEX

All this discussion of women worrying about making sure that men are
sexually satisfied raises the possibility that this idea of marital sexuality
as a strategy to build a strong relationship is just a new version of the
old idea that women have to be sexually available to their husbands.
The way women talk about saying no to sex, however, makes it clear
that there is a genuinely new element here. This talk of pleasure is not

just a reworking of the idea that women must *cumplir* to include more diverse practices, sources of knowledge, and consumer goods, with the same underlying idea that women refuse to satisfy men's sexual needs at their own peril.

The women who talked about intimacy-oriented sexual relationships all said that they could say no when their husbands tried to initiate sex, and none reported ever having been forced to have sex. Furthermore, several could not even imagine having sex if they did not desire it. The classic refrain with which men told their wives that they should go along or they would be forced to was "*eres mi mujer, por eso me casé contigo*" (you are my woman, that's why I married you). I asked one young woman in Atlanta:

> J: And what about "I am your husband, that's why I married you"?
> R: Well, that may be why you married me, but, well, no. If I am not in the mood [*si yo no tengo ganas*], then no. How is it possible, that just because you married someone—it's not as if I'm some straw doll, that only exists to satisfy him.

Some said that if they said no several nights in a row, their husbands might joke with them about looking for it elsewhere, but all felt that they had the right to decline on the grounds that they were not in the mood without necessarily driving their husbands into another woman's arms. When I asked if their husbands might force them to have sex, they responded by telling me that was unthinkable or, in some cases, by laughing at the idea. For them, sexual intimacy is so strongly defined as an interaction the value of which depends on mutual desire that sex without *ganas* (desire) is absurd. This was true across the field sites; women in the Mexican field sites were as likely to articulate a right to say no as were their sisters in Atlanta.

Several of the women who said that being forced to have sex was unthinkable responded by saying that "it would be like rape." One young woman in Atlanta told me that when she got married her older sister (who lives in California) told her on the telephone that "even if I didn't feel like it, I should just satisfy him," but that she disagreed with her: "I said, 'No, how could I do a thing like that without desire?'" At the same time, a few of the same women who laugh off the possibility of marital rape have experienced other kinds of violence from their husbands, ranging from a slap "to calm her down" to a much more intense beating. Both men and women may see sexual violence as categorically separate from other kinds of violence; one of the staunchest defenders of a man's right to slap his wife also said that it was extremely important to respect her by not forcing her to have sex against her will. Although most of the women in this group were not routinely subject to physical violence from their husbands, some clearly were. It seems that men and women have come to see sexual violence as anathema in the companionate marriage in a way that other forms of violence are not.

For the older women, the primary goal in a marital sexual relationship was to please one's husband and thus prevent infidelity, so not being in the mood to have sex is irrelevant. The women whose narratives suggested a more reproductively oriented sexuality either said that they never said no to their husbands (other than to tell them when they were menstruating) or—for those who said they had tried to say no—they talked about having been forced to have sex. Some of the younger women did talk about times when they were not particularly in the mood to have sex, but they allowed their husbands to convince them (they say, "*me saca las ganas,*" he wakes up my desire), but this seems more an issue of foreplay than of force. Saying no when one is not in the mood also implies the more affirmative possibility of women articulating and owning their own desire, of an active female sexuality separate from a woman's duty to please her husband.[12]

One woman in Atlanta explained her right to say no to sex by saying, "I am the owner of my body." Later on, I discuss the implications of this idea of physical autonomy for women's contraceptive method preferences in the United States. The idea that a woman has the right to say no to sex—definitely not a right her mother would have claimed—could certainly be used to challenge men's perceived "right" to physically discipline their wives. Those few couples in which there is no question of sexual violence but still the lingering threat of other kinds of force may exemplify relationships with aspects of both newer and older bodily ideologies. Rather than seeing these marriages—in which sex must be mutual and consenting but men still slap their wives to calm them down—as contradictory because they do not fit an American model of companionate marriage, we might view these marriages as an expression of broader contradictions in the social construction of gender, in which dreams of egalitarian intimacy coexist with persistent gender inequality. These few men may have ceded to women the right to consent to sex because it allows for a kind of sexual relationship that is otherwise impossible, but they do not see it as in their best interests to cede total control over their wives' bodies.

THE SOCIAL CONSTRUCTIONS OF SEXUALITY

My goal here is not merely to describe these changes in sexuality, but also—by focusing a careful eye on which women are the most vociferous proponents of conjugal intimacy—to construct an argument about *why* sexuality is changing, and for whom. To some extent, the fact that a woman chooses to emphasize the bonds of pleasure rather than (or in addition to) the bonds of children depends on what her husband is like; for example, the woman whose husband became angry and jealous the one time she tried to initiate sex learned quickly that he was not interested in having a relationship of intense intimacy with her, that by showing her desire she risked losing the moral power of acting with vergüenza without any corollary gain of intimacy through confianza. The woman who rebuffed her husband's attempts at foreplay, in contrast, may have felt that for her it was safer to rely on respect rather than risk intimacy. Both of these sexualities—the more reproductively oriented one, and the more intimacy-focused one—can be interpreted as women's strategies, processes through which they imagine and create themselves as sexual beings in response to the specific demands of marital relationships.

The structural differences between the two groups of women suggest, however, that factors other than men's personalities are shaping this cultural transformation. Those women who had more than a ninth-grade education (who had finished middle school) were the most articulate spokespeople for intimate sexuality and marital union. Some of these more educated women had gone to the local Catholic high school, and they spoke in particular about what their teachers had told them about how uplifting it could be for couples to share sex that is meaningful and tender rather than sex that just satisfied physical needs. For others, the effect of education seemed to be through increased literacy, which meant that they had the ability to read books and women's magazines through which they could explore these issues on their own at more length. Finally, the government's official program of sex education for all sixth graders may also be an important social factor. The quality of lessons taught varies widely and the curriculum is limited to the most basic information on puberty and reproduction, but this generation is the first to have received any formal sex education at all (the program was initiated in the 1970s as part of the national population control program), and school-based sex education has certainly communicated to a generation of students that sex and reproduction can be discussed publicly by respectable people.[13]

The Mexican media, particularly since the arrival of satellite TV in the area, is a major purveyor of information about sexuality. Several of the life history informants' mothers, for example, credited the television as being primarily responsible for how young women today know all about sex when they marry. In January 1998 when I visited Degollado and Mexico City, the newspaper columns were abuzz with the scandal created by the telenovela of the moment, which portrayed a middle-aged woman abandoned by her husband; in revenge she had taken a lover who was her children's age and brought him to live with them. Another example of the media's role might be the June 1997 issue of *Men's Health/Hombre Saludable,* a men's magazine sold on newsstands throughout Mexico, which carried an article titled *"Satisfacción Sexual Garantizada,"* purporting to tell men the secrets they need to make their sexual partner happy. A closer look at the masthead reveals a sexologist among the permanent editorial staff, and nearly every issue features some similar article about sexual "success." Of course, these cultural changes are inextricably intertwined with social and economic change; people would not be influenced by the images available on satellite TV if disposable income (for most families, sent by men in the North) did not allow them to purchase the satellite dishes that loom over so many homes throughout Mexico.

There were a number of women with only a sixth-grade education, however, who spoke at length about the centrality of sexual intimacy in their own marriages, underlining the extent to which generation is perhaps the central factor in this paradigm shift. Most of the women who talked about sexual intimacy were younger than thirty-five, and none of them was older than forty. Since I argued earlier that there has been a generational paradigm shift in marriage, it is hardly surprising that generation again emerges here as a key factor in shaping the meaning of physical intimacy within marriage.

Time is not by itself a force for change, of course, so the cohort differences direct our attention to the specific social changes that have promoted these new ideas about marital sexuality. Neolocality—couples living alone in their own home immediately after marriage, rather than in the groom's parents' home as was traditionally the case with all but the wealthiest families—promotes a level of conjugal intimacy otherwise impossible. Several couples mentioned enjoying being able to have sex without worrying about in-laws who might listen. The rise in neolocal marriage, in turn, reflects the effect both of migrant remittances and of the relative weakness of the peso, which means that hard-earned dollars buy more bricks and gravel in Mexico. D'Emilio has argued that urbanization and wage labor facilitated the development of homosexual identities and practices in mid-twentieth-century America as "capitalism allowed individuals to survive beyond the confines of the family" and thus to create small urban communities of sexual choice.[14] Similarly, I am arguing here that changes in the Mexican location of this transnational community have restructured heterosexuality through an increased emphasis on the social, economic, and affective self-sufficiency of the marital dyad.

The social organization of space within these houses also teaches young couples about sexual intimacy—and about privacy in general. Transformations in residential architecture in migrant-sending communities mean that in newer homes the bedrooms are connected via hallways (rather than having people walk through one room to get to another), there is at least one bathroom indoors (and sometimes more), and internal doors are made of wood rather than just a curtain hanging in a doorway. The layout of these modern homes in Mexico—which echoes the design of the homes in which their families may live in Atlanta—shapes these young couples' experiences of personal privacy and shared sexual intimacy.

Women also learn about sex by shopping; there is a wide variety of sexy lingerie available for purchase in Degollado and La Piedad (the town where people from the rancho go to shop), as of course there is in Atlanta. One woman joked about her sisters teasing her about which set of underwear she would buy for her wedding night, and while she insisted that they stop teasing her because it was embarrassing, she admitted that she did go ahead and buy some. Now her husband picks out her lingerie, and though she says she still sometimes feels embarrassed to don his choices, he tells her that as long as they keep their sartorial tastes a secret, she is his wife and should not be ashamed to please him. Other women also talked about choosing lingerie, wanting to walk a fine line between being sexy enough and being too sexy; one young woman in Atlanta, for example, said that beige and pink and even black lingerie was nice, but that red was definitely too much.

In addition to the media and the marketplace, the Catholic Church has also promoted this new vision of marital sexual intimacy. There are several ways that couples get direct messages about sexuality from the Catholic Church, but the form of communication most relevant here is the series of discussions about marriage and family life that couples are required to attend before being married in the church. All but one of the married women in the study wed in Mexico, so regardless of where they lived while interviewed, their experiences in these discussions are entirely reflective of attitudes among church leaders in this region of Mexico. These meetings are led not by priests but by married couples chosen by priests as exemplary in their own marriages.

For the most part, of course, the church has stood firmly behind its vision of reproductive sexuality as the only legitimate practice, opposing modern contraceptive technologies on the grounds that they promote sexual relations based solely on pleasure. At the same time, however, the message that most of the young women seem to have received through the classes is a sort of adaptation of the idea of a pleasure-based bond to Catholic ideas about the sanctity of the marital relationship. Even the older women recalled having been instructed that it was their holy obligation to be sexually available to their husbands; one woman, for example, recalled a priest telling her that if she were making tortillas, washing, or cooking and her husband arrived home wanting to have sex she was required to interrupt whatever she was doing to respond to him. Younger women reported this same message from the discussion groups, but with a new twist. When I asked one woman in her early thirties what she had learned in the discussions, she said, "They told us that the man is like a pickup truck, that heats up right away, and that women are like big trailer trucks that take a long time to warm up, so you need to turn them on ahead of time. I didn't understand this at the time, but now I do see that we are like that, that we do need caresses and kisses."[15] Similarly, another woman reported being told in a church discussion group that "the man also needs to take the woman into account, not just show up and want it right away. They said, 'Remember that a flame needs you to blow on it a little so it will really burn. If you throw a log on and don't blow on the fire, it will go out, so you need to give a little puff so that it starts well.'" Other women had similar memories of the discussions. Several specifically mentioned hearing about a woman's right to consent, creating a somewhat contradictory message in which a woman is supposed to drop whatever she is doing to satisfy her husband sexually, but at the same time sex is supposed to be an expression of shared desire. The Catholic Church seems to have responded to these new ideas about sexual pleasure by reinforcing the importance of mutuality and women's autonomy, though still subsumed within a rubric of reproductive sexuality.[16]

Migration experience also plays a role—albeit a minor one—in women's adoption of this new set of sexual strategies. In particular, the experience of working outside the home in a factory exposed some women to a range of casual conversations about sexual variety and sexual pleasure that is rare in semirural Mexico. Two women, for example, said that they learned that women have orgasms by listening to their coworkers' conversations, by "speaking with more open-minded people." Another woman talked about speaking "even with women from the street" about the kinds of sexual variety men like, though she did not make it clear under what circumstances she had encountered them. Furthermore, the woman who asserted that she was "owner of her own body" did not come up with that idea on her own; she said she learned it from a domestic violence counselor with whom she has an ongoing telephone relationship. In the past, she said her husband forced her to have sex: "When he wanted to, he would take me, even if it was against my will. . . . He would get mad, and even beat me up. He said it has to be when he wants it, and not when I want it. But not now. Now we do it when I want to and if not, he just goes away. That's how it's supposed to be, according to this, because if you are the owner of your body then why should another person be bossing you around and using it?" When I asked her what made her suddenly feel that she was the owner of her body, she said, "The counselor that I have, she tells me that one should not be so submissive with a man. He always says that I belong to him because he supports me, that I am his like a piece of furniture to use, but that's not what I am." Although marital rape is not widely prosecuted in the United States (and although it is also illegal in Mexico), Mexican women in the United States express ideas about women's sexuality that assume a moderately greater amount of physical autonomy. The underlying discourse here is one of property rights, and the position she takes seems much more reflective of North American feminist messages about women being owners of their own bodies than by Mexican ideas about men's control over their wives' bodies as expressed through such phrases as "mi mujer."

While at first it may seem surprising that this was the only difference between the women in the U.S. and Mexican field sites in terms of their overall attitudes about sexuality, after a bit of reflection it becomes clear that it would be quite surprising if repeated analysis had revealed greater ones. First of all, the primary force shaping women's attitudes is generation, and since all of the young women grew up in Mexico—regardless of where they live now—we should expect to find that migration has as minimal effect on attitudes toward sexuality as it had on marital goals. Migration does not change women's goals, but rather its effect can be seen in terms of the resources on which women can rely to reach those goals. Similarly, migration's consequences are much more clearly visible in how women use this ideology about companionate marriage and sexuality in their relationships.

It is possible, of course, that there were differences between the groups in terms of specific behaviors like anal or oral sex. Bronfman and Minello, for example, found that the privacy and anonymity of migration encouraged men to experiment with new sexual behaviors, and the same could certainly be true for women, but as none actually admitted directly to engaging in these behaviors it is hard to know.[17] Furthermore, even if there were significant behavioral differences, it is likely that they would still be framed by the same shared discourse about how sexual intimacy promotes marital ties.

For some women, sexual intimacy has replaced paternal obligation as a rhetorical strategy for explaining women's claims on men, in spite of the fact that many of these young women continue to be entirely economically dependent on their husbands. There is a certain amount of bravado in the words of one young woman, with neither working papers nor a driver's license nor even the most rudimentary command of English:

> Look, I've told him very clearly, "The day that you no longer care for me, go with all the freedom in the world and find yourself someone you love, someone you desire. Don't think that you are with me out of obligation, not for the kids and not for me." Just like if one day I no longer feel the same for him, I'll tell him. I don't want him to be with me out of obligation, neither during the day nor at night, never, not as a husband or in any other way. If we are together, it's because we care for each other, because we still feel something, not because it's a routine or an obligation.

If in fact her husband did find someone else he desired, she would be hard pressed to support herself. It is one thing for a woman who is economically self-sufficient to speak of marriage as a purely affective partnership, but quite another for a woman with no work experience and young, dependent noncitizen children (who do not qualify for Medicaid, WIC, or AFDC) to do so.[18] Several of the younger life history informants in both Mexican and U.S. field sites took this position. Women seemed to see the idea of being with a partner purely out of choice and mutual desire as elevating, and the alternative—which would be to use their mothers' generation's rhetoric about obligation—as debasing, not just old-fashioned but somehow less prestigious. They may adopt the rhetoric of companionate marriage, without having the resources on which to depend if a man calls their bluff, because they still feel some benefit in terms of the identity it allows them to imagine and project; men and women use a discourse of gender to make claims about modernity and thus social status. To talk about bonds composed purely of affection allows them, at least in their conversation with other women, the momentary creation of a powerful, independent identity as a woman who has the luxury of choosing for love as opposed to obligation.

This is not a story about a generational shift from sexual oppression to liberation. As Foucault and others have pointed out, a modern sexuality is not one that is freer but rather one that is diffusely regulated by ideologies, discourses, and institutions such as law, medicine, and public health.[19] This regulation of sexuality normalizes certain sexual behaviors and relationships and places others in the category of transgression; it proposes a set of expectations for how people will act and what they will feel. That sexuality remains every bit as constructed as it was in the past becomes clear if one pauses to think about the limits and boundaries that continue to be placed on sexual relationships. Women are hardly encouraged to explore their sexuality outside marriage, or in a way that emphasizes pure lust and passion divorced from emotion. Some women may prefer other ways of creating emotional intimacy with their spouses, and may even find the focus on the importance of mutual pleasure oppressive. Men, too, are instructed that there is a proper way to experience marital sexuality with one's wife; they are suddenly presented with the task of integrating sexuality and emotion. For both men and women, there is also a total screening off of homosexual desire.

Structural and ideological changes have changed the range of options available to women and men as they create relationships with each other. This new, intimacy-oriented sexuality is a strategy, an invention that takes place at the intersection of specific historical changes and individual struggles to create satisfying and secure relationships. This new Mexican understanding of marital sexuality does not obviate the ideas of the earlier generation but rather lies alongside them as an ideological option on which women can draw to interpret and justify their behavior. In addition, however, to being a key finding in and of itself, these ideas about marriage and marital sexuality are the cultural context within which couples form their family size and contraceptive method preferences.

CHAPTER 8

Fertility Decline, Contraceptive Choice, and Mexican Companionate Marriages

The younger women would agree with their mothers that *los hijos son la felicidad de la casa* (children make for a happy home), but they want much less of this happiness than did their parents. Young couples' interest in delaying a first birth and their decisions to space births, to have fewer children overall, and to build more emotionally complex relationships with those children take on new meaning when analyzed in light of the broader trend toward companionate marriage. The life history informants' mothers, who managed their fertility using breast-feeding or sterilization, had an average of almost nine surviving children each. The life history informants, admittedly much earlier in their reproductive careers, have an average of three children, and none of the younger ones want more than four or five.

These families, though, are not just smaller—they are different.[1] These changes can only be understood in light of the social and sexual relations implied by the Mexican companionate marriage. Specifically, the emphasis on socially constructed (as opposed to blood-based) ties between spouses and between parents and children promotes smaller families with different kinds of relationships. The ideal family has become one in which the primary bond is the parents' relationship, and the secondary bonds are those that the parents deliberately construct through giving their children love and understanding (*cariño* and *comprensión*).

BACKGROUND ON FERTILITY LEVELS AND TRENDS

Fertility has fallen markedly in Mexico during the past three decades, as Table 8.1 demonstrates. In the United States, recent National Center for Health Statistics (NCHS) data on births of Hispanic origin notes that Mexican women have the highest fertility of any Hispanic group in the United States, with a TFR of 3.2.[2] The fertility of Hispanic women is increasingly in the public eye—the NCHS report on Hispanic fertility cited here was covered in a half-page article on the National page of the *New York Times*—as both the number of Hispanic births and the proportion of total births in the United States that are to Hispanic women have increased during the past decade. Currently more than 12 percent of U.S. births (and more than 10 percent of births in the four most densely populated counties in metro Atlanta) are to Mexican or Mexican-origin women. The 1995 fertility rates for all Mexican women in the United States were 10 percent higher than 1989 rates for the same group (3.2 versus 2.9), with the greatest increase among women ages fifteen to nineteen, who showed a 32 percent increase in age-specific fertility rates, from 94.5 to 124.6 per 1,000. (By way of comparison, the age-specific fertility rate for white, non-Hispanic fifteen- to nineteen-year-olds was 39.3.) Mexican women born in Mexico were also the likeliest of any Hispanic subgroup to have a fourth or higher-order birth; 16.8 percent of births to this group of women were fourth or higher order, compared to 13.8 percent of all Hispanic births and 9.6 percent of all non-Hispanic U.S. births.

In spite of the ways that migrant selectivity complicates comparisons between migrants and nonmigrants, demographers have found that Mexican women's fertility does decline with migration.[3] It is unlikely that this decline is merely a result of migrant selectivity—first, because Mexican women who migrate tend to be more like their peers than women in other migrant groups, and second, because migrant streams tend to become more heterogeneous over time, so if anything the migrant selectivity would decrease rather than increase. Measurable declines in migrant fertility could also be due to a temporary disruption of family formation processes while couples migrate.[4] Assuming that differences between migrants and nonmigrants are neither artifactual nor temporary, lower fertility among migrants might reflect cultural change and the assimilation by migrants of "American" ideas about contraceptive use and ideal family size, or it might be more of a question of struc-

TABLE 8.1. TOTAL FERTILITY RATES:
JALISCO AND MICHOACÁN (STATES)
AND MEXICO (NATIONAL), 1960–97

	Jalisco	Michoacán	National
1960	7.3.	7.6	7.0
1970	6.8	7.2	6.3
1980	4.9	5.3	4.3
1990	3.7	3.9	3.3
1995	3.1	3.0	2.8
1997	2.9	2.9	2.6

SOURCES: 1960–80 data: Banamex, México Social, 1996; 1990–97 data: Consejo Nacional de Población.

tural forces, with immigrant fertility falling in response to the greater opportunities for economic and educational achievement in their new homeland.[5]

It does appear that the life history informants who formed or are forming their families in the United States will have lower completed fertility than their peers in Mexico, but these women's repeated moves to Mexico and back make it hard to know who exactly to compare to whom, and the small sample size further cautions against drawing conclusions about migration and fertility decline. Furthermore, changes in migration due to the immigration reforms of the 1980s mean that younger women were more likely to migrate immediately after marriage, whereas many of their older peers lived in Mexico for years while waiting for their papers. These younger women in Atlanta seem to want fewer children than the older women who formed their families in Mexico and then moved to Atlanta, but this is likely to be the effect of generational changes in fertility goals rather than migration. Finally, comparisons are complicated because only the oldest women in the study have finished childbearing. This study, then, has little to contribute to debates about whether Mexican women's fertility declines are real or artifactual.[6] However, I do show two major changes—related both to generation and to migration—in how women understand the ideal family. First, in contrast to their mothers and most of the older informants who were eager to conceive as soon as possible after marriage, some young couples talked about delaying the first birth—a decision with im-

portant symbolic and demographic implications.[7] Second, the younger
generation imagines an ideal family about half the size of their parents';
most of them talked about wanting three to five children. These changes
relate both to the new ideal of companionate marriage and to migration
experience.

MAKING TIME FOR A COURTSHIP AFTER MARRIAGE

There is strong social pressure to have a child soon after marriage in
this transnational community. This was the area in which my own life
history (married in July 1993, still not pregnant as of July 1997) was
subject to the most intense scrutiny during the fieldwork. Once people
discovered I was married, it was open season—even for people I had
just met—to explore why a woman would be married for so long
without having a child. I was repeatedly taken aback by the way in
which Mexicans, usually so painstakingly polite in ways that Americans are not, felt free to ask questions that even my mother-in-law and
my own parents felt were none of their business.[8] My struggle to explain and justify my own behavior focused my attention on what
seems to be a relatively new idea in this community, that a newly married couple might want time to get to know each other and to learn to
get along. All seemed unconvinced by my explanation that I wanted to
finish graduate school before having a baby, but some of the younger
women responded more warmly to my explanation that my husband
and I wanted some time to enjoy being married before rushing into becoming parents.[9] I could tell that this was an idea that made sense to
many women, even to those who had had their first child ten months
after marriage, because when I framed my own experience this way
women frequently responded by telling me their own stories about delaying, or not delaying, or wanting to delay but becoming pregnant
anyway. As I slowly realized how different this was from how most of
their mothers had approached the early years of marriage, I incorporated questions about the idea of *convivencia* (being together [without
children]) early in marriage into my interview guides and casual conversations.

To understand how noteworthy it is that some women would even
consider delaying the first birth, it is important to describe the strong
pressure that there was (and, to some extent, still is) for couples to have
a first child immediately after marriage. Doña Chuyita, now in her six-

ties, remembers her anguish at still not being pregnant fifteen months after her marriage:

> No, I didn't get pregnant. I even remember that one day I was picking through the beans and I had just gotten my period, [and I said to myself] "Ay, well I have to tell him, too bad" because I had been like eight days late, and so we thought, finally.... So then I told him, "What do you think, I have my period again," and he said, "Well, maybe you're going to be barren, maybe you're not going to be able to have kids." Ay, and I felt that really hurt me, it felt really hard for him to say that to me. "So, if I am not going to have kids then you're going to leave me, no?" [And he said] "No, I wouldn't leave you, never." He said, "Look at Lucrecia who never had kids and they are together."... And then soon after that I get pregnant.

He said he would not have left her, but others told stories of men who sought out other women to fulfill their desire for children. The fear that a man whose desire for children is not satisfied by his wife will look for another woman runs through women's explanations of how many children they would like and even affects the methods that women choose.

The older life history informants said that it never occurred to them to delay the first birth—that the whole point of marriage is to have children. Mariana, living in Atlanta and at forty-eight pregnant with her ninth child, critiqued the government-sponsored family planning campaigns in her rancho by saying she did not know "why the president worries so much about us—if you get married, you know what you are headed for." Her cousin Guadalupe explained that she never thought of using a method because "I think that when you get married, that's what you're thinking about, that it's the first thing that's going to happen."

Several of the life history informants, now in their late thirties or early forties, now seem to regret having their children immediately after marrying. Lucha said, "Yes, I thought I was going to have children... because I saw that all the women who got married had their first baby right away, so I said, 'Well, I will too.' " When she was considering leaving her second husband to go back to her first, I asked her if she thought she'd have another baby with him right away, and she was emphatic that this time she would wait: "I would take precautions for about two years, yeah, because you need to enjoy at least two years." She also said that she would advise her daughters not to conceive a first child immediately after marrying.

Eva had her first child immediately after marrying, but would now advise her daughter to wait, to take some time to enjoy marriage—she

said she never had the time to enjoy her own. Claudia's first child was
born nine months after her wedding and she said she has really suffered
as a mother, raising her children alone in the rancho while her husband
works in a factory in Illinois and they wait for her green-card application to be approved. She was emphatic that once they were living together again she would not get pregnant right away: "We have not enjoyed our marriage." And when I asked Victoria if she had thought
about waiting for a bit before getting pregnant, she said no, but then
characterized her behavior as *muy mensita* (really stupid).

Those who did want to delay the first birth explained their desire in
terms of their marriage. Although Isabel got pregnant soon after her
marriage, she said that they had wanted to wait: "Well, to enjoy life at
first, like that, alone and recently married and all—supposedly we were
going to wait four years, that was always the plan, that after four years
we were going to get pregnant with the first, to enjoy ourselves and all
that." Beneath the idea of enjoying oneself as a couple lies the suggestion that there is work to be done in these first few years—that is, that
investing time in getting to know one's partner lays the foundation for
the marriage. Mercedes said that they wanted to have time to get to
know each other, and when I asked her to expand on that she said:

> It means you know if you are going to get along with your partner…that
> you have a good relationship, a stable one. Because if you get married, and
> get pregnant right away, you don't get to know each other, you don't get to
> know him as a spouse, but rather you get to know him right away as a fa-
> ther. I think you should go in stages, enjoy marriage in stages more than
> anything. So that first you say, he's a good husband, I've known him for
> three years as a spouse and he's the greatest, so then you know we can get
> along, we agree on a lot of things, we have the same opinions and
> everything. Then that's the moment to get pregnant with a child.

As with the idea that a satisfying sexual relationship is the fruit of deliberate effort, the implication here is that a marital relationship takes
conscious effort, that getting along is something that young couples
need to learn to do rather than an automatic product of work well done
and roles respectfully filled. Her comments are echoed by the concerns
of Blanca, who said to me in the months before her marriage that she
and her husband wanted to "get to know each other better, to enjoy
being a couple, because they say—and I know—that it's hard to settle in
together, and just imagine having a child right away."

Patricia recounted how she and her husband had not agreed about
delaying the first birth but how she had gotten her way:

He really wanted a baby, ever since we got married he wanted one right away, but I did not because I was working, and I said to him that I did not want kids so soon, that I wanted to enjoy—even if for only a year—my marriage. That is, just the two of us together, because having a child is a responsibility, and a worry that you have all the time and all....Well, so I held out a year and I felt really good. It's not that my daughter is an inconvenience or anything, now we are really happy with her, but it's really nice to be alone, to enjoy being a couple for a while, that's why I didn't want to have kids right away. He did want to, and I didn't, and whenever I was late he would always say to me "I hope you are."

As an anniversary present on their first wedding anniversary, Patricia gave her husband the news that she was pregnant. They courted while they were college students, and as young marrieds they both worked full time in professional jobs. Their relationship was based on clearly articulated (though not always realized) principles of equality in decision making, so they compromised and waited a bit before the first child—perhaps not as long as she would have liked, but certainly longer than her husband wanted.

Diana, in contrast, could not convince her husband of the importance of having time to *conocerse* (get to know each other) as a couple. Both from El Fuerte, they headed north soon after their marriage. Recounting their discussions about the first child, she said, "I wanted to spend some time just the two of us, and to have one later, but in the beginning I did not want to have one right away....I did tell him, but he said no, because if I took precautions then maybe later I would not be able to have one, or something like that. That was why he said it was better to have one....Yeah, and then later we could take precautions, but that we have one first." Why was Patricia able to convince her husband to wait while Diana was unable to convince hers? Neither Diana nor her husband had more than a primary-school education, and even that was from a rural primary school, in contrast to Patricia and her husband's private, college-level education. Furthermore, Patricia's husband may have felt they had more to enjoy. They were living alone as newlyweds, their combined incomes provided for meals out and day trips, and the rhythm of their life as professionals in small-town Mexico allowed ample time for the pleasures of creating the intimacy for which Patricia was arguing. Diana and her husband, in contrast, left soon after their wedding to live with family in a crowded apartment in Los Angeles. He was working six days a week as a manual laborer, and she worked as well for a time in a factory. In spite of the relatively much higher wages they were earning, costs were higher as well: they had to pay off the coyote who had smuggled them both over the border and save to buy a car, more a necessity than a luxury both in Los Angeles and Atlanta. Her arguments for prolonging the honeymoon may have rung hollow as they worked to scrape by in their new home.

For a woman who migrates with her husband but without any of her own family or the resources (English skills, driver's license, working papers) necessary to enjoy the possibilities for independence offered by life in the United States, the loneliness and boredom of being shut in a small apartment or a trailer all day alone can be intense. As one woman who got pregnant as a newlywed soon after arriving in Atlanta said, "When I got here, I was so alone, not working, not doing anything just alone, shut in,... that's why we tried right away." In addition, women who migrate this way are far more dependent on their husbands than they might be if the couple had remained in Mexico. For a migrant woman with few resources, having a child right away may appeal both as a more concrete way to formalize the marriage and as the only way a woman can feel like she is contributing productively to the establishment of their household.

Those who began trying to conceive immediately after marriage also feared that delaying a first birth could endanger one's fecundity. Diana's husband's concerns were shared by others with whom she spoke as a newlywed, who told her that the pill or Depo-Provera were too risky.[10] Concerns about contraceptive side effects, always significant, play an especially important role in shaping women's method preferences early in the marriage. Couples fear that a hormonal method such as oral contraceptives will impair fecundity, and so sometimes (as was the case with at least one of the life history informants) women get pregnant even though they had wanted to delay because they are using a less reliable method.

These worries are shared by women as well as by men. Diana's friend in Mexico, Pilar, argued to her husband that they should have a child right away: "He said to me, that why didn't we wait, that I should wait a year without having kids, so that we could get used to each other to be closer, just the two of us alone. But I said to him, 'What if I take precautions now, and then when I want them God will not give them to me? No, it's better like this [with nothing] and if God wants to give them to me, well, he should give them to us, and if not, well, too bad.'" Women and men fear that using a technological or hormonal contraceptive method could cause infertility, but they also fear that delaying a first birth is a particularly egregious violation of their promise to accept all the children that God will send them. Some spoke about wanting to know right away, as one woman put it, "if the machinery was working" but their anxiety is clearly about the metaphysical as much as the physical. It was bad enough, they suggested, to be infertile, but even worse might be the potential knowledge that it was one's own fault, caused by the selfish pursuit of personal or conjugal pleasure. As one woman whose first child was born soon after marriage and who, after fifteen years, now has seven children said, "I'd say that the first one, you shouldn't take any precautions.... You don't know if you'll be able to, so then if you are using something and then you can't, you might say that maybe it was because of what I did.... So I would say that you should have the first one when God wants to give it to you, and then later you can use something because you know you are going to be able to.... Many do use something to enjoy themselves and that's ok, but then maybe when they want one they will not be able to have one."

This widespread anxiety about infertility indicates the continued importance of having children. Some women also said that their husbands were concerned about their own fertility, so that they felt the added pressure of putting their husbands' personal fears to rest in addition to dealing with their own worries. Others who had children right away said that they had not known as young brides that it was possible to limit fertility, that they had never even thought about it, or just that they had really wanted to have a child right away. Only three of the women actually did successfully delay. Another three said that they or their husbands had wanted to, and several more said that in retrospect they wished that they had. Seventeen of the twenty-four married, fertile life history informants, by contrast, had their first child before their first wedding anniversary (see Table 8.2).

So, although the idea of having time to enjoy being together before becoming parents may be evocative for younger women, it is not something that all or even most of them are actually doing. In looking at how those who delayed are different, the strongest patterns seem to be the combined effects of generation and migration. All six of those who delayed or tried to are younger than thirty-five. They spoke strongly in favor of companionate marital ideas, although many of those who wanted to get pregnant right away did so as well. Clearly, though, the very fact that some women can articulate and justify this desire to delay a first birth is integrally related to the ideology of companionate marriage, based as it is on the idea that the deepest marital bonds are those of emotion and intimacy.

TABLE 8.2. LIFE HISTORY INFORMANTS' FERTILITY HISTORIES AND IDEALS

Age	Parity	Ideal Number of Children	Mother's Parity	Delayed First?	Interviewed In
Under 20	1	4–5	10	No	Mexico
Under 20	1	Didn't say	13	Yes	Atlanta
Under 20	Not married	3–4	12	Not Married	Mexico
20–29	1	4	3	No	Mexico
20–29	1	3–4	7	Yes	Atlanta
20–29	1	Her, 3; him, 3+	11	No, but he wanted to	Mexico
20–29	1	3	8	No, but she wanted to	Atlanta
20–29	3	No more	8	No	Atlanta
20–29	2	4–6	8	No	Atlanta
20–29	2	4	7	Yes	Atlanta
20–29	3	3	13	No, but wishes she had	Atlanta
20–29	1	4	10	No	Atlanta
20–29	2	4	6	No	Atlanta
20–29	2	4	11	No	Mexico
30–39	2	Her, 4; him, 2	6	No	Mexico
30–39	6	Her, 3; him, 6	5	No, but wishes she had	Atlanta
30–39	4	2	5	No	Mexico
30–39	7	Not clear	13	No	Mexico
30–39	3	4	7	No, but tried	Mexico
30–39	4	No more	13	No, but wishes she had	Atlanta
30–39	0	Some (infertile)	12	Not Married	Mexico
Over 40	10	No more	13	No	Mexico
Over 40	8	No more	4	No	Mexico
Over 40	8	All that God sends	8	No	Atlanta
Over 40	3	No more	11	No, but wishes she had	Atlanta
Over 40	1	Not Married	11	Not Married	Mexico

Furthermore, all three of those who delayed live in Atlanta (though Patricia was already pregnant by the time she moved there), as do four of the six women who say that either they or their husbands wish they had. Women in Atlanta may have experienced (as I did) a slackening of the intense social pressure to produce a first child, which many women feel in Mexico. Lucha's comment that she will encourage her daughters to delay a first birth, but that ultimately it would depend on what sort of men they marry suggests another possibility: that the strategy a woman chooses to build her marriage on in the early years depends not just on her individual characteristics but also on what approach she thinks will be most successful with her husband.

The childless family is still incomplete. The phrase "to have a family" (*tener familia*), which is a more common idiom among older women than among the young and educated, is still understood by all to mean having a child. Women need to provide their husbands with sons and daughters, and their parents and in-laws with grandchildren, in order to become fully adult members of the community. Children create kinship ties to in-laws and strengthen those with one's own kin; even in an era of declining fertility, babies are tangible evidence of the bonds between adults.[11] This combined model of kinship, in which people draw both on new ideas about emotional bonds and on older ideas about blood bonds, is yet more evidence of a syncretic mixing of the new and the old rather than an absolute adoption of North American ideals of the modern family.

There are other reasons not to delay the first birth. A child solidifies a woman's status as a señora; many of the women interviewed said that men treat you with more respeto once they see you with a child, and other women offer you more confianza—that is, a child, rather than marriage, is the true mark of adulthood. Furthermore, having a child legitimizes a married woman's obvious sexual experience; by bearing a child she proves that her body's power is employed in useful, socially approved ways rather than in purely selfish, even potentially destructive, ways.[12] The fact that women in Atlanta are more willing even to entertain the idea of delaying suggests that motherhood and adult personhood might not be so tightly woven together for women in Atlanta as they are for women in Mexico. These young migrant women are the same ones who prefer the risk of contraceptive side effects (including infertility) to the risk of unwanted births. Women in the United States lean more toward affective strategies for building the companionate marriage, while their sisters in Mexico seem to have adopted the focus on affective bonds without moving away from their reliance on the bonds of parenthood.

"THEY DON'T JUST LIVE ON FOOD"

> Three is more than enough.... We want them to have a little bit of what we did not—more than anything, we want them to study, and if we have a lot of kids we wouldn't be able to spend much time with them.... Imagine, if you have ten, you won't be able to give them the same things as if you have five. They say, "Where two can eat, so can three," but it's not true. They do eat, but they won't be full, they won't be satisfied.
>
> Then, you have to think, they don't just live on food. If you have ten, you won't be able to take care of them the same way as five. Just imagine, you work eight hours, and you won't even be able to spend two or three hours with them, because you get home, you have to do the housework, and they need attention too. They need your care, that you talk to them and help them progress, show them how things are—so that they do not grow up like us, with blinders on their eyes, just waiting to see what happens. So you have to make sure that they are more open-minded, that they feel that they have your help. If you need to talk with your mother and you always see her working... you are never going to go up to her and ask her, "Mom, why is it that way?" because she will say to you, "Child, I don't have time right now. The little one is dirty, I need to change him."

Many of the life history informants' mothers did manage their fertility through some combination of prolonged breast-feeding and medically indicated surgical sterilization, but they still had an average of 8.7 children surviving infancy. Their daughters, in contrast, react with horror to the idea of having anywhere near as many children as did their mothers. The difference should not be understood as the transition from a state of natural fertility to one of controlled fertility, since all of the older women tried at different points in their marriages to manage their fertility.[13] When I interviewed Mariana in 1995 she told me that she was still hoping to have another child, but was waiting until they had paid off their trailer; sure enough, when we spoke in the spring of 1998 she told me she was expecting her ninth child in June (they had taken out a three-year mortgage). Furthermore, many of these women's mothers, though claiming that they welcomed all the children that God sent them (as they had promised to do when they were married), saw no contradiction in helping shape divine will through prolonged breast-feeding or surgical sterilization.

Some explain the change in terms of the high costs of child rearing, of wanting give their children things (like shoes and education) that

Drawing 8.1. Perla's Life. Perla's drawing suggests the intertwining of fertility decline, aspirations for social mobility, and interpersonal relations based on warmth and intimacy. The first frame shows her sitting close to her husband, as their children play with toys that she and Francisco as children could not have afforded. The caption reads: "My husband and I playing with our children." The second frame shows Francisco completing their house in the imagined future. Visible in the formal living room are an overstuffed (and likely untouched) couch and a smiling family portrait, while her child is shown in the schoolhouse seated next to a teacher. The captions read: "To have my house" and "To give education to my children."

were beyond their parents' reach.[14] Even more intriguing, however, are those women who argue that the most compelling reason to limit family size is to enjoy a new model of family relations (see, for example, Drawing 8.1). These women (eleven of the eighteen who expressed a definite preference for a family of two to five) talk about wanting to have time to get to know their children as people and guide their developing personalities, without being distracted by an endless round of diapers and bottles. Some explicitly contrast the kind of time they would like to spend with their children with what their mothers could give them, while others talk about how much little children need love and attention. Others speak about making sure that they have time for their husbands—that is, remaining a couple in addition to being coparents. These women's words suggest an important dimension of fertility decline that has received scant attention from observers of such changes: the link between a desire for smaller families and the desire for different sorts of relationships among people in those families.

Younger women critiqued the Mexican proverb "*donde comen cuatro, comen cinco*" (where four eat, five can eat too), which implies that it is always possible to squeeze enough food out of the pot to feed another child. The women who focused on the expense of large families spoke about how this proverb was not true, but those women who emphasized a different kind of relationship said that it was beside the point. As Clara said, "I don't think that the material stuff is so important.... I'll give them all of the little that I have economically, but all of the love that I can, and to understand them, to have them trust me."

Five of the oldest life history informants had families much closer to the size of their mothers'. All were older than thirty-five, and either from poor families in la colonia or from the rancho. Even these women are divided, however, on the question of ideal family size. Mariana at forty-eight years speaks as a representative of the older generation:

> They say that the small family lives better, that you can give them more schooling, you can give them more of everything they want, and if you have a lot of kids you can't give them schooling, or what they need to eat, or what they want to wear, or the toys they want.... Well I think that those who have larger families, in my experience we live much better than those with small families.... I haven't lacked for anything, I haven't needed to bother anyone asking for help and all that and why is that? Because I have my large family. God has not failed me with sustenance for my children. It's a lot of work but we can do it—if I need help, I say "Child, come help me," and if I didn't have all those children who would I call to, to ask for help? I'd be alone.... For me, it's been very peaceful, very happy, my large family, and I feel really content, really proud of my house, full of voices.... Small families might have everything, but it's not for me.

Mariana told me that, after their first child was born, her husband said to her, "We have to accept all the children that God sends us, and where two or three can eat, so can many. God will help us provide for them." Others tried at certain points (unsuccessfully) to limit their family size. Norma said that her husband had always argued for accepting "all the children that the Lord sends, and I said fine, but no, later I got fed up." Although she said she had had enough after six pregnancies, she never suggested to her husband that they limit their fertility. Instead, she waited until after the seventh, when he suggested that they might do so and she agreed with him. Concha, who had a hysterectomy after her ninth child, had been trying to figure out how to stop having children since after her seventh pregnancy (sixth child). For medical reasons she could not use hormonal methods, she was never offered an IUD, and for religious reasons she did not dare consider surgical sterilization until after her last pregnancy when her doctor was emphatic that due to her weak heart she might not survive another pregnancy.

Two others wanted to stop after three, but neither did. One could not convince her husband to have fewer children, and while she managed some child spacing by taking the pill, her last three children were conceived during her husband's surprise homecomings after migratory separations. The other woman's husband supported the idea of a smaller family, and they combined coitus interruptus (CI) with breast-feeding to achieve some measure of birth spacing, but she had never quite gotten up the courage to use a more effective method. She frequently did not have enough to feed her children (the only times I ever saw all of them eat until they were full was when I brought them food), but at the same time she seemed proud of her large family. She said that at the birth of her last child the doctor asked her: "How many of your children have been wanted [*deseados*]?" and she said:

> Well, none of them.... Loved, yes, but wanted, none of them, nor planned. Once you have them you love them. They say that it is nicer when you plan them and all, but I say that even though I have not wanted them, now I really love them, as if I had planned them.... And I'd even dare have another one, or a couple...to show them that I am good for something, even if just to have kids.... Feeding them is what worries me—giving them clothes and shoes, well, they can always go around barefoot or with broken sandals, dirty or whatever, but food is the most important thing.

These older life history informants and their mothers articulate strong reasons to space children—especially the physical difficulty and economic burden of short birth intervals—but they do not see compelling reasons for having smaller families. Producing large families gives a woman the chance to show that she is "good for something." These women are proud of both the biological act of reproduction and the constant physical labor of maintaining a clean, well-dressed, well-fed, and well-mannered brood; for many of them, child rearing has been their career. If having children is the physical and social act that lies at the heart of constructing a family, then it is hard for these women to imagine a good reason to limit births, short of dire health consequences for not doing so.

The younger women concentrate more on the importance of forging and maintaining affective bonds with one's husband. They also see having children as an integral part of family building, but on a much more limited scale. Some emphasize modern children's needs; as one woman said, "Before, they did not give them everything. They did not send them to school much, and they did not have a lot of clothes [*muchos cambios*], or shoes, or toys. You want to give your kids what you did not have. So you buy them more, and can you imagine buying so much for all of them?" These women's words imply that one motivation for smaller families is the possibility of living in some way other than just barely scraping by—that is, the enticement of having something left over for pleasure or diversion. As Lucha said, she did not want any more children "because I was working, and just paying one bill after another, and there was nothing left over."

Diana makes even clearer that the idea is not just to have enough to eat but rather "so that they live well, and so we do too, so that more or less we can satisfy their whims, and if you have lots [of kids] then you can't." Diana's idea that a parent ought even to acknowledge a child's whims, much less worry about satisfying them, is a new one. It implies that children are small individuals with particular tastes and desires, as it does that one of the responsibilities of parenting is not just basic feeding and clothing but rather providing *muchos cambios* (lots of clothes) to change into and tasty things to eat—illustrated, for example, by the new practice of children's birthday parties among Degollado's elite (see Photo 8.1). Even in their discussions of the change in purely material costs of child rearing, women talk not so much about the rising cost of basic items as they do of an expanded idea of what is "basic." Their words hint at a new kind of parenting.

The women who talk explicitly about wanting time to attend to their children as individuals are even clearer about the way a certain kind of affectivity is only possible with smaller families. As Juana, mother of four, said, the goal is "to give fewer children more love" or as Isabel, mother of three, noted, "I think that with fewer, you enjoy them more." Lourdes, eager as she was as a fifteen-year-old newlywed to make sure that the machinery was working, is now just as sure that she wants to wait a good while before having the next one, and not have more than four or five altogether. She explains their preferences by talking about her in-laws: "His mother never hugged them, and his father even less, he didn't love them at all....He [her husband] says their parents never paid any attention to them."

Women in Atlanta share these ideas about the specific ways in which the smaller family lives better. As Beatriz, Lourdes's sister, said:

We grew up without a lot of things—never lacked for food or clothes, thank God, but we did miss love and attention....If you have one child there on the side, and another crawling, and a third in bed, and you are pregnant again, which of all of them are you going to pay attention to? Ultimately, to none of them, because you are trying to take care of all of

Photograph 8.1. Birthday Party. Better-off families in Degollado have adopted the American custom of celebrating
children's birthdays. Here, Diana and her younger brother
Ulysses blow out the candles at their shared birthday party.

them. When my mother was pregnant, and had one still in her arms, and
another crawling and a fourth just barely learning to walk, she would get
really anxious. Sometimes the oldest would scream, and wake up the little
one, and then it was just anger and mistreatment instead of attention and
tenderness. So I don't know, but that's why I would like my son to be two
or three, so that he could talk and take care of himself a little bit, and not
have them a year apart...that seems really hard to me.

Most of the life history informants said that the era of the man who
wanted his wife pregnant every year was long gone. The only man who
initially said that he wanted a dozen children recanted as soon as he saw
how much work it was to support and take care of even two. In some
cases, men wanted even fewer children than their wives.

Women's discussions of parenting echo the ideal of marital confianza:
I heard the same emphasis on spending time together, on open communication, and on emotional support. Women, who hoped that their husbands would also form these new kinds of confianza relationships with
their children, said a father's job is the same as a mother's: to create relationships based on love and understanding. As Esperanza noted, "It
should be the same, so that they have a lot of trust for both of them. I
wouldn't like to feel as if they love me more, as if they have more trust in

me—I'd like them to trust us both the same, to talk to us both the same."
(Younger women hope that their husbands will have the same kind of
warm, close relationship with their children as they do, but women do
not expect their husbands to share equally in the gendered work of child
rearing. Most of them took for granted that they would be primarily responsible for the daily minutiae of caring for their children. When their
husbands contributed by helping, they viewed it as just that—help.)

Finally, women talk about having fewer children than their mothers
did so that they will have time to continue with what Eva referred to as
"*un noviazgo después de ser casados*" (a courtship after marriage).
These modern marriages need constant maintenance in order to succeed. Esperanza, who at the time of the interview was trying to get pregnant with their first child, talked about her fears that after having a
child their marriage might change: "I wouldn't like to stop paying attention to my husband because of my child. I'd like to be able to divide
things well, make time for my child without neglecting him. . . . It would
be really bad to ignore him, to leave him alone because all day the child
needs one thing or another, and to neglect my relationship as his
spouse." The idea that a child could get in the way of a married couple's
relationship—or even that a man or woman might feel jealous of the attention a spouse pays to the children—is only conceivable within this
new paradigm of companionate marriage.

Several women mentioned wanting three or four, or four or five,
rather than specifying an exact number. Their goal is to have a family
that is small enough to facilitate their marital and social mobility goals,
but also large enough to meet other important criteria. Blanca, whose
mother had seven and who even before marriage agreed with her husband that they should not have more than three or four, explained to me
that one needs to balance between the fact that "it's really hard to be a
parent" and the appeal of a large family, "that when they are older they
all get together, they talk and joke, they enjoy being together, you go out
and it is a nice family, not just with only two, or even one." Others,
however, talked about how even smaller families of three or four children could provide a satisfying kind of convivencia (being together). Esperanza, who proudly showed me her baby daughter when I returned to
visit Degollado in January 1998, said that three or four "is enough to
complete a family, to enjoy being together, to go on excursions." Rosa,
whose second daughter was born in 1997, said that she thinks that four
children is "a complete family; with that many I will know what it's like

to be a mother, and they will know what it's like to have siblings, and then grandchildren will come along and all that, that would be good enough to build a family."

The importance of having enough children is not just to provide them with the pleasure of being together; women also talked about how children without siblings are more likely to be *egoísta* (selfish). Siblings keep each other from being lonely, but they also force each other to learn to share. As Beatriz said, "It's the same, one more or one less. However, if you wish for four and you get eight, well, where four eat, four more are not going to fit, right?" The exact number women end up with depends on compromising with a spouse, on the sex of the existing children, and, of course, on the efficacy of whatever method of fertility regulation they are using since none of these women say they would consider terminating an unplanned pregnancy.[15]

Generational differences were evident even in how women frame the value of child spacing. A number of the life history informants' mothers mentioned that they had used breast-feeding to space their births, though not everyone achieved the same level of success with this method. All of them were acutely aware of the intervals: when I asked them if their children were *seguiditos* (right after one another), they could immediately recall their fertility histories. Diana's mother, Catalina, recounted to me "it went ok for me" when she breast-fed, because "all of them were like that, two years apart." Another one said that try as she might, "*no me valía*" (it didn't work for me), and so none of her birth intervals were as long as two years. The older women talked primarily about the physical hardship of closely spaced births, while the younger women focused more on not being able to meet a child's emotional needs and on missing out on the pleasure of each baby. As Pilar said, the bad thing about having children who are "right after each other" is that "you do not enjoy the little child, you have to neglect him to take care of the other one.... What I want is to give all my time to the child, like that, to take better care of him." Younger women discussed ideal birth spacing in terms of the relationships between parents and children, as well as between siblings. They wanted siblings to be far apart enough in age to take care of each one well, but close enough in age so that they could be companions for each other.

Both older and younger women mentioned wanting to stretch out the years they have children at home so as to avoid being left *sola* (alone).[16] Stretching them out became even more important when there were fewer

Drawing 8.2. "When We Are Old." In this drawing, a married woman in Degollado imagines herself in the future, after her children are grown. The caption reads "Tratando de ser un ejemplo para nuestra familia cuando este grande y ocupen de nosotros" (Trying to be an example for our family when I am old and they need us). Clearly, her hope is that their marital companionship will sustain them through the years after their children are gone.

altogether. Regardless of their age, women always referred to having their last child marry as the moment when they are left alone, when they have no one in the house (they say, "ya no tengo nadie en la casa"). No matter how many you have, they say, in the end you are alone. That even younger women say this indicates that in spite of all the emphasis on conjugal intimacy and companionship, children still provide women with an intensely satisfying and deeply important kind of relationship, one without which they feel quite literally alone. The sadness that the Mexican parents in this community expressed at watching their children grow up seems quite distinct from the bittersweet mixture of joy and wistfulness that many North American parents seem to feel at a child's passage through time. Drawing 8.2 illustrates one woman's hope for peaceful companionship with her husband after their children are grown.[17]

Concerns about the number and spacing of children among younger women direct our attention to the ways in which the family is the crucible for the culturally constructed individual. Women imply that there are specific lessons about personhood that they want to teach their children (such as the pleasure of being with others and the value of sharing and companionship within the family), which reflect broader Mexican cultural ideals about human relations. The implicit contrast here is to my own frame of reference as a native North American; when my peers talk about child spacing, for example, they are much likelier to talk about wanting birth intervals that minimize the psychological trauma to the older child and lessen sibling rivalry. These sorts of differences underline the way in which an equivalent demographic outcome—for example, the two- or three-child family—could be the result of broadly variable motivations.

"IN THIS COUNTRY, TO HAVE FOUR IS LIKE HAVING A LOT"

It is complicated, for a number of reasons, to compare the fertility of the life history informants in Atlanta with women's fertility in Mexico. First of all, given the levels of movement between the Mexican and U.S. field sites, any moment chosen to make the comparison is somewhat arbitrary. Since the formal end of fieldwork for this study, two of the life history informants in Atlanta have made supposedly permanent moves to Mexico, only to return within several months. Two of those interviewed in Mexico subsequently made what seem likely to be permanent moves north to join their husbands. Two other women who left Atlanta in December 1997 had yet to return as of April 1998, and it was not clear what their plans were. Several others had, over the course of their marriage, moved back and forth several times, so some of their children were born in Mexico and others in the United States, or else they were conceived in Mexico but born in the United States. Just as the women themselves will not stand still to be counted, neither will their fertility; continued contact with the life history informants after the formal end of fieldwork means that I know that a number of babies have been born or conceived since I first filled in a matrix of demographic characteristics of the informants. At this microlevel of analysis, the variety of women's experiences is so striking that patterns are all but unobservable; it becomes hard to see the forest for the trees.

The question of selection bias, which usually bedevils studies of migration and fertility, is less of a problem due to the matched samples. Each woman either comes from the same natal family as her match or else one that is quite similar. The two samples, therefore, grew up with approximately the same kinds of resources and opportunities, and with the exception of one pair all of the women are within a year or two of their match in terms of years of completed schooling. They are more or less similar in age: six of the life history informants in Mexico are older than their matches in Mexico, while five are younger and two are the same age. Comparing the women solely on the basis of current residence when interviewed, the group in Atlanta had an average parity that was a bit lower than the group in Mexico: 2.7 compared to 3.2. Five women in the Mexican field sites had more children than their matches in Atlanta, while two had fewer and the rest had the same number. Comparing the groups on the basis of where women lived at the time they were interviewed but leaving out Susana and Soledad (who were not married) and Guadalupe (who was infertile), the women in Atlanta had an average of 3.0 children each, while those in Mexico had an average of 3.7.

Looking at fertility in terms of where families were formed gives a different result: those who formed their families entirely in the United States have an average parity of 2.3, while those who formed them going back and forth had an average of 3.8 and those who did so entirely in Mexico had an average of 4.0 children each. However, given that changing immigration patterns mean that the younger women (who are likelier anyway to have lower fertility because of generational changes in ideals) are precisely those who are also more likely to have migrated with their husbands, the fertility differentials that appear when women are separated into groups by migration experience are more likely a product of generation than of migration per se. Although the average parity of the thirteen life history informants interviewed in Atlanta is only a bit lower than that of those in the sending communities (2.7 compared to 3.2), the two women who stand out in the Atlanta group are Mariana and Eva. Mariana, who is in her late forties and just recently moved to Atlanta with her children after receiving their legal residence papers, is pregnant with her ninth child. Eva, in her midthirties with six children, has split the eighteen years since her marriage shuttling back and forth between Degollado and the Salinas Valley. When Mariana and Eva are removed from the Atlanta group, the average fertility drops to 1.9.

While the preceding discussion suggests that Mexican women in Atlanta may have somewhat lower fertility than their Mexican peers, a study with this sample size cannot generate generalizable data on fertility differences—nor was that my goal. Furthermore, whatever change there might be is slight compared to the much more significant generational change in women's actual and desired fertility. My focus, though, was on the social context of reproduction, and the fieldwork did point to a number of immediate economic and more long-term social influences that shape fertility preferences. In Atlanta, for example, paid labor outside the home is much less easily integrated with the work of child rearing. Women in Atlanta cannot bring their children to work with them, as they often can in Mexico, and child care can be an enormous expense. In Degollado and El Fuerte child care is much less of an issue; some women who work, like Isabel, can bring their children to play while they mind the store, while others can have older children or a relative watch the younger ones. It is also, as several women noted, more expensive to raise children in the United States than in Mexico; not only must one provide the same basics of food and clothing as in Mexico, but also children are likely to develop more expensive "whims," such as Nintendo games and rollerblades.

Social pressures for higher fertility in Mexico and lower fertility in the United States also come into play. In Mexico, the pressure to have a first child is more acute. Women are also aware that fertility norms in the United States are different. Patricia, for example, said that while she would like to have four children, she will wait and see how it feels to have two or three, "because sometimes they say that four is a lot—in this country, to have four children is like having a lot." It is possible, then, that women who migrate have fewer children not just to help ensure their children's upward mobility but for their own.

In summary, there is a marked cohort difference in desired fertility, which suggests a reevaluation of how people are constructing families: they are having fewer children, and at least considering having them later, in order to create solid ties based on a new kind of confianza relationship with their husbands and children. Women who migrate are perhaps a bit bolder in adopting these new strategies than their sisters. The few who actually delay a first birth rather than just talk about it are migrants, and migrants also seem to have lower fertility.

Cultural Logics of Contraceptive Choice

B: Well, they can also take care of you.

J: How is that, that they take care of you?

B: That is, I heard about it from a friend. Really nice—we were talking
about how to take care of yourself, and she says to me: "No, he
takes care of me," and...I said, "What do you mean, he takes care
of you?" She said, "If we have sex, he feels when it is the moment
when the sperm are going out, and instead of giving them to me, [he
comes] outside...[and] if you do it that way, you are not the only
one worrying about it, he is also worrying about it. He needs to be
attentive and alert." And it seems really nice to me, the idea that he
would care about it too, and not just me.

Differences between older and younger women's fertility control
strategies reflect the generational change in ideal family size. Older
women breast-fed for birth spacing, and some eventually had surgical
sterilization; their daughters are much more likely to use a technological
method and to think about limiting their family size after three or four
births as opposed to after ten or twelve. Table 8.3, which summarizes life
history informants' fertility control histories, reveals three patterns that
merit analysis. First, women interviewed in Atlanta share with their sisters in Mexico these modern ideas about the role of sexuality in marriage,
but the different social setting—and especially differences in their relationships with the Catholic Church—facilitates their use of technological
methods. (The term "technological method" is used here to include all of
what are usually called "modern methods," in contrast to "traditional"
methods. I choose not to use the modern/traditional dichotomy in the
sense that it is usually used because methods that are usually lumped together as "traditional" in fact differ in important ways in terms of how
women use them in pursuit of modern relationships.) Second, couples
who use either withdrawal or rhythm for fertility regulation are using
these "traditional" methods to build a modern marriage—that is, one
that emphasizes pleasurable conjugal sexuality as a route to a stronger relationship. Third, some traditional methods are more modern than others; women distinguish between different ways that their husbands take
care of them, and they are quite aware of the different implications of
rhythm and withdrawal for the actual experience of having sex.

"It's Not Secure, It's Risky":
Migration-Related Differences in Method Preference

Women interviewed in Atlanta were much more likely to be using technological methods.[18] Several women in the Mexican field sites tried
technological methods for birth spacing, but only one of the informants

TABLE 8.3. METHOD EXPERIENCE AND PREFERENCES AMONG LIFE HISTORY INFORMANTS

	Women in Atlanta			Women in Degollado/El Fuerte	
ID No.	Current Use	Other Methods Tried	ID No.	Current Use	Other Methods Tried
1	Rhythm	Condoms (–)[a]	1A	Pregnant, not currently using	None
2	IUD (+)[b]	Pills	2A	Surgical sterilization	Breast-feeding
3	Pills (+)	IUD	3A	CI (–)	Pills (–)
4	CI and rhythm or condoms (–)	Pills	4A	CI and rhythm (–)	None
5	Pills	Condoms (–), depo (–)	5A	Pregnant, not currently using	Pills (–), CI (+)
6	CI (all month) (–)	None	6A	CI and rhythm (+)	None
7	Pills	Foam, condoms (–), CI (–)	7A	Surgical sterilization	IUD (+), Depo (–), Rhythm (–), Pills (–)
8	Never pregnant	None	8A	Not married	Not Married
9	Surgical sterilization	CI (–), rhythm and billings, pills (–) and foam (+), depo (+), condom (–)	9A	Not married	Not Married
10	Depo (+)	Rhythm, pills (–)	10A	Rhythm (–)	None
11	Pills	None	11A	Trying to conceive, not currently using	Rhythm (–), pills (–)
12	Rhythm (+)	None	12A	CI (–)	Breast-feeding, migrant separation
13	Rhythm and condoms	None	13A	CI (–)	Condoms (–)

[a] A minus (–) indicates that the woman said she and her husband did not like the method.

[b] A plus (+) indicates that the woman said she and her husband liked the method.

used such a method for any length of time. In contrast, seven of the twelve fertile women interviewed in Atlanta have used either pills, Depo, or the IUD, and six of the twelve were using them currently.

The greater reliance of Mexican women in Atlanta on technological methods for child spacing cannot be explained by saying they find the methods less risky. Most of the life history informants, whether in the Mexican field sites or in Atlanta, believed that technological methods of fertility regulation are extremely dangerous. Women mentioned the possibility that an IUD will become stuck in a fetus' forehead (*encarnada*), thus causing the child to be born bearing the mark of his or her mother's recklessness in a way that cannot be hidden.[19] Oral contraceptive pills, women said, cause the uterus to "rot" (*pudrir*), or to become permanently incapable of accepting sperm; intriguingly, many women said that Mexican physicians had been the ones to tell them about the dangers of the pill.[20] Condoms break, women say, and Depo-Provera causes weight gain and uncomfortably long, irregular menstrual periods.

The women in Atlanta did not deny the dangers of using technological methods, but they focused on the dangers of the ones they were not using or had not tried: women who liked the pill spoke about how sick they got when they tried Depo, and those who had been happy with an IUD were emphatic about the dangers of the pill. Furthermore, they referred to another risk, less frequently mentioned by their sisters in Mexico: the risk of a mistimed pregnancy. As one woman in Atlanta, who went on the pill before her wedding, said: "Pills give me a bad feeling... imagine that they made me feel bad, or that they affected me, ... that I got thinner or fatter, like the experiences that I have seen. The nun told us that we should use the natural method, Billings. I was looking into it and she gave us a pamphlet that I was studying, and it seems to me like the most appropriate, the best method, but it's not secure, it's risky, and I'm not like that... [I don't menstruate] every thirty days, my cycle can get shorter, I don't know how to regulate it." Women in Atlanta also worry about contraceptive side effects, but they weigh those fears against the newly perceived risk of exercising less-than-perfect control over pregnancy timing.

Participant observation ruled out the greater accessibility of technological methods in Atlanta as a reason for these migration-related differences. As with all health care, women have better access to reproductive health care in Mexico than they do in the United States.[21] In Atlanta a woman who wants to take the pill or get a shot of Depo needs to find out where reproductive health services are offered, make an appointment (in English), have money to pay for the office visit, bring a translator in case one is not offered, arrange for transportation to the clinic, and then brave a Pap smear in order to get six months' to a year's worth of pills. If she wants to use Depo, she needs to do this every three months. In Degollado, in contrast, hormonal methods are available over the counter; no office visit, translator, Pap smear, or transportation is required. In El Fuerte access is even easier; local family planning campaigns targeting rural women send health promoters door to door, offering oral contraceptive pills.[22] Even IUDs are easier to get in the sending communities, where women do not face the barriers of language and transportation. Women in the Mexican field sites are not choosing to have their husbands take care of them because of problems with access to modern methods.

One key social-context related difference is in the way the Catholic Church regulates sexuality and reproduction (both directly and indirectly) in Mexico. On a daily basis the Catholic Church permeates the rhythms of daily life in the Mexican field sites in a way that it does not in the United States. Sundays in rural Mexico are organized around religious observance: all excitement clusters in the plaza and the public spaces just outside the church, and most families plan their Sunday leisure activities around attending Mass. Both sacred and secular time are marked by the tolling of church bells (which mark the hour by quarters and ring in a special pattern to announce the beginning of Mass, the moment when the wafer and wine are consecrated, or news of a death).

Although some Mexican women in Atlanta continue to rely on the church for spiritual and social support, Sundays in Atlanta are nothing like Sundays in Mexico. For many women, it is the only day of the week that they and their husbands do not work from dawn to dusk. In Atlanta, Sunday is the day for weekly food shopping and the chance for a meal in a restaurant, rather than for Mass followed by tacos in the plaza. Women who are not especially religious may have gone to church anyway in Mexico, even if all they did was to look around to see who had new shoes, but in Atlanta there are ample other choices for entertainment. Furthermore, as Lucha said, ruminating about the effect of the relative luxury in which many migrants in Atlanta live, "here we do not lack for anything, and so we forget about God, and there [in Mexico], with everyone the way they are, so poor and everything, that's why they remember God."

Not attending church regularly means forgoing the weekly reminder of having to sit while others stand to take communion, perhaps the moment when women feel their transgression most acutely—and at least some of those women who do attend Mass in the United States continue to take communion even if they are using a technological method. In Degollado and El Fuerte, in contrast, women using a technological method of contraception (or men whose wives are doing so) are prohibited from taking communion. The only life history informant in the Mexican field sites who had used a technological method had to discontinue because she and her husband had been invited to be godparents; although the priest instructed them in the rhythm method, she got pregnant almost immediately after having her IUD removed.

Women in Atlanta also have more privacy. This may be the only way in which technological methods are more accessible in Atlanta: most service providers in the local clinics and pharmacists do not speak Spanish, much less know women's families, so if a woman does decide she wants to use a technological method it is much less likely that her neighbors would necessarily need to know about it.[23] Although some asserted that who takes communion and who does not in Mexico is private, at least one woman admitted that who sits and who stands does not escape the notice of others: "There are some who don't tell anyone [they are using a technological method] and they take communion. So you say, 'Look, she is using something and still taking communion.'" Others have discussed how a more diffuse community gives migrants the sense that it is possible to try out things they might not have done in Mexico.[24] This could certainly be the case with technological methods of contraception as well.

Women in Atlanta regard both their bodies and their potential fertility more as their own private property and less as something held in joint ownership with their husbands. Women were asked whether they would use a contraceptive method to which their husbands objected and whether they would use a method secretly in case of a disagreement. Some said it should be up to the husband, others posited an ideal of joint decision making, and still others said that although mutual agreement would be ideal, they would use a method in secret rather than having more children than they wanted. A few said that women should decide because they bear the physical hardship of pregnancy and childbirth and do most of the work of raising the children.

The group who said that it absolutely must be a joint decision was split between the Mexican and U.S. field sites, but all who said it should be the man's choice alone were in Mexico, while most of those (nine out of twelve) who said that if push came to shove they would use a method in secret were in Atlanta. It is impossible, of course, to use either of the nontechnological methods in secret, while it is eminently possible to use Depo, the IUD, or even the pill without a man's knowledge, so it is not surprising that the same group who had tried these methods could imagine using them. However, this points to something much deeper than just whether a woman would dare use a method that she considers both a sin and potentially hazardous to her health: it suggests that Mexican women in the United States may be reimagining their bodies and their fertility as individual property, rather than looking at them as a conjugal resource.

"Like That, . . . You Are Not Fighting with Him": Using Traditional Methods to Build a Modern Marriage

Women who use nontechnological methods like the way that they emphasize that fertility regulation is a joint decision. The word that women use most commonly to talk about all contracepting is *cuidar* (to take care of). Women use the phrase *él me cuida,* he takes care of me, to refer to both coitus interruptus and rhythm, and their explanations of their method choice suggest that they are referring both narrowly to their joint commitment to regulating fertility and more broadly to the idea that they are being taken care of by their husbands.[25] Although most of the women who were currently using either rhythm or withdrawal were in Mexico, seventeen of the twenty-three fertile married women have tried being taken care of by their husbands, and so here I explore the broad appeal of these methods to a group of women so committed to demonstrating their marital modernity.

Women gave three reasons for preferring to be taken care of by their husbands. First, women in Atlanta and the Mexican field sites who preferred nontechnological methods often referred to their lack of side effects. Women whose husbands forbid them to use a technological method because of the danger seemed to experience their husbands' preference as a gesture of caring and protectiveness, as almost a tender shepherding of their shared resources.[26] Given that women who used technological methods also referred to their side effects, it seems curious that for some women these physical risks would seem compelling while others would not find them to be so. One possibility is that risk must be socially contextualized, that it is not possible to understand how women's perception of risk—a cultural factor—relates to their behavior without knowing more about the relative value of fertility in that particular social context.

That women in the United States value the individual control and possibilities for sticking more closely to a specific number, while their sisters in Mexico emphasize the importance of sharing fertility control decisions with their husbands, suggests that fertility has a slightly different value for women in the Mexican field sites than it does in Atlanta. In the Mexican field sites, women are less worried about controlling their fertility than they are about impairing it; it is a precious resource. In Atlanta, women have resources other than fertility, and it is less clear that fertility is as much of a resource as it would be in Mexico: they are isolated from their extended families and (at least some of them) are trying to coordinate full-time work in the formal sector with child care and other domestic responsibilities.

Second, women want to use a method that is not a mortal sin. All of the women—both those who use or have used nontechnological methods and those who rely on the pill, the IUD, Depo, or condoms—acknowledge the moral superiority of using a method that is not prohibited by their religion. All of the women learned about basic church doctrine in Mexico, and all of them (including the one who married in Atlanta) had been instructed in nontechnological methods and believed that these were the only methods approved by the church.[27] Part of the risk of using a technological method is that a woman might provoke divine wrath by showing the hubris of trying to take total control over her fertility. In other words, women see the possibility of side effects in moral as well as physiological terms; any physical discomfort or consequent infertility that might be thought to occur as a result of using a prohibited method could very well be read as divine punishment. The risk of an unplanned pregnancy—which women know is inherent in using CI or rhythm—seems to give them a modicum of comfort with the idea that they are trying at all to prevent a pregnancy. (This fear of invoking divine wrath is particularly acute before the first birth: of all the women in the study, including those women in Atlanta who eventually became enthusiastic users of technological methods, only one dared use a technological method before her first birth. All the others waited until they had proven their fertility through a first birth—and, perhaps, appeased the divine by becoming mothers in addition to wives.) The inefficiency of their chosen method means that they are not going back altogether on their promise to accept all the children that God sends, only making it a little more difficult to receive them. The technical failure rate of these methods, in other words, contributes to their appeal.[28]

Third, women talk about the value of being taken care of by one's husband in terms of the companionate marriage. Women say that these methods resonate with the way sexuality has been redefined as a crucial part of the conjugal bond. When a woman's husband "takes care of her," she experiences in an intensely physical way her husband's commitment to developing a shared, nonreproductive sexuality. Since these methods depend for their success on cooperation and communication, there is also no implication that a woman might be leaving her husband unsatisfied by not giving him another child. Beyond the health and moral risk of a technological method, then, one might also note a kind of marital risk—that is, the risk that women who are socially and economically dependent on their husbands feel they would be taking by claiming fertility as an individual, as opposed to a jointly held, domain. As one woman said, she likes having her husband take care of her (cuidarla) because "like that,...he does not say to you, 'why don't you want any more kids?' You are not fighting with him." These methods make fertility regulation a shared project, the embodiment of a joint commitment to building a certain kind of family and a certain kind of marriage. The physical restraint of desire becomes a private performance of a shared goal—the goal of having a different kind of marriage and a more modern kind of family.[29]

"Who Would Want to Miss the Best Part?"
Rhythm versus Withdrawal

Women refer to rhythm and withdrawal the same way—as being taken care of—but of the eleven using nontechnological methods, four strongly preferred CI, while seven favored rhythm. Among the women who prefer rhythm, most abstain completely during the fertile days in the middle of their menstrual cycle, while a few of the couples use CI or condoms during that time. Those who favor rhythm say that sex with condoms or withdrawal is not as satisfying as without using anything, but they also say that it is better than nothing and is what makes using rhythm possible at all. As one woman said, neither she nor her husband could hold out for this additional week: "How could I stand it?" (¿cómo me voy a aguantar?), she asked, laughing.

Using withdrawal means a woman never has to say no to her husband; in contrast, those who use rhythm organize their sexual intimacy around a shared ability to restrain desire. This latter choice implies quite a different vision of men's and women's sexual needs and abilities to control themselves—that is, that for somewhere between one and two out of every four weeks, they will be able to dominate their sexual urges (some couples abstained for up to six days on either side of the estimated day of ovulation, while others only did for three days). For all of them this was in addition to the other monthly period of abstinence during menstruation.

Those who prefer rhythm place a premium on the quality of sex, on the idea that both partners must be physically satisfied, rather than on the frequency of sex. As one said, "Once a drop or two has come out of him, who would want to miss the best part?" (*Ya con un chorrito que se le sale, ¿quién va a querer perderse lo mejor?*). As another said, "Look, talking frankly, I don't like withdrawal, because you end up halfway there [*se queda uno a medias*], and they can maybe come but what about you?" Others talked more about their husbands' dissatisfaction with the method, or said that men would not have the self-control: "Do you think that right then, in the middle of things, that they'll pull out? Well, no—what's the whole point?"[30]

"Life Is Not All about Pleasure"

Those who preferred withdrawal agreed that neither men nor women experienced the same degree of sexual satisfaction as when the man ejaculates inside the woman's vagina—nor did they even argue very strongly for the method's efficacy. As one woman said, "These ways that he takes care of me, we've been doing it since the first, and now I have seven, and if he keeps taking care of me like that I'll end up with twelve....I think it's hard for them, because it's the time when they are most excited,...so sometimes they slip up....It's just when it feels the best for them, and even for you." Those using withdrawal, however, spoke proudly of the sacrifice their husbands were making on their behalf. In the words of one woman: "They say that they do not enjoy it as much as with nothing—so then let them not enjoy it. Supposedly they do not feel the same...but let them take care of it." Another said that although she would use pills or Depo if he preferred not to take care of her, she liked feeling that he put her welfare before his own pleasure: "I feel that he is very responsible....Many men do not want to take precautions this way because they do not get the same satisfaction or something, and well, you don't either, but life is not all about pleasure" (*pero no toda la vida es gozar*). Women in this community talked about how pain in childbirth forges a love between mother and child that can never be broken. Here, similarly, they spoke about the way a physical experience shapes emotion: "And I say to him, well, I suffered a bit more [in the birth], and he says, 'you're right'...and like that, he suffers too." Women who like withdrawal experience their husbands' ability to keep fertility control goals foremost in their minds in a moment of intense temptation as an act of love and caring. Women's discussions of their husbands' sacrifices, though, might just be an attempt to put a positive spin on men's unwillingness to restrain themselves: one of the women who uses withdrawal, in fact, said that the reason they did not use rhythm is that she does not trust her husband's willingness to cooperate by following her calendar.[31]

So what do we know about social differences among these couples that might explain differences in the way that they choose to act out this ideology of love, sex, and marriage? Compared to those women who liked rhythm, the four who preferred withdrawal had marriages that were much more focused on respeto and less on confianza. They said that this method was their husbands' choice, and this deference to men's decision making was emblematic of their generally more hierarchical marital style. Three of them said they had been forced to have sex, and it was not at all clear that any of them really enjoyed the sexual relationship. Their discussion of withdrawal draws on *some* of the ideas in the discourse of companionate marriage, such as the value of nonprocreative sexuality to strengthen the marital tie, but for them ultimately it seems that sexual satisfaction is just one more of the services a dutiful wife must provide her husband.

Those women who were using or had used rhythm, in contrast, were fully engaged in building companionate—even somewhat more egalitarian—relationships with their husbands. They spoke about the importance of their own pleasure, both in explaining their preference for rhythm over withdrawal and in describing the difficulty of enduring abstinence. Generally, they were more likely than users of withdrawal to speak their minds and to have husbands who would listen. Coitus interruptus, which allows men constant sexual access to their wives while complicating mutual sexual satisfaction, is much more traditional. Rhythm, which teaches men and women to force their bodies to wait for sex but then values pleasure over self-control during actual intercourse, is a "traditional" way of expressing consummately modern ideas about sexuality and marriage.

All of these younger women, regardless of their method choice, talk about the importance of sexual and emotional intimacy in marriage, and they all interpret their contraceptive choices within this discourse of marriage, pleasure, and intimacy. However, social context—especially the role of the Mexican Catholic Church in regulating sexuality and reproduction and the increased privacy and autonomy that characterize migrant women's lives—leads some women to express their desire for a companionate marriage and modern sexual intimacy trying to delay the first birth, using a technological method, and understanding their reproductive potential as subject to their own individual will. By contrast, the comparison group in Mexico seemed less committed to a firm separation of sexual intimacy from reproduction and more invested in emphasizing the shared control of fertility. Both of these approaches to building a marriage and a family fit squarely within the discourse of the Mexican companionate marriage, but at the same time they show how women highlight those aspects of the discourse most useful to them, given their circumstances and resources.

CHAPTER 9

Conclusions

MIGRATION

The changes in the lives of Mexican men and women who migrate highlight the importance of exploring how social and economic context may affect communities of people who are culturally similar but who live in different places. Specifically, differences between the two communities in the spatial organization of social life, in women's economic opportunities, in the role of the Catholic Church in organizing and regulating daily life, and in perceived legal protections against family violence facilitate independence for some migrant women.

A finding that merits further investigation is the way in which men and women in the three field sites talked about migration and domestic violence. As others have noted in passing, migrants from many countries share the idea that divorce, disobedience, and disintegration are prevalent in the United States because children learn to dial 911 and women learn about temporary restraining orders.[1] Amuchástegui, drawing on the work of Stuart Hall, discusses that a key feature of modern states is that they regulate individual behavior directly, as opposed to through families or other institutions. A man is not king of his domain in the United States, because the state, local, and federal laws see each member of the family as having his or her own set of individual rights and responsibilities. As Amuchástegui writes:

Another characteristic of post-industrial societies which is just beginning to spread through various sectors of Mexican society is the direct participation of the state in people's lives, especially in what were at one time private spheres—such as sexual activity or family relationships—which encourages a sense of individualism and free will at the same time as it favors the defense of vulnerable populations, such as women and children. Instead of a face-to-face relationship between the individual and the state, diverse Mexican cultures generally place great importance on belonging to families and groups, so that the intervention of public agencies is frequently mediated by collective structures which, although not organized for the purpose of taking care of the citizenry, may soften the effects of policies.[2]

Amuchástegui's argument suggests that the relationship between modern states and the development of autonomous individuals is not an unmitigated good. On the one hand, as Mexican migrants are wont to point out, it may be that women feel more protected from domestic violence under these modern regimes. On the other hand, Mexican families may have been organized better to shelter their children from economic shocks than those north of the border.[3]

The fact that migrants to the United States from so many other locations have made similar observations about domestic violence, though, suggests that it may be worth exploring the effects of an imagined America on the processes of migrant settlement—and even more broadly on meaning making throughout this transnational community. It was clear to me in Degollado, for example, that men's comments about domestic violence were spoken in dialogue with the implied difference in its acceptability in the United States. Migrants' persistent emphasis on domestic violence laws speaks to the intertwining of gender and citizenship. Men may perceive that migration limits their domestic power, but women also complain about how migration limits their power to control their children, suggesting that the imagined relationship between individuals and the government—or, put differently, people's perceptions about modern citizenship—may be one of several cultural factors that affects migrants' experiences of settlement.

My work also suggests that there cannot be a single answer to the question of how migration shapes gender: in general migration may expand women's economic opportunities, but there are still significant forms of social stratification within the immigrant community. María, for example, earned more than her husband and was the driving force behind both their recent purchase of a house in the middle-class suburb of Norcross and their opening a restaurant of their own. Clara, by contrast, spoke almost no English and, with three children younger than age five, almost never left her ramshackle trailer unless accompanied by her husband. The idea that women automatically benefit from migration draws on the assumption that they are moving from a society rigidly controlled by tradition and machismo to one of unlimited economic opportunity and gender equality. Some women prosper in Atlanta, while others do not, and the reasons for women's assorted successes and failures lie as much in women's individual courage to risk getting on a bus alone without being absolutely sure of the final destination as they do in the material resources they bring with them (kin, papers, work experience).

Rebhun found that her informants in northeastern Brazil "speak as if each city generates its own figurative temporal wheel, forming the proudly modern center of a circle that grows more old-fashioned the further out you travel from it."[4] Mexicans in these transnational communities clearly also imagine that spatial wheel, seeing their rural homes as inherently less modern, and they express their yearnings for modernity through mastery of a gendered idiom. But in critiquing the way that feminist researchers have explored the effect of gender and migration, I am in effect saying that it is us, too, and not just our informants, whose understandings about the world draw unexamined assumptions about how some places are inherently more modern than others.

Any examination of how locations differ must be grounded in history, in the way the sending community itself is changing. Women from Degollado and El Fuerte who live in Atlanta have somewhat more latitude to negotiate for a certain kind of marriage than do their sisters or sisters-in-law still living in Mexico, but if we were only to look at the migration-related differences, we would miss the ways in which women's marital goals in both these locations have changed. My focus on location, furthermore, includes recognizing the importance of receiving location: one of the big stories from the U.S. 2000 census was the diversification of migrant-receiving communities. As small towns and large cities across the United States see growing concentrations of Mexican immigrants, social scientists may be called to question what we have learned about the settlement processes of immigrant families; ideas about what factors facilitate or constrain economic and social integration may depend as much on the specific social context and moment in the economic cycle at which the data were collected as they do on the values and social organization of any particular immigrant community. Therefore, the diversification of immigrant-receiving locations provides us with new opportunities to test—and to complicate—our ideas about the immigrant experience in America. María and her sisters have already moved to the suburbs and purchased their own homes, several men from Degollado have become quite successful as subcontractors in the Sheetrocking business, and men from El Fuerte have benefited from the Georgia Department of Transportation's seemingly never-ending commitment (and bountifully deep pockets) for building new roads and improving old ones—none of which would likely be possible without Atlanta's peculiar mix of economic strength, geographic dispersion, and weak commitment to public transportation.

IMPLICATIONS FOR SEXUALITY RESEARCH

Making the Familiar Strange: Examining Heterosexuality

The very idea that women in some far corner of the globe might be stigmatized because they trade sex for money implies that there are other, more proper valuables for which sex might be traded (like love). Here I have explored how people experience and put into motion this idea that sex is the currency of love. A vast body of research has explored the meaning, social context, and historical determinants of men's sexual relationships with other men.[5] This work on men has directed us to think about the strategic and situational nature of sexual identity, how sexual behavior maps onto social space, the ways in which sexual relationships can simultaneously inscribe and transgress power relations, and the links between urbanization, industrialization, and the development of sexual identities and communities. Since the mid-1980s, feminist scholars and social historians have mined similar themes.[6]

Curiously, though, this rich body of theory has not for the most part been applied to anthropological or public-health analysis of heterosexual behavior, which is not only a hegemonic structure but also likely to be statistically the most common category of sexual behavior. Social scientists seem to have taken as self-evident the fact that heterosexual relationships cover some ill-defined domain that includes pleasure, emotional closeness, and biological "drives." Only in groups whose sexuality is seen as a social problem (such as teenagers and poor women) has there been any serious discussion of cultural and social aspects of nonreproductive sex.[7] Reproductive behavior among heterosexuals has been studied exhaustively (again, especially focused on those whose reproduction is perceived to be problematic or on behaviors that are in and of themselves public health concerns), but the meanings of those sexual relationships, and the social factors that shape those meanings, have gone largely unattended.[8] Most of what we know about sexuality comes from research on sexualities that are visible because they seem problematic to at least someone—gay sex, sex with a risk of diseases, commercial sex, or sex among the poor, sex that we can in some way think about as an identity or a risk group. The sex about which we know the least, and the sex that has been made invisible and normalized by this attention to nonhegemonic sexualities, is married, heterosexual, middle-class sex.[9]

There are, of course, important theoretical reasons to study a wide range of sexualities; even beyond a desire to make sure that the ethnographic record does not contribute to making nonheterosexual behavior invisible, scholars have seen in both men's and women's same-sex relationships an opportunity to study the intertwining of resistance and desire. To some extent, this focus on same-sex sexual relationships (most of which has been about men's same-sex relationships) may be related to the sociology of sexuality researchers and to the field's early ties to the gay liberation and feminist movements.[10] Also, perhaps it has been hard to generate interest in researching a behavior that is prescribed rather than prohibited, a behavior that is not supposed to have any bad consequences, and a behavior that—according to our own culturally constructed models—is not very interesting anyway. Furthermore, for scholars interested primarily in sexuality, studying homosexual relationships has offered the chance to study relationships that are, at least on the surface, perhaps a bit easier to study as sexual relationships because they are not also reproductive relationships (which is not to say that people in nonheterosexual relationships do not reproduce, either at all or biologically, because they certainly do. However, they do not reproduce biologically through their relationships with each other.) Although those engaged in same-sex sexual relationships still juggle multiple projects—building identities and communities, seeking pleasure, preventing diseases—the fact that at least they are not also sites for sexual reproduction has perhaps made them more appealing as an object of study to scholars whose primary interest is sexuality, rather than reproduction.

Anthropologists begin by asking *why* about the most taken-for-granted aspects of everyday life, and so that in itself is a reason to explore sexuality and marriage. There is also a fundamental theoretical reason, however, to extend all the insight gained about the factors shaping modern gay sexuality to our study of heterosexuality: they have experienced parallel transformations. D'Emilio writes about how industrialization and urbanization in mid-twentieth-century America made it "possible to release sexuality from the 'imperative' to procreate. Ideologically, heterosexual expression came to be a means of establishing intimacy, promoting happiness, and experiencing pleasure. In divesting the household of its economic independence and fostering the separation of sexuality from procreation, capitalism has created conditions that allow some men and women to organize a personal life around their erotic/communal attraction to their own sex."[11] In other words, the same social transformations that made it possible for homosexuality to become an identity, rather than just a type of behavior, also transformed heterosexual relationships into an arena within which people consciously and deliberately do the work of building and maintaining relationships. "Love makes a family" is not just a slogan of the American gay pride movement—it is a description of a new and modern way of thinking about kinship as socially constructed. Much ink has been spilled on sex work (critiqued in de Zalduondo), but we should turn our gaze also toward the work of sex, the way in which people—gay and straight, rich and poor—use sex to build social ties.[12] To be sure, that is not all that they are doing: sex remains the way that most couples make babies and is still for some the only coin they have to trade for survival. The challenge, then, is to combine these insights about sex as intimacy work, as reproductive work, and as work. For some Mexican couples, having sex has been redefined as doing the work of intimacy. Women in this transnational community are imagining families united by bonds of love and confianza, and they are building those families in ways that make room for the conjugal intimacy that nourishes those bonds.

Strategic Pleasures

This book raises a number of issues relevant to how women bargain and negotiate in sexual relationships. First, the goals toward which women strategize do change, and any research that looks at marriage should attend to the social and historical construction of marital ideals. Although most people in Degollado and El Fuerte get married now, just as they did a century ago, this demographic continuity obscures important cultural changes in what people expect from that relationship. In turn, those differences are crucial to understanding changing demographic behaviors, such as declining fertility.

Similar findings about changing marital ideology in locations as diverse as Nigeria, Egypt, New Guinea, and in historical research on marriage in Europe and North America, suggest that further attention could be paid to links between widespread processes such as industrialization and technological change and ideologies of the nuclear family. The point is not that Mexicans are adopting wholesale some universally homogeneous ideal of family relations, but rather that given similar social changes (fertility decline, industrialization, education) they are actively transforming a globally available ideology into the specifically Mexican companionate marriage. The intertwining of gender and modernity makes companionate marriage seem a strategy for social mobility; remaking marriage—and themselves—through these more companionate relationships is one way for men and women to show that they too belong to modernity.

Second, I have explored how bargaining styles are culturally variable, describing a generational change in *how* women bargain, from trying to get what they want por las buenas, by getting on their husbands' good sides, to asserting that they too have a right to speak, to share their *opiniones*. Similarly, we see a change from the old way of choosing a novio, in which women did exert control but did so within an ideology of female passivity, to the new way in which women's will is much more explicit. A criticism of bargaining theory has been that it assumes a typically North American kind of individualism and confrontation, but I show here that it is not necessary to make those assumptions; I describe the ways that women bargain without direct confrontation and the ways they frame their bargains as not just in their own interest but in the interests of their children and family.

Third, those interested in what women and men bring to the bargaining table should attend as closely to nonmaterial resources as they do to material ones, looking more amply at all of the exchanges that occur as part of the marital bargain, including the affective ones. I have shown here how some men's love for their wives creates a sort of moral bargaining power for women. Pilar's husband let her tell him to find his own socks—though he could probably have forced her to get up and find them for him—because he loves her and wants her to feel respected. Oscar helps Blanca around the house and cooks for her on his days off, not because she makes him do it, but rather because it is part of being the kind of husband, and thus the kind of man, he dreams of being. Though he could probably enforce a Mexican version of *purdah* through violence, Pedro lets Josefina spend much of the day in the street, running invented errands (and strengthening her social networks) because, as he says, he felt his heart pierced by Cupid's arrow the first time he saw her. Changes in the ideology of masculinity and the feelings men and women have for each other lead to marital bargains that could not be predicted by looking solely at differential resource levels and changing opportunity structures.

Fourth, much attention has been paid to the changing value of fertility as a resource, whether in terms of the value of child labor, social capital to build family ties, or old-age security. Less attention has been given to sexuality per se as a resource, and one of the questions with which I began this study was whether women who had more limited access to other resources were more likely to use their sexuality as a resource—that is, to trade it strategically for other things they needed—than women who had more resources. My thinking was that women who had options that might make it possible for them to walk away from their husbands, for example, might be more likely to see sexuality as an arena for pleasure and intimacy. In a sense, the answer to this was a qualified yes. Young women in both the Mexican and U.S. field sites invest time and energy in creating a sexuality that will serve as a sort of marital glue, a confirmation of the physical and emotional confianza at the heart of these new marriages, but those who could walk away from their marriages, if push came to shove, emphasized themes of mutuality and equality, while women who were more dependent focused more on sexuality as a means of keeping their husbands happy.

In another sense, though, this question was packed with assumptions that are a product of my own social location. To think of sexuality as a resource only under conditions of relative poverty and dependence implies that the invisible reference group—middle-class professional women—get to do what they really want to do, that their (our) behavior is only shaped by culture whereas those of the women we study is also shaped by class. It may be more useful to see all sexuality as strategic. The question, then, is not how women or men with few other resources rely on their sexuality as a resource, but rather how everyone does. This directs us to explore the local meanings of any sexual relationship by asking what it is that people get out of that specific interaction. It is true that some people may need to use their bodies to get food, shelter, clothing, or protection, while others use their bodies more to express love, seek pleasure, and build intimacy. However, as Sobo has pointed out, even women in the most precarious economic circumstances may choose to see sex as a way of finding love rather than a route to economic security.[13]

Furthermore—and this is where my interest in companionate marriage might hit a bit closer to home—even women living lives of relative privilege, whether in developed or rapidly industrializing nations, continue to face persistent gender inequality in varying degrees. To be sure, women do the work of love out of genuine affection, but it seems no accident that love and emotion have become a feminine specialization and that supermarket shelves brim with women's magazines in both English and Spanish, promising tips on how to bring the spice and excitement back into the marital bed, and thus strength to the marital hearth.[14] To insist that sex is only strategic for poor women helps us avoid the fact that building relationships through shared pleasure is just a more sophisticated way of ensuring that same security and social status. It also, even more problematically, reserves true love as a privilege for those who can afford it, rather than seeing all heterosexual relationships as something of a leap of faith, an attempt to bridge the gulf of gender inequality in pursuit of a marriage of true minds.

Private Revolutions

I have focused here on intimate matters and private spaces, concentrating on the homes, heads, hearts, and bodies of Mexican transnational families. Some of the public spaces and institutions that shape their private lives have been very evident in these pages (the church and the promenade through the plaza come to mind), but others—the terror of the border and the long walk through a snake-infested desert, guided by coyotes who are their only protection but who also at any moment might turn on them and become rapists and robbers; the places María, Mercedes, Guadalupe, and Rosa spend their days, stooping, lifting, and comforting as nursing-home workers and day-care providers, assembling and checking on the factory floor; and the places in which their husbands labor as *sheetrockeadores, plomeros,* and construction workers—have been noticeably absent. My primary goal here has been to describe how generation and migration interlock to form the social context of reproductive health practices in this community, but, secondarily, I have tried to place these intimate transformations in gender and sexuality within broader economic and social change. In future research I hope to weave the threads of political economy here into a cloth with a clearer pattern.

No research project can accomplish everything simultaneously. My interest in political economy has evolved—with the discipline's—during the past several years.[15] I make this point both to lay out my tentative direction for future research and to point out that the social construction of sexuality and the cultural construction of sexuality—terms that are often used interchangeably in sexuality research—are really quite distinct. The cultural construction of sexuality directs us to look at symbolic and ideological aspects of sexual behavior, relationships, and identities. The best work in this genre reminds us that these cultural meanings are historically contingent and that the local is inextricably intertwined with broader regional or even global forces. In the past decade there has been a great deal of interest within public health in how locally variable ideas about sex and sexual relationships shape behavior (a cultural view of sex), but there has been very little work on more social aspects of sexuality. It goes without saying that much of this research on sex and culture has been in the service of explaining the failure of our prevention programs to stem the HIV pandemic, as I am certainly not the first to point out.[16]

This is certainly an improvement over thinking about sex as exposure to the risk of conception, as demographers have traditionally done. But all this attention to culture and ideology can produce static, ahistorical portrayals of sexual cultures. The problem is not just that it leads to bad research, to work that reifies sexuality; it also leads to what Paul Farmer calls an "exaggeration of personal agency."[17] Consider the African-American women in east Baltimore or in the south Bronx who are infected with HIV at a rate almost twenty-five times higher than white women who live only 5 miles away[18]—what these women think about sex and relationships is probably not irrelevant to the risk of becoming infected with HIV, but it is not the whole story either. Culture, and its programmatic corollary cultural appropriateness, have been embraced because they are an easy pill for us to swallow in public health. They suggest that if we capture just the right culturally appropriate perspective, if we could just tell people how to be healthy in the right words, they would listen and all would be well. A social perspective on sexuality, in contrast, might force us more in the direction of political economy. This would present a challenge to the status quo of public health because of late most applied public health (with the exception perhaps of environmental and occupational safety and health) has focused primarily on improving the public health through changing individual behavior—that is, improving population health by asking people to make themselves healthier, one by one by one.

This overemphasis on culture and cultural appropriateness results from several factors: first, our own American largely unexamined—and culturally constructed—ideas about the importance of individual choice in shaping behavior. Rayna Rapp calls this the "discourse of choice," critiquing the overemphasis on the choices individuals make and the relative neglect of the contexts of those choices in understanding the behaviors that shape health. She also explores our peculiarly American fascination with a sort of Horatio Alger–like, pull yourself up by your own bootstraps model of the individual production of health.[19] Simon Watney very aptly calls this the "look after yourself" model of health education.[20] A focus on cultural appropriateness without attention to social inequality suggests that it would be possible to make behavioral science–based interventions work in diverse populations by adapting and translating our messages. Without a more social theory of sexuality in public health, the only role for anthropologists is that of cultural emergency workers, translating exhortations for better behavior into the globe's many languages. The shift toward a more companionate ideal of marital relations is, to be sure, a cultural one, but to see women's interest in being taken care of by their husbands, or their embrace of a smaller family ideal, as solely a product of ideological change is to miss the ways in which these cultural transformations are inextricably intertwined with the social changes that have occurred in this transnational community throughout the past several decades.

The "Discourse of Desire": Still Missing

In 1988, Michelle Fine wrote in the *Harvard Educational Review* about the "missing discourse of desire" in adolescent sexuality education programs. The point she made, which is generalizable beyond programs targeted to adolescents, is that public health programs designed to protect young women's sexual and reproductive health have been hampered by an inability to acknowledge that young women might actually want to have sex. Since that time, there have been some interchanges among those interested in HIV prevention as to whether vulnerable women have sex primarily for love or for money, but Fine's critique still applies: the primary public health discourses about women's sexuality are framed in terms of victimization.[21] Furthermore, the "love or money" controversy presents a false dichotomy. Sexual intimacy provides people with an opportunity to express love, satisfy desire, secure resources, and impose power—sometimes all four simultaneously. We should be wary of any theoretical model of sexuality that, if it were applied to our own relationships, we would find deeply insulting or overly simplistic.

The younger Mexican women with whom I spoke demonstrated amply a sense of sexual subjectivity. Although I was warned by senior anthropologists who had worked in Latin America that it might be hard to get Mexican women to talk about sex, this was hardly the case: I think in particular of the mischievous smile on the face of one when she recalled to me the week her first child had been conceived. We had been discussing the complex art of timing the conception of one's child so that his or her birth would fall near a desired date (she, for example, wanted him to be born near her husband's birthday), and she was explaining to me that women tend to plan these things more after moving to the United States. I asked her if she remembered exactly the week of his conception, which had after all been several years before our conversation, because they had waited patiently to have sex until the right day. Standing outside her trailer, her eyes lit up and she laughed as she told me, "Oh no, Jennifer, I remember because we did everything that week [*hicimos todo*], all week."

I remember also the rapt attention in the knitting store as a young married woman told of her experiences giving her husband oral sex. I remember the many jokes women told me about sex—about penises too large or too small and about women who wanted too much sex, or not enough, or with the wrong person, as well as the many clever sexual puns I heard, whose only point sometimes seemed to be to show that one could use words not otherwise heard in polite company. And I remember the laughter with which one woman in Degollado responded when, after she complained that her husband had not given her a birthday gift, her neighbor asked if he had at least given her *el regalo de los pobres* (the gift of the poor).

Sexuality, Fertility, and Contraceptive Choice

My final point in terms of sexuality is that the contextualization of women's contraceptive choices has implications beyond explaining the specific patterns found in these communities. During the past decade, anthropologists have argued persuasively that to understand fertility trends and differentials we must begin by "situating fertility."[22] Absent from even these finely detailed explorations of the local meanings of reproduction, however, is much acknowledgment of the fact that when women and men make choices and strategize about fertility, they are also having sex—frequently messy, sometimes passionate, occasionally forced, but always a physical and emotional experience of some immediacy. With a few exceptions, when sexuality is invoked in relation to contraceptive methods, it is to explain patterns that are seen as problematic—for example, the reluctance of men to use condoms is often described as due to some local cultural construction of sexuality.[23] Sexuality deserves a much more central role in our analyses of contraceptive behavior. Sexuality is clearly not the only factor that influences method choice. Obviously, political-economic factors (such as insurance reimbursement and access to medical facilities) play a part, as do broader structures of gender inequality, but to understand why some traditional methods are more modern than others, or why Blanca in Atlanta uses the pill while her sister Isabel in Degollado prefers rhythm, we need to remember that fertility goals are interwoven with other short- and long-term objectives: individual and mutual pleasure, the strengthening of intimate relationships, and the construction of a modern self.

IMPLICATIONS FOR RESEARCH ON GENDER

Gender and Power in Public Health Research

The variation in men's marital goals underlines the importance of including men's diverse voices in research on gender inequality; it hardly seems possible to develop a socially and historically grounded portrait of how gender is negotiated at the microlevel without having a better understanding of men's goals and strategies.[24] This is not a new point, to be sure, but it seems one that feminist scholars have been slow to integrate in more than a token way (for example, in their otherwise excellent research, Rapp, Pesquera, and Petchesky and Judd all either ignore men entirely or else only include them in the most cursory way).[25]

Including men's perspectives might more accurately represent the microprocesses of household negotiation, but we should not mistake Oscar's and Sergio's claims of mutuality and cooperation for relationships in which women have access to the same socially structured sources of power as men. Subsequent to the 1994 International Conference on Population and Development, public health researchers have paid increasing attention to the negative effects of gender inequality on reproductive health—through, for example, men's opposition to family planning or refusal to wear condoms.[26] The way in which a shift toward a more companionate marital ideal may coexist with continued gender inequality suggests that those interested in using gender analysis to study women's reproductive health (or, for that matter, men's reproductive health) should expand their horizons beyond inquiring about household decision-making practices.[27] Even relatively equitable practices may be simply the result of men's preferences; some of the young couples presented here are building marriages that feel quite different than their parents', but the underlying shift—particularly for those couples who remain in Mexico—is more one of style than of power.

Most of this research linking gender inequality to undesirable reproductive health outcomes has focused on men's and women's attitudes and microlevel domestic processes, but gender inequality at the household level is inseparable from men's greater access to economic and social resources outside the household.[28] These Latino men, invisible yet omnipotent in public health research, are the same ones standing *agachados*, trying to make themselves unobtrusive, on the corner of Shallowford Road and Buford Highway in Atlanta, hoping that a contractor will slow down enough to allow them to jump up on the back of his truck, signing up for a day of hard labor at uncertain pay. To the extent that, around the world, individual ideas about masculinity and femininity are being transformed, we need to know more about how these ideological changes are shaped by changes in gendered opportunity structures.

Gender, Representation, and Modernity

When Mexican women and men in El Fuerte, Degollado, and Atlanta spoke to me about marriage, sexuality, and love, they were deliberately using a discourse of gender to locate themselves in time, to show me whether they were traditional or modern. Rather than taking their words to be simple factual descriptions of life in their community, I read their words as a way of positioning themselves in terms of a discourse—in which they assumed I would also participate—in which certain forms of masculinity and femininity are more modern, and thus inherently superior. This awareness of how people use gender to represent themselves strategically suggests that exploring directly the "biases" that shape how women and men choose to portray themselves is one way to see subtle (and not-so-subtle) transformations in gendered ideologies. It is certainly intriguing that gender and modernity should be so tightly interwoven in the minds of men and women in this community, and we should not take as self-evident that Yulissa gave her heart to the handsome blond doctor from Mexico City, rather than to Ignacio, because he was somehow inherently more desirable. The question of why it might make sense to viewers that he was more desirable, why Francisco insisted so vehemently that he was not macho, are some of the questions with which I end this project.

Gutmann elegantly reviews the intellectual and social histories through which the idea of Mexican machismo came to dominate U.S. social science research on Latino masculinities.[29] Based on my work in this community, I might add yet another reason that these ideas about Mexican women as completely subjugated by men have so captured the imaginations of researchers in the United States. The way older women spoke about being kidnapped, the way Pedro spoke about Josefina "not letting him" go out drinking after work, and the way I myself learned to use the excuse that I was expecting a phone call from my husband to beg off unwanted social obligations in Mexico—all of these examples suggest that perhaps in Mexico women and men have a more subtle understanding of the complex relationship between how people talk about power and actual individual autonomy. Researchers in the past may not have seen women's power in Mexico because they may have had too ethnocentric an idea of what power might look like. In spite of the interest within public health in teaching women in developing countries to "negotiate" for condom use, my experience was that almost every one of the women with whom I spoke had something to teach me about negotiating. True, this skill in negotiating may derive in some part from a history of approaching the table with the cards stacked against them, but still, there was a sophistication to these women's understandings of how to create a sense of common good in the daily give-and-take of marriage that was new to me, schooled as I have been by American ideas about the need to demonstrate power through words in addition to actions.

In the introduction, I raised the question of why people choose to reinvent the world through gender and sexuality, through creating what they perceive to be modern relationships, rather than by striving to be modern workers or citizens. First, one reason may be that these domestic paths to modernity seem, on the ground, to be primarily a question of individual preferences, and thus more within the control of people with rather limited resources. People may prefer to reinvent gender in the privacy of their own homes, or in the plaza, rather than to struggle with large, powerful institutions (political systems, the labor market) in pursuit of seemingly unattainable changes. Although these changes in gendered practices are not at all trivial, they are quite precarious and are merely a first step toward a world in which men and women feel happy sitting down at the bargaining table (or at the kitchen table) because they each hold good cards, rather than just because they are holding hands as they play.

Second, these Mexican men and women may use gender and sexuality to lay claim to modern personhood as a postcolonial response to the way that European and American people have, for centuries, used these same arenas of gender and sexuality as a way to emphasize the strangeness and supposed lack of civilization among inhabitants of Latin America, Africa, and Asia.[30] Researchers (anthropologists among them) and colonizers from the developed world have persistently used discussions of gender and sexuality to characterize people from the developing world as backwards, primitive, traditional, and uncivilized. A parallel development in the field of reproductive health and fertility has been the growing ideological prestige of low fertility: during the past two centuries fertility has tended to decline first among the ruling class, and "reproductive stigma" has come to attach itself to those who are perceived to be unable, or unwilling, to control their bodies in this new modern way.[31] Inevitably, one of the various lenses through which people viewed me was as a representative of those same researchers, colonizers, and family planners. Seen this way, the insistent efforts of these men and women to convince me that they have modern bodies, modern loves, and modern sex could be understood as their response to a conversation they did not start and in which they perceive themselves, perhaps rightly, to be at a permanent disadvantage. Laying claim to modern intimacy and modern gender identity is a strategy to claim citizenship in a global community that may be otherwise inaccessible to them; cell phones and beepers are expensive, but hugs and kisses are free.

Third, a set of issues specific to the relationship between Mexico and the United States overlays the way gender and sexuality have been used discursively around the globe to "other" colonized peoples. Although the men and women with whom I spoke were unlikely to have read either Octavio Paz or Oscar Lewis, they were certainly aware of North American perceptions about machismo in Mexico. As Gutmann also found, their claims to a gendered modernity could be seen as a working through of concerns about national identity, a way to contest Mexico's relationship of political and economical subordination to, and dependence on, the United States.[32]

By pointing out that the adoption of more modern gender identities is not the same as achieving change in the underlying social and economic structures, I do not meant to suggest that cultural changes are unimportant. The way people build identities, perceive ideologies, and engage in discursive struggles has critical implications for how they live their lives. When María, for example, responded to her husband's refusal to continue to drive her to work by buying her own car and teaching herself to drive, she was at least in part trying to show him that she was a modern woman who could not be pushed around. In *The History of Sexuality,* Foucault argued that the history of modern sexuality is not a shift from repression to liberation, but rather a shift from explicit institutional regulation to more subtle regulation via various forms of discourse—among which he would certainly have counted this reformulation of sexuality as a critical means to assert a modern identity.[33] María's story reminds us, though, that the discursive intertwining of gender, sexuality, and modernity can open up spaces for resistance, autonomy, and creativity; in diverse ways, people can use these abstractions in very concrete ways to support their efforts to make choices, seek pleasures, and press for power in ways their parents might not have been able to.

The Perils and Pleasures of a Courtship after Marriage

I have sought throughout these pages to make clear that this is not a story about Mexican women and men blindly adopting U.S.-based ideas about love and marriage, nor is it a tale about companionate marriage as an indicator of gender equality. I set out to learn about sex, reproduction, and migration and was led by my informants to think about love and marriage; this reformulation of my research turned me somewhat bemusedly into a native anthropologist, forced to inquire about the cultural-constructedness of concepts that are just as much a part of my life as they are of my informants'. Although I long to tell a story with a happy ending, I have tried throughout to avoid a modernist sensibility about gender and social change, to remember that good sex and sweet words are nice but not always a sign of equality, and to keep my eyes and ears open to the way in which these Mexican concepts of companionate marriage do not map exactly onto the ideas with which I am more familiar as a participant-observer in American life.

Although women may see a promise of power in these new ideas about confianza, companionate marriage as an ideology has more to say about the emotional intimacy couples can achieve through talking than it does about who gets the last word.[34] Several of the men saw no contradiction between the idea that they and their wives should be loving companions and their insistence that they as men should always have just a bit more power, that ultimately they were the ones who wore the pants. Other couples did seem, within the confines of this same ideology, to have adopted a more egalitarian domestic style—but ultimately that is a man's choice, not a woman's.

Furthermore, the focus on marital companionship emphasizes the extent to which it is a bond of desire rather than of obligation—which may put women in a difficult position when, as is so often the case, desire falters. Several women mentioned that the negative aspect of knowing that they could valerse por si misma (make it on their own) is that their husbands know it too; that is, that seeing their wives work and earn money can diminish men's feeling of obligation to take care of them. Helplessness can be a kind of power too.

This was borne out by what the men said: Sergio, for example, talked about how his friend told him that rather than hit his wife to try to bend her to his will, it was better just to leave her. Mario also said that he would leave his wife if they were unhappy together, that there is no point to being married and fighting all the time. In the United States, the transformation of marriage into a supposedly purely affectionate (as opposed to both affectionate and economic) relationship has lessened women's claim on men's resources after a marriage breaks up. In Mexico, too, there will be gains and losses associated with the paradigm shift toward the companionate marriage: women may gain emotional closeness and (sometimes) a degree of power sharing, but they lose some economic security when it begins to make sense to people that a man would leave a woman, or a woman would leave a man, simply because they no longer enjoy each other's company. The continued incorporation of this ideology, privileging emotional satisfaction over men's responsibility to support their families, leaves women on shaky ground.

Courtship is an inherently unstable relationship; the outcome depends on the capacity of each partner to woo and be wooed, on a woman's ability to give "little looks" without being seen as a rogona, a girl who is looking for it, and on a man's ability to keep asking for a kiss with enough persistence to convince a girl of his interest but without being so persistent as to be insulting. Courtship's implication of impermanence must be part of this story of companionate marriage in Mexico, although by choosing to work primarily with currently married women it was not an aspect on which I chose to concentrate. It is not a coincidence that increasing rates of divorce and separation during the past quarter century have coincided with the popularization of these ideas about marriage. Although predictions are always a risky proposition, it seems safe to say that the development of a companionate ideal of marriage—which is inherently, as Giddens argues, a relationship in which partners' must continually rearticulate their commitment to each other—is likely to presage further increases in rates of marital dissolution in Mexico.[35]

This is neither bad nor good—after all, who am I to say that only women in rich countries should move on to another partner when the current one no longer elicits just that right mixture of confianza, cariño, and respeto?—but women in rural Mexico may be even less well set up than their counterparts in the United States to make it on their own. The policy problem, to the extent that there is one, is not that a man and a woman may choose to part when the magic is gone. Rather, the problem is that these "pure relationships" carry the implication that each partner is equally free to walk away, that each person could make it equally well on his or her own, and that is simply not true in rural Mexico—or, for that matter, in the United States.[36] If push came to shove, these women could support themselves and their children, but with difficulty. (A further consequence of marital dissolution, of course, is the effect on children, although the social scientific jury is still out on the magnitude and long-term implications of divorce for children.[37]) Part of my argument here has been that the enduring difference in threat points—the point at which a spouse would say that he or she would be better off without the partnership—is what makes love into women's work.

I am not saying, though, that women (Mexican or otherwise) are naive dupes of a fairy tale about love. Holding out for love may be a risky proposition, but there are also ways in which it may, in and of itself, increase the range of possibilities for women. Chapter 6 closed with a tale of three sisters, one of whom (Lucha) had left her second husband, Jose, to return to live with her first, Roberto, in a house she had built with her earnings from the factory. Heading south on the bus, she was choosing love over security—but only because she had a bit of security of her own, represented by two pieces of paper: her green card, and her ownership of the house. When I last saw Lucha, though, she was back in Atlanta with Jose, and they were happily playing with their adorable new baby boy. He had gotten enough of a jolt from her leaving, it seemed, to try a bit harder to meet her halfway on her wish for a bit more cariño, tenderness.

A second issue that should cause us to pause before celebrating the global triumph of love is the possibility that the ideological intertwining of love, sex, and marriage may have little effect on men's socially structured access to sex outside of marriage. Indeed, for women in many parts of the world, the behavior that puts them at greatest risk of infection with HIV is unprotected sex within marriage.[38] This is certainly the case for women in rural, migrant-sending communities of Mexico such as Degollado and El Fuerte. In 1987, the first year that AIDS cases were reported in Mexico, the twelve cases from rural areas represented less than .5 percent of the total number of cases. By 1997, the most recent year for which data are available, rural cases accounted for 11.1 percent of new cases. The preponderance of these rural cases is thought to be either men who have become infected in the United States, or the partners of these men.[39] In addition, the rural female-to-male ratio of 1:4, compared to an urban ratio of 1:6, indicates a higher occurrence of heterosexual transmission in rural areas.[40] Taken together, all these data suggest that married women in rural, migrant-sending areas may be at special risk of HIV transmission.[41]

Juan, Francisco, and several others told me that it is the rare man who is faithful to his wife or girlfriend during the long lonely months in the North.[42] The social organization of migration puts migrants' wives at risk for marital transmission, but this risk may be exacerbated by young women's embrace of ideas about companionate marriage.[43] Despite all the emphasis on talk in these modern marriages, young women are perhaps even less interested than were their mothers in communicating about how men manage their desire during these long absences. The older women may not have wanted to know about infidelity because for them it indicated a lack of respect, but for the younger women, for whom sex is the language of love, it is a betrayal of the confianza at the heart of the modern marriage. Younger women say that they would leave their husbands if they learned that they were unfaithful, but they also say, as they close their ears to hurtful gossip, "ojos que no ven, corazón que no siente." Given the reluctance of even those who develop prevention programs to see marital sex as dangerous, it is no surprise that women in these communities are unwilling to spoil their migrant reunions, known locally as being de luna de miel (on honeymoon), with talk of condoms and infidelity. Risks of disease and divorce do represent real dangers of a wholesale embrace of these ideas about love and marriage. Yet another cost may be the weakening of women's ties to other women, as women and men are instructed to find all emotional, social, economic, and moral support within the confines of the conjugal bond.[44]

I am reluctant, though, to end this story of love, sex, and change on such a sour note. Ultimately, I mention these issues not to pass judgment on whether the shift to a more companionate ideal of marital relations is good or bad, but to emphasize that there are both gains and losses, that this is a story about Mexican men and women developing *different* marriages than their parents', not better ones. Furthermore, to focus overmuch on passing judgment on the companionate marital ideal (which we are ill-qualified to do, since after all we share it) is to be distracted from the fact that, for better or for worse, it is increasingly prominent around the world as a framework within which men and women negotiate their relationships with one another.

This is a story about the work of pleasure men and women do to sustain a marriage and about the edge of anxiety in women's voices regarding their ability to measure up to this task. It is a story both about the intertwining of gender and modernity and about how older women and men in Mexico may have had a more subtle understanding of the strategic value of representation than those who traveled south to study them. It is a story about some men and women who risked their lives to start again in a land in which used computers are free for the taking and for a moment in the mid-1990s there seemed to be work for everyone, and about others who, though they have stayed in Mexico, may have deliberately adopted seemingly more equitable patterns of decision making as a way not to get left behind, *para no quedarse atrás*. It is a strangely ironic story, in which very unsexy processes of economic and demographic change have created the conditions in which some couples see good sex and satisfying intimacy not just as ends in themselves, but as useful strategies with which to build a modern family.

Notes

CHAPTER I. INTRODUCTION

1. I am *not* arguing that there is one unitary type of demographic transition with a fixed set of causes and demographic implications (see Szreter, "Demographic Transition")—merely that ideologies of companionate marriage, which vary locally in how they are conceptualized and used, are one important factor in explaining people's desire to have fewer children in the pursuit of a "modern" life.

2. Dixon-Mueller, "Sexuality Connection."

3. Fricke, "Culture Theory"; Greenhalgh, *Situating Fertility;* Pollak and Watkins, "Cultural and Economic Approaches to Fertility."

4. Martin, *Woman in the Body;* Ginsburg, *Contested Lives;* Davis-Floyd, *Rite of Passage;* Gordon, *Woman's Body;* Newman, *Women's Medicine.*

5. Korovkin, "Oral Contraceptives"; MacCormack and Draper, "Female Sexuality in Jamaica"; Coleman, *Family Planning;* Browner, "Gender Roles"; Renne, "Gender Ideology"; Scheper-Hughes and Lock, "Mindful Body"; Sobo, "Condom Use" and *Choosing Unsafe Sex;* Caplan, *Cultural Construction of Sexuality;* Newman, *Women's Medicine.*

6. Vance, "Anthropology Rediscovers Sexuality"; Dixon-Mueller, "Sexuality Connection"; Parker and Aggleton, *Culture, Society and Sexuality.*

7. Reiter, *Toward an Anthropology of Women;* Rosaldo and Lamphere, *Women, Culture and Society;* Ortner and Whitehead, *Sexual Meanings;* di Leonardo, Introduction; Collier and Yanagisako, *Gender and Kinship;* Brinton, "Gender Stratification."

8. Connell, *Masculinities.*

9. Stoler, "Making Empire Respectable"; D'Emilio, "Capitalism and Gay Identity."

10. Stansell, *City of Women* and *American Moderns*; Cott and Pleck, *Heritage of Her Own.*

11. Di Leonardo, Introduction.

12. Connell, *Gender and Power.*

13. Vance, "Anthropology Rediscovers Sexuality," 878.

14. Foucault, *History of Sexuality*; Giddens, *Transformation of Intimacy.*

15. Parker, *Bodies, Pleasures and Passions.*

16. Farmer, *Infections and Inequalities*, 257.

17. For references to homosexuality, see Parker, *Bodies, Pleasures and Passions*; Lancaster, *Life Is Hard*; and Connell, *Masculinities.* See Bledsoe's work on reproduction and family structure in Africa: Bledsoe, *Women and Marriage in Kpelle Society* and "Politics of Children"; Bledsoe, Hill, D'Allessandro, and Langerock, "Constructing Natural Fertility."

18. Nader, "Up the Anthropologist."

19. Some anthropologists do ground their explorations of sexuality in specific historical contexts, but these have primarily been studies in Europe and America (see Schneider and Schneider, *Festival of the Poor*; an exception to this focus on Europe and America is Parker, *Bodies, Pleasures and Passions*). Social historians have also dealt with changes in how sexuality and gender are understood and regulated (see Weeks, *Sex, Politics and Society*; Peiss, *Cheap Amusements*; D'Emilio and Freedman, *Intimate Matters*; see also D'Emilio, "Capitalism and Gay Identity")—but again, these studies have tended to concentrate on settings in the developed world.

20. Marriage is not, of course, the only context for sexual and reproductive behavior for Mexican women, but it remains the primary context for Mexican women's sexual intimacy and reproduction, and thus the primary focus of the study. Homosexual relationships, both among women and men, are not addressed at all here, though there were certainly both men and women in Degollado with publicly acknowledged nonheterosexual identities. For discussions of how discourses and practices of men's sexual relations with each other reflect on Latin American masculinities, see Hirsch, "Mexican Dirty Jokes"; Lancaster, *Life Is Hard*; Parker, *Bodies, Pleasures and Passions* and *Beneath the Equator*; and Carrier, "Mexican Male Bisexuality."

21. Blanc, "Power in Sexual Relationships."

22. Kippax et al., "Women Negotiating Heterosex."

23. Bargaining theory draws on the economic and sociological traditions that approach people as rational actors seeking to maximize their own utility; see Collins, "Sexual Stratification." My use of bargaining theory brings together the feminist critique of Becker's New Home Economics (see Isvan, "Reproductive Decisions"; Marx Ferree, "Beyond Separate Spheres"; Folbre, "Hearts and Spades"; Dwyer and Bruce, *Home Divided*; Blumberg, "Income Under Female Versus Male Control"; Manser and Brown, "Household Decision-Making"; Sen, "Economics and the Family") with social science literature that looks at sexual and reproductive behavior as well as other aspects of women's lives as strategies (see Nathanson and Schoen, "Bargaining Theory"; Bledsoe, *Women and Marriage in Kpelle Society*; Browner and Lewin, "Female Altruism Reconsidered"; González de la Rocha, *Resources of Poverty*; Hoodfar, *Marriage and*

the Market). Feminists critical of New Home Economics take issue with the assumption that members of a household agree on the optimal way to use their limited resources. Whereas econometric applications of bargaining theory are concerned with modeling mathematically how individual access to resources shapes domestic bargaining power, my use of bargaining theory borrows only the idea of unequal bargaining power based on resources.

24. Bledsoe, *Women and Marriage in Kpelle Society;* Browner and Lewin, "Female Altruism Reconsidered"; Nathanson and Schoen, "Bargaining Theory"; González de la Rocha, *Resources of Poverty;* Hoodfar, *Marriage and the Market.*

25. Nathanson and Schoen, "Bargaining Theory," 287.

26. Sobo, "Condom Use" and *Choosing Unsafe Sex.*

27. Crow, "Concept of Strategy," 14.

28. Isvan, "Reproductive Decisions"; Manser and Brown, "Household Decision-Making."

29. Pahl, "Allocation of Money"; Benería and Roldán, *Crossroads of Class and Gender.*

30. Hartmann, "Family as Locus"; Young, "Gender Inequality"; Mahoney, *Kidding Ourselves;* Pesquera, "He Wouldn't Lift a Spoon."

31. Sobo, "Condom Use" and *Choosing Unsafe Sex.*

32. Inhorn, *Infertility and Patriarchy.*

33. Nencel, "Men's Sexual Selves."

34. Simmons, "Companionate Marriage," 54–55.

35. Ibid., 55.

36. Gordon, *Woman's Body.*

37. Trimberger, "Greenwich Village," 134.

38. Gordon, *Woman's Body.*

39. Masters and Johnson, *Pleasure Bond,* 253.

40. Giddens, *Transformation of Intimacy,* 12.

41. Inhorn, *Infertility and Patriarchy;* Schneider and Schneider, *Festival of the Poor;* Gillis, "Gender and Fertility Decline."

42. Bott, *Family and Social Networks,* 198.

43. Ahearn, "Love Keeps Afflicting Me"; D. J. Smith, "These Girls Today"; Wardlow, "All's Fair"; Yan, "Triumph of Conjugality"; Collier, *Duty to Desire;* Rebhun, *Heart Is Unknown Country.*

44. Skolnik, *Embattled Paradise,* 17.

45. Caldwell, "Demographic Transition Theory," 346.

46. Thadani, "Logic of Sentiment," 486.

47. For example, see Greenhalgh, *Situating Fertility,* 5–6.

48. Harvey, *Condition of Postmodernity,* 12–13.

49. See, for example, Knauft, *Exchanging the Past;* Wardlow, "All's Fair"; Smith, "Courting for Love"; Chan, "Love and Jewelry."

50. For research that has explored how people in Latin America use a discourse of gender to assert traditional or modern identities, see Rebhun, *Heart Is Unknown Country;* Stephenson, *Gender and Modernity;* González Montes, "Intergenerational and Gender Relations"; Mummert, "From *Metate* to *Despate*"; Martínez Vázquez, "Mujeres ejecutivas"; Parker, *Beneath the Equa-*

tor; Amuchástegui, *Virginidad e iniciación sexual;* Gutmann, *Meanings of Macho.* Research on gender and social change in Mexico is discussed at some length in Chapter 5, below.

51. For a review of the vast social science literature on gender and change in Latin America, see Flora, "Beyond Exploitation and Integration." In Mexico, notable works looking at how social and economic change have reshaped gender relations include Gutmann, *Meanings of Macho;* Stephen, *Zapotec Women;* González de la Rocha, *Resources of Poverty;* Fowler-Salamini and Vaughan, *Women of the Mexican Countryside;* Benería and Roldán, *Crossroads of Class and Gender;* Fernández-Kelly, *We Are Sold;* Tiano, *Patriarchy on the Line.*

52. Collier, *Duty to Desire,* 6.

53. For a discussion of the modernist assumptions underlying theories of fertility decline, see Greenhalgh, *Situating Fertility,* 5–12.

54. Knauft, *Exchanging the Past, Critically Modern.* In addition to the literature on transformations in gender relations cited above in note 50, a second important theme in discussions about the emergent Mexican modernity is how the political and economic inequalities of Mexico's relationship with the United States in particular, and the developed world in general, have shaped (and distorted) the processes through which Mexico has modernized. See, for example, García Canclini, *Hybrid Cultures* and *Transforming Modernity;* Lomnitz, "Decadence in Times of Globalization"; and Bartra, *Cage of Melancholy.*

55. Collier, *Duty to Desire,* 10.

56. Gutmann, *Meanings of Macho.*

57. Glick Schiller, Basch, and Blanc-Szanton, "Transnational Perspective on Migration"; Portes and Borocz, "Contemporary Immigration."

58. For example, see Rouse, "Mexican Migration" and "Making Sense of Settlement"; R. C. Smith, "Los ausentes siempre presentes" and "Transnational Localities."

59. Kearney, "Invisible Hand"; Portes and Bach, *Latin Journey;* Smith and Guarnizo, *Transnationalism from Below;* Portes, Guarnizo, and Landolt, *Ethnic and Racial Studies.*

60. Pessar, "Introductory Remarks"; Mahler, "Engendering Transnational Migration" and "Transnationalizing Research"; Hirsch, "*En el norte la mujer manda*"; Grassmuck and Pessar, *Between Two Islands.*

61. A conference organized by Patricia Pessar and Sarah Mahler at Yale in February 1999, "Engendering Transnational Migration," addressed intersections between gender and transnational migration. See Pessar and Mahler, *Identities.*

62. Guzman, "Census 2000 Brief."

63. U.S. Bureau of the Census, "Table DP-1: General Population and Housing Characteristics: 1990, Alabama"; "Table DP-1: General Population and Housing Characteristics: 1990, Georgia"; "Table DP-1: General Population and Housing Characteristics: 1990, North Carolina"; "Table DP-1: General Population and Housing Characteristics: 1990, South Carolina"; "Table DP-1: General Population and Housing Characteristics: 1990, Tennessee"; "Table QT-P3: Race and Hispanic or Latino Origin: 2000, Alabama"; "Table QT-P3: Race and Hispanic or Latino Origin: 2000, Georgia"; "Table QT-P3: Race and

Hispanic or Latino Origin: 2000, North Carolina"; "Table QT-P3: Race and Hispanic or Latino Origin: 2000, South Carolina"; and "Table QT-P3: Race and Hispanic or Latino Origin: 2000, Tennessee."

64. *Atlanta Journal Constitution,* "Metro Area Grows"; *Atlanta Journal Constitution,* "Hispanic Voter Drive"; U.S. Bureau of the Census, Census 2000 Redistricting Data.

65. For histories of migration between Mexico and the United States, see Hondagneu-Sotelo, *Gendered Transitions;* Massey, "New Methods and Findings" and "Settlement Process"; Massey et al., *Return to Aztlan,* "Theories of International Migration," and "Continuities in Transnational Migration"; Durand, *Más allá de la línea;* Davis, *Mexican Voices.*

66. *Atlanta Journal Constitution,* "Tortilla Plant," "Sign of the Times," and "Immigrants Facing Loss of Benefits."

67. INEGI, *Jalisco XI Censo, Jalisco XII Censo.*

68. INEGI, *Michoacán XI Censo.*

69. I use the terms "anthropologists" and "demographers" as shorthand for referring to the respective qualitative and quantitative, or ethnographic and statistical, research traditions. The opposition between the two is necessarily oversimplified: many anthropologists are quite comfortable with the use of statistical inference in their research, and demographers are increasingly interested in incorporating ethnographic research methods into their methodological toolbox (Selby, Murphy, and Lorenzen, *Mexican Urban Household;* González de la Rocha, *Resources of Poverty;* Kertzer and Fricke, *Anthropological Demography*). Among anthropologists who collaborate across disciplinary lines there is a tradition of systematic sampling to increase generalizability (Selby, Murphy, and Lorenzen, *Mexican Urban Household;* Uribe-Salas, "HIV Infection among Sex Workers").

70. Kertzer and Fricke, *Anthropological Demography.*

71. In response to these problems of representation and interpretation, cultural anthropologists have experimented with narrative strategies that deliberately undercut authorial authority (for example, Abu-Lughod, *Writing Women's Worlds;* Wolf, *Thrice Told Tale*). These experimental ethnographies make fine reading (for example, Wolf, *Thrice Told Tale;* Behar, "My Mexican Friend"), but they are hardly suitable as documents on which to base public health or immigration policies.

72. See also Johannsen's useful discussion in "Applied Anthropology" about how to incorporate some of the insights of interpretative ethnography in applied anthropology.

73. U.S. Bureau of the Census, "PCT19: Place of Birth for the Foreign-Born Population," 126.

74. Guzman, "Census 2000 Brief."

75. Mathews et al., "Monthly Vital Statistics Report."

76. Sebert, "Needs Assessment."

77. Wolf, *Thrice Told Tale.*

78. Martin, "Rethinking Contingencies."

79. See also Johanssen, "Applied Anthropology."

80. Hondagneu-Sotelo, *Gendered Transitions;* Massey et al., *Return to Aztlan;* Mummert, "Reshaping Gender Relations"; Fernandez, "Migración hacia Los Estados Unidos"; Trigueros and Rodríguez Piña, *Migración en el Occidente de Mexico;* Alarcon, "El proceso de norteñización."

81. To say something is ethnographically generalizable—for example, that the concepts of *confianza* (trust) and *respeto* (respect) represent an organizing system for social relationships—does not mean that different women cannot use that organizing system to justify and explain contradictory behavior.

82. Katz Rothman, *Tentative Pregnancy,* 18–19.

83. Bernard, *Research Methods.*

84. Massey, "Ethnosurvey in Theory and Practice"; Cornelius, "Interviewing Undocumented Immigrants"; Rouse, "Mexican Migration" and "Making Sense of Settlement."

85. Cornelius, "Interviewing Undocumented Immigrants."

86. The comments people made about the Mexican community were filtered through their particular social relationship to it. Although health and social service workers were politically committed to helping people they spoke of as their ethnic kin, at the same time many of them were individually invested in preserving social differences between themselves, as English-speaking, middle-class, and American-born, and the people they serve—which meant not going outside whatever professional relationships they might have with their clients to find out perhaps the most salient part of a Mexican immigrant's identity, his or her hometown. Similarly, the list from the Consulate was mired in the internal politics of the Mexican community, and the extent to which the priests interviewed were knowledgeable about the community depended heavily on their individual vision of the role of the church in social action versus spiritual salvation.

87. Although El Fuerte is only about twenty minutes by car from Degollado, it lies across the border in Michoacán and "belongs" (*pertenece*) instead to a small city in that state. Consequently, there is no local bus service between El Fuerte and Degollado, so people from El Fuerte do not go to the market in Degollado and only rarely even go there for the annual fiestas in December. Social ties between El Fuerte and Degollado are limited in Mexico and almost nonexistent between their residents living in Atlanta. Even within Degollado, residents make a sharp distinction between el pueblo, which are the blocks surrounding and downhill from the main square, and *las colonias,* which are uphill and consist of lots that during the past two decades have been given to people by the government. The town has paved streets, and water runs to fill each house's tank every three or four days. In the colonia, streets are not paved, and in the areas where there is water in every house (in the newer colonias, there is only a common tap) it does not run more than weekly, and sometimes less frequently. Migrants in Atlanta from the colonias and from the pueblo do not socialize much—and when they do, those from the colonia still remember that they would not have dared enter the houses of the women from the pueblo, while those from the town know they would not have deigned to return the visit. The three separate communities in Mexico (rancho, colonia, and pueblo) each have their equivalent sister community in Atlanta.

88. Separate procedures for informed consent were carried out for each sister, and Mexican contacts were told that a recommendation from their sisters did not put them under any obligation to participate in the interviews.

89. Scheper-Hughes talks about being a "good enough" ethnographer, which I find an apt phrase to describe my approach. Her point is that we can simultaneously admit that all representation is partial and still argue that some representations are more complete than others. Scheper-Hughes, *Death without Weeping*, 28.

90. Mintz, *Worker in the Cane*; Behar, *Translated Woman* and "My Mexican Friend"; Shostack, *Nisa*.

91. Abu-Lughod, *Writing Women's Worlds*; Gulati, *Profiles in Female Poverty*.

92. See Hirsch, "Migration, Modernity and Mexican Marriage," for Spanish and English versions of the ethnographic field guides from the interviews with the life history informants and their mothers and husbands.

93. I did not even ask to interview the husbands of the two women who were unhappiest in their marriages, nor did I press to interview the husbands of those women who told me that their husbands were not willing to be interviewed because they were very *vergonzosos* (ashamed or bashful). *Vergüenza* acknowledges sexual or social hierarchy; I understood them to mean either that the sexual politics of being interviewed by (and thus having to be alone with) a strange woman was too awkward, or that being interviewed by someone with more education was too uncomfortable. More than anything, however, which men were interviewed reflects my own patterns of time allocation during fieldwork. I spent more time with the families in Mexico at night, when the men were around, and so had more opportunities to develop a casual acquaintance with them during the course of my many visits. Consequently, I interviewed six out of a possible nine life history informants' husbands in Mexico, but only two out of the possible thirteen in Atlanta.

94. Gittlesohn et al., *Listening to Women*; Chambers, "Rural Appraisal."

95. Knitting also helped me deal with the boredom of fieldwork. As anyone who has ever spent time in the field will attest, not every conversation feels earth-shatteringly important.

96. Knitting yarn can cost a dollar or two per 100-gram ball, and I gradually understood that crocheting is a much more widespread skill. The women who knit tend to be from wealthier families than those who only know how to crochet. Still, the fact that I was trying to learn about any needlework at all was significant, and women saw it as perhaps natural that a gringa would gravitate toward a more prestigious, complicated, and expensive kind of needlework.

97. Once I was pregnant I did not have much time to knit because I was writing my dissertation, but I made sure to tell the life history informants with whom I have spoken since Isaac's birth that my mother, together with various friends and relatives, has provided him with a closet full of handmade sweaters and baby blankets. Several of the life history informants also knitted for him.

98. I finally put to rest their lingering doubts as to my domestic abilities when I baked baskets of Christmas cookies for all of my life history informants and many of their mothers while I was in Degollado. I used the same tactics in

Atlanta, where I regularly brought women freshly baked cookies or brownies. There is some irony to the fact that I, as a Jewish woman, tried to establish a gendered connection with these women by baking and delivering twenty-six baskets of Christmas cookies. None asked me about this, however, since it was unimaginable to them that someone would not celebrate Christmas (see note 100 below). Furthermore, the Christmas cookies were successful as a gift because of the prestige in Mexico of foreign goods and practices, known as *malinchismo*. Exchanging baskets of homemade baked goods is an American, not a Mexican, Christmas practice (only in the past decade have indoor ovens become a common feature in Mexico kitchens, and most households use them as a convenient, rodent-free storage area rather than for baking or roasting). For the women to whom I delivered these baskets, baking brownies, chocolate chip cookies, and sugar cookies was an exotic and impressive feat. Furthermore, the red-and-green embroidered napkins lining the baskets (which I had ordered especially for this purpose) were meant to be used later as tortilla napkins, giving these women—only one or two of whom had adopted the gringo practice of seasonal holiday decorations—an opportunity to participate in this exotic foreign ritual.

99. In the interest of showing people that I did have a family, my father had come to visit me earlier that fall. People did seem glad to have some man to attach me to in their minds, and his enthusiasm for the local cuisine confirmed in many people's minds that I came from good stock, but still my father's visit did not have nearly the reassuring value that my husband's did. I heard comments about his piercing blue eyes from many who had not even seen him in person, but his visit seemed to have raised more questions than it answered. For example, if I was really married, why was my father still responsible for me rather than my husband? Furthermore, what kind of family did I come from that my father had time to travel now that he was retired, while my mother was at home working?

100. The kinds of questions people asked me about Judaism varied from moderately complicated (such as "Well, you may be Jewish, but don't you still believe in the Virgin?" and "Why do you eat pork if you are Jewish?") to deeply troubling ("Why did you kill Jesus?"). In all fairness, several of the times I was asked the latter question, others came to my rescue and said that the local priest had noted during a recent Easter sermon that in fact Jews did not kill Jesus. Conversion anxiety in this part of Mexico runs high, so I learned to point out that I was born Jewish and that my religion represents the continuation of my parents' tradition rather than a rejection of it; people seemed to see religious converts as inauthentic theological opportunists—in addition, to be sure, to their fear that if I were a convert I might start proselytizing.

101. See Paz, *El Laberinto de la Soledad;* and Gutmann, *Meanings of Macho.*

102. Although the IRB did not suggest changing the name of the Mexican research sites to further protect women's identities, I had initially thought that I might. The women, however, were emphatic in their desire to have their community identified so that outsiders would know about their experiences as Mexican women. The most recent AAA statement on research ethics instructs an-

thropologists that their plans for human subjects' protection should incorporate the desires of those interviewed, so I eventually abandoned the names I had invented for Degollado and El Fuerte. As the women I interviewed told me, changing the names of their towns did nothing to protect them, since if people were not from their town they would not recognize them anyway.

103. Brettell, *Politics of Ethnography;* Scheper-Hughes, *Saints, Scholars and Schizophrenics.*

CHAPTER 2. "HERE WITH US"

1. Even those who work in the fields or in construction in the United States come back with lighter skin, explaining that the sun does not burn them like it does in Mexico. This attention to skin color draws on ideas about color and class, which are somewhat different from the social construction of race in the United States. See Lancaster, *Life Is Hard,* 211–34. When I have returned for subsequent visits, I have been subject to the same inspection as any return migrant. People told me how much better I looked than when I had gone home last time, commenting especially (and particularly mercilessly, I thought) on my hair, the color of my skin and its relative smoothness, my weight, and which of the clothes I brought were new.

2. Fried tacos in this part of Mexico are soft tortillas filled with seasoned mashed potatoes (and sometimes crumbled, cooked chorizo), rolled up, fried in lard, and eaten with a thin, very spicy tomato-based *salsa* and shredded cabbage. Thick cornmeal cakes made from *masa,* called *sopes,* are usually covered with refried beans and melted cheese and served with cabbage and salsa. *Pozole* is a hominy, pork (usually pig's head), and chile soup, which is served with a squeeze of lime, chopped onion, shredded cabbage, fresh cilantro, and (for those with something to prove) more ground chiles added to taste. In this part of Mexico it is often served with *tamales* (cornmeal mixed with chile-spiced pork or chicken and steamed in softened corn husks), which are added whole, dumpling-style, to the steaming bowl of soup. All of these foods are nighttime, special occasion treats, typically served at *posadas* before Christmas or during the occasional dinner out. They are the *antojitos* (tasty treats) of which immigrants dream. Most immigrants continue to cook using the same recipes in the United States that they did in Mexico, but they complain that the food tastes different: the meat is not as fresh; the cheese is pasteurized; the tortillas are made from dried ground corn instead of freshly ground corn; the water tastes of chemicals. While on vacation in Mexico, they revel in the tastes and smells of *real* Mexican food, which means they are home.

3. Durand, *Más allá de la línea.*

4. Anyone, of course, is free to attend whichever Mass they please, but the songs and homily at the 7:30 Mass are directed more toward teenagers from Degollado, most of whom would not be caught dead at the noon Mass anyway because they feel somewhat superior in terms of sophistication to those who live in the ranchos (although their own parents may have been born in these same ranchos). They make fun of their dress and speech, and it is not uncommon to a hear a young mother scold a child who has just done something rude or is

being too shy to greet someone properly by saying, *"no seas ranchero(a)"* (don't act like you're from a rancho). The evening Mass also gives adolescents an excuse to at least pass through the plaza at night, when it is infinitely more exciting than during the day.

5. In November and December I was frequently asked whose wife I was; that is, people assumed the obvious explanation for the presence of a gringa during the fiestas, which is that I had married a young man from the town and was back to meet my new in-laws.

6. Mummert, "Western Rural Families"; Durand, *Más allá de la línea*, 161.

7. *Carnitas* are accompanied by tortillas, refried beans, white rice, avocado slices, jalapeños in vinegar with cauliflower, onions, and carrots, and a slice of wedding cake. They make the menu of choice for local weddings.

8. Rostas, "Gendered Imagery."

9. A local handicraft, strips of dried cactus fiber from the *maguey* plant (also used to make tequila) are woven into leather in a custom design (someone's initials, a horse or a rooster, the brand of a ranch). Belt buckles are the most common, but the store that sells them also had saddles, holsters, and other leather goods for sale (no cell phone holders yet during my fieldwork, but I expect to see them on my next visit). The buckles are large in diameter and present almost a codpiece effect visually; they are also quite expensive (can cost several hundred dollars) and are frequently one of the first luxury goods that a male migrant will send money home to have made so that he can wear it on his arrival home.

10. Goldring, "Blurring Borders" and "Gendered Memory"; R. C. Smith, "Los ausentes siempre presentes" and "Transnational Localities."

11. Every year several men are chosen as the organizers of the fiesta in the rancho. They must choose and hire musical entertainment, collect the money necessary to decorate the streets and the chapel and to buy fireworks, and feed the musicians (this latter task they delegate to their wives). They also sell permits for the food stands, rides, and games that are set up in the paved space outside the chapel. Although it is a great honor to be chosen, it is also an enormous burden, given the extent to which reputation and prestige depend on a well-organized fiesta. In 1996 one of the life history informants' fathers was among the men chosen as an organizer. As is common among organizers, he lived in the United States (in this case, in Atlanta), where he was better positioned than if he were in Mexico to ask those who have money to contribute their share. Had he lived in the rancho, he would have had little likelihood of finding other families with cash to contribute and no way to generate the income himself to make up for any potential shortfall in fund-raising. This is a good example of how local status systems in Mexican migrant towns are inextricably connected to the rhythms of migrant life.

The tension between the migrants' influence and their nostalgia for what they imagine to be authentically Mexican manifests itself in El Fuerte in the struggle over the dates of the annual fiesta. In the past, the fiesta in El Fuerte has been February 9 and 10, which are the days on the Catholic calendar dedicated to Nuestro Señor del Perdón, the patron saint of the rancho. Although the dates in February may have been convenient for men who spent six months a year as

agricultural workers in the Salinas Valley, they are considerably less so for the
new generation of migrants who have full-time jobs in construction, restaurants, and factories. Furthermore, men and women who have settled in the
United States as families are likely to have school-aged children. While hijos
ausentes from Degollado do not look askance at taking their children out of
school a week early in order to reach Mexico in time for the last day or two of
the fiestas (and then to stay and enjoy the parties that continue through the
posadas on December 16, Christmas, and New Year's), most parents do not
want their children to miss school for the entire month of January. Some migrants quit their jobs in December and return in February hoping to find a new
one, but others have begun to argue that it would be better for both the town
and the migrants to switch the fiesta to mid-December or early January. As of
1999, the date remained unchanged.

   12. Inhorn, *Infertility and Patriarchy.*

   13. Although men (and a few women) have been traveling to the United States
from this part of Mexico since at least the days of the Mexican Revolution, earlier in the century the exchange rate between the peso and the dollar was less un-
even, so that migration was more of a seasonal survival strategy and less of a
means to amass the significant amount of capital (now $10–$15,000USD) necessary to build a house.

   14. González, *San José de Gracia;* Pader, "Spatiality and Social Change."

   15. Alarcon, "El proceso de norteñización."

   16. *Compadrazgo* is a tradition of selecting godparents for a religious ceremony, such as a baptism, first communion, or wedding, which then incorporates these people into one's kinship network (see Mintz and Wolf, "Ritual Co-
Parenthood"; and González de la Rocha, *Resources of Poverty*). The
godparents of one's children become one's *compadres* (literally, coparents). This
can be a hierarchical, patronage sort of relationship, but in Degollado and El
Fuerte people are more likely to choose compadres with whom they already
have some sort of kin or friend relationship (aunts or uncles, newly married
sisters- or brothers-in-law, neighbors, and, less commonly, friends).

   There is a baroque quality to current uses of compadrazgo: a wedding
might have *padrinos* (godparents) of the wedding rings, the ring-pillow, the
unity candle, the *lazo* (a rope or a lasso, used to symbolically tie the couple together during the Mass), the real bouquet, the artificial bouquet, the veil, the
bride's shoes, the photo album, the guest book, the goblets used for the toast,
the dance music, the mariachis, the liquor, the cake, and, of course, several sets
of *recuerdos*. This multiplication of compadres is a recent development, which
may be related in part to the growing phenomenon of weddings as a public
spectacle of a couple's future mastery of consumer culture. An alternative explanation would be that multiple sets of compadres are a deliberate strategy for
widening and strengthening social networks at just that point in a couple's life
(as newlyweds, parents of young children) that they are most likely to need help.
Furthermore, Mexicans now seek compadres for events that previously passed
with less pomp and circumstance such as primary-school graduation and
confirmation. Josefina joked with me, after I accompanied her to the town hall
to register her son's birth, that now I was her *comadre de registro*.

17. When I asked in interviews how people changed when they went north, I was hoping for answers about values and customs. Instead, people in the Mexican field sites talked more about how some return-migrants *presumen del norte* (brag about having been in the United States). This newly acquired snobbery takes multiple forms: pretending not to recognize people in the street and thus not greeting them or returning their greetings; complaining loudly and constantly about how boring small-town life is compared to the excitements of the city and the mall; pretending to have forgotten Spanish, pausing and saying "umm" in English rather than "*este*" as native Spanish speakers do; pretending to have learned English, dropping words such as *el mall* and *los taxes* into conversation with locals who are sure not to understand, or else substituting words from Chicano Spanish such as *parquear* instead of *estacionar* and *freezear* rather than *congelar. Parquear* is the Spanishization of the English word "park"; the Spanish word is *estacionar.* Similarly, *freezear* (to freeze) substitutes in Atlanta for *congelar* (Spanish for to freeze). Other notable new Spanish words I have heard in Atlanta include *beepear* (to call with a beeper), *sheerockeador* (a man who works in Sheetrock), and *roofeador* (a roofer). (Lopez Castro argues, however, that return migrants are not so much showing off by using this Spanglish vocabulary as they are trying to express a particular set of experiences that do not fit within their regular Spanish vocabulary and frame of reference. See Lopez Castro, "Lenguage y migración.")

18. Durand, Parrado, and Massey, "Migradollars and Development."

19. *Ejido* possession of land was more successful in some areas than in others; so, for example, the land near El Fuerte went directly from being part of a large hacienda (an estate with title granted by the king of Spain or his representative) to being broken up for sale into smaller, private parcels. Just across the border in Jalisco, however, most of the land around Degollado was owned by the local ejido. For a discussion of the history of ejidos, see Keen and Wasserman, *History of Latin America,* 258–93; on the Mexican Revolution and land reform, see Womack, *Zapata and the Mexican Revolution.*

20. Thanks to Gillian Feeley-Harnik for reminding me to pay close attention to what people see as worthy of display in their homes. It took me a while to recognize these overcrowded, often rickety pieces of furniture as deserving of ethnographic note, since initially they seemed to contain many of the same items found in an American living room, and thus not to be obviously "folkloric" (as opposed to, for example, Salvo's book, *Home Altars of Mexico*). This blindness on my part, no doubt, comes from enduring stereotypes about the indigenous and what is ethnographically meaningful. It is also akin, in some way, to Blanca's and Patricia's surprise, when they came to my house, that my husband and I should have decorated our house with antiques and folk art. They were expecting my house to look modern, just as I had expected their relatives' houses in Mexico to look more traditional.

21. The only item I ever saw on a shelf in Atlanta that did not seem to work was a molded plastic model of a computer, the mastery of which is a distant dream for most immigrants. Early in my fieldwork, Father Carlos at the Catholic Mission in Doraville asked me if I could help them get some used computers so they could do basic computer training programs. Given the rate at which

computer equipment becomes superannuated, they soon had more old computers than they knew what to do with.

The computer training program was interesting in several ways. First, part of what Mexicans find miraculous about life in the United States is the accessibility of slightly used consumer goods that can be acquired cheaply at *las yardas* (yard sales); in Mexico their owners would cling to them as precious. The computers are just another example of the much lower relative value of electronic equipment, clothes, toys, and cars in the United States in comparison to Mexico. See Rouse, "Making Sense of Settlement." Second, I wondered what computer training actually does for Mexicans immigrants who work as manual laborers in the United States and generally have limited formal education. Since most Mexicans in Atlanta work in a variety of manual trades (landscaping, Sheetrock, roofing, masonry, road crews, light factory work, and restaurant and hotel work) and since most of the software they taught at the mission was so out of date as to be practically useless (for example, versions of DOS from the late 1980s), one possibility is that the value of the computer training is less in the mastery of practical, immediately applicable skills and more in the arena of mastery of modernity—that is, a reinforcing of the value of discipline, hard work, self-improvement, and engagement with science as the path to success in el norte. This interpretation is reinforced by the rules of the classes: students who do not do their homework assiduously and practice in the times allotted are not allowed to advance in class.

22. Many women cross-stitch or buy sets of tortilla napkins for themselves before they marry. One woman who eloped rather than marrying "properly" laughingly told me that when she married they had "nothing, not even a napkin."

23. Mauss, *Gift*.

24. One time at Doña Elena's house I asked her about cross-stitch patterns because her daughter, Josefina, had told me she wanted to make me a set of pillowcases as a gift and that her mother had many patterns from which to choose. Doña Elena opened a wardrobe to reveal perhaps fifty sets of pillowcases and coverlets stored away, some new and others yellowing with age. Each told a story about a relationship; one was a gift from a daughter, another from a daughter-in-law, a goddaughter, or a granddaughter. It was clearly a wealth of tributes, one from which she derived enormous value in having as opposed to using.

25. Migrants frequently travel to San Juan de los Lagos during visits home to express their gratitude for a safe sojourn in the United States. See Durand and Massey, *Miracles on the Border*. San Juan de los Lagos is a popular pilgrimage destination; people go on bus tours or, less frequently, will fulfill a vow they have made to the Virgin by traveling there on foot (it is several days' journey on foot). Pilgrims bring no food, counting on the kindness of strangers as they walk, and they sleep under the stars. This is one way that people fulfill a *promesa* (vow) that they make to a particular virgin or saint. There are many kinds of promesas people make, most of which involve some kind of sacrifice or discomfort. Mercedes, for example, promised the Virgin that if she had a baby

she would not cut her hair for five years. Her son turned one in June 1997, and by November of that year her hair stretched past her lower back.

26. Rodríguez, *Our Lady of Guadalupe.*

CHAPTER 3. FROM *RESPETO* (RESPECT)
TO *CONFIANZA* (TRUST)

1. This chapter deals almost exclusively with courtship in Degollado and El Fuerte, since all but one of the life history informants met and courted while still in the sending communities.

2. INEGI, *VII Censo, Estado de Michoacán,* 375; *Michoacán XI Censo,* 46.

3. INEGI, *VII Censo, Estado de Jalisco,* 445; *Jalisco XI Censo,* 18.

4. Corona Vargas, "Resquicios en las puertas."

5. Rodríguez, personal communication with author.

6. CONAPO, *Nupcialidad en México.*

7. CONAPO, *Remesas enviadas a México.*

8. Parker, *Beneath the Equator.*

9. Rebhun, personal communication.

10. The word in Spanish is *llevada* or *robada. Llevar* means to carry off, and *robar* in this sense means to steal a person (as opposed to stealing something that belongs to that person). Neither stealing nor robbing has this connotation in English, however, and so I have translated it variously as either carrying them off against their will or kidnapping.

Luis González, in his classic 1974 microhistory of a nearby town in Michoacán (*Pueblo en Vilo,* translated into English as *San José de Gracia*), writes that the frequency with which men carry weapons publicly has decreased enormously in the past generation. The only people I saw carrying a gun were the few town policemen, though I also did not make a practice of staring at men's pockets as this would have been easily misinterpreted. Alan Lujambio, the son of the woman with whom I lived in Degollado, told me that men carry guns less than they did in the past for economic, not legal reasons—that *la crisis* has made bullets too expensive to waste (except, of course, for the eve of September 16th and New Year's Eve, when men in the streets fire into the air with an abandon that made me cringe).

11. Simplistic, pan-Latin conceptions of Marianismo as a cross-cultural complex sanctifying women's suffering and passivity (that is, Stevens's *Marianismo*) have given way to research on women in Latin America showing how women actively strategize to reach clearly articulated individual or group goals. See Ehlers, "Debunking Marianismo"; Bourque and Warren, *Women of the Andes;* Nash and Safa, *Sex and Class in Latin America* and *Women and Change in Latin America;* Fernandez-Kelly, *Women and Industry;* Stephen, *Zapotec Women;* Beneria and Roldan, *Crossroads of Class and Gender;* Fowler-Salamini and Vaughn, *Women of the Mexican Countryside.* However, some of the mothers of the life history informants did imply that they found moral power through accepting the suffering in their marriages, and Melhuus has also discussed the way that Mexican women derive a certain kind of power from their ability to *aguantar* (to suffer) for the sake of their children. See Melhuus,

"Meanings of Gender." One of the themes in the Virgin of Guadalupe story with which Mexican women seem to connect most deeply is the holiness of her suffering (for her son), and they seem to see their own suffering, similarly, as making them almost into their children's personal saints. This idea of suffering as a maternal resource, rather than solely as an outcome of domestic power-lessness, reminds us of the importance of grounding applications of bargaining theory with ethnographic research on the local diversity of resources.

12. In one house there was an airbrushed-looking photo of an extremely handsome young man, who I had always assumed was an old-time movie star until one time I asked the señora who he was. She laughed and told me it was her husband, saying something like, "Don't you see it's not worth marrying for good looks?"

13. A man's ability to support a family should not be confused with his cur-rent economic status; several of the life history informants said that they did not pursue noviazgos with young men who came from families with money, because they did not want to appear *interesada* (greedy). Although marrying a hard worker is encouraged, marrying for money is frowned upon, and several women told me stories about women and men who had married for money only to experience subsequent tragedy and heartbreak.

14. In quotations in which the other speaker's pseudonym begins with a let-ter other than "J," as here, I identify myself with a "J" and the speaker by her (or his) first initial. In quotations in which the speaker's pseudonym begins with a "J," I identify myself by my initials J. H.

15. An American joke about the three kinds of married sex that people have in their houses illustrates particularly well the domestic-spatial organization of sexuality: "At first, there's kitchen sex, when you're still so crazy for each other you'll just lay down on the floor and do it. Then there's bedroom sex, when you're still mildly hot for each other but you have little kids, so the only time you can have sex is early Saturday morning with the doors locked while the kids watch cartoons. Finally, there's hallway sex, when you pass each other in the hallway and are so pissed off, all you say is 'Fuck you!'" Aside from depending on a shared (cynical) vision of the chronology of marital sexuality, the joke's (limited) humor draws on the assumption that the listener also takes for granted the relative sexiness of having sex in the bedroom versus on the kitchen floor.

16. Parker, *Bodies, Pleasures and Passions.*

17. Research on modern and historic carnivals has discussed public displays of sexuality as challenges to political or social order. See Parker, *Bodies, Plea-sures and Passions;* Davis, *Fiction in the Archives;* Lancaster, *Life Is Hard* and "Homosexual Stigma," 110. An example in the modern United States would be the gay-pride parades that take place in urban settings across the United States in June, at which floats of men in S&M gear pass cheering couples of gay yup-pies holding hands: these parades are a public challenge to dominant ideas about sexuality. In an urban park in the United States hardly anyone raises an eyebrow at a heterosexual couple lying embraced and kissing on a blanket (it is so normal as to be invisible), but the same seen in broad daylight in Degollado would have approximately the same impact as a gay couple lying entwined on

a blanket would have in Cobb County, Georgia—that is, it would cause a riot, and someone would likely call the police.

18. For those families wealthy enough to have a residential phone line, the telephone is playing an increasing role in courtship. Norma, in El Fuerte, had a daughter who was not quite ten, and several sons a bit older, and as soon as their phone was installed she began to complain about how her children monopolized the phone, and how girls in the rancho were doing something previously unheard of—calling boys on the phone to talk! Telephone conversations provide a previously unparalleled new opportunity for the development of premarital intimacy.

19. They say "*ojos que no ven, corazón que no siente*" (eyes that do not see, heart that does not feel). See Hirsch et al., "Cultural Constructions of Sexuality."

20. This is similar to how abortion among adolescents has become a focal point for policy debates about adolescent sexual behavior in the United States, as if without the incriminating evidence of a pregnancy it is possible to ignore their sexual activity. See Nathanson, *Dangerous Passage*.

21. Another way in which people fail to see sex is when they say as adults that when they were children they never noticed their parents having sex and to deny as parents that their children might ever notice them having sex. Until recently it was very common in Mexico for whole families to sleep in a single room (though generally with separate beds for male and female children), and many couples still keep young children in their room until they are two or three, but none of the women with whom I talked said that they had ever seen their parents having sex. One of the few women who admitted worrying that her young children might see them having sex was not worried that they would be traumatized by the sight. Rather, her concern was that they might unknowingly embarrass their parents by telling other people what they had seen—that is, by making what is private public.

22. Rouse, "Mexican Migration"; Goldring, "Blurring Borders" and "Gendered Memory"; da Matta, cited in Rebhun, *Heart Is Unknown Country*, 113.

23. Mexican men and boys use large key rings as a favorite adornment, putting the keys in their front pants pocket and letting the plastic or metal hang outside. Aside from its phallic symbolism, I interpret this as a gendered flaunting of their freedom of movement. Married women, when they have keys, carry them in their hand or in their purse rather than in a pocket (it is only recently that married women in Degollado and El Fuerte have started wearing pants instead of skirts, but I think that the public key display is at least at much symbolically as it is sartorially determined). Unmarried girls almost never have a key to their family's front door. The gendered nature of public space is further underlined by the fact that little boys are allowed to urinate in the street from a very young age, whereas girls are never allowed this dubious pleasure. Even aside from the toilet-training message that boys can satisfy themselves immediately whereas girls need to learn to wait, it is thought to be amusing if slightly naughty for little boys to expose their penises to the general public, whereas a girl who pulled up her skirt to urinate in public would be reprimanded and told that she lacked vergüenza.

24. One of the life history informants in Mexico talked specifically about how she does not like to have her five-year-old daughter visit her friends in their homes; she seemed to feel that even entering a home that was not one's own put her daughter's moral and physical innocence at risk. More commonly, many women talked about how working as a domestic servant was an option of last resort because (even aside from the danger of actual sexual violence), one's reputation was inherently damaged by entering the house of a man to whom one was not related. One woman who raised eight children on her own said that she preferred to have her daughters sit up all night hunched over sewing machines than to let them work as *muchachas* (servant girls) in another man's house. I, of course, spent most of my fieldwork entering into other people's houses, but I was careful never to enter if the señora was not home, since even accepting an invitation from a man to sit down and talk could easily be misinterpreted.

25. See Macleod, *Accommodating Protest.* Elisha Renne has referred to women's use of the veil as a sort of "moral mobile home." See Renne, "Gender Roles and Women's Status."

26. Fears about incest are used to justify gendered child-care arrangements: older girls can change diapers and baby-sit for either boys or girls, but older boys are only asked to take care of their baby brothers.

27. Douglas, *Purity and Danger.*

28. The shift in residential architecture both in Degollado and (to a lesser extent) in El Fuerte described in the previous chapter indicates changing ideas about the relationship between the house (that is, the family) and society. The more traditional house is an inward-looking house, but people would also move their chairs out onto the sidewalk to enjoy the late afternoon breeze, to crochet, and to chat with the neighbors. The house itself was more separate from the street, but people used the space outside their houses. As noted previously, the new style is reminiscent of houses in the United States. These newer-style houses cut people off from the communal life of the street; people sit on their living room couches staring at the TV, rather than monitoring their neighbor's behavior, or even interacting with their neighbors at all.

29. The mothers need to balance their own wishes to grant their daughters greater latitude than they perhaps enjoyed against the risk of angering their husbands. If a girl should run away with her boyfriend while she was seeing him without her father's permission, it becomes the mother's fault.

30. Private spaces such as cars or indoor rooms are still generally off-limits to novios, on the assumption that any couple presented with the opportunity to have sex will in fact do so. At the time I was in Degollado, there was an apocryphal story circulating about a couple (each married to someone else) who had been found having sex in the church during the day, causing the priest to start locking the doors between Masses rather than leaving the building open and unattended. Two of the life history informants admitted to having gotten in a car alone with their boyfriends in Degollado, but they knew that this was scandalous behavior on their part.

Generally the attitude about riding in cars is that if a woman would get in a car alone with a man, she would do anything with him. The one time I did accept a ride from a man (the son of a couple who had invited me to have lunch with them in their home), I was half-jokingly, half-seriously scolded by Alan for being *volada* (wild); he said if I did it again he would be forced to tell my husband. The eroticization of riding in a car holds true for almost any man and any woman: even the eminently respectable woman I lived with told me how in her ladies' church group no one wanted to be seen sitting in the front seat when the priest was driving them to a meeting in another town, even though there were clearly other women in the car and their male companion was a priest.

The disco in Degollado is more private than the plaza because it is indoors and generally frequented only by unmarried teens and some young married couples. In the rancho there is nothing like the disco. Neither El Fuerte nor Degollado has a motel (motels that charge by the hour and cater to couples having pre- or extramarital sex are found in larger cities in Mexico), but there are several in the city where people from El Fuerte go to market.

31. Stephen, *Zapotec Women*; González, *San José de Gracia*; Gutierrez, *When Jesus Came*; Lauria, "Interpersonal Relations in Puerto Rico."

32. De Zalduondo and Bernard have explored how the ideology of female passionlessness helps women in Haiti use sexual access as a bargaining chip. See de Zalduondo and Bernard, "Sexual Economic Exchange." Ortega, Amuchástegui, and Rivas found that women in several Mexican communities said that they got very little pleasure from sex, but the authors failed to consider ways in which women's claims of lack of desire may be, in and of themselves, strategic self-representations. See Ortega, Amuchástegui, and Rivas, "Negotiating Women's Rights."

33. Petchesky and Judd, *Negotiating Reproductive Rights*.

34. From the Spanish *fajarse*, which means either to belt or to wrap up.

CHAPTER 4. "*YA NO SOMOS COMO NUESTROS PAPAS*"

1. Folbre, "Hearts and Spades"; Dwyer and Bruce, *Home Divided*; Beneria and Roldan, *Crossroads of Class and Gender*; Gutmann, *Meanings of Macho*.

2. Connell, *Gender and Power*.

3. Breckon, "A Local Wife"; Schneider and Schneider, *Festival of the Poor*; Wardlow, "All's Fair"; Maggi, "Heart-Struck"; Yan, *Private Life under Socialism*; Collier, *From Duty to Desire*; Rebhun, *Heart Is Unknown Country*; D. J. Smith, "Sexual Relationships," "These Girls Today," "Courting for Love," and "Modern African Society."

4. *Quién manda* describes the communication of orders and desires from one person to another, so being *el* (or *la*) *que manda* is a relational—as opposed to an absolute—quality. There is also a spatial dimension to this relationship: the question "*¿quién manda?*" implies the longer, more complete question "*¿quién manda en tu casa?* (who gives the orders in your house?). It is distinct from (though obviously related to), for example, the *cabeza principal*, the head of the house (literally, the first head), which describes the person who has public and legal responsibility for a household. All of the life history informants distinguished between el que manda and the cabeza principal in a way that suggests that the question of the private microprocesses of negotiation over domestic decision making is conceptually separate from the issue of ultimate responsibility for a family's material well-being. The cabeza principal, in contrast

to the person (or persons) who gives orders, is the cabeza principal all the time, wherever he goes, regardless of his relationships to others. Regardless of their ideas about gender politics, all but one of the women asked said that their husbands were the cabeza principal of the family. Even if women earn money, men still have more prestige socially, more physical mobility in public, and greater access to money in an emergency, which makes them the cabeza principal. Another phrase men use that seems roughly equivalent to cabeza principal is *el jefe de la casa*. This discussion of the fine points of who gives the orders is a good reminder of the usefulness of ethnographic research on demographic categories such as head of the household. See Szreter, Dharmalingam, and Sholkamy, *Qualitative Demography*.

5. Blanca told me about how she had fought with Oscar during their engagement because he asked her to bring him a beer one day when they were relaxing at his house. By asking her to wait on him in front of his brothers, she felt that he was trying to assert before they were even married that he had the right to demand that she serve him, and so she refused. He said that she was being overly sensitive, that he was not trying to make a point about anything but was just asking her a favor, as she might ask him a favor. The fact that she refused is meaningful in light of what it might mean for any of a number of the other women to refuse such a request: if a man asks his wife for a favor in front of his friends, his respectability would be at stake if she said no. Furthermore, since he might already be drinking, an outright refusal might easily provoke violence, to be subsequently blamed on his drunkenness. I heard Blanca's story as her making a point about how different she hoped her marriage would be from this stereotypical scenario.

6. Exploring changes in marriage and gender further back in time is beyond the scope of this project, but in *San José de Gracia: Mexican Village in Transition*, González gives a beautifully detailed portrait of the social and cultural changes (wrought by two hundred years of historical change) in daily life in western Mexico.

7. Women continue to bear primary responsibility for the myriad tasks of social reproduction, though the nature of some of those tasks has changed in important ways. See Marroni de Velasquez, "Rural Society and Domestic Labor"; Mummert, "From *Metate* to *Despate*"; Gutmann, *Meanings of Macho*, 252. Most women in Degollado buy tortillas now from the corner tortilla shops, but particularly in the ranchos there are still some women who make their own tortillas, especially when their husbands are home from the United States. Similarly, a generation ago women used to take their clothes to the river to wash them in the running water and beat them on the rocks, but now it is more common for women to have washing machines; however, most still scrub clothes in the wash basin before putting them in the machine, and many of these machines have to be filled with water by hand, so they seem only marginally less labor-intensive. (Although the shift from grinding one's own corn to buying tortillas and from communal washing to the rinse-and-spin cycle may have made women's daily routines less arduous, they have isolated women by placing the tasks of social reproduction more firmly within the individual household. All of the life history informants' mothers recalled early-morning trips to the mill.

When asking a neighbor if she has heard a choice bit of gossip, sometimes women will still open with *"¿fuiste al molino?"* [Did you go to the mill?]—that is, assuming that if she had gone to the mill that morning she would already have heard it.)

Women's responsibility for the minutiae of social reproduction is reflected in the way people talk about and observe child rearing. The phrase for a person who has committed an extremely rude act is *que poca madre* (sometimes abbreviated to *que poca*), which means literally "how little mothering." Women's production of clean, well-mannered children is reflected in daily indicators such as whether they greet adults with a handshake and say "excuse me" when they walk between two adults who are talking (Mexican standards for children's manners far surpass middle-class American standards) and whether (in spite of the intermittent availability of water during the dry season) their clothes are clean and well-ironed and their hair is neatly combed and (for girls) arranged in braids or barrettes.

8. Temporary labor migration to the United States presents the most extreme version of this gendered division of labor in which the woman is responsible for social reproduction and the man for production. The mothers of the life history informants formed their families at the height of the Bracero program (1942–64), so ever-greater numbers of men from Michoacán and Jalisco were making the annual trip to el norte, but relatively few women were doing so (only in the 1990s did married women begin to accompany their husbands north in significant numbers). This meant that the mothers of the life history informants and many other women of their generation—much more so than either the generation that preceded or followed them—were likely to spend large portions of every year apart from their husbands. While the men are away, women have a great deal more control over their daily routines. They come and go as they please without asking permission and they worry less about having food prepared at exact times (they do not neglect their children, but neither do they need to have the food ready and piping hot the minute men walk in the door for lunch). Women in this situation have more leisure time while their husbands are away (less laundry, less elaborate food preparation) and more autonomy to make decisions. See González de la Rocha, "El poder de la ausencia."

9. Abu-Lughod, in *Writing Women's Worlds,* described a similar situation in which women feel they stand to gain more by complying with modesty requirements than by resisting them.

10. Renne, "Gender Ideology."

11. Stern, in his reading of nineteenth-century Mexican court cases, found similarly that under certain circumstances women could counter their husbands' power over them by calling on the help of their own fathers and brothers, local female networks, institutions such as the church or the police, or even the specter of supernatural retribution. See Stern, *Secret History of Gender.*

12. The literal translation of this phrase is "it's more the noise than the nuts." It seems to refer to the fact that when cracking nuts one makes a lot of noise and commotion but that the nutmeats themselves are relatively small. Nuts (as in English) are a stand-in here for testicles, so that the sense of the

phrase is that even though men make a lot of commotion about their manliness, when it comes down to it their actual nuts are not that big.

13. In spite of the long hours and arduous labor associated with washing by hand, cooking large meals, mopping up rivers of mud in the rainy season, and battling penetrating dust in the dry season, neither these women nor anyone else with whom I spoke accorded the same status to the chores of social reproduction as they did to paid work. This is indicated even by what the chores are called—not *trabajo* (work) but *quehacer,* which translates more or less as "things that must be done."

14. Gutmann, *Meanings of Macho.*

15. One of the life history informants had a full-time maid, and another had a part-time (three mornings a week) maid to do the heavy cleaning.

16. The interviews with men covered migration, marriage and gender, and fertility control. The following material draws on formal interviews with the eight men who consented to be interviewed (out of a possible twenty-two husbands) as well as on informal conversations with these men and others in the families of the life history informants.

17. Gutmann, *Meanings of Macho;* Mirandé, "Que gacho es ser macho" and *Hombres y Machos;* Melhuus and Stølen, Introduction.

18. Only Oscar used moral language to talk about shared decision making and his wife's independence. He said that being a good husband consisted of three things: "not going around with other women, and to treat the woman well, to respect her rights," and then he elaborated by saying that her rights included the freedom to speak her mind, to make financial decisions, and to control her own movements. Rhona Mahoney, writing about the experiences of women in rich countries, has described the power women can derive from a shared moral language about gender and fairness (for example, a shared understanding that it is fair for parents to divide child-care responsibilities). See Mahoney, *Kidding Ourselves.* In a multicountry study of how women in the developing world negotiate for control of their reproductive choices, Petchesky, Judd, and others from the International Reproductive Rights Action Group trace the importance of this rights-based language as a moral resource in women's strategic negotiations. See Petchesky and Judd, *Negotiating Reproductive Rights.*

19. Josefina constantly amazed me with her resourcefulness and ability to laugh in the face of bad luck. When, after a nine-hour sojourn (including four hours on the bus) for a prenatal care visit, she was told in one pharmacy after another that the 50-peso note she had hidden in her shoe all day had gotten so worn out that she could not use it to buy the prenatal vitamins the doctor had prescribed, she laughed at herself (*"que pendeja soy"*—what an idiot I am) and kept trying until she found a pharmacy that would accept it. All of which is to say, the reader should take this story of Pedro's drinking and violence as one piece in the depiction of her story but not as a tale of her victimhood.

20. Mirandé, "Que gacho es ser macho" and *Hombres y Machos.*

21. The younger women may have feared that I, as a gringa, would judge them or, for those in Atlanta, that I would turn in their husbands to the police. Furthermore, they might have been ashamed to tell me stories of domestic vio-

lence because they felt that they were ultimately the ones who had pushed their husbands too far (*darles motivo*) and so had asked for it. One of the few who admitted that her husband had actually hit her was Josefina, who was probably the woman with whom I became the closest. Several others denied to me that their husbands had ever hit them, in contrast to what others had told me about them.

22. There were two life history informants whose husbands had beaten them severely (at least two that I knew about), but neither even asked her husband if he would be interested in being interviewed.

23. Marital rape is an important topic in terms of discussions of women's physical and sexual autonomy; I discuss women's and men's ideas about women's right to say no to sex much more thoroughly in Chapter 7; I only bring it up here because the contrast between Juan's strong statement about his wife's right to say no to sex and his belief in his right to slap her is so striking.

24. Gutmann, *Meanings of Macho*.

25. Mahoney, *Kidding Ourselves*.

26. The idea that men's power is rooted in their productive capacity is an ideological power play in and of itself, rather than merely a statement of fact. To argue that earning money is men's source of power obscures the labor of social reproduction, which falls mostly on women—that is, there is some sleight-of-hand involved in the argument that men's work gives them the right to rule, while women's work merely gives them the right to expect to be supported. Furthermore, people break these "rules" all the time. Half of the life history informants in Mexico were earning some money, as were eleven out of the thirteen women in Atlanta.

27. Zelizer, "Social Meaning of Money."

28. Doubtless women have their own reasons for wanting an independent income, but they score no points as women for doing so. The essence of their nature as women is supposedly fulfilled through motherhood and housekeeping. As Zavella has pointed out, this creates a sort of double-bind for women, in which this understanding of women's income as "extra" facilitates their working at all by making their income much less threatening to men's power, but the fact that it is only acceptable for women to work so long as they do not fail to fulfill their "real" responsibilities means that they are never directed to take the sort of full-time, high-paying jobs that would give them the economic power to actually challenge their husbands. See Zavella, *Women's Work*.

29. Pedro had to be persistent with Josefina, since when they met she had another boyfriend. In contrast to Pedro's discussion of sentiment, Josefina talked about strategy in recounting their courtship narrative: as a sign of his love, Pedro was willing to ask for her hand formally (braving her father), and to have married correctly (*casarse bien*) is a lifelong marker of respect afforded to precious few girls in la colonia. The danger of running away with the other was that he would have sex with her and then leave her (as men sometimes do), and so various members of her family counseled her to choose Pedro, because he was showing her more respect. In spite of all the talk about love at first sight, then, it is important to remember that in a social setting in which women need

men more than men need women, marrying for love is a luxury not all women can afford.

30. I greatly regret not having asked them all to talk about men they admired.

31. This analysis follows in the tradition of Jane and Peter Schneider's *Festival of the Poor*, which looks at the connections between historical change, the adoption of self-consciously "modern" stances, and people's experiences of intimacy and sexual relations. Jane Collier presents a finely detailed portrait of similar changes in rural Spain in *From Duty to Desire*.

32. There is a carefully coded language to the gifts, which women do not seem to want to explain to men—the satisfaction lies in men knowing how to do it without being told. Women will let their birthdays or wedding anniversaries pass unnoticed (though with hurt feelings) rather than remind their husbands of the date. The one time Pedro bought her flowers, Josefina angrily rejected them because they were carnations instead of roses. Another time he bought her a pair of earrings he had seen her admiring, but she soon gave them to a friend; she said they caught her eye because of their gaudy glitter, and he should have known they were not her style. The gifts signify to women that their husbands know them in some deep, authentic way, that they will go out of their way to make them feel loved, and that they know that their duty as husbands is not just to support their wives but to cherish them.

33. Rouse, "Mexican Migration."

34. Of course, there is no plaza in Atlanta. The plaza, with its public rituals of courtship, is a key location in rural Mexico for the social reproduction of gender. The lack of noncommercial public space in migrant-receiving communities such as Atlanta is a key component in how migration reconstructs gender. This is clearly also a process by which larger structural forces discipline migrants into becoming obedient workers, but it seems important to allow for men's agency by reflecting on the reasons men might see it as in their individual strategic advantage to adopt this change in style.

35. Recall my discussion in note 23, Chapter 3, in which I observed that Mexican men and boys use large key rings as a favorite adornment.

36. The comparison between Pedro and Sergio raises the possibility that there is some relationship between changes in masculinity, rising participation in wage labor, and the concomitant decline in family-based agricultural work.

37. Alarcon, "El proceso de norteñización"; Lopez Castro, "Lenguaje y migración"; Goldring, "Blurring Borders."

38. Alarcon, "El proceso de norteñización"; Goldring, "Blurring Borders," 183.

39. Mahler, "Transnationalizing Research"; Pessar, "Situating Gender"; Rebhun, *Heart Is Unknown Country*.

40. Gutmann, *Meanings of Macho*.

CHAPTER 5. REPRESENTING CHANGE

1. Thorton, "Developmental Paradigm."

2. Bernard, *Research Methods*.

3. Austen, *Northanger Abbey.*

4. Hirsch, "Mexican Dirty Jokes."

5. Gutmann, *Meanings of Macho.*

6. Sex ratios at birth tend to hover between 102 and 107 (that is, between 1,020 and 1,070 men for every 1,000 women). See Miller, *Endangered Sex,* 40. In the overall population, demographers see sex ratios lower than 90 or above 105 as needing an explanation; the two most likely are war or, as is the case here, migration. By way of comparison, the sex ratios in postwar USSR were 81.9. See Shryock and Siegel, *Materials of Demography,* 110.

7. CONAPO, *Mortalidad.*

8. Banamex, *México Social.*

9. Mummert, "Western Rural Families," 23.

10. Mummert, "From *Metate* to *Despate,*" 205.

11. Ibid., 207.

12. Grimes, *Crossing Borders,* 95–96, 104.

13. González-Montes, "Intergenerational and Gender Relations," 185.

14. Vásquez-García, "Mujeres que 'respetan su casa,'" 180.

15. Amuchástegui, *Virginidad en México.*

16. Hubbell, "Values under Siege," 13.

17. LeVine, Sunderland, and Tapia Uribe, "Marital Morality," 183.

18. Ibid., 201. Similarly, women in Degollado and El Fuerte whose husbands migrate expressed a strong preference not to know about whatever liaisons they may have formed while apart. For the older women, sexual infidelity was never welcome, but it hardly ranked as a reason to leave a man. For the younger women, however, infidelity was a betrayal of the confianza on which the union depended. See Hirsch, Higgins, Bentley, and Nathanson, "Constructions of Sexuality."

19. Chant, "Household Survival Strategies," 226, and "Women's Work."

20. Martínez-Vásquez, "Mujeres ejecutivas," 277.

21. Rodríguez-Dorantes, "Las jefas de familia."

22. González-Montes, "Intergenerational and Gender Relations," 188.

23. UNIFEM/ INEGI 1995, cited in Rodríguez-Dorantes, "Las jefas de familia," 201.

24. Gutmann, *Meanings of Macho,* 221, 243.

25. Hubbell, "Values under Siege"; Chant, "Women's Work" and "Household Survival Strategies"; Mummert, "Western Rural Families" and "From *Metate* to *Despate.*"

26. Gutmann, *Meanings of Macho,* 251–53.

27. See Gutmann, *Meanings of Macho;* Tiano, *Patriarchy on the Line;* Mummert, "From *Metate* to *Despate*"; Chant, "Single-Parent Families," "Family Formation," "Women's Work," and "Household Survival Strategies." Much of this work on the relationship between wage labor and gender transformations suffers from the problematic assumption that capitalist industrialization promotes gender equality. Tiano discusses the ways in which wage labor simultaneously opens up new possibilities for women and endeavors to regulate their behavior through gendered ideologies (Tiano, *Patriarchy on the Line*).

28. Trying to complicate Das and Jesser's argument that industrialization has contributed to the rise of the nuclear family by weakening extended families, Chant notes that it is unreasonable to accept a new paradigm in which the nuclear family is normative, given the large—and growing—percentage of all families that are single-parent families throughout Latin America. See Chant, "Single-Parent Families" and "Family Formation"; Das and Jesser, *Family in Latin America*, cited in Chant, "Single-Parent Families."

29. De la Peña, "Ideology and Practice," 226.

30. Ibid., 226–27.

31. See Safa, "New Women Workers." González de la Rocha writes about "El poder de la ausencia" (the power of absence), by which she means that men's extended absences during migration leave women in charge and give them an expanded sphere for decision making and individual autonomy.

32. De Barbieri, "Sobre géneros, prácticas y valores," 98.

33. Ibid.

34. Arias, cited in ibid.

35. Montesinos-Carrera, "La identidad masculina," 23.

36. D.J. Smith, "Courting for Love," 11–12.

37. Wardlow, "All's Fair," 1, 4.

38. Chan, "Love and Jewelry," 2.

39. Ibid., 14.

40. See also Collier, *Duty to Desire*, on Spain; Cole, *Women of the Praia*, on Portugal; Rebhun, *Heart Is Unknown County*, on Brazil; Parikh, "Love Letters," on Uganda; Ahearn, "Love Keeps Afflicting Me" and "Invitations to Love," on Nepal; Maggi, "Heart-Struck," on Pakistan; Reddy, "Bonds of Love," on India; Inhorn, *Infertility and Patriarchy*, on Egypt; Yan, "Triumph of Conjugality" and *Private Life under Socialism*, on China; and Jankowiak, *Romantic Passion*, on love.

41. See Gillis, Tilly, and Levine, *Declining Fertility*; Skolnik, *Embattled Paradise*; Simmons, "Companionate Marriage"; Gordon, *Woman's Body*; Schneider and Schneider, *Festival of the Poor*; Stone, *Family in England*; Shorter, *Modern Family*; Stansell, *City of Women*.

42. Gregg, "Liberdade," 7.

43. Ibid., 5, 10.

44. Kandiyoti, cited in Gregg, "Liberdade," 2.

45. Erikson, *What Is Love*, 14, 16.

46. Junge, "Competing Discourses," 8.

47. Reddy, "Bonds of Love."

48. D.J. Smith, "These Girls Today" and "Courting for Love"; Wardlow, "All's Fair"; Parikh, "Love Letters."

49. Yan, "Triumph of Conjugality."

50. D.J. Smith, "These Girls Today" and "Courting for Love"; Collier, *Duty to Desire*; Rebhun, *Heart Is Unknown Country*; Maggi, "Heart-Struck."

51. Collier, *Duty to Desire*.

52. Hirsch and Wardlow, *Modern Loves*.

CHAPTER 6. *"EN EL NORTE LA MUJER MANDA"*

1. For example, Grassmuck and Pessar, *Between Two Islands.*
2. Hirsch, "Gender, Generation and Geography."
3. Behar, *Translated Woman;* Rouse, "Mexican Migration."
4. Cole, *Women of the Praia;* Collier, *Duty to Desire;* González de la Rocha, "El poder de la ausencia."
5. Cole, *Women of the Praia,* 87.
6. The life history informants' comments about how migration to the North has changed their lives reflect how they actually feel about their lives and a deliberate process of identity construction. When María insisted to me that "when women come here, they stop being so blind," she was talking about her own experiences *and* trying to shape my perception of her, in addition to making a general sociological observation. Similarly, when a woman who drives, works full time, and expects her husband to make the beds on his day off told me that women do not change at all when they go north, she seemed as much as anything to be insisting on the integrity of her authentic Mexican identity—that is, to be saying that she is still the same person, in spite of the many ways her life is different in Atlanta than it was in Degollado.
7. Between the time the fieldwork was completed (the summer of 1997) and 1999, two of the thirteen women interviewed in Atlanta made supposedly permanent moves to Degollado, only to return subsequently to Atlanta. Others had returned to Mexico and as of 1999 were still there, and still others interviewed in Mexico had come north. Furthermore, four of the life history informants interviewed in Atlanta had visited Mexico at least once during the fifteen months of my fieldwork, and Soledad, who lives in Degollado, traveled to Atlanta with her mother to visit her sisters for a month in the summer of 1997.
8. A family's migration history is related in complex ways to their local social status and economic security. Historically families with limited economic power and social status would be the ones most likely to look toward migration as a means to improve their lot, so that to say that a woman married into a family with strong migrant ties would imply that she married into a poor family with little to offer locally in terms of work opportunities for her husband. Following this logic, to say conversely that she married into a weakly developed migrant network would also be to say that she married into a locally powerful, important family and thus would have little reason to go north in the first place. However, some families in Degollado and El Fuerte have used their savings from trips north to buy land and start businesses, thus raising their social and economic status. So even if there is a complex and perhaps at this level of analysis inextricably intertwined relationship between a family's economic position and its history of migration, it still seems that migration history should be taken into account on its own.
9. Dwyer and Bruce, *Home Divided;* Dinerman, "Patterns of Adaptation."
10. *Atlanta Journal Constitution,* "Immigrants Facing Loss of Benefits"; *New York Times,* "Illegal Workers" and "Pregnant Wait."
11. Durand, *Más allá de la línea.*

12. Cornelius, "Los migrantes de la crisis." The intent of the 1986 Immigration Reform and Control Act (IRCA) was to limit undocumented immigration by imposing fines on employers who knowingly hired undocumented workers. However, the amnesty provision of the IRCA—which resulted in the provision of visas to 2.7 million people who could prove that they resided in the United States prior to 1986—is considered by many to have promoted undocumented migration, as some newly legal migrants brought their families to the United States, and others who did not qualify for that amnesty came in the hopes that they might qualify for a future one. See Smith and Edmonston, *The New Americans*, 20–75.

13. Hondagneu-Sotelo, *Gendered Transitions.*

14. Some of the women seemed close to their husband's sisters (*cuñadas*). Much less common is any exchange of favors between wives of brothers. In Spanish, this relationship is known as *concuñas*. Though these would also be called sisters-in-law in English, in Mexico it is a distinct, and much more problematic, relationship. Particularly in the past when women who married into a family would all live under the same roof in the patrilocal joint household, this relationship was thought to be rife with potential for backbiting, gossip, and competition to *quedar bien con la suegra* (get in good with the mother-in-law), and women both in Atlanta and in the field sites in Mexico had endless stories about difficulties with their husband's brothers' wives.

15. González de la Rocha, "El poder de la ausencia."

16. Cornelius, "Los migrantes de la crisis"; Chávez, "Settlers and Sojourners."

17. Hirsch, "Gender, Generation, and Geography."

18. Hondagneu-Sotelo, *Gendered Transitions.*

19. González de la Rocha, "El poder de la ausencia"; Cornelius, "Los migrantes de la crisis"; Cerrutti and Massey, "Female Migration."

20. The border itself seems cast in the popular imagination as a gendered zone, a sort of intensified version of the street, with a much greater danger for women than for men. As news reports, oral histories, folklore, and personal communications suggest, the crossing can be fatal, even for men (see Davis, *Mexican Voices;* Massey et al., *Return to Aztlan*), but popular wisdom has it that the danger is far greater for women because they stand to lose not just their lives but their honor. People say, "*Los coyotes son muy abusados*" (the smugglers will really take advantage of you). As is palpable to anyone who has stood on *la linea* watching the *pollos* mass for their midnight dash into the desert, the border feels like a strange, wild, liminal zone where all the respeto of Mexico abruptly gives way to the anonymity and moral disorder of life on the other side. Mexicans talk about how this lack of respect in the United States endangers women.

21. Durand, *Más allá de la línea,* 157; Cerrutti and Massey, "Female Migration."

22. González de la Rocha and Escobar, *Mexico's Economic Crisis.*

23. *New York Times,* "Exodus of Migrant Families."

24. Rouse, "Mexican Migration."

25. During the 1990s, as part of the enforcement of immigration laws in Georgia, the requirements necessary to get a driver's license in Georgia were made more stringent to prevent undocumented migrants from getting licenses. In 2000, under the sponsorship of the local business communities, both North Carolina and Tennessee passed legislation that made it possible to apply for a driver's license without being a citizen or legal resident, but the law in Georgia continued to prevent undocumented immigrants from getting licenses there.

26. Of course, not all men in Mexico face these pressures to act out a certain kind of masculine identity. Earlier, I contrasted the experiences of Sergio, who as his own boss and an independent contractor can take his wife, Juana, with him to visit clients during the day, with those of Pedro, who as a construction worker has to face his coworkers' taunts when he refuses to join them for a drink after work.

27. Billings is the name for the version of the rhythm method approved by the Catholic Church.

28. There are Jehovah's Witnesses knocking on doors in Degollado and El Fuerte, but "*los halelujas*" have barely gained a toehold in these Mexican field sites.

29. This threat only carries weight, of course, if one believes strongly enough in the efficiency with which court-ordered child-support arrangements are enforced; ironically, then, a threat such as this might be more effective among Mexican immigrants than it would be to a man who was a native-born American, because most immigrants have formed their impressions of the regulatory power of the U.S. government based on their contacts with the INS (and in comparison to the sometimes formidable inefficiency of their own government). It seems it never would have occurred to either of them, as it did to me, that men succeed all the time in evading child-support payments.

30. Other research with Mexican battered women in Atlanta confirms that women earning more than their husbands is a risk factor for domestic violence. See Perilla, Bakeman, and Norris, "Culture and Domestic Violence." In Perilla's research, women who earned more than their husbands were more likely to have suffered domestic violence than women who did not earn more. "Mutuality," an indicator that measured the extent to which the couple felt that they made decisions together and whether the man regarded his wife more as his companion than as his servant (*criada*), was a mitigating factor in these couples; to some extent a greater measure of mutuality negated the effect of income disparity.

31. Grassmuck and Pessar, *Between Two Islands.*

32. The phrase "to let her work" is a direct translation of the Spanish *dejar que trabaje.* The implication that men (either fathers or husbands) can and should control whether a woman works outside the home obscures the fact that women's paid work is a topic of intense negotiation. Juana, Isabel, Josefina, Mercedes, and Perla have all been involved at times in income-generating work that their husbands preferred they not do; thus when a man says that he "lets" his wife work, it could either mean that he has the power to decide and he gave her permission, or that he does not have the power to decide but wishes to cover

that up. A woman would never say that she "lets" her husband work, of course, because being a man means having both the right and the obligation to work.

33. The phrase that those in Degollado used to measure the entirety of my time "in the community," counting both the time in Atlanta and in Degollado.

34. González de la Rocha, "El poder de la ausencia."

CHAPTER 7. SEXUAL INTIMACY IN MEXICAN
COMPANIONATE MARRIAGES

1. My questions about women's sexual relationships with their husbands covered their wedding night, verbal and nonverbal communication about sex, sexual preferences and satisfaction, pleasure, foreplay and sexual activities other than vaginal intercourse, and potential problems in the sexual relationship (see Hirsch, "Migration, Modernity, and Mexican Marriage"). As one of the women said—and it should be noted that it was only in the sixth interview that she made comments of this ilk—"*son bien atrevidas, tus preguntas*" (your questions are really bold [*atrevida* could also be translated as audacious, so I am giving myself the benefit of the doubt here]). To protect women's privacy, the quotes in this chapter are attributed in only the most general terms. In contrast, the questions asked in the interviews with men were much less personal—I would have been run out of town if I went around interviewing men about foreplay and their wedding night experiences—and so their quotes are attributed by name. Material in this chapter and the one that follows was presented in papers at the 1998 meeting of the American Anthropological Association and at the 1999 IUSSP meeting in Cairo, at seminars in the Departments of International Health and Anthropology at Emory University, and in an article in *Culture, Health and Society* (Hirsch and Nathanson, "Some Traditional Methods"). Along the way, I received input from many generous readers, and I would particularly like to acknowledge the comments of Hania Sholkamy, Bill Hanks, and Tom Fricke, as well as five anonymous reviewers.

2. There is a growing recognition that sexuality per se is a valid and important category of inquiry within public-health research. See Dixon-Mueller, "Sexuality Connection"; Zeidenstein and Moore, *Learning About Sexuality.* Early public-health research on sexuality tended to define it rather narrowly as a domain of behaviors or (slightly more expansively) as a category that includes norms and relationships; see, for example, Ford and Norris, "Urban Hispanic Adolescents"; Moran and Corley, "Sexual Information, Attitudes, and Behaviors"; Scott et al., "Adolescents' Beliefs." Here, sexuality is defined as the behaviors, emotions, and ideas people have about physical relations with others; it includes both extremely concrete issues, such as the specific behaviors people expect in a sexual interaction with another person (for example, Gagnon and Simon, *Sexual Conduct;* Laumann et al., *Social Organization of Sexuality*) and more abstract issues such as what motivates people to have sex (that is, culturally variable ideas about the social and biological sources of sexual desire, and how those desires vary by gender [for example, Snitow, Stansell, and Thompson, *Powers of Desire;* Vance, "Anthropology Rediscovers Sexuality"]).

3. This is not a perfect question, of course, since women do not ejaculate and so a "no" on a woman's part could either mean that only men ejaculate or that only men have orgasms.

4. One woman said, for example, that she literally had no idea that they were going to even sleep in the same bed; she just thought they were going to live in the same house, and she was going to cook and clean for him, and when they wanted to have a baby "[she] really thought that they sold them in La Piedad."

5. Goldstein, "AIDS and Women in Brazil," and Rebhun, *Heart Is Unknown Country*, both working in Brazil, had similar findings about generational differences in women's willingness to admit to sexual knowledge. This is just another example of why it is critical for those conducting research on sexuality (whether survey or ethnographic) to think about how people's responses are shaped by their desire to represent themselves to the interviewer.

6. There is an obvious contradiction in saying that the confianza a couple shares implies that their sexual behavior is private, and at the same time reporting on how women talked about that sexual behavior with their friends and in interviews with me—after all, if it were really so secret, how could they talk about it? Within the culturally specific meanings of confianza, however, sharing information with some people in certain circumstances does not violate that trust. When one woman's husband made a comment about her lack of vergüenza in front of her children, it was hurtful because of both the speaker and the audience: under the terms of confianza, a woman's husband is absolutely the last person who should reveal her sexual behavior. Women talked repeatedly about how the most important condition for participating in any kind of behavior that could be interpreted as lacking in shame (for example, initiating sex or expanding their sexual repertoire) is the trust that their husbands will not throw it in their faces (*echarles en cara*) in public. So for that woman's husband to have mentioned her behavior in front of their children—the very people who should have the most respeto for her, and therefore be least exposed to evidence of her sexuality—was truly a cruel move on his part. When a woman reveals something about her own sexual experience to a group of gathered friends, it has a totally different meaning than it would if her husband divulged the same information. He would be risking his wife's respectability, whereas she is merely sharing with her friends. For a man to tell something to other men makes it public in a way that it does not when a woman tells the same thing to other women.

Less personal discussions about sexuality—and sexual joking in particular—frequently serve as indicators of confianza among women more or less of the same age and marital status. In many of the all-female social events I attended, the conversation would turn quickly to sexual joking; these jokes—which women found hilarious—marked a kind of equality among the group, signifying the lack of a hierarchy that might be violated by the mention of sexual topics.

7. Being *un gallo jugado* (literally, a cock that has been played) has the same meanings in Spanish as it might in English. Furthermore, the rooster is a familiar symbol of oversexed masculinity in Mexican popular culture, figuring

prominently in everything from *albures* (a dozens-like verbal game revolving around the "joke" of anal rape) (see Hirsch, "Mexican Dirty Jokes") to the unforgettable vision of a man tenderly kneeling down to suck the blood out of the mouth of his dying cock during a cockfight.

8. Mexican men use the word "friend" (*amiga*) to describe relationships with women that may or may not be sexual but that have not been formalized into a noviazgo. The connotation is not, as it is in English, one of emotional intimacy, but rather one of informality. In the interviews, when men talked about being close to their wives, they would use words such as *pareja* (partner) or *compañera* (companion) more commonly than amiga, and in fact the implied informality of the term seems to suggest a certain lack of respect. In her research on the different kinds of relationships Mexican migrant men in Los Angeles have with women other than their wives, Harvey et al. also found that amiga was, as a category, considerably less formal and committed than novia. See Harvey et al., "Reproductive Decision-Making."

9. Nencel, "Men's Sexual Selves."

10. The most common way of saying this is "*si no te dan de comer en la casa, comes en la calle*" (if they don't feed you at home, you'll eat in the street). Women can also use culinary metaphors to remind their husbands of their conjugal duties; one woman recounted to me how she jokingly let her husband know that he ought to spend more time at home by telling him, "*Ceno a las nueve, estes o no estes*" (I eat dinner at nine, whether or not you are home).

11. A woman's physical need for sex can explain, though not justify, her infidelity. Pedro said that if a woman's husband does not fulfill his obligations (*no le cumple*) and she is very *temperamental* (hot) (which he implies is not the norm), her nature may drive her to infidelity. Francisco also hinted that women as well might have a physical need for sex. The word he uses, *atender,* means in this context to acknowledge and satisfy a partner's sexual needs. Some women run around on their husbands "because they are tricky, they like it" but others, he said, are forced into infidelity because their husbands neglect them: "There are many men who prefer a bottle of booze to taking care of their wife" (*atender a la mujer*). No doubt so that I would not confuse him with one of those pathetic creatures, he continued, telling me that if he were forced to choose between a woman and a bottle of booze, he would take (and presumably take good care of) both.

12. These times when women say no because they are not in the mood should not be confused with saying no because they have their period or during the forty days after the birth of a child, *la cuarentena,* when a man is also supposed to let his wife rest. All of the women in the study, regardless of generation, said that it was not only disgusting (*cochino*) to have sex while menstruating, but that it could also harm a man's health and lead to dark blotches on his face, known as *paño*. Since women are frequently regarded as themselves more open (*abierta*) and thus more vulnerable to disease during menstruation, it is interesting that in this case the threat is to the man's health—of course, the risk of bearing a sign on his cheeks or forehead of having done something widely said to be disgusting gives the prohibition more weight. The only variety in terms of attitudes toward sex while menstruating was that one of the older women said

that while one was not supposed to have sex while menstruating, men did not always accord their wives this respect—that is, that sometimes they would force them—and several of the younger women noted that while they did not have sex on the heaviest days of their period, they would sometimes not wait until it was completely over.

13. Corona Vargas, "Resquicios en las puertas."

14. D'Emilio, "Capitalism and Gay Identity," 242. See also Katz, "Invention of Heterosexuality."

15. The metaphoric connection between heat and sexuality is even stronger in Spanish. To be *caliente* means either to have a high temperature or to be in an excited state sexually but is generally taken to mean the latter (as any beginning Spanish speaker who has ever made the mistake of announcing to a crowded room that he or she is caliente will remember with painful clarity). To be cold (*frio*), similarly, suggests a lack of sexual desire. See Currier, "Hot-Cold Syndrome"; Anderson, "Humoral Medicine"; Messer, "Hot and Cold"; Logan, "Hot-Cold Theory of Disease"; Lopez Austin, "Los puestos complementarios." In future work I hope to explore gender, sexual aspects of hot-cold balance, and generational changes in physiological models of desire in greater depth.

16. Similarly, Linda Gordon notes that American Protestant churches in the 1920s and 1930s also worked to harness the discourse of conjugal desire in the service of strengthening the family. See Gordon, *Woman's Body,* 256.

17. Bronfman and Minello, "Hábitos sexuales."

18. Even then, as Rhona Mahoney points out in *Kidding Ourselves: Babies, Breadwinning and Bargaining Power,* a woman who is technically capable of supporting herself and her children can over time make choices in her marriage that make her more and more dependent economically on a spouse with whom she was economically equal the day they wed.

19. Foucault, *History of Sexuality;* Gallagher and Laquer, *Modern Body;* Weeks, *Sex, Politics and Society;* Giddens, *Transformation of Intimacy;* D'Emilio, "Capitalism and Gay Identity."

CHAPTER 8. FERTILITY DECLINE, CONTRACEPTIVE CHOICE, AND MEXICAN COMPANIONATE MARRIAGES

1. To the extent that demographic studies of fertility decline around the world have focused on social relationships at all, they have concentrated primarily on those between parents and children (for example, Caldwell, *Theory of Fertility Decline*), or on the implications of microlevel gender inequality for women's use of contraceptive methods (see Blanc, "Power in Sexual Relationships," for a review of this literature). Here I follow the lead of anthropologists (for example, Schneider and Schneider, *Festival of the Poor*) and social historians (for example, McLaren, "Sexual Politics"; Gillis, "Gender and Fertility Decline"; Seccombe, "Changing Conjugal Relations") to argue that people's changing relationships with their children cannot be analyzed in isolation from the other relationships in their family, in particular the conjugal bond. Some scholars, of course, have made a connection between marital characteristics and fertility, raising questions about gender, power, and fertility decline (see Safilios-

Rothchild, "Female Power"; Mason, "Status of Women" and "Women's Social Position"). These studies of gender and fertility decline have been somewhat unidimensional—or even ethnocentric—in that they have concentrated on narrowly constructed measures of power and autonomy rather than conducting a more multidimensional analysis of marriage as an institution as suggested by Connell in *Gender and Power* or looking at what it means to individual actors to build their families (Schneider and Schneider, *Festival of the Poor*). Even more sophisticated studies of women's empowerment and fertility (for example, Federici, Mason, and Sogner, *Women's Position*), which employ multiple measures of gender inequality in marriage rather than simplistic notions of women's status, tend not to include the ways in which marriages are both institutions that reproduce gender-based social stratification *and,* at the same time, fields of social relations in which people have affective and identity goals.

2. See Mathews et al., "Monthly Vital Statistics Report." Data on long-term trends in births of Hispanic origin are not available because only since 1989 have all of the states with a significant number of Hispanics been tracking Hispanic-origin births at all, and only recently have those data distinguished different Hispanic groups. These data, it should be noted, only count as "Hispanic" those births on which the mother is known to be Hispanic. A child whose father is a first-generation Mexican immigrant will not be counted as Hispanic unless his mother is Hispanic.

3. See Kahn, "Immigrant and Native Fertility"; Stephen and Bean, "Fertility of Mexican Women"; Bean and Swicegood, "Mexican-American Fertility Patterns." Analyses of the 1980 U.S. census data suggested that women of Mexican origin in the United States were in fact more similar to their peers in Mexico in terms of criteria such as educational background—that is, they were less highly selected—than women in many other immigrant groups, but this very well may have changed since then (see Kahn, "Immigrant Selectivity"). The composition of migrant streams changes over time: initially those leaving a town in Mexico might be those with the resources necessary to migrate and the family connections in el norte, but over time migrants are more widely drawn from the local population (see Massey et al., *Return to Aztlan*). This may be even more true in the post-IRCA era: the characteristics of male migrants from Mexico changed in the years following immigration reform and the currency shocks of the late 1980s and early 1990s, suggesting that migrant flows grew to include previously nonmigrating groups such as the urban middle class. So little research was done on women's migration from Mexico prior to the mid-1980s that any discussion of how the population of female migrants has changed remains speculative.

4. See McKinney, "Migrant Fertility in Senegal." The sometimes prolonged spousal separations that are a common part of family stage migration lend some ethnographic weight to the possibility, as do the comments made by a number of life history informants, that on being reunited with their husbands in the United States they would wait for a time before conceiving their next child.

5. Neither of these approaches is without its flaws. The first assumes an unrealistic amount of homogeneity in both the sending and receiving cultures, as well as assuming that there is in fact some degree of contact between migrants

and natives. These first-generation immigrants speak little English, and for the most part I was the only American woman they knew well, so they could hardly be called assimilated. The second approach, directing our attention to structural forces, assumes that all migrants will in fact become structurally integrated. Portes and others have pointed out how even among Hispanic migrants there are widely ranging experiences with structural integration. See Portes and Bach, *Latin Journey;* Portes and Rumbaut, *Immigrant America;* Fernandez-Kelly, *For We Are Sold.*

6. One possibility that seems potentially very fruitful would be retrospective fertility and migration histories with Mexican women in the United States and in Mexico who have completed childbearing. Although there are not enough older women from Degollado and El Fuerte in Atlanta to do this, there certainly are enough in some of the other receiving communities, such as Chicago.

7. For further discussion of the demographic significance of the first birth, see Hirsch, "Un noviazgo."

8. I frequently complained to Evita and to several of the other informants with whom I felt confianza about the *pinche gente tan metiche* (the damn nosy people) who kept demanding that I justify my fertility behavior. I felt the pressure much more intensely in Mexico than I did while conducting fieldwork in Atlanta. In part, this may have been because it was more apparent to those I knew in Atlanta that I did have a husband and an extended family; several of the life history informants visited me at home, and others hustled me out of their houses at 4 or 4:30 so I would not get stuck in traffic on my way home to make dinner for my husband. People in Atlanta may also have felt less free to try to fit me into their social categories when we were on what was clearly my turf rather than theirs. The social contact, of course, was also less intense; while at home in Atlanta I could leave "the field" every day (though sometimes "the field" called me at home late at night to wake me up) in a way that was only possible in Mexico during my occasional weekend escapes to Guadalajara.

9. People did seem to understand the importance of a college degree, but when they found out not only that had I graduated from college a decade prior to beginning the project but that the degree I was currently seeking would make me into some kind of doctor who could not cure anyone, they were generally reduced to bemused laughter and speculation on how different life really is in the United States. I eventually gave up trying to explain my professional plans to those around me.

Tellingly, when I did get pregnant, the most common reaction to the news was for people to say "*¿está contentísimo tu señor, no?*" (your husband is delighted, isn't he?). They generally seemed to think it was quite selfish of me to have made him wait so long. Both in the Mexican field sites (which I deliberately visited while pregnant to show off my belly) and in Atlanta, people were relieved that, after pushing the envelope on the amount of time one might enjoy as a childless couple, I had finally seen fit to give my husband every man's heart's desire. Some couples do delay the first birth for a year or two, but for us to have gone four years without producing a child was thought by all to be a bit much.

10. Potter, "Outmoded Contraceptive Regimes."

11. Schoen et al., "Americans Want Children."

12. Szasz, personal communication.

13. Bledsoe et al., "Constructing Natural Fertility."

14. This change should be read not merely as an economic change, a transition from "quantity" children to "quality" (Easterlin and Crimmins, *Fertility Revolution*) but also as a cultural response to that change, as a redefinition of what it means to be a good parent and as a deliberate statement about being a modern person, the kind of person who knows how to produce a child who can succeed in a world that demands different skills and resources.

15. None of the women discussed markedly strong gender preferences such as those that researchers have found in South Asia (for example, Miller, *Endangered Sex*), but modest gender preferences did enter into couples' overall family-building plans. There seemed to be an assumption that men prefer boys and women prefer girls, so that in a family with no sons the husband might press for more children, while in one with no daughters it might be the wife who argues for trying for another. Second, a number of the women seemed to talk about wanting to have children in *parejitas* (literally, little couples), so that they would mention wanting to have "one little couple" (that is, a boy and a girl) or "two little couples" (two and two). I also discussed abortion and menstrual regulation with the life history informants, but there is not room here to do justice to the complexity of their ideas about health and menstrual regularity. For the moment, it must suffice to note that all of them stated strong opposition on moral grounds to the idea of an induced abortion.

16. In families of three or four, closely spaced births could mean that a woman's children were all in school ten years after her marriage and all out of the house after twenty. Isabel, for example, said she wanted four children but hoped to wait at least five years between the first two and the second two. Running through women's comments is a theme about the pleasure of having a little one to kiss and cuddle. In fact, when women talk about wanting a subsequent child, they discuss it in terms of an *antojo,* which is also the word people use for any nonstaple food that is craved for the special pleasure of eating a treat, whether sweet, salty, fried, or spicy. Mariana, now expecting her ninth child, said she could not resist the antojo of having one more child, now that her youngest son was in kindergarten.

17. The U.S. version of companionate marriages does not deny the pleasures of parenting, but it does emphasize more strongly the primacy of the bond between the couple. Although American parents talk about the sadness of the empty nest, they also joke about freedom. (As one joke goes, a minister, a priest, and a rabbi are debating when life begins. The priest says, "Life begins at conception." The minister says, "No, life begins at quickening." The rabbi says, "No, you're both wrong, life begins the day you drop the last kid off at college and the dog dies.") The difference in emphasis is also exemplified by how parents act at weddings. At weddings in the Mexican field sites, I was struck (particularly in El Fuerte) by the general assumption that a wedding was a thoroughly sad occasion for the parents of both the bride and the groom, as opposed to the bittersweet experience it is thought to be in the United States. Sometimes the bride's parents did not even attend the weddings because they said it was too sad for them to see their daughter get married, while at others

they went to the Mass but did not stay for the party; they felt that by delivering her to the altar in white they had discharged their responsibilities. (The groom's parents are forced to attend, since they host the party after the wedding.) Weddings in the United States are certainly an emotional time for a family, and many parents cry during wedding ceremonies, but they are generally expected to act joyful at the wedding itself.

18. To some extent this is supported by survey data from the National Survey of Family Growth and the Mexican Consejo Nacional de Población, which shows that Mexican women in Mexico were more likely than "Hispanic" women in the United States to be using nontechnological methods (see Table 8.4). There are a number of problems with comparing the data; "Hispanic women" includes women who are not of Mexican origin at all, as well as those who are second generation, and excludes women whose fathers but not mothers are of Hispanic origin. Still, it is interesting that more than 12 percent of women in the CONAPO data were using "traditional methods," while the number using abstinence in the NSFG was much lower. Even if users of withdrawal were classified as "other" (5.1 percent), this would still mean that the total use of "traditional" methods among Hispanic women in the United States is 8.8 percent, much less the 12.3 percent in Mexico.

The Mexican data also provide a useful reminder that our emphasis here on the continued importance of nontechnological methods needs to be seen in the context of the striking rise in overall method use and the relative decline in importance of nontechnological methods in Mexico. Between 1976 and 1997, the percentage of women in unions ages fifteen to forty-nine using any method went from 30.2 percent to 68.5 percent, and the percentage of overall users who rely on traditional methods declined from 23.3 percent to 12.3 percent. Taken from CONAPO, "Planificación familiar."

19. The forehead, *la frente,* is used idiomatically in a way that suggests that it is a part of the body that reveals one's essence and heritage. For example, María frequently talked about how no matter how long she lives in the United States, no one will ever mistake her for an American, *"con el nopal que traigo en la frente"* (with the cactus that I have on my forehead). (The *nopal,* or prickly pear cactus, is considered a symbol of Mexican-ness: the eagle on the Mexican flag is depicted standing atop a nopal, and it is one of the Mexican delicacies that immigrants always talk about craving while in culinary exile in the United States.)

20. Potter, "Outmoded Contraceptive Regimes."

21. Chavez, Flores, and Lopez-Garza, "Immigrants and U.S. Health Services"; Hirsch, "Mexican Marriage"; Georgia Department of Human Resources, "Access to Health Care"; Sebert, "Needs Assessment"; *Atlanta Journal Constitution,* "Global Atlanta."

22. This may not be the wisest policy in terms of protecting women's overall reproductive health—cervical cancer, detectable through Pap smears, is a leading cause of death among Mexican women of reproductive age. See Langer and Romero, "Salud reproductiva."

23. The exception, of course, is that women with limited English skills sometimes need to call on a neighbor or friend to help them get to a clinic or to

TABLE 8.4. COMPARISON OF CONTRACEPTIVE METHOD PREFERENCES, HISPANIC WOMEN IN THE UNITED STATES AND WOMEN IN MEXICO

Method	Percentage of Contraceptors Using That Method	
	NSFG (Hispanic Women)	CONAPO
Female sterilization	33.1	44.7
Male sterilization	6.4	1.8
Pill	31.4	10.2
IUD	1.9	20.8
Diaphragm	1.5	N.A.
Condom	17.1	N.A.
Periodic abstinence	3.7	N.A.
Other	5.1	N.A.
Injection	N.A.	4.6
Condom and foam	N.A.	5.7
Traditional methods	N.A.	12.3
Total	100	100

SOURCES: L.S. Peterson, *Contraceptive Use in the United States, 1982–90* (Hyattsville, Md.: Vital and Health Statistics, National Center for Health Statistics, Centers for Disease Control and Prevention, 14 February 1995); and CONAPO, *Planificación familiar* (Mexico City: Consejo Nacional de Población, 1997).

translate for them once they are there, and this certainly can compromise their privacy.

24. Bronfman and Minello, "Hábitos sexuales."

25. Santow, "Coitus Interruptus"; Schneider and Schneider, *Festival of the Poor.*

26. Comments such as these sometimes made me feel that these women's husbands were being controlling. The fact that the women themselves experienced their husbands' preferences as an expression of caring should alert us to the culture-bound nature of the assumption, almost universally made by family-planning programs, that female-controlled methods are inherently empowering to women. The underlying premise is that women are more able to make the choices they desire when they do so individually; in situations such as the one described here, though, marital fertility may be a significant resource for women precisely because of men's investment in it, and thus there may be real benefits to a method that is not female controlled. For a further discussion of this, see Luker, *Taking Chances,* and Nathanson, *Dangerous Passage.*

27. Although coitus interruptus is not in fact a method of which the Catholic Church approves, for the most part women seemed not to be aware of this

(or to have conveniently ignored this bit of information). The extent to which women see both rhythm and withdrawal as morally equivalent—and innocent—is revealed by the fact that women who use these methods will frequently say that they are doing nothing to control their fertility. They say *no agarro nada* (I don't touch anything) or *no tomo nada* (I am not taking anything) when in fact they faithfully count the days between menstrual cycles or encourage their husbands to withdraw before ejaculating. The same, it should be noted, is true of women who breast-feed; they rarely included this as a method for fertility control even when they were doing it deliberately for this purpose. Many of the life history informants knew older women who had sought permission from a priest for sterilization after being told by a doctor that a subsequent birth would endanger their health, but few of them dared seek such permission for themselves.

28. Eighteen percent of typical users of withdrawal are estimated to become pregnant in their first year of relying on this method. See Hatcher et al., *Technologia anticonceptiva*, 449.

29. Schneider and Schneider, *Festival of the Poor.*

30. Just who gets to *gozar*, to enjoy (also a synonym for "to come"), while using this method merits further exploration. If simultaneous orgasm is not a priority, it is possible for women to have an orgasm (or several) and then for men to withdraw and ejaculate outside the vagina. However, if (as some of the life history informants suggested) intercourse is regarded as most satisfying when the couples experience simultaneous orgasm (which seems unlikely if not impossible if they are using withdrawal), coitus interruptus becomes more of a mutual sacrifice. Some women said in their discussions of sexual pleasure that their partners would let them have an orgasm first (to make sure they got a chance to have one at all) before ejaculating themselves, while others talked more about the importance of having a simultaneous orgasm. It was not clear how widespread this privileging of simultaneous orgasm was, but if it is widely shared then that would mean that women also see CI as inherently unsatisfying to women, not just to men.

31. Of course, they do not need to abstain from sexual intimacy altogether, but merely from intercourse. However, none of the women suggested that they used nonpenetrative forms of mutual sexual satisfaction during their fertile periods: several of the women said that they alerted their husbands that the day of their ovulation was approaching by telling them not to come near or even to try to touch them. Though perhaps this possibility could have been explored in greater depth, comments such as this certainly imply that if they are not having intercourse, they are not doing much else either during that time.

CHAPTER 9. CONCLUSIONS

1. Foner, "Immigrant Family"; Goldring, "Gendered Memory"; Grimes, *Crossing Borders;* Kibria, cited in Foner, "Immigrant Family"; Fadiman, *Spirit Catches You.* Violence, of course, still occurs in these immigrant families (see, for example, Perilla, Bakeman, and Norris, "Culture and Domestic Violence"), and may even become more prevalent with long-term settlement (according to

Lown and Vega, "Physical Partner Abuse," second-generation Mexican immigrant women are twice as likely to experience violence from their intimate partners as are first-generation women). Rather, the striking similarity of these observations point to violence's power as a symbol of how people perceive the different role of families in the United States.

2. Hall, cited in Amuchástegui, *Virginidad en México*, 36. Quote from Amuchástequi, 36 (translation mine).

3. Chant, "Women's Work" and "Household Survival Strategies"; González de Rocha, *Resources of Poverty*.

4. Rebhun, *Heart Is Unknown Country*, 2.

5. Parker, *Bodies, Pleasures and Passions;* Lancaster, *Life Is Hard;* D'Emilio, "Capitalism and Gay Identity"; Carrier, "Mexican Male Bisexuality" and "Sexual Behavior in Mexico"; Almaguer, "Chicano Men"; Connell, *Masculinities.*

6. Rich, "Compulsory Heterosexuality"; Smith-Rosenberg, *Disorderly Conduct;* Peiss, *Cheap Amusements;* Snitow, Stansell, and Thompson, *Powers of Desire;* Stansell, *City of Women* and *American Moderns;* Weeks, *Sex, Politics and Society.*

7. On adolescents, see Luker, *Taking Chances;* Thompson, *Going All the Way;* Nathanson, *Dangerous Passage.* On poor minority women, see Worth, "Sexual Decision-Making"; Kline, Kline, and Oken, "Sexual Choice"; Sobo, "Condom Use" and *Choosing Unsafe Sex.*

8. On adolescent sexual behavior, see Santelli et al., "Adolescent Sexual Behavior"; Donovan, "Special Analysis"; on abortion, see Henshaw, "Teenage Abortion"; and on fertility and contraceptive use, see Feyisetan and Casterline, "Fertility Preferences."

9. Important exceptions, of course, are the work of Giddens, *Transformation of Intimacy,* and Foucault, *History of Sexuality*—but these are the theoretical benchmarks. We do have the tools, theoretically, to analyze heterosexuality but few have set these tools to work.

10. Vance, "Anthropology Rediscovers Sexuality."

11. D'Emilio, "Capitalism and Gay Identity," 241.

12. De Zalduondo, "Prostitution Viewed Cross-Culturally."

13. Sobo, "Condom Use" and *Choosing Unsafe Sex.*

14. Cancian, "Feminization of Love."

15. See Parker, "HIV/AIDS Research"; Farmer, *Infections and Inequalities.*

16. Vance, "Anthropology Rediscovers Sexuality"; Parker and Aggleton, *Culture, Society and Sexuality.*

17. Farmer, *Infections and Inequalities,* 84.

18. CDC, "AIDS Cases and Rates."

19. Rapp, *Testing Women,* 226.

20. Watney, "Safer Sex as Community Practice," 411.

21. For example, Kline, Kline, and Oken, "Sexual Choice"; Worth, "Sexual Decision-Making"; Sobo, "Condom Use" and *Choosing Unsafe Sex.*

22. See Bledsoe et al., "Constructing Natural Fertility"; Greenhalgh, *Situating Fertility;* Kertzer and Fricke, *Anthropological Demography.*

23. Dixon-Mueller, "Sexuality Connection"; Petchesky and Judd, *Negotiating Reproductive Rights.*

24. Of course, women also bargain with other women—as relatives, friends, and lovers.

25. Rapp, *Testing Women;* Pesquera, "He Wouldn't Lift a Spoon"; Petchesky and Judd, *Negotiating Reproductive Rights.*

26. See Blanc, "Power in Sexual Relationships," for a review.

27. Hirsch, "AIDS Risk Behavior."

28. Soler et al., "Relationship Dynamics." Mason ("Balance of Power") and Amaro ("Love, Sex and Power") take a more expansive view of gender inequality and thus are exceptions to this literature.

29. Gutmann, *Meanings of Macho,* 221–42.

30. See, for example, Stoler, "Politics of Race and Sexual Morality"; Lavrin, *Sexuality and Marriage;* Schiebinger, *Nature's Body;* Trouillot, "Anthropology and the Savage Slot."

31. Schneider and Schneider, *Festival of the Poor,* 9–11; see also Thorton, "Development Paradigm."

32. Gutmann, *Meanings of Macho.*

33. Foucault, *History of Sexuality.*

34. Collier, *Duty to Desire,* 113–52, discusses in great detail the tension between the fact that women in rural Spain perceive these marriages to be more egalitarian and her observation that there are a number of ways in which women in these modern families are more dependent on their husbands than women were in the past.

35. CONAPO, "La Nupcialidad en México"; Giddens, *Transformation of Intimacy.*

36. Giddens, *Transformation of Intimacy,* 58.

37. Cherlin, "Going to Extremes."

38. UNAIDS, "Men and AIDS."

39. In 1995, one study revealed that 25 percent of rural AIDS cases were among men who had been in the United States, while only 6 percent of urban cases reported travel to the United States; therefore, a substantial portion of these rural cases are likely to be related to temporary migration. See Magis-Rodríguez et al., "Rural AIDS Cases in Mexico." In Jalisco, Mexico (the state in which Degollado is located), one study found that half of reported AIDS cases had traveled to foreign countries. See Díaz-Santana and Celis, "AIDS and Migration." In neighboring Michoacán, where El Fuerte is located, Pineda found that 39 percent of those with AIDS had traveled to the United States. See Pineda, cited in Bronfman, Sejenovich, and Uribe, *Migración y SIDA.*

40. Magis-Rodríguez et al., "AIDS Cases in Rural Mexico," "Rural AIDS Cases in Mexico," and *Rural AIDS Cases in Mexico.*

41. Santarriaga et al., "HIV/AIDS in a Mexican State"; Mishra, Conner, and Magaña, *AIDS Crossing Borders;* Bronfman and Minello, "Hábitos sexuales"; Bronfman, Sejenovich, and Uribe, *Migración y SIDA.*

42. Research in progress, however, suggests that a good proportion of men do manage to resist the temptations of easy gringas. A survey with a convenience sample of two hundred married or partnered Mexican migrants in Atlanta found that only 38 percent reported having had sex while away from home. (See Hirsch, Yount, Chakraborty, and Nyhus, "AIDS-Risk Behavior

among Mexican Migrants.") This underlines the importance of looking for social and cultural factors that operate at the microlevel to create intracultural diversity in sexual risk behavior. What puts Mexican men who are labor migrants at risk for HIV infection, however, are not just cultural factors such as their beliefs about sexuality and masculinity, but also the fact that they are in the United States having sex with casual partners, rather than at home having sex with their wives, and they are here because they are building our roads, mowing our lawns, plucking our chickens, and busing our tables in restaurants. See Hirsch, "AIDS Risk Behavior."

43. Hirsch, Higgins, Bentley, and Nathanson, "Constructions of Sexuality."

44. Collier, *Duty to Desire;* de Barbieri, "Sobre géneros, prácticas y valores."

Glossary

A ESCONDIDAS in secret
ABIERTA open-minded (literally, open)
ADIÓS greeting: hello or good-bye
AGACHADO bent over, humbled
AGUANTAR to suffer or endure
AGUANTARLO to put up with something
AL OTRO LADO on the other side (in the United States)
ALBUR a joke or riddle, frequently sexual in nature, sometimes hostile
AMABLE nice
AMERICANA/O person from the United States (though literally means a person
    from the Americas)
AMIGA friend
APRETADA uptight
AQUI TRAIGO LOS PANTALONES, Y BIEN PUESTOS here I wear the pants, and I
    wear them well
ARROCES party favors from a wedding (literally, "rices"; sometimes favors are
    filled with rice)
ATENDER to take care of
ATENIDO used to being waited on
AVENTADAS very wild
BAILE dance
BAJIO western central region of Mexico
BESO kiss
BRACERO U.S. government program to import workers from Mexico
CACHETADA a slap
CALLE street
CARIÑO warmth, tenderness

CARNITAS deep-fried pork meat

CASA house

CASARSE BIEN to get married properly

CHINGAR to fuck or to beat

COLONIA newer, less prestigious districts of Degollado (literally, neighborhood)

COMPADRES, COMPADRAZGO kin relationship shared by adults when one is the godparent of another's child. Compadres refers to the people themselves; compadrazgo, to the type of relationship.

COMPAÑERA companion

COMPRENSIÓN understanding

CONCUÑAS sister-in-law (wife of husband's brother)

CONFIANZA trust, intimacy

CONGELAR to freeze

CONOCERSE to get to know each other

CONVIVENCIA living together, spending time together

CRIADA servant or maid

CUARENTENA forty-day period following childbirth

CUATES friends, buddies

CUIDAR to use contraception (literally, to take care of)

CUIDARLA to take care of her (refers to rhythm or withdrawal methods)

CUMPLIR to fulfill a duty or responsibility

CUÑADA sister-in-law (either brother's wife or husband's sister)

DAR LA VUELTA promenade around the plaza

DEJADA easily pushed around (literally, past participle of *dejarse*, to let oneself [be pushed around])

DEJARSE to let oneself be overpowered

DESAHOGO alleviation of distress, relief

DESCARGO unloading or release

DESEADOS wanted

DESVERGONZADAS shameless

DETALLISTA thoughtful

DICHOS sayings

DIVERSIÓN entertainment, amusement

DONDE COMEN CUATRO, COMEN CINCO where four eat, so can five

ECHARLES EN CARA to throw something in someone's face

EGOÍSTA selfish

EJIDO Mexican system of communal land ownership

EL HOMBRE NO PIERDE NADA, LA MUJER PIERDE TODO men have nothing to lose, women have everything

EL HOMBRE TIENE QUE MANDAR the man has to give the orders

ÉL ME CUIDA he takes care of me (refers to rhythm or withdrawal methods)

EL QUE TE TOCA he for whom you are destined

EL REGALO DE LOS POBRES the gift of the poor (sex)

EN EL NORTE LA MUJER MANDA in the United States, women give the orders

ERES MI MUJER, POR ESO ME CASÉ CONTIGO you are my wife, that is why I married you

ES UN ALBUR it is a riddle or a joke (refers to marriage)

ES UNA CRUZ it is a cross [to bear]

ESTACIONAR to park

ESTADOUNIDENSE person from the United States

ESTAR JUNTOS to be together

ESTE this

FAJE petting

FRACASAR to fail (literally); figuratively, to have a child outside of marriage

FREEZEAR to freeze (migrant colloquialism)

GANAS desire (sexual)

GARBANZOS chick peas

GOLPE a blow

GOZAR to enjoy (refers to sexual pleasure, orgasm)

GRINGA/O foreigner, especially one from the United States; sometimes used disrespectfully

HACER EL AMOR to make love

HAY QUE CUMPLIR one has to do one's duty

HIJOS AUSENTES, LOS the absent sons (and daughters)

HOMBRES FAMILIARES family men

INGRATAS disagreeable

IRSE to run off together, to elope

LA FAMILIA ES TU PEOR ENEMIGO the family is your worst enemy

LAZO rope used in Mexican wedding ceremonies to unite a couple symbolically

LLEVADA carried off, or kidnapped

LO FÍSICO physical things

LO GRINGO American things

LO MEXICANO Mexican things

LOS HIJOS SON LA FELICIDAD DE LA CASA children are the happiness of a house

MADRINA godmother

MAGUEY type of cactus from which tequila is made

MANDAR to give orders, be in command

MANDILÓN a man who lets himself be bossed around by his wife (literally, a big apron wearer)

MANDO command or control

MARIACHI type of Mexican music

MEJOR SOLA QUE MAL ACOMPAÑADA better alone than in bad company

MENSITA stupid

MIGRA United States Immigration and Naturalization Service

MUCHACHAS unmarried girls

MUJERES DE LA CALLE women of the street

NADIE SE METE CONTIGO nobody bothers you

NO ME VALÍA it did not work for me

NORTEÑAS women in the United States

NORTEÑOS people returning from the North (used to refer to returned migrants)

NOVIAZGO courtship

NOVIO/A boyfriend/girlfriend or fiancé(e)

NUESTRO SEÑOR DEL PERDÓN Our father of forgiveness

OBLIGACIÓN obligation
OJOS QUE NO VEN, CORAZÓN QUE NO SIENTE eyes that don't see, heart that doesn't feel
OPINIONES opinions
PADRINOS godparents
PARA NO QUEDARSE ATRÁS so as not to get left behind
PAREJA partner, spouse
PARQUEAR to park (migrant colloquialism)
PEREGRINACIÓN DE LOS HIJOS AUSENTES religious procession sponsored by absent sons (and daughters)
PIÑATA hollow papier-machê figure filled with candy
PITEADO handicraft of dried cactus woven into leather
PLAZO engagement period
POR LAS BUENAS through the good way
POSADAS parties during the days leading up to Christmas
POZOLE hominy, pork, and chile soup
PRETEXTO excuse
PROMESA religious vow
PUEBLO town (as opposed to people from outlying neighborhoods)
QUEDADAS unmarried women (derogatory)
QUEHACER housework
QUEMADA literally, burned; figuratively, having one's reputation spoiled
QUIEN MANDA who gives the orders or makes the decisions
QUINCEAÑERAS fifteenth birthday party
RANCHO rural settlement
REBOZO shawl
RECOGIDA EN MI CASA safely back at home
RECOGIDAS, LAS literally, prison inmates; idiomatically, good girls, girls who are well behaved
RECUERDOS party favors
RESPETO respect
RESPETUOSO respectful
ROBADA stolen, kidnapped
ROGONAS women who beg for it (sex or intimacy)
SABERSE LLEVAR to know how to get along
SALIR to go out, to leave
SALIR ADELANTE CON MIS HIJOS to make it with my children, to carry on to support my children [without a man]
SECUNDARIA middle school
SEGUIDITOS close together (refers to birth spacing)
SENTIMIENTOS feelings
SEÑORA married woman
SEÑORITA unmarried girl
SINVERGÜENZA shameless
SOLA alone
TAMALES cornmeal seasoned with meat or cheese and sauce and steamed in corn husks

TELENOVELAS soap operas
TENER FAMILIA to have children (literally, to have a family)
TENER RELACIONES to have [sexual] relations
TERMINAR literally, to finish; refers to orgasm
TÚ you, informal
TÚ TE LO BUSCASTE, AHORA AGUANTATE you sought him out, now put up with
   it
UNA FALTA DE RESPETO a lack of respecct
UNA HIJA DE FAMILIA an unmarried daughter (literally, a family girl)
USAR literally, to use; older women use this word to refer to sexual intercourse
USTED you, formal
VALERSE POR SÍ MISMA to get ahead on one's own, rely on oneself
VERGÜENZA shame or modesty
VOLADA wild
YARDAS yard sales

References

Abu-Lughod, L. *Writing Women's Worlds: Bedouin Stories*. Berkeley and Los Angeles: University of California Press, 1993.

Ahearn, L. "'Love Keeps Afflicting Me': Agentive Discourses in Nepali Love Letters." Paper presented at the Annual Meeting of the Anthropological Association of America, Philadelphia, Pa., 1998.

——. *Invitations to Love: Literacy, Love Letters, and Social Change in Nepal*. Ann Arbor: University of Michigan Press, 2001.

Alarcon, R. "El proceso de norteñizacion: Impacto de la migracion internacional en Chavinda, Michoacán." In *Movimientos de poblacion en el occidente de Mexico*, ed. T. Calvo and G. Lopez, 337–57. Zamora: El Colegio de Michoacán, 1988.

Almaguer, T. "Chicano Men: A Cartography of Homosexual Identity and Behavior." *Differences* 3, no. 2 (1991): 75–100.

Amaro, H. "Love, Sex, and Power: Considering Women's Realities in HIV Prevention." *American Psychologist* 50, no. 6 (1995): 437–47.

Amuchástegui, A. *Virginidad e iniciación sexual en México: Experiencias y significados*. Mexico City: EDAMEX, 2001.

Anderson, E. A. "Why Is Humoral Medicine So Popular?" *Social Science and Medicine* 25, no. 4 (1987): 331–37.

Atlanta Journal Constitution. "Immigrants Facing Loss of Benefits," 11 January 1995.

——. "Tortilla Plant Is Prospering in Marietta," 21 September 1995.

——. "Non-English, Multilingual Signs Are a Sign of the Times," 28 September 1995.

——. "Taquerias Quickly Taking Hold Here," 9 November 1995.

——. "Metro Area Grows to Three Million: ARC Seeking Ways to Manage Future," 5 October 1998.

———. "Governor Promotes Hispanic Voter Drive," 30 June 1999, home edition.

———. "Global Atlanta: Dose of Spanish Needed; Health Clinics Seek Interpreters as Immigrant Workloads Grow," 2 July 2001.

Austen, J. *Northanger Abbey.* 1818; reprint, New York: Pantheon Books, 1948.

Banco Nacional de Mexico (Banamex). *México Social.* Mexico City: Banamex, 1996.

Barbosa, R.M., and A.P. Uziel. "Gender and Power: Sexual Negotiation in Times of AIDS." Paper presented at Reconceiving Sexuality: International Perspectives on Gender, Sexuality, and Sexual Health, Rio de Janeiro, 14–17 April 1996.

Bartra, R. *The Cage of Melancholy: Identity and Metamorphosis in the Mexican Character.* Trans. C. Hall. New Brunswick, N.J.: Rutgers University Press, 1992.

Bean, F.D., and G. Swicegood. *Mexican-American Fertility Patterns.* Mexican-American Monograph Number 10, the Center for Mexican-American Studies. Austin: University of Texas Press, 1985.

Behar, R. "My Mexican Friend Marta Who Lost Her Womb on This Side of the Border." *Journal of Women's Health* 2, no. 1 (1993): 85–89.

———. *Translated Woman: Crossing the Border with Esperanza's Story.* Boston: Beacon Press, 1993.

Beneria, L., and M. Roldan. *The Crossroads of Class and Gender: Industrial Homework, Subcontracting, and Household Dynamics in Mexico City.* Chicago: University of Chicago Press, 1987.

Bernard, H.R. *Research Methods in Cultural Anthropology: Qualitative and Quantitative Approaches.* 2d ed. Newbury Park, Calif.: Sage, 1994.

Blanc, A.K. "The Effect of Power in Sexual Relationships on Reproductive and Sexual Health: An Examination of the Evidence." Paper presented at meeting, Power in Sexual Relationships, Population Council in Washington, D.C., 1–2 March 2001.

Bledsoe, C.H. *Women and Marriage in Kpelle Society.* Stanford, Calif.: University of California Press, 1980.

———. "The Politics of Children: Fosterage and the Social Management of Fertility among the Mende of Sierra Leone." In *Births and Power: Social Change and the Politics of Reproduction,* ed. P. Handwerker, 81–100. Boulder, Colo.: Westview Press, 1987.

Bledsoe, C.H., A. Hill, U. D'Allessandro, and P. Langerock. "Constructing Natural Fertility: The Use of Western Contraceptive Technologies in Rural Gambia." *Population and Development Review* 20, no. 1 (1994): 81–113.

Blumberg, R.L. "Income under Female versus Male Control: Hypotheses from a Theory of Gender Stratification and Data from the Third World." *Journal of Family Issues* 9, no. 1 (1988): 51–84.

Bott, E. *Family and Social Networks: Roles, Norms and External Relationships in Ordinary Urban Families.* 1957; reprint, New York: Free Press, 1971.

Bourque, S., and K.B. Warren. *Women of the Andes: Patriarchy and Social Change in Rural Peru.* Ann Arbor: University of Michigan Press, 1981.

Brandes, S. *Power and Persuasion: Fiestas and Social Control in Rural Mexico.* Philadelphia: University of Pennsylvania Press, 1988.

Breckon, L. "A Local Wife: Marriage among Three Generations of Khmer in America." Paper presented at the 98th Annual American Anthropological Association Meeting, Chicago, 17–21 November 1999.

Brettell, C. *When They Read What We Write: The Politics of Ethnography.* Westport, Conn.: Bergin and Garvey, 1993.

Brinton, M. C. "The Social-institutional Bases of Gender Stratification: Japan as an Illustrative Case." *American Journal of Sociology* 94 (1988): 300–334.

Bronfman, M., and N. Minello. "Hábitos sexuales de los migrantes temporales Mexicanos a Los Estados Unidos de América: Prácticas de riesgo para la infección por VIH." In *Sida en Mexico: Migración, adolescencia, y genero,* ed. M. Bronfman et al., 1–89. Mexico City: Información Profesional Especializada, 1995.

Bronfman, M., G. Sejenovich, and P. Uribe. *Migración y SIDA en México y América Central.* Mexico City: Angulos del SIDA and CONASIDA, 1998.

Browner, C. "Gender Roles and Social Change: A Mexican Case Study." *Ethnology* 25, no. 2 (1986): 89–106.

Browner, C.H., and E. Lewin. "Female Altruism Reconsidered: The Virgin Mary as Economic Woman." *American Ethnologist* 9, no. 1 (1982): 61–75.

Caldwell, J.C. "Toward a Restatement of Demographic Transition Theory." *Population and Development Review* (September/December 1976): 321–66.

———. *Theory of Fertility Decline.* New York: Academic Press, 1982.

Cancian, F.M. "The Feminization of Love." *Signs: Journal of Women in Culture and Society* 11, no. 4 (1986).

Caplan, P., ed. *The Cultural Construction of Sexuality.* London: Tavistock, 1987.

Carrier, J.M. "Mexican Male Bisexuality." *Journal of Homosexuality* 11 (1985): 75–85.

———. "Sexual Behavior and the Spread of AIDS in Mexico." *Medical Anthropology* 10 (1989): 129–42.

Centers for Disease Control and Prevention (CDC). "AIDS Cases and Rates in Adult/Adolescent Women, by Race/Ethnicity, Reported in 1999, United States (L264 Slide Series through 1999)." Atlanta, Ga.: Centers for Disease Control and Prevention, National Center for HIV, STD, and TB Prevention, Division of HIV/AIDS Prevention, 2000.

Cerrutti, M., and D.S. Massey. "On the Auspices of Female Migration from Mexico to the United States." *Demography* 38, no. 2 (2001): 187–200.

Chambers, R. *Rural Appraisal: Rapid, Relaxed and Participatory.* Institute of Development Studies Discussion Paper Number 311. Brighton, England: IDS, University of Sussex, 1992.

Chan, S.C. "Love and Jewelry: Patriarchal Control, Conjugal Ties and Changing Identities." Paper presented at the 98th Annual American Anthropological Association Meeting, Chicago, 17–21 November 1999.

Chant, S. "Family Formation and Female Roles in Querétaro, Mexico." *Bulletin of Latin American Research* 4, no. 1 (1985): 17–32.

————. "Single-parent Families: Choice or Constraint? The Formation of Female-headed Households in Mexican Shantytowns." *Development and Change* 16 (1985): 635–56.

————. "Women's Work and Household Change in the 1980s." In *Mexico: Dilemmas of Transition*, ed. N. Harvey, 318–54. New York: St. Martin's Press, 1993.

————. "Women, Work, and Household Survival Strategies in Mexico, 1982–1992: Past Trends, Current Tendencies and Future Research." *Bulletin of Latin American Research* 13, no. 2 (1994): 203–33.

Chavez, L. R. "Settlers and Sojourners: The Case of Mexicans in California." *Human Organization* 47 (1988): 95–108.

Chavez, L. R., E. T. Flores, and M. Lopez-Garcia. "Undocumented Latin American Immigrants and U.S. Health Services: An Approach to a Political Economy of Utilization." *Medical Anthropology Quarterly* 6, no. 1 (1992): 6–26.

Cherlin, A. J. "Going to Extremes: Family Structure, Children's Well-Being, and Social Science." *Demography* 36, no. 4 (1999): 421–28.

Cole, S. *Women of the Praia: Work and Lives in a Portuguese Fishing Community.* Princeton, N.J.: Princeton University Press, 1991.

Coleman, S. *Family Planning in Japanese Society: Traditional Birth Control in a Modern Urban Culture.* Princeton, N.J.: Princeton University Press, 1983.

Collier, J. F. *From Duty to Desire: Remaking Families in a Spanish Village.* Princeton, N.J.: Princeton University Press, 1997.

Collier, J. F., and S. J. Yanagisako. *Gender and Kinship: Essays toward a Unified Analysis.* Stanford, Calif.: Stanford University Press, 1992.

Collins, R. "A Conflict Theory of Sexual Stratification." *Social Problems* 19 (summer 1971): 5–20.

CONAPO. *Mortalidad.* Mexico City: Consejo Nacional de Población, 1997.

————. *Planificación familiar.* Mexico City: Consejo Nacional de Población, 1997.

————. *La nupcialidad en México: Patrones de continuidad y cambio en el último cuarto de siglo.* Mexico City: Consejo Nacional de Población, 1999.

————. *Las remesas enviadas a México por los trabajadores migrantes en Estados Unidos.* Mexico City: Consejo Nacional de Población, 1999.

Connell, R. W. *Gender and Power: Society, the Person and Sexual Politics.* Stanford, Calif.: Stanford University Press, 1987.

————. *Masculinities.* Berkeley and Los Angeles: University of California Press, 1995.

Cornelius, W. A. "Interviewing Undocumented Immigrants: Methodological Reflections Based on Fieldwork in Mexico and the U.S." *International Migration Review* 16 (1982): 378–411.

————. "'Los migrantes de la crisis': The Changing Profile of Mexican Migration to the United States." In *Social Responses to Mexico's Economic Crisis*, ed. M. González de la Rocha and A. Escobar Latapí, 155–93. San Diego: Center for U.S.-Mexican Studies, University of California at San Diego, 1991.

Cornwall, A. "Body Mapping in Health RRA/PRA." In *RRA Notes, Number 16: Special Issue on Applications for Health*, 69–115. London: International

Institute for Environment and Development, Sustainable Agriculture Program, 1992.

Corona Vargas, E. "Resquicios en las puertas: La educacion sexual en Mexico en el Siglo XX." In *Antología de la sexualidad humana, Tomo III,* ed. CONAPO, 681–733. Mexico City: Editorial Porrúa, 1994.

Cott, N. F., and E. H. Pleck. *A Heritage of Her Own: Toward a New Social History of American Women.* New York: Simon and Schuster, 1979.

Crow, G. "The Use of the Concept of Strategy in Recent Sociological Literature." *Sociology* 23, no. 1 (1989): 1–24.

Currier, R. L. "The Hot-Cold Syndrome and Symbolic Balance in Mexican and Spanish-American Folk Medicine." *Ethnology* 5, no. 3 (1966): 251–63.

Das, M. S., and C. J. Jesser, eds. *The Family in Latin America.* New Delhi: Vikas, 1980.

Davis, M. P. *Mexican Voices, American Dreams: An Oral History of Mexican Immigration to the United States.* New York: Henry Holt, 1991.

Davis, N. Z. *Fiction in the Archives: Pardon Tales and Their Tellers in Sixteenth-century France.* Stanford, Calif.: Stanford University Press, 1987.

Davis-Floyd, R. *Birth as an American Rite of Passage.* Berkeley and Los Angeles: University of California Press, 1992.

De Barbieri, T. "Sobre géneros, prácticas y valores: Notas acerca de posibles erosiones del machismo en México." In *Normas y prácticas: Morales y cívicas en la vida cotidiana,* ed. J. M. Ramírez-Sáiz, 83–105. Mexico City: Porrúa/Universidad Nacional Autónoma de México, 1990.

De la Peña, G. "Ideology and Practice in Southern Jalisco: Peasants, Rancheros, and Urban Entrepreneurs." In *Kinship, Ideology and Practice in Latin America,* ed. R. T. Smith, 204–34. Chapel Hill: University of North Carolina Press, 1984.

De Zalduondo, B. O. "Prostitution Viewed Cross-culturally: Toward Recontextualizing Sex Work in AIDS Intervention Research." In *Culture, Society and Sexuality: A Reader,* ed. R. Parker and P. Aggleton, 307–24. London: UCL Press, 1999.

De Zalduondo, B. O., and J. M. Bernard. "Meanings and Consequences of Sexual Economic Exchange: Gender, Poverty and Sexual Risk Behavior in Urban Haiti." In *Conceiving Sexuality: Approaches to Sex Research in a Postmodern World,* ed. J. H. Gagnon and R. G. Parker, 157–80. London: Routledge, 1995.

D'Emilio, J. "Capitalism and Gay Identity." In *Culture, Society, and Sexuality: A Reader,* ed. R. Parker and P. Aggleton, 239–47. London: UCL Press, 1999.

D'Emilio, J., and E. Freedman. *Intimate Matters: A History of Sexuality in the U.S.* New York: Harper and Row, 1988.

Di Leonardo, M. Introduction to *Gender at the Crossroads of Knowledge: Feminist Anthropology in the Postmodern Era,* ed. M. di Leonardo. Berkeley and Los Angeles: University of California Press, 1991.

Díaz-Santana, D., and A. Celis. "AIDS and Migration in Jalisco, Mexico: Their Relation with Risk Factors." *International Conference on AIDS* 5 (1989): 1057 (abstract number T.H.H.P.20).

Dinerman, I.R. "Patterns of Adaptation among Households of U.S.-bound Migrants from Michoacán, Mexico." *International Migration Review* 12, no. 4 (1978): 485–501.

Dixon-Mueller, R. "The Sexuality Connection in Reproductive Health." *Studies in Family Planning* 24, no. 5 (1993): 269–82.

Donovan, P. "Special Analysis: Falling Teen Pregnancy Birthrates: What's Behind the Declines?" *The Guttmacher Report* 1, no. 5 (1998).

Douglas, M. *Purity and Danger.* London: Routledge, 1978.

Durand, J. *Más allá de la línea: Patrones migratorios entre México y Estados Unidos.* Mexico City: Consejo Nacional para la Cultura y las Artes, 1994.

Durand, J., and D.S. Massey. *Miracles on the Border: Retablos of Mexican Migrants to the United States.* [Tucson: University of Arizona Press,] 1995.

Durand, J., E. Parrado, and D.S. Massey. "Migradollars and Development: A Reconsideration of the Mexican Case." *International Migration Review* 30, no. 2 (1995): 423–44.

Dwyer, D., and J. Bruce, eds. *A Home Divided: Women and Income in the Third World.* Stanford, Calif.: Stanford University Press, 1988.

Easterlin, R.A., and E.M. Crimmins. *The Fertility Revolution: A Supply-Demand Analysis.* Chicago: University of Chicago Press, 1985.

Ehlers, T.B. "Debunking Marianismo: Economic Vulnerability and Survival Strategy among Guatemalan Wives." *Ethnology* 30, no. 1 (1991): 1–16.

Erikson, P.I. *Latina Adolescent Childbearing in East Los Angeles.* Austin: University of Texas Press, 1998.

Fadiman, A. *The Spirit Catches You and You Fall Down: A Hmong Child, Her American Doctors, and the Collision of Two Cultures.* New York: Farrar, Straus and Giroux, 1997.

Farmer, P. *Infections and Inequalities: The Modern Plagues.* Berkeley and Los Angeles: University of California Press, 1999.

Federici, N., K. Mason, and S. Sogner. *Women's Position and Demographic Change.* Oxford: Oxford University Press, 1993.

Fernandez, C. "Migracion hacia Los Estados Unidos: Caso de Santo Ines, Michoacán." In *Movimientos de Poblacion en el Occidente de Mexico,* ed. T. Calvo and G. Lopez, 113–24. Zamora: Colegio de Michoacán, 1988.

Fernandez-Kelly, M.P. *For We Are Sold, I and My People: Women and Industry in Mexico's Frontier.* SUNY Series in the Anthropology of Work. Albany: State University of New York Press, 1983.

Fernandez-Kelly, M.P., and D. Schauffler. "Divided Fates: Immigrant Children in a Restructured U.S. Economy." *International Migration Review* 28, no. 4(108) (winter 1994): 662–89.

Feyisetan, B., and J.B. Casterline. "Fertility Preferences and Contraceptive Change in Developing Countries." *International Family Planning Perspectives* 26, no. 3 (2000).

Flora, C.B. "Beyond Exploitation and Integration: New Scholarship on Women in Latin America." *Latin American Research Review* 33, no. 2 (1998): 245–57.

Folbre, N. "Hearts and Spades: Paradigms of Household Economics." *World Development* 14, no. 2 (1986): 245–55.

Foner, N. "The Immigrant Family: Cultural Legacies and Cultural Changes." *International Migration Review* 31, no. 4 (1997): 961–74.

Ford, K., and A. Norris. "Urban Hispanic Adolescents and Young Adults: The Relationship of Acculturation to Sexual Behavior." *Journal of Sex Research* 30, no. 4 (1993): 316–23.

Foucault, M. *The History of Sexuality: Volume 1, An Introduction.* New York: Random House, 1978.

Fowler-Salamini, H., and M. K. Vaughn, eds. *Women of the Mexican Countryside, 1850–1990.* Tucson: University of Arizona Press, 1994.

Fricke, T. "Culture Theory and Population Process: Toward a Thicker Demography." In *Anthropological Demography: Toward a New Synthesis,* ed. D. Kertzer and T. Fricke, 248–77. Chicago: University of Chicago Press, 1997.

Gagnon, J. H., and W. Simon. *Sexual Conduct: The Social Sources of Human Sexuality.* Chicago: Aldine Publishing Company, 1973.

Gallagher, C., and T. Laquer, eds. *The Making of the Modern Body: Sexuality and Society in the Nineteenth Century.* Berkeley and Los Angeles: University of California Press, 1987.

García Canclini, N. *Transforming Modernity: Popular Culture in Mexico.* Trans. Lidia Lozano. Austin: University of Texas Press, 1993.

———. *Hybrid Cultures: Strategies for Entering and Leaving Modernity.* Trans. C. L. Chiappari and S. L. López. Minneapolis: University of Minnesota Press, 1995.

Georgia Department of Human Resources, Division of Public Health. *Access to Health Care by Limited English Proficient Populations in Georgia: A Report of the Bilingual Health Initiative Task Force.* Atlanta, Ga., 1994.

Giddens, A. *The Transformation of Intimacy: Sexuality, Love, and Eroticism in Modern Societies.* Stanford, Calif.: Stanford University Press, 1992.

Gillis, J. R. "Gender and Fertility Decline among the British Middle Classes." In *The European Experience of Declining Fertility, 1850–1970,* ed. J. R. Gillis, L. A. Tilly, and D. Levine, 32–46. Cambridge, Mass., and Oxford, England: Blackwell, 1992.

Gillis, J. R., L. A. Tilly, and D. Levine, eds. *The European Experience of Declining Fertility, 1850–1970.* Cambridge, Mass., and Oxford, England: Blackwell, 1992.

Ginsburg, F. D. *Contested Lives: The Abortion Debate in an American Community.* Berkeley and Los Angeles: University of California Press, 1989.

Gittelsohn, J., M. E. Bentley, P. J. Pelto, M. Nag, S. Pachauri, A. D. Harrison, and L. T. Landman. *Listening to Women Talk about their Health: Issues and Evidence from India.* New Delhi: The Ford Foundation and Har-Anand Publications, 1994.

Glick Schiller, N., L. Basch, and C. Blanc-Szanton, eds. *Towards a Transnational Perspective on Migration: Race, Class, Ethnicity and Nationalism Reconsidered.* Annals of the New York Academy of Sciences, vol. 645. New York: New York Academy of Sciences, 1992.

Goldring, L. "Blurring Borders: Constructing Transnational Community in the Process of Mexico-U.S. Migration." *Research in Community Sociology* 6 (1996): 69–104.

————. "Gendered Memory: Constructions of Rurality among Mexican Transnational Migrants." In *Creating the Countryside: The Politics of Rural and Environmental Discourse*, ed. M. DuPuis and P. Vandergeest, 303–29. Philadelphia, Pa.: Temple University Press, 1996.

————. "The Power of Status in Transnational Social Fields." *Comparative Urban and Community Research* 6 (1998): 165–95.

Goldstein, D. M. "AIDS and Women in Brazil: The Emerging Problem." *Social Science and Medicine* 39, no. 7 (1994): 919–29.

González, L. *San José de Gracia: Mexican Village in Transition.* Trans. J. Upton. Austin: University of Texas Press, 1974.

González de la Rocha, M. "El poder de la ausencia: Mujeres y migración en una comunidad de los Altos de Jalisco." In *Las realidades regionales de la crisis nacional*, 317–34. Zamora: El Colegio de Michoacán, 1993.

————. *The Resources of Poverty: Women and Survival in a Mexican City.* Cambridge, Mass.: Blackwell, 1994.

González de la Rocha, M., and A. Escobar Latapí. *Social Responses to Mexico's Economic Crisis of the 1980s.* San Diego: Center for U.S.-Mexican Studies, University of California at San Diego, 1991.

González-Montes, S. "Intergenerational and Gender Relations in the Transition from a Peasant Economy to a Diversified Economy." In *Women of the Mexican Countryside, 1850–1990*, ed. H. Fowler-Salamini and M. K. Vaughan, 175–91. Tucson: University of Arizona Press, 1994.

Gordon, L. *Woman's Body, Woman's Right: Birth Control in America.* 1976; rev. ed. and reprint, New York: Penguin Books, 1990.

Grassmuck, S., and P. R. Pessar. *Between Two Islands: Dominican International Migration.* Berkeley and Los Angeles: University of California Press, 1991.

Greenhalgh, S. "Toward a Political Economy of Fertility: Anthropological Contributions." *Population and Development Review* 16, no. 1 (1990): 85–106.

————, ed. *Situating Fertility: Anthropology and Demographic Inquiry.* New York: Cambridge University Press, 1995.

Gregg, J. " 'He Can Be Sad Like That': *Liberdade* and the Absence of Romantic Love in a Brazilian Shantytown." Paper presented at the 98th Annual American Anthropological Association Meeting, Chicago, 17–21 November 1999.

Grimes, K. M. *Crossing Borders: Changing Social Identities in Southern Mexico.* Tucson: University of Arizona Press, 1998.

Gulati, L. *Profiles in Female Poverty.* Delhi: Hindustan Publishing Company, 1981.

Gutierrez, R. *When Jesus Came, the Corn Mothers Went Away: Marriage, Sexuality, and Power in New Mexico, 1500–1846.* Stanford, Calif.: Stanford University Press, 1991.

Gutmann, M. C. *The Meanings of Macho: Being a Man in Mexico City.* Berkeley and Los Angeles: University of California Press, 1996.

Guzman, B. *Census 2000 Brief: The Hispanic Population.* Washington, D.C.: U.S. Bureau of the Census, GPO, 2001.

Hartmann, H. I. "The Family as the Locus of Gender, Class, and Political Struggle: The Example of Housework." *Signs* 6, no. 3 (1983): 366–94.

Harvey, D. *The Condition of Postmodernity*. Cambridge, Mass.: Blackwell Publishers, 1989.

Harvey, S. M., et al. *Context and Meaning of Reproductive Decision-making among Inner City Mexican Immigrant Couples*. CONRAD/Centers for Disease Control, Subcontract CSA 94-155, Final Report. Los Angeles: The Pacific Institute for Women's Health, 1997.

Hatcher, R. A., D. Kowal, F. Guest, J. Trussell, F. Stewart, G. K. Stewart, S. Bowen, and W. Cates. *Tecnologia anticonceptiva: Edicion internacional*. Atlanta, Ga.: Printed Matter, 1989.

Henshaw, S. K. "Teenage Abortion and Pregnancy Statistics by State, 1992." *Family Planning Perspectives* 29, no. 3 (1997).

Hirsch, J. S. "Between the Missionaries' Position and the Missionary Position: Mexican Dirty Jokes and the Public (Sub)version of Sexuality." *Critical Matrix: Princeton Working Papers in Women's Studies* 5 (spring/summer 1990): 1–27.

———. "Migration, Modernity and Mexican Marriage: A Comparative Study of Gender, Sexuality and Reproductive Health in a Transnational Community." Ph.D. diss., Dept. of Population Dynamics. Johns Hopkins University, 1998.

———. "*En el norte la mujer manda*: Gender, Generation and Geography in a Mexican Transnational Community." *American Behavioral Scientist* 42, no. 9 (1999): 1332–49.

——— "'Un noviazgo después de ser casados': Companionate Marriage, Sexual Intimacy, and the Modern Mexican Family." Paper presented at International Union for the Scientific Study of Population (IUSSP) seminar, "Social Categories in Population Studies," Cairo, Egypt, 16–18 September 1999.

———. "'Because He Misses His Normal Life Back Home': Masculinity, Sexuality and AIDS Risk Behavior in a Mexican Migrant Community." *Migration World Magazine* 29, no. 4 (2000): 30–32.

Hirsch, J. S., and C. A. Nathanson. "Some Traditional Methods Are More Modern Than Others: Rhythm, Withdrawal and the Changing Meanings of Gender and Sexual Intimacy in Mexican Companionate Marriage." *Culture, Health and Sexuality* 3, no. 4 (2001): 413–28.

Hirsch, J. S., and H. Wardlow, eds. *Modern Loves: Romantic Courtship, Companionate Marriage, and the Political Economy of Emotion*. Unpublished manuscript.

Hirsch, J. S., J. Higgins, M. E. Bentley, and C. A. Nathanson. "The Cultural Constructions of Sexuality: Marital Infidelity and STD/HIV Risk in a Mexican Migrant Community." *American Journal of Public Health* 92, no. 8 (August 2002): 1227–37.

Hirsch, J. S., K. Yount, H. Chakraborty, and C. Nyhus. "'Because He Misses His Normal Life Back Home': Sexuality, Loneliness, and AIDS-Risk Behavior among Mexican Migrants in Atlanta." Paper presented at 129th Annual Meeting of the American Public Health Association, Atlanta, Ga., 21–25 October 2001.

Hondagneu-Sotelo, P. *Gendered Transitions: Mexican Experiences of Immigration*. Berkeley and Los Angeles: University of California Press, 1994.

Hoodfar, H. *Between Marriage and the Market: Intimate Politics and Survival in Cairo.* Berkeley and Los Angeles: University of California Press, 1997.

Hrdy, S. *Mother Nature: A History of Mothers, Infants, and Natural Selection.* New York: Pantheon Books, 1999.

Hubbell, L. J. "Values Under Siege in Mexico: Strategies for Sheltering Traditional Values from Change." *Journal of Anthropological Research* 49, no. 1 (1993): 1–16.

Inhorn, M. *Infertility and Patriarchy: The Cultural Politics of Gender and Family Life in Egypt.* Philadelphia: University of Pennsylvania Press, 1996.

Instituto Nacional de Estadistica, Geografia E Informatica (INEGI). *VII censo general de poblacion, 1960, estado de Jalisco.* Mexico: Estados Unidos Mexicanos, Secretaria de Industria y Comercio, Direccion General de Estadistica, 1960.

———. *VII censo general de poblacion, 1960, estado de Michoacán.* Mexico: Estados Unidos Mexicanos, Secretaria de Industria y Comercio, Direccion General de Estadistica, 1960.

———. *Jalisco: Resultados definitivos, datos por localidad (integracion territorial), XI censo general de poblacion y vivienda.* 1990.

———. *Michoacán: Resultados definitivos, datos por localidad (integracion territorial), XI censo general de poblacion y vivienda.* 1990.

———. *Jalisco: Resultados definitivos, datos por localidad (integracion territorial), XII censo general de poblacion y vivienda.* 2000.

———. *Michoacán: Resultados definitivos, datos por localidad (integracion territorial), XII censo general de poblacion y vivienda.* 2000.

Isvan, N. A. "Productive and Reproductive Decisions in Turkey: The Role of Domestic Bargaining." *Journal of Marriage and the Family* 53 (1991): 1057–70.

Jankowiak, W., ed. *Romantic Passion: A Universal Experience?* New York: Columbia University Press, 1995.

Johannsen, A. M. "Applied Anthropology and Post-modernist Ethnography." *Human Organization* 51, no. 1 (1992): 71–95.

Junge, B. "Competing Discourses of the Gay Male Subject: A Foucaultian Analysis of the Bareback Sex Debates." Paper presented at the 98th Annual American Anthropological Association Meeting, Chicago, 17–21 November 1999.

Kahn, J. R. "Immigrant Selectivity and Fertility Adaptation in the United States." *Social Forces* 27, no. 1 (1988): 108–28.

———. "Immigrant and Native Fertility During the 1980s: Adaptation and Expectations for the Future." *International Migration Review* 28, no. 3 (1992): 501–19.

Katz, J. N. "The Invention of Heterosexuality." *Socialist Review* 20 (1990): 7–34.

Katz Rothman, B. *The Tentative Pregnancy: Prenatal Diagnosis and the Future of Motherhood.* New York: Penguin Books, 1987.

Kearney, Michael. "From Invisible Hand to Visible Feet: Anthropological Studies of Migration and Development." *Annual Reviews in Anthropology* 15 (1986): 331–61.

Keen, B., and W. Wasserman. *A Short History of Latin America.* Boston: Houghton Mifflin, 1984.

Kertzer, D., and T. Fricke. *Anthropological Demography: Toward a New Synthesis.* Chicago: University of Chicago Press, 1997.

Kippax, S., et al. "Women Negotiating Heterosex: Implications for AIDS Prevention." *Women's Studies International Forum* 13, no. 6 (1990): 533–42.

Kline, A., E. Kline, and E. Oken. "Minority Women and Sexual Choice in the Age of AIDS." *Social Science and Medicine* 34, no. 4 (1992): 447–57.

Knauft, B. M. *Exchanging the Past: A Rainforest World of Before and After.* Chicago: University of Chicago Press, 2002.

Knauft, B. M., ed. *Critically Modern: Alternatives, Alterities, Anthropologies.* Bloomington: Indiana University Press, 2002.

Korovkin, M. A. "Oral Contraceptives in a Southern Italian Community." *Current Anthropology* 27, no. 1 (1986): 80–83.

Lancaster, R. N. *Life Is Hard: Machismo, Danger, and the Intimacy of Power in Nicaragua.* Berkeley and Los Angeles: University of California Press, 1992.

———. " 'That We Should all Turn Queer?': Homosexual Stigma in the Making of Manhood and the Breaking of a Revolution in Nicaragua." In *Culture, Society, and Sexuality: A Reader,* ed. R. Parker and P. Appleton, 97–115. London: UCL Press, 1999.

Langer, A., and M. Romero. *Diagnostico en salud reproductiva en Mexico. Reflexiones: Sexualidad, salud y reproduccion* 1, no. 3 (1994): 1–64.

Laumann, E. O., J. H. Gagnon, R. T. Michael, and S. Michaels. *The Social Organization of Sexuality: Sexual Practices in the United States.* Chicago: University of Chicago Press, 1994.

Lauria, A. "*Respeto, Relajo* and Interpersonal Relations in Puerto Rico." *Anthropological Quarterly* 37, no. 2 (n.d.): 53–67.

Laurin, A., ed. *Sexuality and Marriage in Colonial Latin America.* Lincoln: University of Nebraska Press, 1989.

LeVine, S. E., C. C. Sunderland, and F. M. Tapia Uribe. "The Marital Morality of Mexican Women: An Urban Study." *Journal of Anthropological Research* (1986): 183–202.

Logan, M. "Anthropological Research on the Hot-Cold Theory of Disease: Some Methodological Suggestions." *Medical Anthropology* 1, no. 4 (1997): 87–112.

Lomnitz, C. "Decadence in Times of Globalization." *Cultural Anthropology* 9, no. 2 (1994): 257–67.

Lopez Austin, A. "Los puestos complementarios: La parte feminina del cosmos." *Arqueologia Mexicana* (n.d.): 6–13.

Lopez Castro, G. "Lenguage y migración." In *Lenguage y tradicion en Mexico,* ed. H. Perez, 285–95. Zamora: El Colegio de Michoacán, 1989.

Lown, E. A., and W. A. Vega. "Prevalence and Predictors of Physical Partner Abuse among Mexican American Women." *American Journal of Public Health* 91, no. 3 (2001): 441–45.

Luker, K. *Taking Chances: Abortion and the Decision Not to Contracept.* Berkeley and Los Angeles: University of California Press, 1975.

MacCormack, C., and A. Draper. "Social and Cognitive Aspects of Female Sexuality in Jamaica." In *The Cultural Construction of Sexuality,* ed. P. Caplan, 143–65. London: Routledge and Kegan Paul, 1987.

Macleod, A. E. *Accommodating Protest: Working Women, the New Veiling, and Change in Cairo.* New York: Columbia University Press, 1991.

Maggi, W. R. "Heart-Struck: Love Marriage as a Marker of Ethnic Identity among the Kalasha of Northwest Pakistan." Paper presented at the 98th Annual American Anthropological Association Meeting, Chicago, 17–21 November 1999.

Magis-Rodríguez, C., A. del Rio-Zolezzi, J. L. Valdespino-Gomez, and M. L. Garcia-Garcia. "AIDS Cases in Rural Mexico." *Salud Publica de Mexico* 37 (1995): 615–23.

Magis-Rodríguez, C., et al. "Rural AIDS Cases in Mexico." Abstract presented at the 12th World AIDS Conference, Vancouver, 28 June–3 July 1998.

Magis-Rodríguez C., E. B. Garcia, E. R. Nolasco, P. U. Zuñiga. *Rural AIDS Cases in Mexico.* Mexico City: CONASIDA, 2000.

Mahler, S. J. "Engendering Transnational Migration: A Case Study of Salvadorans." *American Behavioral Scientist* 42, no. 4 (1999): 690–719.

———. "Transnationalizing Research on Migration and Gender: Notes and Queries from a Case Study of Salvadorans." Paper presented at Engendering Theories of Transnational Migration conference, Yale Center for International and Area Studies, Yale University, 5–6 February 1999.

Mahoney, R. *Kidding Ourselves: Babies, Breadwinning, and Bargaining Power.* New York: Basic Books, 1995.

Manser, M., and M. Brown. "Marriage and Household Decision-making: A Bargaining Analysis." *International Economic Review* 21, no. 1 (1980): 31–44.

Marroni de Velasquez, M. D. G. "Changes in Rural Society and Domestic Labor in Atlixco, Puebla, 1940–1990." In *Women of the Mexican Countryside, 1850–1990,* ed. H. Fowler-Salamini and M. K. Vaughan, 210–24. Tucson: University of Arizona Press, 1994.

Martin, E. *The Woman in the Body: A Cultural Analysis of Reproduction.* Boston: Beacon Press, 1987.

———. Participant in Discussion, "Domestic Cycles, Family Strategies, and Reproductive Behavior: Rethinking Contingencies." Conference on Anthropological Demography, Brown University Conference Center, Providence, R.I., 3–5 November 1994.

Martínez-Vásquez, G. "Mujeres ejecutivas: En la búsqueda del equilibrio entre trabajo y familia." In *Familias y mujeres en México,* ed. S. González Montes and J. Tuñón, 239–80. Mexico City: El Colegio de México, 1997.

Marx Ferree, M. "Beyond Separate Spheres: Feminism and Family Research." *Journal of Marriage and the Family* 52 (1990): 866–84.

Mason, K. O. "The Status of Women: Conceptual and Methodological Issues in Demographic Studies." *Sociological Forum* 1, no. 2 (1986): 284–300.

———. "The Impact of Women's Social Position on Fertility in Developing Countries." *Sociological Forum* 2, no. 4 (1987): 718–45.

———. "HIV Transmission and the Balance of Power Between Women and Men: A Global View." *Health Transition Review* 4 (supplement, 1994): 217–40.

Massey, D. S. "The Settlement Process among Mexican Migrants to the United States: New Methods and Findings." In *Immigration Statistics: A Story of Neglect,* ed. D. B. Levine, K. Hill, and R. Warren, appendix C. Washington, D.C.: National Academy Press, 1985.

———. "The Settlement Process among Mexican Migrants to the United States." *American Sociological Review* 51 (1986): 670–85.

———. "The Ethnosurvey in Theory and Practice." *International Migration Review* 21, no. 4 (1987): 1498–1522.

Massey, D. S., R. Alarcon, J. Durand, and H. González. *Return to Aztlan: The Social Process of International Migration from Western Mexico.* Berkeley and Los Angeles: University of California Press, 1987.

Massey, D. S., J. Arango, G. Hugo, A. Kouaouci, A. Pellegrino, and J. E. Taylor. "Theories of International Migration: A Review and Appraisal." *Population and Development Review* 19, no. 1 (1993): 431–66.

Massey, D. S., L. Goldring, and J. Durand. "Continuities in Transnational Migration: An Analysis of Nineteen Mexican Communities." *American Journal of Sociology* 99, no. 6 (1994): 1492–1533.

Masters, W. H., and V. E. Johnson. *The Pleasure Bond: A New Look at Sexuality and Commitment.* Boston: Little, Brown, and Company, 1974.

Mathews, T. J. et al. *Monthly Vital Statistics Report: Births of Hispanic Origin, 1989–95.* Hyattsville, Md.: National Center for Health Statistics, Centers for Disease Control and Prevention, 12 February 1998.

Mauss, M. *The Gift: The Form and Reason for Exchange in Archaic Societies.* 1950; reprint, New York: W. W. Norton, 1990.

McKinney, B. "The Impact of Rural-Urban Migration on Migrant Fertility in Senegal." Sc.D. diss., Johns Hopkins University, Dept. of Population Dynamics, Baltimore, Md., 1992.

McLaren, A. "The Sexual Politics of Reproduction in Britain." In *The European Experience of Declining Fertility, 1850–1970,* ed. J. R. Gillis, L. A. Tilly, and D. Levine, 85–180. Cambridge, Mass., and Oxford, England: Blackwell, 1992.

Melhuus, M. "Power, Value, and the Ambiguous Meanings of Gender." In *Machos, Mistresses, Madonnas: Contesting the Power of Latin American Gender Imagery,* ed. M. Melhuus and K. A. Stølen, 230–59. New York: Verso, 1996.

Melhuus, M., and K. A. Stølen. Introduction to *Machos, Mistresses, Madonnas: Contesting the Power of Latin American Gender Imagery,* ed. M. Melhuus and K. A. Stølen, 1–33. New York: Verso, 1996.

Messer, E. "The Hot and Cold in Meso-American Indigenous and Hispanicized Thought." *Social Science and Medicine* 25, no. 4 (1987): 339–46.

Miles, M. B., and A. M. Huberman. *Qualitative Data Analysis: An Expanded Sourcebook.* Newbury Park, Calif.: Sage, 1994.

Miller, B. *The Endangered Sex: Neglect of Female Children in Rural North India.* Delhi: Oxford University Press, 1977. Reprint, Ithaca, N.Y.: Cornell University Press, 1981.

Mintz, S. *Worker in the Cane: A Puerto Rican Life History.* New York: W. W. Norton, 1960.

Mintz, S., and E. Wolf. "An Analysis of Ritual Co-parenthood (*Compadrazgo*)." *Southwest Journal of Anthropology* 6 (1950): 341–68.

Mirandé, A. "*Que Gacho Es Ser Macho:* It's a Drag to be a Macho Man." *Aztlan* 17, no. 2 (1986): 63–89.

———. *Hombres y Machos: Masculinity and Latino Culture.* Boulder, Colo.: Westview Press, 1997.

Mishra, S., R. Conner, and R. Magaña, eds. *AIDS Crossing Borders: The Spread of HIV among Migrant Latinos.* Boulder, Colo.: Westview Press, 1996.

Montesinos-Carrera, R. "Cambio cultural y crisis en la identidad masculina." *El Cotidiano* 11, no. 68 (1995): 20–27.

Moran, J. R., and M. D. Corley. "Sources of Sexual Information and Sexual Attitudes and Behaviors of Anglo and Hispanic Adolescent Males." *Adolescence* 26, no. 104 (1991): 858–64.

Mummert, G. "Reshaping of Gender and Generational Relations among Rural Mexican Migrants to the U.S." Paper presented in the panel Restructuring of Class and Gender Relations among Latino Immigrants in the U.S., Seventeenth International Congress of the Latin American Studies Association, Los Angeles, Calif., 24–27 September 1992.

———. "Changes in the Formation of Western Rural Families: Profound Modifications." *DemoS* 6 (1993): 23–24.

———. "From *Metate* to *Despate:* Rural Women's Salaried Labor and the Redefinition of Gendered Spaces and Roles." In *Women of the Mexican Countryside, 1850–1990,* ed. H Fowler-Salamini and M. K. Vaughan, 192–209. Tucson: University of Arizona Press, 1994.

Nader, L. "Up the Anthropologist: Perspectives Gained from Studying Up." In *Anthropology for the Eighties.* New York: Free Press, 1982.

Nash, J., and H. Safa, eds. *Sex and Class in Latin America.* Cambridge, Mass.: Bergin and Garvey, 1980.

———. *Women and Change in Latin America.* Cambridge, Mass.: Bergin and Garvey, 1986.

Nathanson, C. A. *Dangerous Passage: The Social Control of Sexuality in Women's Adolescence.* Philadelphia, Pa.: Temple University Press, 1991.

Nathanson, C. A., and R. Schoen. "A Bargaining Theory of Sexual Behavior in Women's Adolescence." Proceedings of the 1993 General Conference of the International Union for the Scientific Study of Population, Montreal, Canada, 1993.

Nencel, L. "'*Pacharacas, Putas* and *Chicas de su Casa*': Labeling, Femininity and Men's Sexual Selves in Lima, Peru." In *Machos, Mistresses, Madonnas: Contesting the Power of Latin American Gender Imagery,* ed. M. Melhuus and K. A. Stølen, 56–82. New York: Verso, 1996.

New York Times. "New Tactic Is Used Against Illegal Workers," 26 September 1995.

———. "Caught in Storm, the Pregnant Wait," 16 October 1996, national edition.

———. "An Exodus of Migrant Families Is Bleeding Mexico's Heartland," 17 June 2001, final edition.

Newman, L. F. *Women's Medicine: A Cross-cultural Study of Indigenous Fertility Regulation.* New Brunswick, N.J.: Rutgers University Press, 1985.

Ortega, A. O., A. Amuchástegui, and M. Rivas. "'Because They Were Born from Me': Negotiating Women's Rights in Mexico." In *Negotiating Reproductive Rights: Women's Perspectives across Countries and Cultures,* ed. R. P. Petchesky and K. Judd, 145–79. London: Zed Books, 1998.

Ortner, S. B., and H. Whitehead. *Sexual Meanings: The Cultural Construction of Gender and Sexuality.* Cambridge: Cambridge University Press, 1981.

Pader, E. J. "Spatiality and Social Change: Domestic Space Use in Mexico and the United States." *American Ethnologist* 20, no. 1 (1993): 114–37.

Pahl, J. "The Allocation of Money and the Structuring of Inequality Within Marriage." *Sociological Review* 13, no. 2 (1983): 237–62.

Parikh, S. A. "What's Love Got to Do with It? Love Letters and Romance among Youth in Uganda." Paper presented at the 98th Annual American Anthropology Association Meeting, Chicago, 17–21 November 1999.

Parker, R. *Bodies, Pleasures and Passions.* Boston: Beacon, 1991.

———. *Beneath the Equator: Cultures of Desire, Male Homosexuality, and Emerging Gay Communities in Brazil.* London: Routledge, 1999.

———. "Sexuality, Culture, and Power in HIV/AIDS Research." *Annual Review of Anthropology.* 30: 163–79, 2001.

Parker, R., and P. Aggleton. *Culture, Society, and Sexuality: A Reader.* London: UCL Press, 1999.

Paz, O. *El Laberinto de la Soledad.* 1950; reprint, Mexico: Fondo de Cultura Economica, 1986.

Peiss, K. *Cheap Amusements: Working Women and Leisure in Turn-of-the-Century New York.* Philadelphia, Pa.: Temple University Press, 1986.

Perilla, J., R. Bakeman, and F. Norris. "Culture and Domestic Violence: The Ecology of Abused Latinas." *Violence and Victims* 9, no. 4 (1994): 325–39.

Pesquera, B. M. "In the Beginning He Wouldn't Even Lift a Spoon." In *Situated Lives: Gender and Culture in Everyday Life,* ed. L. Lamphere, H. Ragoné, and P. Zavella, 208–22. New York: Routledge, 1997.

Pessar, P. "Introductory Remarks: Engendering Transnational Migration." Panel at 1997 Annual Meeting of the Anthropological Association of America, Washington, D.C., 19 November 1997.

———. "Situating Gender within a Transnational Social Field: Guatemalan Refugees and Returnees." Paper presented at Engendering Theories of Transnational Migration Conference, Yale Center for International and Area Studies, Yale University, 5–6 February 1999.

Pessar, P., and S. Mahler, eds. *Identities: A Journal of Studies in Culture and Power.* Forthcoming.

Petchesky, R.P., and K. Judd, eds. *Negotiating Reproductive Rights: Women's Perspectives across Countries and Cultures*. London: Zed Books, 1998.

Peterson, L.S. *Contraceptive Use in the United States, 1982–90*. Hyattsville, Md: Vital and Health Statistics, National Center for Health Statistics, Centers for Disease Control and Prevention, 14 February 1995.

Pineda, T., B. Loeza, R. Heredia, N. Vazquez, and V. Hernandez. *Perfil del michoacano emigrado a Los EUA y el impacto de la epidemiologia del VIH/SIDA en la región*. III Congreso Nacional de Investigación Sobre Salud, Mexico, 1992.

Pollak, R.A., and S.C. Watkins. "Cultural and Economic Approaches to Fertility: Proper Marriage or *mésalliance?*" *Population and Development Review* 19, no. 3 (1993): 467–96.

Portes, A., and R.L. Bach. *Latin Journey: Cuban and Mexican Immigrants in the United States*. Berkeley and Los Angeles: University of California Press, 1985.

Portes, A., and J. Borocz. "Contemporary Immigration: Theoretical Perspectives on Its Determinants and Modes of Incorporation." *International Migration Review* 23, no. 3 (1989): 606–30.

Portes, A., L.E. Guarnizo, and P. Landolt, eds. *Ethnic and Racial Studies*, special issue, 22, no. 2 (1999).

Portes, A., and R.G. Rumbaut. *Immigrant America: A Portrait*. Berkeley and Los Angeles: University of California Press, 1990.

Potter, J.E. "The Persistence of Outmoded Contraceptive Regimes." *Population and Development Review* 25, no. 4 (1999): 703–40.

Rapp, R. *Testing Women, Testing the Fetus: The Social Impact of Amniocentesis in America*. London: Routledge, 2000.

Rebhun, L.A. *The Heart Is Unknown Country: Love in the Changing Economy of Northeast Brazil*. Stanford, Calif.: Stanford University Press, 1999.

———. Personal communication with author. 2000.

Reddy, G. "*Pyar ke rishte* [Bonds of love]: The Desire for Companionate Marriages among the Hijras of Hyderbad." Paper presented at the 98th Annual American Anthropological Association Meeting, Chicago, 17–21 November 1999.

Reiter, R. *Toward an Anthropology of Women*. New York: Monthly Review Press, 1975.

Renne, E.P. "Gender Ideology and Fertility Strategies in an Ekiti Yoruba Village." *Studies in Family Planning* 24, no. 6 (1993): 343–52.

———. "Gender Roles and Women's Status: What They Mean to Hausa Muslim Women in Northern Nigeria." Paper presented at IUSSP workshop, Social Categories on Population Studies, Cairo, Egypt, 15–18 September 1999.

Rich, A. "Compulsory Heterosexuality and Lesbian Existence." In *Culture, Society and Sexuality: A Reader*, ed. R. Parker and P. Aggleton, 199–225. London: UCL Press, 1999.

Rindfuss, R.R., and S.P. Morgan. "Marriage, Sex, and the First Birth Interval: The Quiet Revolution." *Population and Development Review* 9, no. 2 (1983): 259–78.

Rodríguez, Gabriela. Personal communication with author. January 1998.

Rodríguez, J. *Our Lady of Guadalupe: Faith and Empowerment among Mexican-American Women*. Austin: University of Texas Press, 1994.

Rodríguez-Dorantes, C. "Entre el mito y la experienca vivida: Las jefas de familia." In *Familias y mujeres en México*, ed. S. González Montes and J. Tuñón, 195–237. Mexico: El Colegio de México, 1997.

Rosaldo, M., and L. Lamphere, eds. *Woman, Culture and Society*. Stanford, Calif.: Stanford University Press, 1974.

Rostas, S. "The Production of Gendered Imagery: The Concheros of Mexico." In *Machos, Mistresses, Madonnas: Contesting the Power of Latin American Gender Imagery*, ed. M. Melhuus and K.A. Stølen, 207–27. New York: Verso, 1996.

Rouse, R. "Mexican Migration and the Social Space of Postmodernism." *Diaspora* 1, no. 1 (1991): 8–23.

———. "Making Sense of Settlement: Class Transformation, Cultural Struggle, and Transnationalism among Mexican Migrants in the United States." In *Towards a Transnational Perspective on Migration*, ed. N. Glick Schiller, L. Basch, and C. Blanc-Szanton, 25–52. New York: Annals of the New York Academy of Sciences, vol. 645, 1992.

Safa, H.I. "The New Women Workers: Does Money Equal Power?" *NACLA Report on the Americas* 27, no. 1 (1993): 24–29.

Safilios-Rothchild, C. "Female Power, Autonomy, and Demographic Change in the Third World." In *Women's Roles and Population Trends in the Third World*, ed. R. Anker, M. Buvinic, and N. Youssef, 117–31. London: Croon Helm, 1982.

Salvo, D., et al. *Home Altars of Mexico*. Albuquerque: University of New Mexico Press, 1996.

Santarriaga, M., et al. "HIV/AIDS in a Migrant Exporter Mexican State." *International Conference on AIDS* 11 (1996): 414 (abstract number Tu.D.2906).

Santelli, J.S., L.D. Lindberg, J. Abma, C.S. McNeely, and M. Resnick. "Adolescent Sexual Behavior: Estimates and Trends from Four Nationally Representative Surveys." *Family Planning Perspectives* 32, no. 4 (2000).

Santow, G. "Coitus Interruptus in the Twentieth Century." *Population and Development Review* 19, no. 4 (1993): 767–92.

Scheper-Hughes, N. *Death without Weeping: The Violence of Everyday Life in Brazil*. Berkeley and Los Angeles: University of California Press, 1993.

———. *Saints, Scholars and Schizophrenics: Mental Illness in Rural Ireland*. Berkeley and Los Angeles: University of California Press, 2001.

Scheper-Hughes, N., and M. Lock. "The Mindful Body: A Prolegomenon to Future Work in Medical Anthropology." *Medical Anthropology Quarterly* 1, no. 1 (1987): 6–41.

Schiebinger, L. *Nature's Body: Gender in the Making of Modern Science*. Boston: Beacon Press, 1993.

Schneider, J., and P. Schneider. *Festival of the Poor: Fertility Decline and the Ideology of Class in Sicily, 1860–1980*. Tucson: University of Arizona Press, 1996.

Schoen, R., et al. "Why Do Americans Want Children?" *Population and Development Review* 23, no. 2 (1997): 333–58.

Scott, C. S., L. Shifman, L. Ordd, R. G. Owen, and N. Fawcett. "Hispanic and Black American Adolescents' Beliefs Relating to Sexuality and Contraception." *Adolescence* 23, no. 91 (1988): 667–88.

Sebert, A. "Needs Assessment for Reproductive Health among Latinas: Cobb, DeKalb, Fulton, and Gwinnett Counties, Georgia." Master's thesis, University of Michigan, 2000.

Seccombe, W. "Men's 'Marital Rights' and Women's 'Wifely Duties': Changing Conjugal Relations in the Fertility Decline." In *The European Experience of Declining Fertility, 1850–1970,* ed. J. R. Gillis, L. A. Tilly, and D. Levine, 66–84. Cambridge, Mass., and Oxford, England: Blackwell, 1992.

Selby, H., H. Murphy, and S. Lorenzen. *The Mexican Urban Household: Organizing for Self-Defense.* Austin: University of Texas Press, 1990.

Sen, A. "Economics and the Family." *Asian Development Review* 1 (1983): 14–26.

Shorter, E. *The Making of the Modern Family.* New York: Basic Books, 1975.

Shostack, M. *Nisa: The Life and Words of a !Kung Woman.* Cambridge, Mass.: Harvard University Press, 1981.

Shryock, H., and J. S. Siegel. *The Methods and Materials of Demography.* Condensed edition by E. G. Stockwell. San Diego, Calif.: Academic Press, 1976.

Simmons, C. "Companionate Marriage and the Lesbian Threat." *Frontiers* 4, no. 3 (1979): 54–59.

Skolnik, A. *Embattled Paradise: The American Family in an Age of Uncertainty.* New York: Basic Books, 1991.

Smith, D. J. "Courting for Love and Marrying for Children: Romance, Parenthood and Gender in Contemporary Igbo Marriages." Paper presented at the 98th Annual American Anthropological Association Meeting, Chicago, 17–21 November, 1999.

———. " 'These Girls Today *na war-o*': Premarital Sexuality and Modern Identity in Southeastern Nigeria." *Africa Today* 47, no. 3 (1999): 141–70.

———. "Romance, Parenthood and Gender in a Modern African Society." Paper presented at the annual meeting of the Population Association of America, Los Angeles, Calif., in March 2000.

———. "Sexual Relationships and Social Change: Linking Fertility Preferences and Contraceptive Use to the Social (Re)Construction of Gender and the Individual." Unpublished manuscript, Emory University Dept. of Anthropology. N.d.

Smith, J. P., and B. Edmondston, eds. *The New Americas: Economic, Demographic, and Fiscal Effects of Immigration.* Washington, D.C.: National Academy Press, 1997.

Smith, M. P., and L. E. Guarnizo. *Transnationalism from Below.* New Brunswick, N.J.: Transaction Publishers, 1998.

Smith, R. C. "Los ausentes siempre presentes: The Imagining, Making and Politics of a Transnational Community Between New York City and Ticuani, Puebla." Working papers on Latin America, Columbia University, Institute for Latin American and Iberian Studies, New York, 1992.

———. "Transnational Localities: Community, Technology and the Politics of Membership Within the Context of Mexico and U.S. Migration." *Comparative Urban and Community Research* 6 (1998): 196–238.

Smith-Rosenberg, C. *Disorderly Conduct: Visions of Gender in Victorian America.* Oxford: Oxford University Press, 1985.

Snitow, A., C. Stansell, and S. Thompson, eds. *Powers of Desire: The Politics of Sexuality.* New York: Monthly Review Press, 1983.

Sobo, E. J. *Choosing Unsafe Sex: AIDS-Risk Denial among Disadvantaged Women.* Philadelphia: University of Pennsylvania Press, 1995.

———. "Finance, Romance, Social Support and Condom Use among Impoverished Inner-City Women." *Human Organization* 54, no. 2 (1995): 115–28.

Soler H., D. Quadagno, D. Sly, K. Riehman, I. Eberstein, and D. Harrison. "Relationship Dynamics, Ethnicity, and Condom Use among Low-Income Women." *Family Planning Perspectives* 32, no. 2 (2000): 82–88, 101.

Stansell, M. C. *City of Women: Sex and Class in New York, 1789–1860.* New York: Alfred A. Knopf, 1986.

———. *American Moderns: Bohemian New York and the Creation of a New Century.* New York: Metropolitan Books, 2000.

Stephen, E. H., and F. D. Bean. "Assimilation, Disruption and the Fertility of Mexican Origin Women in the United States." *International Migration Review* 26, no. 1 (1992): 68–88.

Stephen, L. *Zapotec Women.* Austin: University of Texas Press, 1991.

Stephenson, M. *Gender and Modernity in Andean Bolivia.* Austin: University of Texas Press, 1999.

Stern, S. *The Secret History of Gender: Women, Men and Power in Late Colonial Mexico.* Chapel Hill: University of North Carolina Press, 1995.

Stevens, E. "*Marianismo:* The Other Face of *Machismo* in Latin America." In *Male and Female in Latin America,* ed. A. Pescatello, 89–101. Pittsburgh, Pa.: University of Pittsburgh Press, 1973.

Stoler, A. L. "Making Empire Respectable: The Politics of Race and Sexual Morality in Twentieth-century Colonial Cultures." In *Situated Lives: Gender and Culture in Everyday Life,* ed. L. Lamphere, H. Ragoné, and P. Zavella, 373–99. London: Routledge, 1999.

Stone, L. *The Family, Sex and Marriage in England, 1500–1800.* New York: Harper and Row, 1979.

Szreter, S. "The Idea of Demographic Transition and the Study of Fertility Change: A Critical Intellectual History." *Population and Development Review* 19, no. 4 (1993): 659–701.

Szreter S., A. Dharmalingam, and H. Sholkamy, eds. *Qualitative Demography: Categories and Contexts in Population Studies.* Oxford: Oxford University Press, forthcoming.

Thadani, V. "The Logic of Sentiment: The Family and Social Change." *Population and Development Review* (1978).

Thompson, S. *Going All the Way: Teenage Girls' Tales of Sex, Romance and Pregnancy.* New York: Hill and Wang, 1994.

Thorton, A. "The Developmental Paradigm, Reading History Sideways, and Family Change." *Demography* 38, no. 4 (2001): 449–66.

Tiano, S. *Patriarchy on the Line: Labor, Gender, and Ideology in the Mexican Maquila Industry.* Philadelphia, Pa.: Temple University Press, 1994.

Tienda, M., and K. Booth. "Gender, Migration and Social Change." *International Sociology* 6 (1991): 51–72.

Trigueros, P., and J. Rodríguez Piña. *Migracion en el Occidente de Mexico.* Ed. G. Lopez Castro. Zamora: El Colegio de Michoacán, 1988.

Trimberger, E. "Feminism, Men, and Modern Love: Greenwich Village, 1900–25." In *Powers of Desire: The Politics of Sexuality,* ed. A. Snitow, C. Stansell, and S. Thompson, 131–52. New York: Monthly Review Press, 1983.

Trouillot, R. "Anthropology and the Savage Slot: The Poetics and Politics of Otherness." In *Recapturing Anthropology: Working in the Present,* ed. R. G. Fox, 17–44. Santa Fe, N.M.: School of American Research Press, 1991.

UNAIDS. Men and AIDS—A Gendered Approach: 2000 World AIDS Campaign. Available at http://www.unaids.org.

Uribe-Salas, F. "Low Prevalences of HIV Infection and Sexually Transmitted Disease among Female Commercial Sex Workers in Mexico City." *American Journal of Public Health* 87, no. 6 (1997): 1012–16.

U.S. Bureau of the Census. "Table DP-1: General Population and Housing Characteristics: 1990, Alabama." Data Set: 1990 Summary Tape File (STF-1)—100-Percent Data. Washington, D.C.: Government Printing Office, 1990.

———. "Table DP-1: General Population and Housing Characteristics: 1990, Georgia." Data Set: 1990 Summary Tape File (STF-1)—100-Percent Data. Washington, D.C.: Government Printing Office, 1990.

———. "Table DP-1: General Population and Housing Characteristics: 1990, North Carolina." Data Set: 1990 Summary Tape File (STF-1)—100-Percent Data. Washington, D.C.: Government Printing Office, 1990.

———. "Table DP-1: General Population and Housing Characteristics: 1990, South Carolina." Data Set: 1990 Summary Tape File (STF-1)—100-Percent Data. Washington, D.C.: Government Printing Office, 1990.

———. "Table DP-1: General Population and Housing Characteristics: 1990, Tennessee." Data Set: 1990 Summary Tape File (STF-1)—100-Percent Data. Washington, D.C.: Government Printing Office, 1990.

———. Summary Tape File 3. Washington, D.C.: Government Printing Office, 1990.

———. *Current Population Reports, P23–183: Hispanic Americans Today.* Washington, D.C.: Government Printing Office, 1993.

———. Census 2000 Redistricting Data (PL 94–171) Summary File, Table PL1. Population by Race and Hispanic or Latino Origin, for the 15 Largest Counties and Incorporated Places in Georgia, 2000. Washington, D.C.: Government Printing Office, 2000.

———. "PCT19: Place of Birth for the Foreign-Born Population [126]—Universe: Foreign-born Population." Data Set: Census 2000 Summary File 3 (SF3)—Sample Data. Washington, D.C.: Government Printing Office, 2000.

———. Public Law 94–171 Summary File, 2000. Washington, D.C.: Government Printing Office, 2000.

———. "Table QT-P3. Race and Hispanic or Latino Origin: 2000, Alabama." Data Set: Census 2000 Summary File 1 (SF1) 100-Percent Data. Washington, D.C.: Government Printing Office, 2000.

———. "Table QT-P3. Race and Hispanic or Latino Origin: 2000, Georgia." Data Set: Census 2000 Summary File 1 (SF1) 100-Percent Data. Washington, D.C.: Government Printing Office, 2000.

———. "Table QT-P3. Race and Hispanic or Latino Origin: 2000, North Carolina." Data Set: Census 2000 Summary File 1 (SF1) 100-Percent Data. Washington, D.C.: Government Printing Office, 2000.

———. "Table QT-P3. Race and Hispanic or Latino Origin: 2000, South Carolina." Data Set: Census 2000 Summary File 1 (SF1) 100-Percent Data. Washington, D.C.: Government Printing Office, 2000.

———. "Table QT-P3. Race and Hispanic or Latino Origin: 2000, Tennessee." Data Set: Census 2000 Summary File 1 (SF1) 100-Percent Data. Washington, D.C.: Government Printing Office, 2000.

Vance, C. "Anthropology Rediscovers Sexuality: A Theoretical Comment." *Social Science and Medicine* 33, no. 8 (1991): 875–84.

Vásquez-García, V. "Mujeres que 'respetan su casa': Estatus marital de las mujeres y economía doméstica en una comunidad nahua del sur de Veracruz." In *Familias y mujeres en México,* ed. S. González Montes and Julia Tuñón, 163–93. Mexico City: El Colegio de México, 1997.

Wardlow, H. "All's Fair When Love Is War: Attempts at Companionate Marriage among the Huli of Papua New Guinea." Paper prepared for presentation at the 98th Annual American Anthropological Assocation Meeting, Chicago, 17–21 November 1999.

Watney, S. "Safer Sex as Community Practice." In *Culture, Society and Sexuality: A Practical Beginning,* ed. R. Parker and P. Aggleton, 405–15. London: University College of London Press, 1999.

Weeks, J. *Sex, Politics and Society: The Regulation of Sexuality Since 1800.* New York: Longman, 1981.

Wolf, M. *A Thrice Told Tale: Feminism, Postmodernism, and Ethnographic Responsibility.* Stanford, Calif.: Stanford University Press, 1992.

Womack Jr., J. *Zapata and the Mexican Revolution.* New York: Vintage Books, 1968.

Worth, D. "Sexual Decision-making and AIDS: Why Condom Promotion among Vulnerable Women Is Likely to Fail." *Studies in Family Planning* 20, no. 6 (1989): 297–307.

Yan, Y. "The Triumph of Conjugality: Structural Transformation of Family Relations in a Chinese Village." *Ethnology* 36, no. 3 (1997): 191–212.

———. *Private Life under Socialism: Love, Intimacy and Family Change in a Chinese Village, 1949–1999.* Stanford, Calif.: Stanford University Press, forthcoming.

Young, G. "Gender Inequality and Industrial Development: The Household Connection." *Journal of Comparative Family Studies* 24, no. 1 (1993): 1–20.

Zavella, P. *Women's Work and Chicano Families: Cannery Workers of the Santa Clara Valley.* Ithaca, N.Y.: Cornell University Press, 1987.

Zeidenstein, S., and K. Moore, eds. *Learning about Sexuality: A Practical Beginning*. New York: The Population Council and International Women's Health Coalition, 1996.

Zelizer, V. A. "The Social Meaning of Money: 'Special Monies.'" *American Journal of Sociology* 95, no. 2 (1989): 342–71.

Zhao, X. "Demographic Change and the Economic Status of Women in Rural China." Ph.D. diss., Johns Hopkins University, School of Hygiene and Public Health, Dept. of Population Dynamics, 1991.

Index

affectivity, 3, 7–12, 16; courtship, 50–51, 81, 84, 93–94, 102–11, 141, 144; men on, 218–21, 225; and power, 146–47, 178. See also *cariño;* companionate marriage; *confianza* (trust); desire; emotional bonds; friendship; kisses; love; pleasure; sexuality

age: interviewees, 82; at marriage, 82, 83–84, 159. See also children; generational changes; modernity

agriculture, 71, 72, 165, 171, 172

AIDS, 284, 326n39. See also HIV

air travel, transnational, 72

alcohol. See drinking, men's

Alfonso, 199

Amuchástegui, A., 168–69, 265–66

anthropologists, 2, 31, 275, 281, 291nn69,71; fertility studies, 2, 31, 276–77; research methods, 29, 30–34, 269–70, 294n102. See also cultural constructions; ethnography; social construction of gender

architecture, house, 14, 57, 69–71, 69–70, 226, 303n28

Atlanta, 18–25; battered women, 51, 202–3, 314n30; Catholic Church, 21, 51, 152, 193, *193,* 197, 298n21; fertility data, 241, 251–64; home furnishings, 298n21; Immigration and Naturalization Service (INS), 20, 23, 24–25, 33; life history informants, 36–37, 42, 43, 49; Mexican community, 21–23, 23–25, 34, 292n87; population

of Hispanics, 19–22, 21–22; Protestant churches, 21-22; public/private/street/ house, 192–97, 258, 309n34; religious procession, *196;* soccer teams (Latino), 33, 34, 75; trailer parks, 23, 24, 183; transportation, 22, 23, 24, 188, 192–93, 268. See also transnational community

Austen, Jane, 158

authority: confessional, 197; family, 99, 100, 113–32, 134, 197. See also decision making; ownership; permission; power, gender; rights

autonomy: men's, 123; women's, 35, 134, 168, 202–8, 282, 311n31. See also bodily control; choices; individualism; power, gender; self-confidence; single women

baptisms, of returning migrants' children, 62, 71

bargaining power, 5–9, 280; migration and, 180, 207, 208; theory, 5–9, 208, 271–72, 288n23; of women in labor force, 184, 207. See also gender equality; ideals; negotiating; power, gender; strategies

battered women, Atlanta, 314n30; support group, 51, 202–3. See also violence, domestic

Beatriz, *36;* husband's communication with, 126, 148; mobility, 188; not in labor force, 188, 201–2; parenting, 246–47, 249; transnational trips, 182

357

games: childhood, 41; soccer teams, 33,
34, 75
gay rights movement, 171, 177, 269,
270, 301n17
gender, 2–3, 277–85; cars linked with,
47; childhood games relating to, 41;
defined, 3; house/street, 99–101, 178,
192–97, 302n23; identities, 3, 12,
128–56, 160, 174; interviewed topic,
41; local theories of, 139–40; and migration choice, 163–64, 189; and
nighttime outings, 47, 100, 140; in
public health research, 277–78; segre-
gation by, 41–42, 45, 47–48, 61; social
organization of, 3, 14, 112. *See also*
femininity; gender equality; gender relations; ideals; masculinity; men; social
construction of gender changes;
women
Gendered Transitions (Hondagneu-
Sotelo), 17
gender equality, 9; joint decision making,
123–24, 140, 142, 146, 147, 258–64,
307n18; modernity and, 178, 326n34;
respect asserting, 106. *See also* gender
inequality; mutuality; power, gender
gender inequality, 3, 8, 17–18, 273,
277–78; in birth control, 263, 277–78;
companionate marriage coexisting
with, 10, 112, 123, 140, 147, 156,
174, 178, 223, 277–78, 281–82;
labor/production modes and, 112,
172, 174, 310n27; violence as, 135,
137–38, 156. *See also* gender equality
gender relations: changes in Mexico,
11, 12, 14–16, 115, 158, 163–75; economic changes affecting, 11, 14–15,
16, 158, 165–79; labor/production
modes and, 112, 168, 170–74, 226,
310n27. *See also* affectivity; courtship;
gender; generational changes; ideals;
labor; marriage; modernity; power,
gender; private spaces; public spaces;
sexuality
generalizability, research, 30–32, 202–4,
252–53, 292n81
generational changes, 1, 12–17, 41,
81–84, 89, 157–79, 285; benefits of,
147–56; courtship, 50–51, 61, 81–95,
101–4, 110–11, 158–59, 167, 168–69;
data analysis, 50–51; family ideals,
147, 231–64; female submission,
115–27; housework, 124–25, 306n8;
in living room photographs, 78; marital ideals, 87–93, 111–15, 121–27,
145–49, 160–63, 169–70, 208; marital
power, 14, 115–27, 147; sexuality, 4,

210, 213, 218, 225, 228–30; social
and demographic, 163–75. *See also*
modernity; parents
geography. *See* migration; private spaces;
public spaces; social mobility
strategies; social spaces; transnational
community
Georgia: Hispanic immigrants, 18–25,
19–20, 30; Hispanic population, 18,
19–22, 19–22, 30; immigration laws,
14–15, 20, 183, 185, 191, 313n12,
314n25. *See also* Atlanta
Giddens, A., 4, 10, 283
gifts: among family members, 79–80,
175–76; from men to women, 79, 148,
175–76, 309n32; needlework, 44,
76–77, 293n97, 299n24; party favors,
77–78, 79–80, 207–8
Gillis, John, 11
global ideology, marital, 113, 158,
175–79
godparents, 71, 77, 297n16
González, Luis, 69, 300n10, 305n6
Gonzalez de la Rocha, M., 6, 181, 208,
311n31
González-Montes, S., 168, 169,
171, 172
Gordon, Linda, 9, 318n16
gossip, 99, 192, 284, 306n7
Grassmuck, S., 201
green cards, 183, 188, 207, 283. *See also*
residence papers
Greenwich Village, 9–10
greeting, gender relations, 45, 98
Gregg, J., 176–77
Grimes, K.M., 168
gringa, 47
Guadalupe, 35, 36, 77, 273; and driver's
license, 187; first birth, 235; husband
interviewed, 42; infertile, 252
Gutmann, M.C., *The Meanings of
Macho:* generational changes, 14, 16,
160, 170–71, 280; marital power, 156,
174, 279; quoting from interviews, 54;
violence against women, 137
Gwinnett County, Georgia, 31

Habermas, J., 13
Hall, Stuart, 265–66
Halloween, protest against, 66, 67
handholding, in courtship, 84, 104, 108,
110
Harvard Educational Review, 275
Harvey, D., 13, 15
health: public, 6, 29, 268–69, 273–79,
315n2. *See also* reproductive health
"hidden rationality," 7

Text:	10/13/ Sabon
Display:	Sabon
Cartographer:	Bill Nelson
Indexer:	Barbara Roos
Compositor:	Impressions Book and Journal Services, Inc.